THE STATUS OF THE FAMILY IN LAW AND BIOETHICS

To my parents
Ora and Gadi Gilbar

The Status of the Family in Law and Bioethics

The Genetic Context

ROY GILBAR
Netanya Academic College, Israel

ASHGATE

Published by
Ashgate Publishing Limited
Gower House
Croft Road
Aldershot
Hampshire GU11 3HR
England

Ashgate Publishing Company
Suite 420
101 Cherry Street
Burlington, VT 05401-4405
USA

Ashgate website: http://www.ashgate.com

British Library Cataloguing in Publication Data
Gilbar, Roy
   The status of the family in law and bioethics : the genetic
   context
   1. Genetic screening - Law and legislation - England
   2. Medical ethics - England 3. Informed consent (Medical law)
   - England 4. Domestic relations - England
   I. Title
   344.4'204196

Library of Congress Cataloging-in-Publication Data
Gilbar, Roy.
   The status of the family in law and bioethics : the genetic context / by Roy Gilbar.
       p. cm.
   Includes bibliographical references and index.
   ISBN 0-7546-4545-2
   1.   Informed consent (Medical law)--Great Britain. 2. Medical laws and legislation--
Great Britain. 3. Disclosure of information--Law and legislation--Great Britain. 4.
Medical ethics--Great Britain. 5. Health risk assessment. I. Title.

   KD3410.I54G55 2005
   344.4104'12--dc22

                                                                            2005017367

ISBN 0 7546 4545 2

Printed and bound in Great Britain by MPG Books Ltd. Bodmin, Cornwall.

Contents

Preface   *vii*

1   The Liberal–Communitarian Debate in Medical Law and Ethics   1

2   Formulating a Family in Genetics: A Contextual Framework   43

3   English Tort Law and the Patient's Family Members   77

4   Medical Confidentiality and Genetic Privacy   123

5   Who is the Patient? The Medical Perception of the Family   163

6   The Status of Family Members: Discussion and Conclusions   201

References   *233*
Index   *253*
Index of Cases Cited   *267*

Preface

The book concerns the legal and ethical obligations of doctors and patients in communicating diagnostic and predictive genetic information to the patient's family members. The focus is on two familial tensions. First is the tension between the patient's interest in keeping the information in confidence and the relatives' interest in being informed; second is the tension between the patient's interest in sharing the information and the relatives' interest in remaining ignorant. In these two familial tensions the doctor's professional obligations are investigated. On the one hand, doctors have to respect patient autonomy, confidentiality and privacy, but on the other hand, they may owe a moral and professional duty to help the relatives who may be affected by the information.

The examination of these conflicts is conducted within the liberal-communitarian debate. In this context, the two philosophies hold different perceptions of the individual, his or her autonomy, and the relationship he or she has with others. While, liberals support an individualistic perception of autonomy communitarians and proponents of ethics-of-care perceive this principle relationally.

Within this theoretical framework, this book examines the approach taken by English medical law and ethics to communication of genetic information to family members. Legally, the focus is on tort law (especially the duty of care), and the law of confidentiality. Ethically, it concentrates on the approach taken by the bioethical literature, and more specifically by codes of ethics and professional guidelines.

Subsequently, these legal and ethical approaches are compared to the leading medical model of doctor-patient relationship and the socio-medical empirical studies which examine the views of doctors and patients with regard to communication of medical information to family members. The conclusions arrived at this book is that there is a gap between law and medicine in this area and that this gap should be bridged.

A few people helped me arrive to this stage and it is my pleasant duty to thank them. There are the people in the Department of Law in Queen Mary College University of London. I wish to thank Dr. Paula Giliker, Mr. Jonathan Griffiths, and my friend, Dr. Jill Marshall. I would also like to thank Ms Penney Lewis, a lecturer in the School of Law in King's College London, and Dr. Michael Parker, a reader in medical ethics in Oxford University whose illuminating observations contributed to the completion of this book.

I would like to express my appreciation to Netanya Academic College for its financial support, to Mr Murray Rosovsky for his editorial assistance and to Genoveba Breitstein for her technical help.

Finally, there are two special ladies without whom this book would not have been completed. I would like to express my thanks and love to my wife, Yael, who encouraged me to keep going at difficult times and taught me the practical meaning of family support. Professor Katherine O'Donovan has been an enormous source of inspiration from the early days of my research. It was her unique approach to research and her warm character that led to my decision to write this book.

The law is stated at 1 March 2005.

Roy Gilbar
Tel-Aviv, May 2005

Chapter 1

The Liberal–Communitarian Debate in Medical Law and Ethics

1.1 Introduction

Robert Powell was 10 years old when he died from a condition called Addison's disease. Shortly after his death the doctors explained to the parents why their son had died, presenting them with the medical records. However, a few months later the parents discovered that the doctors had tampered with the medical records to cover up their negligent diagnosis. This caused the parents psychological harm.[1]

Donna Safer was 10 when her father was diagnosed with colon cancer. It was known that that type of cancer had a genetic component, which meant that Donna might inherit it. The doctor did not inform Donna or her mother about the hereditary aspect of the disease and it was not known whether the doctor had informed the father. When Donna was 36 she was diagnosed with the same type of colon cancer as that of her father. When she received her father's medical records she realised that had she been informed in time the disease could have been prevented.[2]

The stories of Robert Powell and Donna Safer raise a significant issue in English medical law and medical ethics: the status of family members in health care. One can think of many situations where the patient's medical condition affects the lives of his or her relatives. For example, when the patient suffers from a serious disease, family members usually change their daily life to provide him or her with care and emotional support. In addition, the patient's condition may affect the relatives psychologically, causing them stress and anxiety when his or her health deteriorates. The above cases present another aspect of this issue, namely that medical information has implications not only for the patient but also for the family members.

Despite the close involvement of family members in a patient's medical care it seems that law and ethics do not pay sufficient attention to their interests. This circumstance can be observed from two perspectives. One is the *doctor–patient* relationship. In this context English courts and professional codes of ethics address the interests of family members in two respects: first, when patients are incapable

---

[1] *Powell v Boldaz* [1998] Lloyd's Rep. Med. 116 (hereafter: *Powell*).

[2] *Safer v Pack* (1996) 677 A.2d 1188 (NJ Super Ct A D) (hereafter: *Safer*).

of giving consent to medical treatment;[3] and second, when the patient's condition endangers the health of his or her family. Yet even in these two categories the interests of family members are not fully recognised. In the former, family members cannot make decisions for incompetent patients; usually the patient's doctors act as a quasi–proxy in accordance with what they believe to be the patient's best interests.[4] In the latter category, when the patient poses a risk to family members, their interests are discussed in three instances: when a mentally– ill patient threatens seriously to harm them; when the patient suffers from an infectious disease; and when the patient suffers from a genetic disorder which may be passed on to other blood relatives. In these circumstances the ultimate authority is given to doctors. They are required to decide, especially when the patient is reluctant to inform the relatives, whether disclosure can save them from serious physical harm.[5]

The limited recognition in the interests of family members can be also seen from the perspective of the *patient–relatives* relationship. Courts hardly interfere with the relationships within families in the medical context. Since the opponents in legal procedures are usually the doctor and the patient or the doctor and the relative, the courts do not come upon circumstances where they are required to discuss the relationship between patients and relatives. By the same token, some professional codes of ethics are focused on the rights of patients vis–à–vis doctors to make informed decisions and not on the implications any decision would have for the relatives.[6]

Yet in the context of the patient–relatives relationship law and medical ethics seem not to speak in one voice. First, there are professional codes of ethics that address the relationship between patients and relatives.[7] Second, there are ethicists who discuss the relevance and significance of the familial relationship when patients are involved in medical decision–making.[8] A gap is apparent between law and ethics: while English law is focused primarily on the doctor–patient relationship, medical ethics addresses, even if not comprehensively, the patient– relatives relationship.

---

[3]   Examples are when an adult patient is incompetent to give consent to treatment, or when the patient is a child too young to understand the implications of the medical decision.

[4]   Kennedy I., Grubb A., *Medical Law*, London, Butterworths (3rd edn., 2000), 831 (Hereafter: Kennedy and Grubb). This position will be changed when the *Mental Capacity Act* 2005 comes into force, probably in 2007.

[5]   The General Medical Council, *Confidentiality: Protecting and Providing Information*, London, General Medical Council (2000), para. 14, 18, 36.

[6]   General Medical Council, *Good Medical Practice*, London, General Medical Council (3rd edn., May 2001); This prevails also in the GMC's guidance on Confidentiality. See Chapter 4 for analysis.

[7]   British Medical Association, *Human Genetics: Choice and Responsibility*, Oxford, Oxford University Press (1998), pp. 21–24.

[8]   Lindemann-Nelson H., Lindemann-Nelson J., *The Patient in the Family*, New York, Routledge (1995) (hereafter: the Lindemann-Nelsons).

The first assumption in this book is that law and medical ethics largely ignore the interests of family members. This assumption will be examined in a specific context, that of communication of genetic information from doctors and patients to family members. It is well established that not only does genetic information affect the individual patient, it has considerable implications for family members. Susceptibility to genetic diseases is transmitted from parents to their offspring in conception, so when a patient is diagnosed as a carrier or as a sufferer of a genetic disorder this implies that his or her family members may suffer from the same condition.

In these circumstances the question whether the interests of family members are fully recognised arises. When genetic information is communicated to the patient but has implications for family members, familial tensions may emerge. There are two possible tensions in this context. First, the patient may perceive the information as personal, and wishes to keep it in confidence, while the relatives may view the information as familial, and demand to be informed. A second tension may arise when the patient who receives the information from the doctor wishes to share it with his or her relatives but they wish to remain ignorant.[9] In a broader sense these familial tensions regarding the access to genetic information concerns the involvement of family members in medical decision–making, namely whether their interests are taken into account in this process. In this chapter the emphasis will be on the first tension.

The assumption that law and ethics do not take the interests of family members seriously at least in the area of genetic information leads to a series of questions which will be examined in this book. First, if it is accepted that law and medical ethics do not fully recognise the interests of family members, the immediate question is why not. A possible hypothesis is that in their underlying philosophy both law and ethics rest on liberal–individualism, which calls on doctors to respect the autonomy of patients to make informed decisions without controlling influences. If this is accepted, the next question is whether this philosophy accords with current medical practices and public views about the involvement of family members. It is assumed that there is a gap between the two because numerous studies indicate that doctors and patients consider the interests of family members during the course of treatment. Lastly, if this assumption is accepted, the final question is whether a different philosophical approach exists that may represent more adequately the practical involvement of family members generally and in the context of genetics particularly. The argument put forward in this book is that values such as solidarity, moral responsibility, care and commitment should be taken into account with liberal conceptions of autonomy and justice when the interests of patients and those of their relatives are considered.

---

[9] A third tension, which will be discussed briefly in this book, is between the interest of the patient in not receiving information from the doctor about his or her condition and the relatives' interest in receiving it.

To sum up, the three hypotheses examined in this work are: (1) English law and medical ethics reflect a liberal–individualistic approach which constricts the interests of family members in knowing and not knowing genetic information. (2) This liberal individualistic approach is not compatible with current views of doctors and patients. Therefore (3) English law and medical ethics should adopt a different approach, which combines communitarian as well as ethics–of–care conceptions with liberal principles.

These three assumptions dictate the structure of this work, whose theoretical framework is laid down in this chapter. The discussion will concentrate on the liberal and communitarian perceptions of the individual and its relationship with others. This will be followed in Chapter 2 by a brief account of genetics, how genetic disorders are manifested and how they affect patients and their relatives. This leads to a fundamental question in this book of what constitutes a family in genetics: is a family in genetics defined by its blood relations or are social bonds important as well? In Chapters 3 and 4 the first two assumptions will be examined, namely whether or not English law and ethics recognise the interests of family members in knowing and not knowing genetic information, and whether this position is based on a liberal discourse. In Chapter 5 the last assumption will be investigated, namely how doctors and patients perceive the role of family members in health care and whether there is a gap between their views and the legal position. This will lead to the final chapter, where some suggestions for a change in the legal position are made.

Focusing on these three assumptions requires beginning with a brief account of the main themes of liberalism, communitarianism, and ethics–of–care. This is the main purpose of this chapter. It will discuss the philosophical debate on the perception of the individual and its relationship with others. In this debate, there is the liberal belief that the individual can choose his or her ends and the communitarian view that the individual is defined by its ends.

Consequently, the first part of this chapter will provide a brief account of liberalism. The second part will examine whether liberal principles are adopted in medical ethics and the law. It will be shown that principles of autonomy and utility underlie the leading ethical position but are less influential in medical law. The analysis of the liberal perception of the individual will lead to the question, discussed in the fourth part, of whether liberal conceptions alone provide a satisfactory solution to familial tension over medical genetic information. Since the answer to this question will be that a liberal approach is not comprehensive enough to deal with this particular subject, a brief account of communitarianism and ethics–of–care will be provided. In the fifth and final part of this chapter some models that apply communitarian conceptions in the specific context of genetics will be examined. The discussion about these models will reflect not only the gap between law and ethics in this area but also the limitations of the legal position with regard to the status of family members.

The discussion in this chapter is brief, as it aims only to set out the complex issues this book raises. The hypotheses put forward in this chapter will be examined in more detail in the subsequent chapters. In addition, the analysis of medical law and medical ethics in this chapter is not comprehensive: it simply aims to illustrate the general attitude to family members.

1.2 Liberalism: The Individual as Autonomous Person

It is difficult to provide a brief account of liberalism, as this branch in political philosophy has many variations.[10] Classical liberals, such as John Locke and Adam Smith, promote the ideas of restricted governmental control, preservation of the rule of law, avoidance of arbitrary power, primacy of private property, freedom to contract, and individuals' responsibility for their own lives.[11] In contrast, modern liberalism limits the scope of freedom of contract and of property rights. Rawls, for example, accepts that personal property is an essential element to individual self–expression.[12] He believes in liberty and justice but he also maintains that inequalities are justified to the extent that they improve the position of the least advantaged. This is not accepted by classical liberals.[13]

There are three different justifications for liberal principles.[14] There are utilitarians, such as Bentham and Mill, who believe that the morally right act is the one which produces the greatest happiness for all members of society. There are libertarians, such as Nozick, who believe that the individual owns his or her rights as a form of private property; and there are those, such as Kant and Rawls, who believe in justice based on a social contract. However, despite the differences between them, the literature perceives these justifications as strands of the liberal approach.[15]

Three conceptions are common to all strands of liberalism: *individualism, universalism*, and *egalitarianism*.[16] In this book the focus will be on *individualism*, as it relates to the perception of the individual and his or her relationships with others.

---

[10] Ryan A., "Liberalism" in Goodin R., Pettit P. (eds.), *A Companion to Contemporary Political Philosophy*, Oxford, Blackwell (1993), pp. 291–312.

[11] Ibid., at p. 293; For a more detailed account of classical liberalism see Gray J., *Liberalism*, Milton Keynes, Open University Press (1986), Chapters 2 & 3.

[12] Rawls J., *A Theory of Justice*, Oxford, Oxford University Press (1971), 272–274.

[13] See Ryan, supra n. 10, at p. 297.

[14] See Gray, supra n. 11, chapter 6, pp. 45–61; see also Kymlicka W., *Contemporary Political Philosophy: An introduction*, Oxford, Oxford University Press (2nd edn., 2002), at p. x where he defines these three approaches as 'three influential defences of liberal democracy'.

[15] See Gray, supra n. 11, at p. ix.

[16] Ibid., at p. x; For a comprehensive analysis of liberalism see Kymlicka W., *Contemporary Political Philosophy: An Introduction*, Oxford, Oxford University Press (2nd edn., 2002), 2–4

Liberals value individual rights and freedom, equality, the conviction that all people are potentially[17] rational, and most importantly the understanding that the individual is first and foremost distinct from others and potentially in conflict with society.[18] When analysing the nature of the individual, liberals argue that people are not only rational but also possess the capacity to choose and to enter into agreements. One of the core perceptions of the liberal tradition is that the individual is pre-social, namely that individuals have a fundamental essence before they enter into society. Thus, what makes one an individual does not depend upon a specific social situation.

The argument that the individual is pre-social prevails in the seminal work of John Rawls, *Theory of Justice*, where he emphasises that justice is the most fundamental principle.[19] Rawls describes a hypothetical situation, 'the original position', where all the participating parties do not know their inherent characteristics, such as race, class, ethnicity, and the like. Thus, the parties to the original position are under what Rawls calls a 'veil of ignorance'. In this position, when they do not know what their social status will be, the primary good the parties are likely to wish for is justice because it will secure their basic needs.[20] In addition, according to Rawls, the parties to the original position are mutually disinterested, and in promoting their goals they do not owe moral duties to each other.[21]

It is apparent from Rawls's theory that the process whereby the parties to the original position reach justice is based on agreement and social contract.[22] Thus, agreement is a fundamental principle in this theory because it leads to justice. Agreements and contracts are perceived as the result of acts of will, whose morality consists in their voluntariness. The act of will leads to the concept of autonomy, namely the notion that the individual determines and chooses his or her way of life. Therefore, from the perspective of autonomy, the individual's obligations to others are to those he or she voluntarily assumes.[23] In other words,

---

[17] There is a dispute whether individuals must exercise their autonomy *rationally* or whether they can act foolishly so long as they do not harm others. This debate exists in the context of the patient's right *not* to know genetic information. For an argument that supports rational choice see: Rhodes R., "Genetic links, family ties, and social bonds: Rights and responsibilities in the face of genetic knowledge" (1998) 23 *Journal of Medicine & Philosophy* 10; for the opposite view see: Takala T., "The right to genetic ignorance confirmed" (1999) 13 *Bioethics* 288.

[18] Frazer E., Lacey N., *The Politics of Community*, Hemel Hempstead, Harvester (1993), 41–53.

[19] Rawls J., *A Theory of Justice*, Oxford, Oxford University Press (1971), 3; still, Rawls justifies an unjust act only if it can improve the least advantaged.

[20] Ibid., at p. 12.

[21] Ibid., at p. 13–14.

[22] Sandel M., *Liberalism and the Limits of Justice*, Cambridge, Cambridge University Press (1982), 105

[23] Ibid., at p. 107.

the individual and the contract are the primary conceptions in Rawls's theory. The individual is prior to his or her ends because he or she chooses them, and the contract is prior to the principle of justice because the parties to the original position agree to it and do not merely find it.

Rawls relies on the work of Immanuel Kant.[24] Kant argues that the individual is always an end in itself and should never be perceived as a means to other people.[25] This Kantian approach (also called deontological) suggests that the individual possesses a will he or she can exercise freely. Thus, Kant argues, the individual is capable of acting autonomously. The most important characteristic of the individual is not the ends he or she chooses but his or her ability to choose them.[26]

The importance of autonomy is evident in the work of Isaiah Berlin. Berlin argues that there are two concepts of liberty. A positive concept of liberty is the individual's freedom to lead his or her ordered form of life[27] which derives from the individual's wish to be his or her own master.[28] A negative concept is absence of interference by others. In his discussion Berlin refers to Mill, who stresses that society should not interfere with the decisions of individuals so long as they do not interfere with the freedom of others.[29]

Yet arguing that liberals perceive the individual as socially unencumbered is not accurate. Following considerable criticism[30] liberals modified their perception of the individual. Rawls, for example, denies that his conception of the individual is individualistic. In his later work he emphasises that he intends his theory of justice to be a political conception, not a general moral approach. Rawls argues that in formulating his conception of justice he has tried to avoid dependence on philosophical claims regarding the essence of the identity of the individual.[31] Focusing on the original position, Rawls explicitly recognises the dominance of the social aspect of life, and observes that the original position generates a social perspective.[32]

---

[24] Rawls's work derived from his dissatisfaction of utilitarianism. See Rawls, supra n.19, at pp. 26–27, 33

[25] See Gray, supra n. 11, at p. 50–51, Frazer and Lacey, supra n. 18, at p. 43–45.

[26] Mulhall S., Swift A., *Liberals and Communitarians*, Oxford, Blackwell (2nd edn., 1996), pp. 43–44; Rawls explicitly relies on Kant in developing his contractual theory. See Rawls, supra n. 19, at p. 11.

[27] Berlin I., *Four Essays on Liberty*, Oxford, Oxford University Press (1969), 131.

[28] Ibid.

[29] Mill J.S., *On Liberty and Other Essays* (London, 1859), Oxford, Oxford University Press (1991), pp. 83–104.

[30] See the discussion about communitarianism in this chapter.

[31] Rawls J., "Justice as fairness: Political not metaphysical" (1985) 14 (3) *Philosophy and Public Affairs* 223, 224–225.

[32] Rawls J., "Kantian constructivism in moral theory" (1980) 77 *Journal of Philosophy* 515, 552, 570.

Rawls was not the only one to clarify his perception of the individual. Other liberals did so as well. They stress the individual's ability to critically evaluate his or her ends.[33] Daniel Bell explains this change in focus, commenting that liberals may accept the social context of the individual, but they also argue that he or she can engage in an autonomous examination and reflection of the relationships he or she has.[34]

These clarifications or modifications made in the liberal discourse did not satisfy the critics. Focusing on the 'original position', Frazer and Lacey argue that it seems inherently unable to generate the social perspective that Rawls now explains it aspires for. Instead, the two critics argue, the parties to the original position must have a particular social standpoint to begin with, and this obviously contradicts the requirement of the veil of ignorance.[35] In addition, as we shall see, communitarians still maintain that individuals cannot distance themselves from close social attachments as they constitute part of their identity and help them exercise their autonomy.

However, liberals sometimes struggle with situations of conflict, especially when the interest of one individual clashes with that of another. For example, in the context of this study the patient's interest in keeping genetic information in confidence may clash with the relatives' interest in receiving this information. In addition, an individual's right may clash with public interest. For example, a policy that enforces screening all newborns for cystic fibrosis may, on the one hand, compromise the autonomy of parents to take decisions regarding their child, but on the other hand it may improve public health in general by controlling the spread of a fatal disease. Does the interest of the patient outweigh the interest of family members in the first conflict? Can the individual's right to autonomy outweigh public interest in the second conflict? Some liberals, such as Ronald Dworkin, acknowledge the force of this argument and make a concession by relying on a utilitarian philosophy.[36] Mill, in "Utilitarianism", argues that the promotion of social utility may lead to the sacrifice of the individual's interests.[37] Hence, the conflict may be resolved by arriving at a decision that causes the least harm to the parties involved. Dworkin agrees that if an individual's right seriously endangers the welfare of the public at large, the

---

[33] Kymlicka W., *Liberalism, Community and Culture*, Oxford, Clarendon Press (1989), 52; see also Dworkin R., "Liberal Community" (1989) 77 *California Law Review* 489.

[34] Bell D., *Communitarianism and Its Critics*, Oxford, Clarendon Press (1993), 9.

[35] See Frazer and Lacey, supra n. 18, at pp. 58–59.

[36] Mason JK., McCall–Smith RA., Laurie GT., *Law and Medical Ethics*, London, Butterworths (6th edn., 2002), 7 provide a brief account on utilitarian approaches.

[37] Mill J.S., *On Liberty and Other Essays* (London, 1859), Oxford, Oxford University Press (1991), pp. 131–201.

public interest should prevail.[38]   Therefore, in the above conflicts the patient's right to confidentiality can be breached if this may prevent greater harm to family members; and the parents' right not to screen their child for CF may be compromised if population screening indeed reduces morbidity and mortality. However, the circumstances where individual autonomy can be compromised should be, according to this approach, extremely rare.[39]

1.3 The Application of the Liberal Approach to Medical Law and Medical Ethics

So far, I have argued that law and ethics failed to recognise the involvement of family members. I assumed that that position derived from reliance on a liberal philosophy, which includes deontological and utilitarian conceptions. Hence, these conceptions were briefly described. Consequently, the next stage is to examine whether these conceptions prevail in medical ethics and law generally. Examining this will provide the basis for the discussion in Chapters 3 and 4, where the legal and ethical attitudes to family members in the context of genetics will be specifically investigated.

1.3.1 Medical Ethics

The most prominent principle in medical ethics today is respect for autonomy.[40] Two components are essential when individuals exercise their autonomy: (1) *Choice*,[41] which includes respect for one's choices and the ability to act without interference by others;[42] and (2) *Agency*, or the capacity to act intentionally.[43] Agency is not under discussion in this work; it is assumed that the patient is competent. By contrast, choice is a central theme in this study and it is viewed as an element of one's identity.[44] Autonomous people are 'choosers', who act intentionally with a substantial degree of understanding and without controlling influences.[45]   Beauchamp and Childress recognise that several professional

---

[38] Dworkin, R., *Taking Rights Seriously*, Cambridge, Harvard University Press (1977), pp. 190–192.

[39] Rawls argues that utilitarians fail to take seriously the distinction between people. See supra n. 19.

[40] Mason, McCall–Smith and Laurie, supra n. 36, at p. 8.

[41] Raz J., *The Morality of Freedom*, Oxford, Clarendon Press (1986), 370–373.

[42] Dworkin G., *The Theory and Practice of Autonomy*, Cambridge, Cambridge University Press (1988), 18–19.

[43] Beauchamp T., Childress J., *Principles of Biomedical Ethics*, New York, Oxford University Press (5th edn., 2001), 58.

[44] This notion is borrowed from Bergsma J., Thomasma D., *Autonomy and Clinical Medicine*, Boston, Kluwer Academics (2000).

[45] See Beauchamp and Childress, supra n. 43, at p. 59.

obligations derive from this principle, including truth–telling, protecting patients' confidentiality, respecting their privacy, and obtaining their consent.[46]

What does autonomy mean in medical ethics? Gerald Dworkin lists twelve different conceptions, to which Faden and Beauchamp add several more.[47] Undoubtedly, the availability of different conceptions does not provide a unifying definition of the principle of autonomy. Although Kant is regularly invoked in support of conceptions of autonomy prevailing in medical ethics and law today, a recent restatement of Kantian autonomy denies that his version is associated with an extreme version of individualism or with ignorance of the ethical importance of emotions and social institutions.[48] Autonomy, as explained by Onora O'Neill, requires not only principles that apply to all but also active concern for others. This view reflects the change in the perception of autonomy. O'Neill, who provides the most recent contribution to the discussion about autonomy, accepts that an individualistic interpretation, which sees the patient as separate from others, where her or his decisions are made independently of, or even indifferently to, others, is insufficient.

If clarity and consistency are sought in this area, where different conceptions of autonomy are available, it is necessary to concentrate on one interpretation. Thus, autonomy as interpreted by Beauchamp and Childress is analysed. There are two reasons for this choice. First, their four principles approach to medical ethics is influential.[49] As one commentator admits, though other approaches to medical ethics exist,[50] the strong impact of their approach is indisputable.[51] Second, the two authors respond to alternative interpretations of autonomy. Recently, they explicitly accepted that respect for patient autonomy must not be excessively individualistic but should take into account the social nature of the individual and the impact of his or her choices on others.[52] They accept in part a critique of individualism admitting that the individual is socially embedded and that his or her

---

[46]   Ibid., at p. 65.
[47]   See Dworkin, supra n. 42, p. 6; Faden R., Beauchamp T., *The History and Theory of Informed Consent*, New York, Oxford University Press, (1986); for a recent discussion see: O'Neill O., *Autonomy and Trust in Bioethics*, Cambridge, Cambridge University Press (2002).
[48]   Ibid., O'Neill, at p. 74.
[49]   Robert Dingwall, "Bioethics" in Pilnick A., *Genetics and Society: An Introduction*, Buckingham, Open University Press, pp. 161–180; Beauchamp and Childress argue that there are four guiding principles in medical ethics: respect for autonomy (i.e., respecting the patient's choice), nonmaleficence (causing no harm to the patient), beneficence (performing affirmative acts to help patients and others), and justice (providing patients with fair, equitable, and appropriate medical treatment).
[50]   See, for example, the discussion between Gillon, Beauchamp, Macklin, Sommerville, Callahan, Campbell, Gardiner, and Harris in (2003) 29 (5) *Journal of Medical Ethics* 267–312.
[51]   Laurie G., *Genetic Privacy*, Cambridge, Cambridge University Press (2002), 189.
[52]   See Beauchamp and Childress, supra n. 43, at p. 57.

identity is considerably affected by the social relationships he or she has with others.[53]

Beauchamp and Childress rely on liberal conceptions when giving their account of autonomy. They adhere to Kant and Mill when justifying respect for autonomy. They emphasise Kant's perception of the individual as an end in itself, and Mill's requirement of non-interference. In addition, relying on Berlin,[54] they argue that the principle of respect for autonomy has two aspects: a negative obligation, namely that autonomous action should not be subject to controlling influences by others, and a positive obligation, which calls for respect in disclosing information and engaging in autonomous decision–making.[55]

A closer look reveals that they focus on the individual patient. This prevails when Beauchamp and Childress discuss voluntariness, which is essential in any conception of autonomy. The two authors argue that the patient acts voluntarily if he or she acts without being under the influence of others.[56] In this context, one would expect the authors to discuss the involvement of family members when the patient makes a decision. However, apart from an initial statement that the patient makes decisions under the influence of family members[57] the authors do not deal with this issue at all. Instead, they focus on the doctor–patient relationship, analysing the circumstances when the doctor unduly influences the patient. Beauchamp and Childress do not define 'controlling influences' when family members intervene in the decision–making process or when the doctor takes their interests into account. By ignoring this issue the authors avoid the question posed in this book, namely 'what is the status of family members when the patient makes a decision?'.

The account provided by Beauchamp and Childress of autonomy implies that when patients have to choose between two or more medical treatments the interests of their family members are not an essential factor. However, the relatives may have various interests: they may prefer the patient to undergo the treatment in hospital owing to their inability to provide him or her with full–time care; or they may prefer the patient to convalesce at home. Yet these considerations, whether perceived as controlling influences or not, are overlooked. Therefore, despite their explicit efforts to display awareness of the social nature of the individual, Beauchamp's and Childress's account of autonomy seems to be situated on the individualistic side of the spectrum for it focuses on the individual patient and his or her relationship with the doctor.

---

[53] Mackenzie C., Stoljar N. (eds.), *Relational Autonomy: Feminist Perspectives on Autonomy, Agency and the Social Self*, New York, Oxford University Press (2000).

[54] See Berlin, supra n. 27, pp. 118–172.

[55] See Beauchamp and Childress, supra n. 43, at p. 64.

[56] Ibid., at p. 93.

[57] Ibid., at p. 95.

Another principle in Beauchamp's and Childress's approach is beneficence.[58] The discussion of this principle is important in the context of this book as it reflects the moral weight given to the interests of others. The two ethicists understand this principle to include acts aimed to benefit those who are the doctor's patients and those who are not. The authors distinguish *general* beneficence, which is directed to all persons, from *specific* beneficence, which is directed to those who have close relationships such as the doctors' patients. They agree that in a close familial relationship or in a doctor–patient relationship the parties are obliged to act in the interests of others. However, they argue that there are limits to beneficence because it is unpractical to owe similar beneficent obligations to patients and to strangers. Therefore, one person (the doctor) has an obligation to benefit the other (the stranger) only if all the following conditions are satisfied: (1) the stranger is at risk of significant harm to life or health or other important interest; (2) the doctor's action is needed to prevent this harm; (3) the doctor's action has a high probability of preventing this harm; (4) the doctor's action does not entail significant risk to himself or herself; and (5) the benefit that the stranger will gain outweighs any injuries and costs that the doctor is likely to incur. Beauchamp and Childress stress that the fourth condition is the most significant. The action would not be morally obligatory if the doctor faced a significant risk in trying to save the stranger's life. Hence, a passer–by does not owe a moral duty to rescue someone drowning in deep water. However, he or she may be morally culpable when failing to save a child drowning in a shallow pool.

Beauchamp and Childress struggle with the question of how wide is the scope of this principle. On the one hand, they admit that the American case of *McFall v Shimp*,[59] where one individual refused to donate bone marrow to his cousin, is a borderline case of specific beneficence as the potential donor was exposed to the low risk involved in anaesthesia.[60] On the other hand, they argue that a psychiatrist has a duty to warn his patient's potential victim or the police, as was held in the well–known case of *Tarasoff*.[61] Ultimately, the authors promote beneficence not by imposing Good Samaritan laws but by providing people protection from legal liability when they decide to render help to strangers.

Reliance on a utilitarian mechanism prevails in Beauchamp's and Childress's approach when there is a conflict between respect for autonomy and beneficence. Such a conflict may arise when doctors face competing obligations, for example, whether to respect a patient's autonomous decision to keep information in confidence or to benefit family members by informing them.[62] When dealing with

---

58 See Beauchamp and Childress supra n. 43, pp. 165–176.
59 *McFall v Shimp* (1978) 10 Pa D & C 3d 90 (Pa Comm Pl).
60 See Beauchamp and Childress, supra n. 43, at p. 172.
61 *Tarasoff v Regents of the University of California* (1976) 131 Cal Rptr 14 (Cal Sup Ct).
62 However, the duty of confidentiality may also involve the principle of nonmaleficence: disclosing medical information to family members without consent may cause harm to the patient. In this context, harm is not limited to physical injury but also includes

this conflict, the two ethicists adopt a utilitarian mechanism, directing to the one act that causes the least harm to the parties involved. When discussing whether *genetic* information should be disclosed to family members the authors justify a breach of patient's right to confidentiality when the patient refuses to disclose and serious physical harm can be avoided.[63]

This mechanism leads to the impression that the interests of family members are less significant than those of the patient, and that the obligation to respect patient autonomy is more important than the obligation to benefit others. Furthermore, the focus on the doctor–patient relationship neglects the social surroundings of this conflict, which may be crucial in understanding the patient's refusal to disclose. In many cases, the patient's refusal may be explained by the nature of the relationship with his or her relatives. Furthermore, this position implies that the patient's identity is fundamentally distinct from that of close others. Though the two authors acknowledge that patients owe a moral obligation to disclose genetic information to their relatives, the underlying reason is the interest in preventing harm (and more specifically physical harm) and not the interest in promoting the mutual familial relationship.[64]

Moving on to the practical aspect, some professional guidelines reflect a patient–centred approach. The guidance of the General Medical Council on good practice is an example.[65] Doctors are instructed to make the care of their patients their primary concern.[66] They have to respect patients' dignity and privacy and protect their confidentiality. They should respect patients' right to be fully involved in decisions about their care.[67] This terminology highlights the rights of the individual patient vis-à-vis the doctor. The guidelines pay little attention to the various needs of those who are closely involved in the patient's care, namely the relatives. The interests of family members when a decision has to be made are limited.[68] When defining what constitutes good communication between doctors

---

psychological harm or interferences with other personal interests. As Ruth Macklin argues, for many doctors this is the most important obligation they owe to patients as it accords with the essence of their profession: Macklin R., 'Applying the four principles' (2003) 29 *Journal of Medical Ethics* 275.

[63] Ibid., at p. 312.

[64] It is important to note at this point that not only do standards of confidentiality affect individual family members but they also affect the public at large. The protection of confidentiality affects the level of public trust in the health care system. From this perspective confidentiality will benefit the public as it encourages people to come forward and receive treatment they would not otherwise get.

[65] General Medical Council, *Good Medical Practice*, London, General Medical Council (3rd edn., 2001). The guidance can be found in the following website: http://www.gmc-uk.org.

[66] Ibid., the introductory para.

[67] Ibid.

[68] A patient–centred approach prevails in the GMC's guidance on confidentiality. See Chapter 4, part 4.2.2.

and patients the GMC states that it involves 'listening to patients and respecting their views and beliefs; giving patients the information they ask for or need about their condition, its treatment and prognosis...'; and 'sharing information with patients' partners, close relatives or carers... by, *having first obtained the patient's consent.*'[69]

To sum up, medical ethics generally relies on liberal conceptions of the individual, which reflect a patient–centred approach. This observation is not based solely on the four principles approach but on the writings of other ethicists and the existence of codes of practice, whose approach will be analysed in subsequent chapters. The purpose of concentrating on the four principles approach and the GMC's guidance was to provide initial indication to support the hypothesis that medical ethics does not devote sufficient attention to family members.[70] One should not infer from this that medical ethics is principlist or that the GMC's guidance is the only practical guidance.

Still, the discussion so far also indicates that recently leading ethicists who rely on deontological and utilitarian approaches have begun to pay more attention to the social nature of the individual.[71] They accept that in exercising autonomy the individual cannot ignore the existence of close others who may be considerably affected by his or her decision. In addition, different approaches to medical ethics do exist, interpreting autonomy differently and stressing that close family members are part of an individual's identity and autonomy.[72] As we shall see in Chapters 3 and 4, this observation is reflected in the specific context of genetics. Some commentators and professional codes of ethics provide a less individualistic interpretation of autonomy, and emphasise other principles such as solidarity and moral responsibility.

1.3.2 Medical Law

One of the most prominent principles in English medical law is consent. This principle governs the relationships between doctors and patients. English law has long recognised that patients have the right to have their bodily integrity protected against invasion by others. Only in limited circumstances can patients be legally

---

[69] Ibid., at para 21 (my italics).

[70] The only major advocate in the UK of the four principles approach is Raanan Gillon. Other leading ethicists do not adhere to it. See the views expressed by other UK ethicists in (2003) 29 (5) *Journal of Medical Ethics* 267–312, and also: Holm S., "Not just autonomy – the principles of American biomedical ethics" (1995) 21 *Journal of Medical Ethics* 332; Parker M., "Introduction" in Parker M. (ed.), *Ethics and Community in the Health Care Professions*, London, Routledge (1999).

[71] See Mason, McCall–Smith and Laurie, supra n. 36, at p. 8; Sommerville A., "Juggling law, ethics, and intuition: Practical answers to awkward questions" (2003) 29 (5) *Journal of Medical Ethics* 281.

[72] See the Lindemann–Nelsons, supra n. 8; Wolf S. (ed.), *Feminism and Bioethics: Beyond Reproduction*, New York, Oxford University Press (1996).

treated without consent. In most cases treatment without consent will be considered battery.

The legal principle of consent reflects the ethical principle of autonomy, more specifically the view that individuals have the right of self–determination with regard to their body. In *Re F*,[73] the famous words of Cardozo J were adopted in an English court: 'Every human being of adult years and sound mind has a right to determine what shall be done with his own body; and a surgeon who performs an operation without his patient's consent commits an assault, for which he is liable in damages'.[74]

The legal requirements for a valid consent are similar to those in medical ethics. Consent has to be (1) given by a competent patient; (2) based on adequate information; and (3) voluntary and not given under the undue influence of others (in short, competence, information, and voluntariness).[75] Since competence is not in question in this study the focus will be on the other two components. As regards information, consent cannot be valid if the patient is not adequately informed.[76] Although this phrase is subject to extensive criticism by the courts[77] and the legal academics[78] it means that the patient must understand adequately the nature of the proposed treatment and therefore relevant information should be disclosed. This implies that the patient has a legal right to receive information and that the doctor has a duty to inform him or her. Failure to do so may result in a claim in negligence or in battery. However, the courts restricted the possibility of patients' bringing a claim in battery. Lord Scarman held that it would be unacceptable to base the law in this medical context on the torts of assault and battery.[79] Kennedy and Grubb argue that a claim in battery concerns information about the nature of and the reason for the physical contact with the patient, while a claim in negligence

---

[73]   *Re F* (*Mental Patient: Sterilization*) [1990] 2 AC 1; [1989] 2 All ER 545, at p. 564; see also *Airedale NHS Trust v Bland* [1993] AC 789; [1993] 1 All ER 821, at p. 866.

[74]   *Schloendorff v Society of New York Hospital* (1914) 211 NY 125, at p. 126; However, it should be stressed that there is a difference between the principle of respect for autonomy and the individual's right to self–determination. Self–determination represents only one interpretation of autonomy. Other possible interpretations are: Berlin's positive or negative liberty, dignity, freedom of the will, integrity, individuality, independence, responsibility, self–knowledge, critical reflection, freedom from obligation, absence of external causation and knowledge of one's own interests. See Dworkin, supra n 42, at p. 6.

[75]   Grubb A., "Consent to Treatment" in Grubb A., (ed.), *Principles of Medical Law*, Oxford, Oxford University Press (2nd edn., 2004), 134 (Hereafter: Grubb).

[76]   Ibid., at p. 171.

[77]   *Rogers v Whitaker* (1992) 109 ALR 625, 633; *Reibl v Hughes* (1980) 114 DLR (3d) 1, 11.

[78]   See Grubb, supra n. 75, at p. 171; and also Mason, McCall–Smith and Laurie, supra n. 36, at pp. 362–3.

[79]   *Sidaway v Board of Governors of the Bethlem Royal Hospital* [1985] 1 All ER 643, 650.

concerns information related to the risks involved in the procedure.[80] In the next part we will concentrate on negligence.

1.3.2.1 Information. The legal ground for a duty to inform is the special relationship existing between doctors and patients. The exclusivity of this relationship will be dealt with further below, but at this point it should be noted that the doctor's duty to inform the patient derives from his or her undertaking to provide services to the patient who seeks professional medical help.[81] Grubb admits that a doctor's duty to inform the patient is affirmative and therefore contradicts the general rule of English law that there is no liability for omissions. However, Grubb argues that in this context English law reflects a pragmatic approach.[82] Whether or not this is the case, the doctor's duty to inform is based on his or her assumption of responsibility to the patient.

Examining the legal standard regarding the range of information doctors have to communicate to their patients, the law discusses three alternatives. First, doctors may have a duty to communicate information which the particular patient wishes to know. This is a subjective test based on a liberal approach for it emphasises the right of the particular patient to determine the range of information disclosed to him or her. A second option is that the doctor will communicate to the patient information which any reasonable patient would wish to know. Grubb argues that this is a compromise because this test acknowledges the patient's right to be informed but prefers a hypothetical reasonable patient over an actual one.[83] Indeed, this approach does not provide the individual patient with exclusive control over the range of information communicated to him or her. The third and final alternative is that the doctor owes a duty to inform the patient according to medical professional standards. Undoubtedly, this test reflects a paternalistic approach, where doctors, relying on their colleagues' view, can decide for patients the range of information disclosed to them.

Interestingly, despite the dominance of the principle of respect for patient autonomy in medical ethics, English law adopted a paternalistic test. In *Bolam v Friern Barnet Hospital Management*[84] it was held that a doctor's conduct would not be negligent if it complies with a practice accepted by responsible body of medical opinion. The range of information disclosed in practice depends upon the view of a responsible body of doctors. Undoubtedly, this paternalistic approach reflected the view of doctors in the 1950s and 1960s that they know what is best for their patients.

The legal position has been developed since *Bolam*. In the landmark case of

---

[80]   See Kennedy and Grubb, supra n. 4, at p. 658.
[81]   See Grubb, supra n. 75, at p. 180.
[82]   Ibid.
[83]   Ibid., at p. 182.
[84]   [1957] 1 WLR 582 (Hereafter: *Bolam*).

Sidaway v Board of Governors of the Bethlem Royal Hospital[85] only Lord Diplock applied the *Bolam* test narrowly. Other judges presented a different approach. For example, Lord Bridge stated: 'A judge might, in certain circumstances, come to the conclusion that the disclosure of a particular risk was so obviously necessary to an informed choice on the part of the patient that no reasonably prudent medical man would fail to make it'.[86] And Lord Templeman held: '... the court must decide whether the information afforded to the patient was sufficient to alert the patient to the possibility of serious harm of the kind in fact suffered'.[87] Lord Scarman, went even further, and delivered what may be considered a dissenting judgement, stating: 'It was a strange conclusion if our courts should be led to conclude that our law... should permit doctors to determine in what circumstances ... a duty arose to warn'.[88]

The decision in *Sidaway* was subject to considerable debate[89] mainly due to the uncertainty it reflects. In any event, it seems that the majority of judges in the House of Lords were not at one with the decision in *Bolam*. Attempting to present a coherent ratio, Kennedy and Grubb interpreted *Sidaway* as suggesting that doctors' views on disclosure of information are not conclusive.[90] However, in a subsequent case the Court of Appeal applied the *Bolam* test strictly.[91]

Consequently, the legal position which existed at the beginning of the 1990s stood in contrast to the ethical position. A gap between these two disciplines prevailed, especially when patient autonomy gained dominance in medical ethics. However, as Grubb comments on the decision in *Gold*, it is difficult to find any explanation for such a significant conflict between the ethical principles and the courts' position.[92] The gap between ethical and legal obligations resulted in confusion: on the one hand, doctors had to respect the decision made by the patient, but on the other hand they were given considerable discretion to decide the range of information provided to him or her.

Yet the legal position was developed further. In *Bolitho v City and Hackney Health Authority*[93] the House of Lords held that the courts and not the doctors had the authority to decide the required standard of care. But as Lord Browne–Wilkinson stated, this case did not concern a doctor's duty to inform but a duty to

---

85   [1985] AC 871; [1985] 1 All ER 643 (HL) (Hereafter: *Sidaway*)
86   [1985] 1 All ER 643, 663.
87   Ibid., at p. 665.
88   Ibid., at p. 654.
89   Kennedy I., Grubb A., *Medical Law*, London, Butterworths (3rd edn., 2000), pp. 691–704.
90   Ibid., at p. 692.
91   *Gold v Haringey Health Authority* [1988] QB 481 (CA) (hereafter: *Gold*); subsequent cases regarded *Gold* as the authoritative interpretation of *Sidaway*. See *Blyth v Bloomsbury HA* [1993] 4 Med LR 151; For a different interpretation of *Sidaway* see: *Smith v Tunbridge Wells HA* [1994] 5 Med LR 334.
92   See Grubb, supra n. 75, at p. 190.
93   [1997] 4 All ER 771; (1997) 39 BMLR 1 (hereafter: *Bolitho*).

provide medical treatment. However, in a subsequent case concerning a doctor's duty to inform, Lord Woolf relied on *Bolitho*. He stated:

> ... if there is a significant risk which would affect the judgment of a reasonable patient, then in the normal course it is the responsibility of the doctor to inform the patient of that risk, if the information is needed so that the patient can determine for him or herself as to what course of action he or she would adopt.[94]

This reflects a shift in the legal position. Lord Woolf's view was similar to the reasonable patient test adopted in the Australian case of *Rogers v Whittaker*,[95] which requires the doctor to communicate material risks which a reasonable patient would wish to know.[96]

What is the legal position after *Sideway* and *Bolitho*? Kennedy and Grubb state that after *Pearce*, the legal position regarding provision of medical treatment, medical diagnosis, and medical information is the same. The position, the two authors argue, derives from a synthesis of the two House of Lords' decisions. In their view this synthesis reflects the explicit recognition by the Court of Appeal in *Pearce* that it is not for doctors to determine the standard of disclosure as it is ultimately for the court.[97]

Do the courts adopt *Pearce*? Sedley LJ in *Wyatt v Curtis* seemed to prefer *Pearce* to *Sidaway*.[98] The House of Lords addressed this issue of the doctor's duty to warn in *Chester v Afshar*.[99] Although the judges did not adopt explicitly the reasonable patient test, their speeches reflect both rejection of the paternalistic reasonable doctor test[100] and emphasis on the patient's right to respect for autonomy.[101] For example, referring to the doctor's duty to warn, Lord Steyn cited Lord Woolf's words quoted above. Referring to *Sidaway* Lord Walker stated that since that decision patient autonomy had gained greater recognition.[102] However, Lord Hope observed that the court in *Sidaway* made a distinction between the right to make the final decision on treatment, which is exclusively the patient's, and the right to decide the range of information disclosed, which is the doctor's.[103]

In the final part of his speech Lord Hope in *Chester* went farther than Lord Woolf in *Pearce*, adopting what may seem the liberal approach recognised in

---

[94]   *Pearce v United Bristol Healthcare NHS Trust* (1999) 48 BMLR 118 (hereafter: *Pearce*).

[95]   *Rogers v Whittaker* (1992) 67 ALJR 47 (HC of A).

[96]   See Kennedy and Grubb, supra n. 4, at p. 708–709; Jones M., "Informed consent and other fairy stories" (1999) 7 *Medical Law Review* 103.

[97]   Ibid.

[98]   *Wyatt v Curtis* [2003] EWCA Civ 1779, para. 19.

[99]   *Chester v Afshar*, (HL), [2004] WL 228913 (hereafter: *Chester*).

[100] See, for example, Lord Steyn's words in para. 16.

[101] Ibid., at para. 18 where Lord Steyn cited from Ronald Dworkin's book *Life's Dominion*.

[102] Ibid., at para. 92.

[103] Ibid., at para. 54.

medical ethics regarding the patient's right to make autonomous decisions. Lord Hope stated that the doctor's legal duty to warn had at its core the patient's right to make informed choice. He continued by saying that patients' views about a particular treatment decision could differ. People may have different hopes, fears, personal circumstances, and above all personal views on whether they should take a particular risk or not. In his view, the law should enable informed choice not only to patients who find it easy to make treatment decisions but also to patients who find it difficult to decide.[104] Reading this speech one may conclude that Lord Hope wished to depart from *Sidaway* with regard to the doctor's authority to decide the range of information disclosed.

In the end, the views expressed by the judges in *Chester* on disclosure reflect the assumption made by Kennedy and Grubb that after *Pearce* the courts would concentrate on the patient's right to make an informed decision and to decide how his or her body will be treated, which would ensure an adequate balance between the doctor's professional discretion and the patient's fundamental rights.[105]

To sum up, the discussion so far indicates that medical law still concentrates on establishing patient autonomy. When viewing other aspects of legal consent, such as the patient's right to refuse treatments proposed by the doctor, it seems that courts only recently began to claw back power from doctors on behalf of patients. The decision in the case of Ms B[106] indicates how difficult it is for patients to exercise their autonomy when doctors take an opposite view. Despite judicial statements which recognise the legal right of patients to make free decisions, patients still have to appeal to the courts in order to exercise their fundamental rights which have long been recognised in the bioethical literature.

A recent case that demonstrates a legal attempt to re-assert patients' fundamental rights is *Glass v United Kingdom*.[107] The unusual circumstances of the case reflect an unbridgeable conflict between the doctors and the mother of a child patient. The doctors placed a Do Not Resuscitate order in the child's file without his mother's knowledge, and administered morphine against her express refusal to allow this method of treatment.

As the circumstances of the case would suggest, the European Court of Human Rights dealt with it in the context of children's consent (which is beyond the scope of this book). But the court also addressed the issue of consent to proposed treatment in general and in light of the European Convention on Human Rights.[108] It found that the doctors had violated Article 8 of the Convention, which protects the individual's right to private and family life, holding that the doctors' decision to impose treatment on the patient against his mother's express refusal (as she was

---

[104] Ibid., at para. 86–87.

[105] See Kennedy and Grubb, supra n. 4, at pp. 709–710.

[106] *Re B (Consent to treatment: capacity)* [2002] 2 All ER 449; although this case dealt with competence and not with questions of information.

[107] *Glass v United Kingdom* [2004] 1 FCR 553 (hereafter: *Glass*).

[108] The European Convention became part of English law in 1998.

the child's legal proxy) amounted to interference with the patient's right to physical integrity. When further examining whether the doctors' interference was 'necessary in a democratic society', as Article 8 (2) requires, the court held that the doctors should not have tried to overcome the mother's refusal of the proposed treatment.

The European court's message in *Glass* regarding the doctor–patient relationship reached an English court. In *R (on the application of Burke) v The General Medical Council*[109] a patient who suffered from a terminal disease sought clarification from the court regarding the circumstances when artificial nutrition and hydration may be lawfully withheld, arguing that the relevant GMC guidance was incompatible with the rights protected in Articles 2, 3, 8, and 14 of the European Convention.

In an exhaustive judgment Munby J dealt with the patient's right to refuse the doctor's proposed treatment. Relying on the decision of the European Court in *Pretty v UK*,[110] Munby J noted that patient autonomy and dignity were both protected under Article 8 of the Convention. The ethical principle of patient autonomy was reflected in the patient's legal right to self–determination, and this right, according to the judge, was protected by both English common law and the European Convention.[111]

In addition, Munby J referred to the relationship between the doctor's duty to disclose and the patient's right to make autonomous decisions, asserting that the ultimate decision should and could be made by the competent patient alone.[112]

Moreover, like the court in the case of Ms B, Munby J set limits on the authority the doctors should have in the medical decision–making process. Accepting that the patient cannot force doctors to act contrary to their professional judgment, he argued that they should transfer the patient to the care of another doctor who was willing to accept the patient's decision. However, Munby J went further still, addressing a situation where the patient chose a particular treatment out of those available to him medically, which was not the one recommended by the doctor. In these circumstances the doctor may not stop treating the patient simply because the patient has not accepted the doctor's recommendation. As Munby J held, there is a sharp distinction between doctors who claim that the patient's choice would offend their conscience and doctors who merely do not see eye to eye with the patient on what the patient's best interests are.[113] Whereas in the former situation the doctor may be entitled to stop treating the patient (but must find another doctor who is willing to assume treatment) in the latter the doctor is

---

[109] *R (on the application of Burke) v The General Medical Council* [2004] EWHC 1879; for a commentary see Fennell P., "The right to require life prolonging treatment" (2004) 12 *Medical Law Review* 306.
[110] *Pretty v UK* [2001] 2 FCR 97, [2002] 2 FLR 45.
[111] Ibid., at para. 80.
[112] Ibid., at para. 97.
[113] Ibid., at para. 191.

not necessarily entitled to stop treating the patient, though the patient may accept that for his or her own benefit he or she should find another doctor.

In this environment, where the courts attempt to establish the fundamental rights of the individual patient vis–à–vis the doctor the interests of the relatives are obviously neglected. Although the courts have accepted that patients often consider how any treatment decision will affect their family,[114] the impression is that they still concentrate on striking a more adequate balance between the doctors' medical authority and the patients' rights. The recent case of *Burke* demonstrates the courts' aim to shift the focus in this context from *Bolam*, which gave considerable authority to doctors, to the patient's right to self–determination, as the mainstream of medical ethics has long recognised. Concentrating on this aspect of the doctor–patient relationship the law does not require the doctor to specify to the patient how any treatment alternative would affect the lives of those who are close to him or her. Instead, the legal debate concentrates on the risks and the chances of the treatment options. Thus, the law hardly grants the relatives any legal status in the medical decision–making process, though as we shall see, in other disciplines their involvement is recognised.

The evident gap between the close involvement of family members in the patient's daily care and the limited authority given to them in the medical decision–making process can be observed in the context of treatment of children. The discussion of children's medical treatment is beyond the scope of this book as it involves issues of competence as well as other complex legal matters; still, a recent English case, which attracted media attention, demonstrates that the courts tend to interfere with the parents' treatment decision regarding their children.

In *Re Wyatt*,[115] a baby girl who was born prematurely suffered from severe respiratory failure for most of her first three months as well as from recurrent infections. Though the doctors were of the view that treating her would be futile, her parents did not lose hope and thought it was their duty to maintain her life and not to let her die.

Simply put, the court had to choose between the doctor's position and the parents' wish. Although the court acknowledged that the parents were closely involved in the patient's care, and that they knew her as no one else did, it preferred to follow the medical view, holding that the parents might project their hopes on to the patient, thus implying that they have different interests which might be in conflict with her interest to die peacefully. In the end the overriding factor that affected the court's decision was the child's quality of life. This factor, which the court called 'intolerability', was dominant in previous cases.[116] Though

---

[114] Ibid., at para. 96 where Munby J cited Lord Scarman in *Sidaway* who argued that the doctor has to provide the patient with information necessary for him or her to consider the medical advantages and risks with other factors such as the family and social responsibilities he or she has.

[115] *Re Wyatt (a child) (Medical treatment: parents' consent)* [2004] EWHC 2247.

[116] *Re J (a Minor) (Wardship: medical treatment)* [1991] Fam 33, at p. 55.

the judge was aware that intolerability and quality of life were subjective factors, and had different meanings for different people, he nevertheless relied on medical opinion when examining whether the patient experienced pain, pleasure, and parental love. The medical view, that the child felt pain but was unlikely to feel pleasure or to respond to her parents, led the judge to his decision. It is interesting that despite the decision in *Glass*, and especially the separate view expressed by Judge Casadevall, who stated that in some cases maternal instinct has more weight than the medical view,[117] the court in *Wyatt* prefer to rely on the doctors' professional view and to interfere with the parent's decision.

However, in the context of the doctor–patient–relatives relationship the implication of the court that the parents may have different interests from those of the child reflects the core perception of the courts of the relationship between the patient and his or her family members, as if they are separate individuals living together and not an intimate community wherein the members constitute part of the individual's personality.[118] Even in areas of law where family members are legally involved in the medical decision–making process their view is rarely accepted.[119]

1.3.2.2 Voluntariness. The attitude to family members in medical law manifests itself in the analysis of the third component of consent, that of voluntariness. Consent is valid only when the patient decides freely without undue influence. In this context, the question whether the influence of family members is undue arises.

The judicial attitude to the patient's family members is observed in *Re T*.[120] In that case a pregnant patient was admitted to hospital following a car accident. After talking to her mother, who was a Jehovah's Witness, she refused a blood transfusion and was told that there was an alternative treatment available. She signed a form refusing consent although the form and its content were not explained to her. She went into labour and a Caesarean section was performed but the baby was stillborn. Her condition deteriorated and the judge at first instance granted a declaration that in the circumstances it would not be unlawful for the hospital to administer a blood transfusion. Although the central issue in this case is the validity of the patient's refusal to consent to administration of blood, it raises

---

[117] See *Glass*, supra n. 107, at para. 2.

[118] The decision in *Wyatt* is indicative. Previous courts' decisions reflect a similar position when the parents' decision contradicted the doctor's view. For summary and analysis see: Fox M., McHale J., "In whose best interest?" [1997] 60 *Modern Law Review* 700, Fortin J., "A baby's right to die" (1998) 10 (4) *Child and Family Law Quarterly* 411, Freeman M., "Whose life is it anyway" (2001) 9 *Medical Law Review* 259 commenting on the unusual case of *Re A (Children) (Conjoined twins: surgical separation)* [2000] 4 All ER 961. A different approach were the court saw the child and mother as "one" is *Re T* [1997] 1 FLR 502, 510.

[119] As Margaret Brazier argues, the courts, with only one exception, rejected the parents' view: See: Brazier M., *Medicine, Patients and the Law*, London, Penguin (2003), 354.

[120] *Re T (adult: refusal of medical treatment)* [1992] 4 All ER 649.

the issue of familial dispute and the status of the family members in the medical decision–making process.

When the case came before the Court of Appeal the judges unanimously upheld the judge's decision. Referring to the status of the patient's family members, the judges held that the mother subjected her daughter to undue influence. While the court treated sympathetically the patient's father and boyfriend, who supported the medical view, hostility was expressed towards the patient's mother because she tried to persuade her daughter to refuse any administration of blood.[121]

It is not surprising that in this conflict between the mother's religious beliefs and the principle of sanctity of human life the court preferred the latter to the former. However, the judgment that the mother unduly influenced her daughter should be examined. Declaring that the patient's decision would have differed from her mother's had she been fully competent helped the court to reach the decision that the blood transfusion should be given. By implication, the court did not give sufficient consideration to the argument that a person's decision is almost always influenced by the views of those who are close to him or her, and that in making important decisions the patient willingly takes relatives' views into consideration. The court did not distinguish between legitimate persuasion and undue influence. It is true that the patient expressed refusal of a blood transfusion following her encounters with her mother, and that she was prone to emotional pressure in her medical condition, but it seems that the court was quick to decide that the mother's persuasion amounted to undue influence. Instead, the court could have detected that the familial dispute only mirrored the dilemma the patient experienced – when still competent – in making a decision. Seeing the familial disagreement in this perspective might not necessarily have led the court to change its decision, but it would have reflected a different approach to the status of family members when patients exercise autonomy. Yet unsatisfactory as the decision in *Re T* may seem, it does reflect the ethical approach to patient autonomy as discussed above.

1.3.2.3 The exclusivity of the doctor–patient relationship. Another important principle in medical law is that the doctor–patient relationship is exclusive. For the doctor this means that he or she owes a legal duty to provide medical care only to the individual patient.[122] The duty derives from the doctor's voluntarily undertaking to treat the patient who seeks professional medical advice.[123] The law describes the relationship not as a contract but as an assumption of responsibility to the patient.[124]

---

[121] Ibid., at pp. 667–8.

[122] *Sidaway v Bethlem Royal Hospital Governors* [1985] AC 871; [1985] 1 All ER 643, at p. 657.

[123] *Capital Counties plc v Hampshire CC* [1997] 2 All ER 865, at p. 883–4 per Stuart–Smith LJ.

[124] *White v Jones* [1995] 2 AC 207 (HL); *Henderson v Merrett* [1995] 2 AC 145 (HL).

The exclusivity of the doctor–patient relationship prevails in the case of *Powell*. In that case, the Court of Appeal rejected the parents' claim. They argued that their discovering that the doctors had misled them after their son's death caused them psychological harm. The Court of Appeal held explicitly that doctors generally owe legal duties only to their patients. Since the claimants in that case were not the patients, the doctors did not owe them any duty.[125] The court held that the fact that the doctors disclosed information to the parents about the patient did not imply that a doctor assumed any responsibility to them. The decision in *Powell* was not exceptional; other cases have supported the conclusion that the legal duties of doctors are directed only to those who are considered patients, especially where there is a possibility of conflict of interest between the minor patient and his or her parents.[126]

A patient–centred approach prevails in *Powell*. The court perceived the patient as separate from his parents and failed to see that they were closely involved in his care. Furthermore, though the court acknowledged that the doctors were in constant contact with the parents it did not infer that doctors assumed responsibility to them. Instead, the court held that there might be circumstances where doctors communicate information to people without the relationship of doctor–patient arising. The decision to dismiss the parents' claim despite their involvement overlooks the view taken by many doctors that illness is a family matter.[127] As will be discussed in Chapter 5, doctors, especially general practitioners, are aware that the patient's illness affects the entire family. Consequently, a gap between law and practice emerges: while the unit of care, according to the legal position, consists of the individual patient alone, many doctors view the family as the unit of care.

To conclude thus far, two assumptions have been made in this chapter. First, it was assumed that law and ethics adopt a patient–centred approach, paying little attention to family members' interests and involvement. Second, it was assumed that this approach is based on a liberal–individualistic philosophy. Therefore, this chapter has examined whether English law and medical ethics adopt liberal conceptions. In this regard a gap seems to separate law and medical ethics. While the leading ethical approach has long recognised the right of the individual patient to make informed and voluntary decisions, the law still struggle to lessen doctors' authority in their relationships with patients. This gap affects the attitude to family members. While medical ethics has become aware of the importance of the social nature of the individual, medical law still perceives the patient as separate from his

---

[125] See *Powell*, supra n. 1, at p. 123–124.

[126] *X (Minors) v Bedfordshire CC* [1995] 2 AC 633, 655; and recently *D v East Berkshire Community Health NHS Trust* [2005] 2 FLR 284 where the House of Lords discussed three different claims of parents for misdiagnosis of child abuse. See also *B v A–G of New Zealand* [2003] 4 All ER 833.

[127] See the discussion in Chapter 5.

or her relatives even when they are closely involved in the patient's medical treatment.

The examination cannot end at this point. Two questions arise: first, can the legal and ethical positions provide a satisfactory solution to the tensions between patients and relatives over access to medical information? Second, do the legal and ethical positions represent the views of doctors and patients in this context? These questions are discussed in the next part.

1.4 Does Liberal–Individualism Provide Satisfactory Guidance?

The liberal perception of the individual as having the freedom to make decisions without controlling influences of others captures only one part of one's identity, that of being separate from others. It overlooks the other part, namely that the individual is a social being and that a significant part of his or her identity is defined by social relationships with others.[128] In any given situation the autonomy of the individual to make free decisions is taken within a social context and has no meaning outside the community in which he or she lives.[129] Thus, autonomy can be fully exercised by interacting with others. Put differently, autonomy as an element of identity not only expresses individuality but also reflects the relationship the individual has with others.

The liberal perception of autonomy raises the question of how it affects familial tensions over access to medical information. As indicated above, some deontological ethicists resolve a tension between the patient's right to confidentiality and the relative's right to be informed by adopting an overriding utilitarian mechanism, which aims to prevent maximum harm to all parties involved.[130]

Concentrating on genetic information, this mechanism limits the various interests that relatives have. For example, a relative's interest in gaining as much information as possible before deciding whether or not to embark upon a demanding career may not be recognised if the guiding principle is avoidance of tangible harm. As Ngwena and Chadwick commented, it is not clear why the interest of the relative to make an informed choice should outweigh the decision of

---

[128] See the Lindemann–Nelsons, supra n. 8, at p. 36.

[129] Donchin A., "Autonomy and interdependence: Quandaries in genetic decision making", in Mackenzie C., Stoljar N. (eds.), *Relational Autonomy*, New York, Oxford University Press (2000), 236, 237–240.

[130] Still, one has to appreciate that in health care settings deontological and utilitarian approaches may clash. An obvious example is a Jehovah's Witness's refusal of a blood transfusion. On the one hand the patient's right to refuse treatment should be respected, but on the other hand, if life can be easily saved utilitarians may argue that blood should be administered. See Macklin R., "Applying the four principles" (2003) 29 (5) *Journal of Medical Ethics* 275.

the patient to keep the information to himself or herself.[131] Therefore, questions remain as to whether the mechanism of prevention of harm strikes an adequate balance between the interests of patients and those of family members, and whether it reflects the complexities involved in the area of genetics. These questions will be examined throughout this book. At this stage it is important to discuss it briefly.

First, medical information affects not only the individual who receives it but also the relationship he or she has with family members. In the context of genetics, lawyers and ethicists concentrate on the effect information exerts on the health of the patient or on that of the relatives, as if these groups are socially unrelated. They do not fully appreciate that medical information may also affect the relationship between them.[132] A decision of one family member to withhold information from another member may have an adverse impact on their relationship. Since in many cases the relatives eventually discover the information (because symptoms become apparent or the relatives themselves are tested) they may experience resentment and anger if the patient has not come forward and disclosed the information voluntarily. Although the decision not to disclose can be legally justified because tangible harm could not be prevented, the relationship between the patient and the relative may suffer. The sensitivity with which patients and family members address genetic information, and the psychological impact it has on their relationship, challenge the assumption that genetic information has implications only for the *physical* health of family members.

Second, as regards medical decision–making, the utilitarian mechanism for resolving a tension between patients and family members does not encompass the complex nature of this process. Patients have an interest in sharing with their relatives the information they receive because they need emotional support to cope with their new genetic status.[133] One study has already indicated that a majority of patients would like a family member to accompany them to the examination room, which is legally perceived as the private sphere of doctors and patients.[134] However, despite this interest in sharing medical information family members have various reasons for not sharing information with their relatives. Parents, for example, are reluctant to disclose information to their children for they want to

---

131 Ngwena C., Chadwick R., "Genetic information and the duty of confidentiality: Ethics and law" (1993) 1 *Medical Law International* 73, 86.

132 Andrews L., *Future Perfect: Confronting Decisions about Genetics*, New York, Columbia University Press (2001), Ch. 3.

133 Bloom J., "The role of family support in cancer control" in Baider L., Cooper C., Kaplan De-Nour A. (eds.), *Cancer and the Family*, Chichester, Wiley (2nd edn., 2000), 53–71, 60; the need to share information to relieve stress and anxiety is also true for family members. See, for example, Beeson R., et al., "Loneliness and depression in caregivers of persons with Alzheimer's disease or related disorders" (2000) 21 *Issues in Mental Health Nursing* 779.

134 Botelho R., et al., "Family involvement in routine health care: A survey of patients' behaviours and preferences" (1996) 42 (6) *The Journal of Family Practice* 572.

protect them from a possible worrisome future.[135] Other family members may feel emotionally estranged from their relatives and thus do not feel morally responsible for communicating information to them. In addition, patients may be angry with their relatives and reluctant to disclose material information to them. Undoubtedly, the medical decision–making process as regulated in medical law does not reflect these various factors.[136]

Practically, doctors have realised that the family is closely involved in patient care.[137] Christie and Hoffmaster acknowledge that when patients seek medical advice they bring to the encounter with doctors not only a medical problem but also a social context, where the familial relationship is a fundamental component.[138] For example, when the doctor arrives to treat a dying patient at home he or she cannot avoid 'treating' her relatives, who provide the patient daily care, by communicating to them essential information and comforting them in this difficult time. In addition, doctors as well as medical students are taught that their medical professional obligations extend beyond the individual patient.[139] This *biopsychosocial* model in health care directs doctors to the ways in which familial function and dysfunction contribute to the patient's medical condition. This approach also makes doctors aware of the various implications the patient's condition has for the relatives' lives.[140] Therefore, medical academics do not question that family members are involved in the medical care of patients. They discuss whether family members are perceived as means to improve the patient's health, or as an end in themselves, viewing the unit of care as consisting of the family, not only the individual patient. In the area of medical information this medical position led a large proportion of doctors, especially general practitioners, to believe that in certain circumstances they would breach patient confidentiality and disclose information to relatives without consent.[141]

---

[135] Robertson J., et al., "BRCA1 screening in women with breast cancer: A patient's perspective with commentary" (2001) 11 (2) *Women's Health Issues* 63.

[136] Reust C., Mattingly S., "Family involvement in medical decision making" (1996) 28 *Family Medicine* 39 found that when patients make a decision they consider how any treatment option will affect their family members. This contests the legal model which focuses on the risk and benefits to the individual patient.

[137] See the discussion in Chapter 5.

[138] Christie R., Hoffmaster B., *Ethical Issues in Family Medicine*, Oxford, Oxford University Press (1986), Ch. 5.

[139] McWhinney I., *A Textbook of Family Medicine*, New York, Oxford University Press (2nd edn., 1997), Ch. 10; Stoudemire A., (ed.), *Human Behaviour: An Introduction for Medical Students*, New York, Lippincott–Raven (3rd edn., 1998), Ch. 9.

[140] Labrecque M., et al., "The impact of family presence on the physician–cancer patient interaction" (1991) 33 *Social Science & Medicine* 1253.

[141] Lako C.J., et al., "Confidentiality in medical practice" (1990) 31(2) *Journal of Family Practice* 167; Geller G., et al., "Physicians' attitudes toward disclosure of genetic information to third parties" (1993) 21 (2) *The Journal of Law, Medicine & Ethics* 238; Wertz D., Fletcher J., *Ethics and Human Genetics: A Cross–Cultural Perspective*, New

To conclude, the socio–medical research briefly reviewed in this part indicates that the legal position does not accord with the practical involvement of family members in health care. While medical law views the patient in isolation, choosing without external influences, in practice doctors and patients appreciate the involvement of family members during illness. As for the ethical position, awareness of the social dimension of autonomy has emerged, but many ethicists still concentrate on the interests and rights of the individual patient, relying on a utilitarian mechanism to solve conflicts between the individuals. Consequently, if it is accepted that the legal and ethical positions do not deal adequately and comprehensively with the complexities of medical practice it is necessary to incorporate another philosophical approach, which may be attuned to the interests of family members. It is suggested that a communitarian philosophy with its perception of the familial relationship should be combined with liberal principles, especially in the context of genetics.

1.5 Communitarianism: The Individual as a Member of a Community

If liberals focus on what separates individuals, communitarians see them as fundamentally attached. During the 1980s communitarians, such as Sandel, focused on criticising the liberal tradition, arguing, for example, that Rawls's theory of justice is limited particularly in situations where people are close to each other.[142] Following the criticism that communitarians do not have any substantive theory,[143] academics such as Bell[144] tried to formulate a communitarian political theory, arguing that the communities of which the individual is a member, such as the family, the workplace, the state and the like, are very important to his or her identity. However, the development of a communitarian theory was subject to criticism. Feminists argued that although communitarians emphasised the importance of social institutions they did not examine these institutions critically, but reinforced the injustices that prevailed in these social institutions.[145] It was argued, for example, that communitarians did not deal with the oppression of women and children in the family.[146] New communitarians, such as Etzioni,

---

York, Springer–Verlag (1989), 16–17; Toon P.D., Southgate LJ., "The doctor, the patient and the relative: An exploratory survey of doctor–relatives relationship" (1987) 4 (3) *Family Practice* 207.

[142] See Sandel, supra n. 22, at pp. 33–34.

[143] See Bell, supra n 34, at p. 28. See also Muller–Okin S., "Humanist liberalism" in Rosenblum N., (ed.), *Liberalism and the moral life*, Cambridge, Harvard University Press (1989), pp. 39–53, 46.

[144] See Bell, supra n. 34.

[145] Held V., *Feminist Morality: Transforming Culture, Society, and Politics*, Chicago, The University of Chicago Press (1993), pp. 189–191; Friedman M., *What are friends for? Feminist Perspectives on Personal Relationships and Moral Theory*, London, Cornell University Press (1993), 72–79.

[146] See Frazer and Lacey, supra n. 18, at pp. 130–142.

responded to this criticism by accepting that women should develop their careers as men did, and that both parents should share responsibility equally in bringing up children.[147]

Taking as a starting point that the individual is first and foremost socially embedded, communitarians, unlike liberals, perceive the individual as situated, embodied, and socially connected.[148] Hence the identity of the individual can only be defined by the relationships with other members of the community he or she lives in.[149] Since the community is part of one's identity one does not freely choose one's own way of life. If individuals are indeed perceived as members of families and other communities, social relationships are often involuntarily picked up during the course of life, and rational choice plays little, if any, role. Taking the familial relationship as an example, the individual does not choose his or her parents or siblings nor does he or she choose to love his or her children. Nevertheless, liberals may assert that ultimately choice has to prevail in the sense that people must have the right to choose and make important decisions in their lives even when this contradicts their social background. Communitarians disagree, arguing that the ability of the individual to choose freely, contrary to his or her background, is limited.

Accepting the importance of social relationships has led communitarians to argue that the communities one lives in are essential for the formulation of one's identity. These communities afford the individual a deeper understanding of himself or herself and what he or she aspires to. According to Bell,[150] these communities are so fundamental to one's identity that abandoning them will throw the individual to a state of severe disorientation and confusion. Being a member of the Smith family or being British is more fundamental to one's identity than it can possibly be articulated.

The significance of the community led communitarians to believe in the primacy of the common good over the right. Since the community has made the individual the way he or she turns out to be, one can argue that what at initially appears as the individual's own assets (i.e., his or her virtues and skills) may be more properly viewed as common assets. The community that shapes the individual's identity shares in his or her achievements.[151] Thus, for communitarians, human flourishing is made possible by social embeddedness. Therefore, the individual has an interest in supporting, encouraging, and maintaining his or her relationships with the communities he or she lives in.[152]

Communitarians' criticism of the atomistic perception of the individual led 'new communitarians' such as Etzioni to argue that Western societies lack

---

[147] Etzioni A., *The Spirit of Community*, London, Fontana Press (1995), pp. 55–56.
[148] See Frazer and Lacey, supra, n. 18, at p. 108.
[149] See Bell, supra, n. 34, at pp. 133–144.
[150] Ibid., at pp. 93–96.
[151] See Sandel, supra n. 22, at pp. 142–144.
[152] Ibid.; and also Bell, supra n. 34, pp. 98–103, 141.

commitment to general welfare, common purposes, education, and public health. Therefore, Etzioni argues, if people are defined by their social relationships and the communities they live in they must acknowledge that as much as they are entitled to fundamental rights they also have moral responsibilities.[153] People should be accountable and morally responsible to other members of their community when they act and make decisions, and this will promote the common good of their community.

However, Communitarians face difficulties when a conflict between individuals in a community emerges. While communitarians concentrate on the importance of the community in one's identity, they provide little discussion for the harm the community can inflict on the individual. As Parker observes, communitarians believe that being a member in a community is always positive,[154] thus paying little attention to the weakest members of the community. Communitarians, critics will argue, fail to see that the principles they promote do not in themselves guarantee justice.[155] Indeed, communitarians face difficulties when dealing with dysfunctional families. Sandel, for example, criticises Rawls's perception of justice even when the family does not function well.[156] Bell argues that the individual has to be true to his or her identity even when he or she does not experience familial love. This, according to Bell, requires the individual not to run away from his or her unfortunate past but to acknowledge the influence of the family and make the best of it. The Lindemann-Nelsons express the same view when discussing a family with a negative influence on the individual.[157]

Taking an extreme version of communitarianism, the impression is that communitarians ignore the achievement of the liberal tradition, that is, recognition that society has to uphold the rights of the individual.[158] However, Bell accepts the feminist criticism of the family.[159] Etzioni too does not ignore the value of personal rights and justice in the family.[160] Yet critics are not satisfied with these concessions, arguing that they do not eliminate the impression that communitarians are *capable* of justifying the oppression of the individual when promoting the shared values of the community.[161]

---

[153] See Etzioni, supra n. 147, at p. 9–11.
[154] Parker M., "Introduction" in Parker M. (ed.), *Ethics and Community in the Health Care Professions*, London, Routledge (1999), 7–8; for a feminist critique see Frazer and Lacey, supra n. 18, at pp. 136– 42
[155] Parker M., "Public deliberation and private choice in genetics and reproduction" (2000) 26 *Journal of Medical Ethics* 160, 162.
[156] See Sandel, supra n 22, at pp. 33–34
[157] See the Lindemann–Nelsons, supra n. 8, at pp. 41–42.
[158] Ibid.
[159] See Bell, supra n. 34, at p. 181; see also Etzioni, supra n. 147, at pp. 55–56
[160] See Etzioni, supra n. 147, at pp. 26 and 63
[161] See Parker, supra n. 154, at p. 9.

The discussion about the individual led to the development of *relational* perception of autonomy.[162] Feminists face the problem of how to merge the view that social relations constitute a large part of one's identity with the values of freedom and autonomy.[163] This problem led Jennifer Nedelsky to argue that the capacity of the individual to find his or her autonomy can develop only in the context of social relationships with others who cultivate this capacity; and that the 'content' of personal autonomy is intelligible through reference to shared social norms and values.[164] Such a relational conception of autonomy means that the concerns of others are taken into account when making decisions.[165] As Donchin sees it, relational autonomy takes into consideration the social relationships that bear on individuals' attempts to be self–governing and responsible people.[166] In a decision–making process the individual considers the interests of those who will be affected by his or her choice, such as family members and other individuals or groups to whom the individual's identity is bound. As Donchin puts it, relational autonomy is both reciprocal and collaborative. It is reciprocal in that it is not solely an individual project but involves a dynamic balance among people who are closely involved in each others' lives; and it is collaborative in that the individual recognises his or her dependence on close intimates when trying to achieve a goal.

However, like the liberal discourse, different conceptions of relational autonomy exist. Commenting on patient autonomy in the family John Hardwig argues that for an individual to be a part of a family he or she is morally required to make decisions thinking not only about what is best for him or her but also what is best for the relevant family members.[167] Yet Hardwig goes even farther, adding that in some cases the interests of the relatives may outweigh those of the individual patient.

This view is extreme. First, it requires relatives to be involved in the decision–making process not only as a source of support to the individual patient but also in their own right. According to Hardwig's account, family members should not be treated as means to the patient's end (recovery) but as end in themselves. In addition, when there is a conflict between the interests of the patient and those of the family members the doctor may be obliged to comply with the interest of the family even when the patient dissents. Undoubtedly, accepting this conception of autonomy ignores the fact that the patient is the vulnerable party and that

---

[162] Mackenzie C., Stoljar N. (eds.), *Relational Autonomy: Feminist Perspectives on Autonomy, Agency and the Social Self*, New York, Oxford University Press (2000).

[163] See Held, supra n. 145, p. 61 and also pp. 188–191 where she provides a critique on the liberal and communitarian perception of the individual.

[164] Nedelsky J., "Reconceiving autonomy: Sources, thoughts and possibilities" (1989) 1 *Yale Journal of Law & Feminism* 7, 11.

[165] Donchin A., "Autonomy and interdependence: Quandaries in genetic decision–making" in Mackenzie and Stoljar, supra n. 162, at p. 236.

[166] Ibid., at p. 240.

[167] Hardwig J., "What about the family" (1990) 20 (2) *Hastings Center Report* 5, 6.

autonomy gives him or her the authority to execute his or her interests vis–à–vis doctors and relatives.

Accepting that the patient is vulnerable leads the Lindemann–Nelsons to view relational autonomy differently. They accept that the interests of family members should be taken into account in the medical decision–making process, but they stress that it is better if their motives and concerns are expressed in the medical encounter, where the intricate network of their relationships can be protected from breakdown by the treating doctors. In a medical decision–making process, where a dispute between the patient and the family members arises doctors should act as mediators, trying to work towards an agreement and mutual compromise.[168]

The conflict raised by Hardwig highlights a key issue in this book: how to solve a conflict between the interests of the patient and those of the relatives. Hardwig's view reflects the communitarian belief that sometimes the common good of the family should trump the individual's rights. He believes that when a family is affected by the patient's decision, the equal moral worth of the interests of the patient and of the relatives requires that they have a say in it.[169] However, the view advocated in this book is that of the Lindemann–Nelsons. Though essentially their underlying position is similar, namely to promote the interests of family members in the medical decision–making process, they seem to provide a more sensible mechanism for this fundamental issue. While Hardwig suggests that the family should make the decision[170] the Lindemann–Nelsons argue for 'reorientation' in the perception of the medical decision–making process[171] by a shift of focus from a patient–centred to a family–based approach.

The Lindemann–Nelsons do not argue that a treatment decision should be imposed on the patient by the family, or that the doctor should be the decision–maker. Instead, they recognise the interests of the patient, arguing that the doctor will have to view carefully the familial relationships and dynamics to avoid abuse of the patient on the one hand, but also must consider the family's interests on the other. Thus, a 'reorientation' of thinking implies that family members will take part in the medical decision–making process when the decision affects them (for example, when a patient wants to recover at home and not in a hospital). However, this does not necessarily imply, as Hardwig argues, that the weight given to the views of the family members is equal to the wishes of the patient. The balance of interests depends on the particular circumstances of each case. A decision is made by taking into account the specific characteristics of the patient's condition together with the nature of the familial relationship as this prevailed in the decision–making process.[172] In the end, the doctor and the patient have to realise that autonomy in the family entails moral responsibilities to others.

---

[168] See the Lindemann–Nelsons, supra n. 8, at pp. 114–117.
[169] See Hardwig, supra n. 167.
[170] Ibid., at pp. 9–10.
[171] See the Lindemann–Nelsons, supra n. 8, at p. 117.
[172] Ibid., at p. 116.

To conclude, the view taken by the Lindemann–Nelsons supports the conclusion reached at the end of this book, namely that the mechanism to solve familial tensions in health care generally and in the context of genetics particularly cannot rely entirely either on a patient–centred or on a family–based approach. A relational conception of autonomy should be adopted which not only respects the right of the patient to choose but also appreciates the significant impact of social relationships when it is exercised.

The conception of relational autonomy was developed in feminist writing, and thus relies significantly on a philosophy of ethics–of–care.[173] The main theme of this philosophy is caring, which refers to emotional commitment to people with whom the individual has social relationships. Obviously, this philosophy shares some of its premises with communitarianism, especially the objection to the perception of the individual as fundamentally separate from others.[174] Proponents of an ethics–of–care appreciate the existence of interpersonal relationship between individuals, and consequently emphasise intimacy, care, love, and commitment as significant values. This philosophy was developed by Carol Gilligan, a psychologist, who through her empirical research discovered that women have a strong sense of responsibility.[175] She found that women perceived morality in terms of responsibility deriving from social relations and care for others, whereas men viewed morality in terms of rights and justice. Like Gilligan, Annette Baier rejected liberal–based principles of justice and autonomy. Instead she argued that decision–making within families is not based primarily on choice but on an intimate relationship of trust and care.[176]

Despite a similar core perception of the individual as socially embedded, there are distinctions between communitarianism and ethics–of–care. First, the philosophy of ethics–of–care provides a critique of communitarianism that fails to deal adequately with the oppression of women.[177] Second, while communitarians establish the relationship of the individual with others on mutual moral responsibility and on the role each member has in the community, proponents of ethics–of–care argue that a sense of commitment derives from emotional attachment to others and from the need to provide and receive care. However, as

---

[173] Mackenzie C., Stoljar N., "Introduction: Autonomy Refigured" in Mackenzie and Stoljar, supra n. 162, at p. 10.

[174] Sherwin S., "Feminism and bioethics" in Wolf S. (ed.), *Feminism and Bioethics: Beyond Reproduction*, New York, Oxford University Press (1996), 47–66.

[175] Gilligan C., *In a Different Voice*, Cambridge, Harvard University Press (1982), 21.

[176] Baier A., "Trust and Antitrust" (1986) 96 *Ethics* 231, 242–243.

[177] Gilligan does not argue that an ethics–of–care and ethics of rights strictly correlate with gender or that all men or women think morally the same. Rather, she argued that men tend to adopt an ethics of rights whereas women tend to adopt an ethics of care. See Gilligan C., Pollak S., "The vulnerable and invulnerable physician" in Gilligan C., Ward J., Taylor J. (eds.), *Mapping the Moral Domain*, Cambridge, Harvard University Press (1988).

will be argued below in the examination of the nature of familial relationships, both communitarian and ethics–of–care conceptions are important.

1.5.1 The Perception of Familial Relationship

The central argument in this book is that family members should gain more recognition than they currently receive in medical law and ethics. This requires recognition that familial relationships are based to a considerable extent on *intimacy*. When people have intimacy with their family members they share with them personal details about themselves as well as mutual experiences and life events. In this relationship people become more vulnerable than in any other type of relationship they have,[178] because they reveal to their close family members their true identity, including their virtues, thoughts, and weaknesses. This ability to have intimacy with others derives, according to proponents of ethics–of–care, from the people's childhood experience of being able to rely on those who are close to them and care for them.[179] Not only have parents or other close relatives provided the individual with basic needs, they also have given him or her emotional support when needed. The relatives' altruistic caring without any expectation of something in return teaches the individual that when he or she needs support there are people who may be willing to provide it.[180] Thus, people learn to care for each other, trust those who are close to them, and share close and mutual relationships. This mutuality enables the individual to reflect on his or her life because close relatives provide him or her with insights to his or her true identity.[181] Through intimacy, close family members gradually shape the individual's identity and even become a part of it.

If people are able to share intimacy with close family members, the decision–making process can be based on mutual compromises that reflect concern for others. Family members may agree voluntarily to compromise their personal preferences somewhat for the benefit of other relatives as they value the relationships with them. Mutual respect and care within the family will lead to a mechanism where in any given situation a different member agrees to forgo his or her desires. As a result decisions within families will be taken through persuasion and mediation and not through confrontation. The autonomy of the individual in the family will be relational and not based solely on personal interests.

---

[178] See the Lindemann–Nelsons, supra, n. 8, at p. 76.

[179] The notion that the combination of mutual caring and sharing personal information are the grounds for intimacy are developed by Blustein J., *Care and Commitment: Taking the Personal Point of View*, Oxford, Oxford University Press (1991), 152–3.

[180] Ibid., at p. 180.

[181] Friedman M., *What Are Friends For? Feminist Perspective on Personal Relationships and Moral Theory*, London, Cornell University Press (1993), at pp. 187–206 argues in detail how friendship, which is based on 'some degree of mutual intimacy', influences and contributes to our moral growth.

However, an inherent limitation of this view is that it is too romantic. Liberal–feminists, such as Susan Okin, contest the argument that the familial relationship can be based solely upon subjective values such as friendship and generosity. Relying on Rawls's theory Okin stresses that justice is a significant principle that should guide the morality of families. She argues that in many cases women and children suffer abuse and violence and when the family breaks down, women are left to bring up the children without financial support. In these cases, Okin argues, the principle of justice is fundamental for it helps weak family members to overcome inequalities to which they are exposed. Furthermore, Okin maintains, justice is important even if there is love in the family. She asserts that affection is not enough to create an adequate and just familial relationship.[182] Indeed, one can imagine a familial relationship which is based on love but nevertheless dominated by one party.

Okin's criticism should be accepted especially in a medical context, where the interest of patients or family members can easily be ignored and their autonomy harmed. In the majority of cases justice can be achieved by the promotion of mutual moral responsibility in the family. Indeed, Hardwig argues that the equal moral worth of the claims made by each family member accords with the inclusion of moral responsibility in the perception of autonomy.[183] Thus, according to Hardwig the patient is morally responsible for his or her family members because the decision affects them as well, and therefore their interests should be taken into account. However, this argument led, as we saw earlier, to a radical view, namely that sometimes the interests of the family should outweigh those of the patient. As noted above, the view taken in this book is that this position goes too far as it may diminish the value of patient autonomy altogether. Instead, the view taken by the Lindemann–Nelsons seems more sensible. The two authors agree that patient's rights must be exercised responsibly, arguing that a just and fair decision does not require forcing the patient to undergo treatment he or she does not want, or imposing on family members an obligation to care for the patient when it significantly compromises their interests. Instead, the decision depends on the nature of the familial relationship, namely whether it is based on intimacy and solidarity or whether the family is a group of individuals who come together simply to maximise their own personal interests.[184] In both types of family a solution may be achieved by a systematic discussion, where patients and family members express their concerns and preferences.

To conclude, the theoretical model of the familial relationship established in this book is based on liberal, communitarian, and ethics–of–care principles. Combining these principles reflects a different approach to the medical decision–making process currently existing in English medical law, which concentrates on

---

[182] Okin–Moller S., *Justice, Gender and The Family*, New York, Basic Books (1989), 31–32.

[183] See Hardwig, supra n. 167, at pp. 7–8.

[184] See the Lindemann–Nelsons, supra n. 8, at pp. 116–117.

the interests of the individual patient. It is appreciated that family members are independent individuals who have different wishes and interests. Hence, their right to make decisions about their health should be maintained and not overridden by the family. However, in the making of such a decision it must also be recognised that it may have implications not only for the individual patient but also for the family members who are closely involved in the patient's life. It may also affect the familial relationship itself. This implies that family members should be involved in the medical decision–making process as well. However, the balance between patient autonomy and the involvement of the family members in the decision–making process is complicated, especially in the area of genetic information where the patient has a legal and ethical right to confidentiality. In this context one must recognise that confidentiality reflects a valid interest of the patient. But it should also be stressed that family members have valid claims on each other that derive from their interdependent relationship. The question of how in practice to manage the tensions between these competing interests will be discussed in subsequent chapters. In the next section several suggestions attempted to present a working model in this area will be reviewed.

1.5.2 Communitarian Models in Genetic Information

Despite the tendency to focus on a patient–centred approach in medical law some bioethicists express a family–based approach in respect of the issue of communication of genetic information to family members. However, these commentators do not present a comprehensive analysis dealing with all the complexities of this issue. The discussion in the following paragraphs will demonstrate this point.

Rosamond Rhodes argues that patients and family members have a duty to know genetic information and share it with their relatives.[185] Rhodes relies on Aristotle, who takes the view that the individual has a responsibility to those who are close to him or her out of a sense of friendship. Aristotle realises that people are bound to express compassion or friendship in their actions toward others to varying degrees depending on the relationship with them. Furthermore, he suggests that the history of the relationship is taken into account and makes a moral difference more than the existence of blood ties. Taken together, the Aristotelian arguments provide guidance in resolving tensions between the patient and the family members. According to this view the patient carries a moral obligation to share genetic information with his or her nephew based on their familial relationship, but his or her moral responsibility may be diminished if he or she has never met him.

Rhodes's reliance on friendship as the foundation of the moral duty to disclose genetic information reflects a communitarian perception of familial relationships.

---

[185] Rhodes R., "Genetic links, family ties and social bonds: rights and responsibilities in the face of genetic knowledge" (1998) 23 *Journal of Medicine & Philosophy* 10.

However, regarding the doctor–patient relationship Rhodes supports a strict rule of confidentiality. She argues that the moral responsibility of one family member to another does not allow doctors to breach the patient's right to confidentiality.[186]

Ann Sommerville and Veronica English attempt to address all sides of the tripartite relationship.[187] In their commentary they present a moderate account of communitarianism, recognising that decisions made by the individual inevitably affect his or her family members and that he or she cannot have rights without bearing some responsibilities. In the specific context of genetics, the limits of the patient's moral responsibility to the relatives and the extent to which it could or should be enforced depend, according to the two commentators, upon the circumstances of each case. They argue that the possibility to make informed decisions should not be exclusive to the patient, who by mere chance is the one to be informed about a condition that affects the relatives. However, when Sommerville and English address the doctor's dilemma they adopt a utilitarian mechanism. When the patient refuses to disclose genetic information to the relatives despite the doctor's efforts to persuade him or her to do so, the ultimate responsibility is cast upon the doctor who has to decide whether to prefer the patient's interests or the relatives'. Assessing the situation, the doctor is required to adopt an objective cost–benefit evaluation, considering whether the disease is curable, how severe it is, and the like.

Consequently, Sommerville and English imply that the patient's moral duty is unenforceable and they are quick to lay the ultimate burden on the doctor.[188] They do not try to investigate how the communitarian model is applied to the relationship between the doctor and the relatives. In this communitarian–utilitarian model the interests of family members are limited because, ultimately, the doctors consider only one criterion: the prevention of harm. Moreover, the criteria the two authors formulate for doctors do not reflect the various implications genetic information has, particularly its effect on the psychological state of the relatives and on the social relationship between them and the patient.

Loane Skene develops a model that perceives genetic information as common to all blood family members (including the patient's spouse in the context of reproduction).[189] Skene suggests that when patients take a genetic test they should be informed prior to testing that family members will have access to the results if and when needed. Practically, the patient has only two options: either to take the test and consent to the possibility that the information will be communicated to other relatives or to refuse to be tested. However, if the patient consents to take the test, his or her privacy may not be entirely breached. When the patient is reluctant

---

[186] Rhodes R., "Confidentiality, genetic information and the physician–patient relationship" (2001) 1 (3) *The American Journal of Bioethics* 26, 27.
[187] Sommerville A., English V., "Genetic privacy: orthodoxy or oxymoron?" (1999) 25 *Journal of Medical Ethics* 144.
[188] Although this assumption may be correct, it deserves closer examination.
[189] Skene L., "Patients' rights or family responsibilities?" (1998) 6 *Medical Law Review* 1.

to inform the relatives his or her doctor is allowed to approach the relatives' doctor and disclose the information without revealing its source (the identity of the patient).

Undoubtedly, Skene's model is family–based for it provides family members free access to the patient's genetic information. It limits the patient's autonomy in controlling access to medical information that derives from decision to take a genetic test. Ultimately, this model promotes the common good of the family at the expense of the patient's right to confidentiality and privacy.

However, Skene's determination that genetic information is common to family members overlooks the implications of the social relationship between family members. In a complementary commentary Skene makes it clear that blood (DNA) and not information is the common thread that turns the group of individuals into a community in the context of genetics.[190] Proponents of ethics–of–care and communitarians will have difficulties in accepting this view of the family, which is not defined socially but simply biologically. Furthermore, the focus in this model is on the *doctor–patient* relationship and not on the *patient–relatives* relationship. Once it is accepted that the information is common to all family members, access will depend primarily on their choice and to a lesser extent on their social relationship with the patient.

David Doukas and Jessica Berg in a recent commentary develop a model of 'family covenant'.[191] They argue that before a particular family member takes a genetic test the other members should agree on how to share the results within the family. In this model the doctor operates as a mediator whose task is to produce a common agreement. The parties to the covenant, namely the family members, undertake to fulfil the provisions of the agreement in the future when the genetic information becomes available. Those among the family members who do not accept this agreement and are not part of it will not have access to the information. However, in this model family members can depart from the covenant when its application to a particular situation does not suit their wishes. The departure may dissolve the covenant. In extreme cases, the doctor can breach the agreement and disclose information to a relative despite the covenant's provisions if the conduct of one of its members offends its integrity.

The model of a family covenant reflects a family–based approach. The parties to the agreement, namely the prospective patient and his or her relatives, are willing to compromise their autonomy for the benefit of others. They realise that

---

[190] Skene L., "Genetic secrets and the family: a response to Bell and Bennett" (2001) 9 *Medical Law Review* 162, 169; Yet in her initial article Skene relies on a communitarian language arguing that this model is based on 'familial and community obligations'. However, in the reply to Bell and Bennett Skene explains that legal change should be based on the fact that blood relatives share genetic material.

[191] Doukas D., Berg J., "The family covenant and genetic testing" (2001) 1 (3) *The American Journal of Bioethics* 2.

mutual agreement is the key to their overall health, as it will benefit them when genetic information becomes available.

Moreover, this model seems to rely on liberal and communitarian conceptions. On the one hand Doukas and Berg stress that the family and not the individual patient constitutes the unit of care, and that the interest of the individual in genetic information can be fulfilled by engaging family members in a collective reflection. On the other hand, they argue that the parties to the covenant can freely *choose* whether or not they would like to participate. The covenant is not based on a sense of solidarity but on a social contract, which is achieved through the personal decision of family members to enter into this familial agreement. The provisions of the covenant are negotiated between the family members and are not pre-determined. These characteristics indicate that the model shares some similarities with Rawls's original position.[192]

The entitlement of family members not to join the covenant implies a distinction between the family as a social unit and the parties to the covenant. Family members can freely decide not to be part of it while still fulfilling their familial responsibilities. The possibility that a covenant may not include all family members indicates that it may not solve familial tensions over genetic information. In addition, it seems that this model does not suit the settings and resources of the NHS. Nevertheless, this model deserves a closer and more detailed examination because unlike other models it attempts to deal with familial tensions over genetic information comprehensively. Such an examination will be conducted in Chapter 6.

Lastly, Graeme Laurie, whose views about communication of genetic information will be thoroughly reviewed in this book, attempts to develop a model which is aware of the various interests of family members.[193] Assuming that disclosure may not only benefit the recipient but may also cause psychological harm, he argues that the decision whether or not to disclose should depend, inter alia, on the possible reaction of the relative when information is conveyed to him or her. For example, Laurie asserts that the fact that the relative is prone to depression should be taken into account when the patient considers disclosure. He argues that being sensitive to the needs of others should guide doctors and patients when contemplating disclosure.[194]

However, despite the sensitivity that Laurie expresses to the interests of family members, his view is heavily influenced by liberal–individualistic conceptions. In his view, privacy, or the individual's sense of being separate from others, is fundamental to his or her survival. Laurie admits that

---

[192] For a discussion of the distinctions between Rawls and Doukas & Berg see Chapter 6.

[193] Laurie G., "Challenging medical–legal norms: The role of autonomy, confidentiality and privacy in protecting individual and familial group rights in genetic information" (2001) 22 *The Journal of Legal Medicine* 1.

[194] Ibid., at p. 51.

intimacy is important to the development of one's identity, but he argues that ultimately the individual can choose whether or not to share his or her intimate emotions with others.[195] Privacy is essential to the moral development of the individual and precedes intimacy.

When discussing the possibility of applying a communitarian model to the context of genetics Laurie argues that it may seem paternalistic, but he admits that it attempts to avoid confrontations within families.[196] Yet he questions whether British society is capable of integrating such an approach as it relies heavily on liberal individualistic conceptions.[197] Laurie's question stands at the core of this book: is it really possible to adopt a communitarian model when English society is individualistic? The answer to this question is that liberal and communitarian conceptions are both valuable when dealing with the issue of communication of genetic information in the family. However, in light the gap between the legal position and the views of patients and doctors the communitarian and ethics–of–care perspectives should be highlighted.

1.6 Conclusion

This introductory chapter prepared the ground for this study within a liberal–communitarian debate. First, it was argued that the interests of family members in genetic information are an important issue, which is insufficiently addressed by law and medical ethics. This neglect, it was assumed, derives from a liberal philosophy which highlights the primacy of the individual as separate from others. Second, it was argued that this approach does not represent adequately the interests of family members because it overlooks the significance of the relationship between them. Instead it was argued that the ethics of families is based on intimacy and moral responsibility. When the individual makes a decision, especially one that affects family members, he or she exercises autonomy *relationally*, reflecting the view that autonomy can exist only in the context of the social relations that nurture it.[198]

Therefore, a brief account of the main conceptions of liberalism, communitarianism and ethics–of–care was provided. The view taken in this book is that combining these conceptions may represent more adequately the interests of doctors, patients, and family members. As Parker observes, one cannot rely either on a liberal–individualist conception of the individual or on an extreme

---

[195] Ibid., at pp. 27–29.
[196] Laurie G., "Genetics and patients' rights: where are the limits" (2000) 5 *Medical Law International* 25, 41.
[197] Ibid., at pp. 41–42.
[198] See Nedelsky, supra n. 164, at p. 25.

communitarian belief that the common good should supersede individual rights.[199]

In the following chapters the hypotheses posed in this chapter will be thoroughly examined and the arguments laid down here will be developed. Before that, a fundamental question has to be addressed, namely who is a family in genetics? Is Loane Skene correct in arguing that DNA constitutes a familial community in genetics? Or is it possible to argue that care, commitment, and mutual responsibility are essential in this context? For this question the characteristics of genetics are significant as they form the specific context in which the discussion takes place. Therefore, it is necessary to know how susceptibility to a genetic disorder is acquired, and what the social and psychological implications of being a carrier or a sufferer are. These issues are discussed in the next chapter.

---

[199] Parker, supra n. 154, at p. 10.

Chapter 2

Formulating a Family in Genetics: A Contextual Framework

The previous chapter set the theoretical framework of this book within the liberal–communitarian debate. Liberals and communitarians hold strong views about individuals and their relationships with others, and they express differing views with regard to the autonomy of patients and their relatives. Whereas some liberals promote an individualistic approach, communitarians and proponents of ethics–of–care adopt a relational perception of autonomy, perceiving close family members as part of the patient's identity and self.

When applying this philosophical debate to the context of this book, there are three preliminary issues which should be discussed before the legal and ethical position of the patient's family members can be examined. These issues are discussed in this chapter. First, it is important to set the context of this book and understand how genetic disorders occur, how they affect family members, and what implications genetic information has for them. Another issue in this context is formulating a workable definition of the terms family member and relative(s). Although genetic information intuitively implies blood relations, it is argued that non-blood relatives, such as spouses or partners, are affected by it as well. The last issue concerns the various interests that patients and family members have in genetic information. Discussing these interests will provide an introduction for the discussion in the next two chapters, which deal with the legal and ethical position of the patient's relatives.

This chapter is accordingly divided into three parts, each addressing one of the three issues outlined above. In the first part a brief account of genetics will be provided. This includes a medical review of genetic disorders and genetic testing, as well as a review of the psychological impact genetic information has on patients and their relationships with relatives. The second part is dedicated to the available definitions of the family in English law. It includes a review of the current position of English law regarding the family and the formulation of a *biosocial* definition, which is adopted in this book. Finally, in the third part of this chapter the interests of the parties in knowing and not knowing genetic information are identified. It will be argued that the discussion in the literature is unsatisfactory because it ignores other interests the parties have.

2.1 Genetics

2.1.1 Some Biological and Medical Facts[1]

The first important point in genetics is to understand what genes are and how they operate. The human body consists of many different cells, which perform specific tasks. Genes transmit the instructions for each cell to perform its assigned tasks. Although almost all cells contain a full set of genes, only those appropriate for a particular type of cell and its functions are operative. Genes are responsible for the development of the human body from the initial stage of fertilised egg to the final stage of fully–grown adult. They continue, throughout life, to provide the information necessary for maintenance and functioning of the body. They are strands of DNA located in the chromosomes that are passed on from the biological parents to their offspring at conception.

The majority of human cells contain two sets of twenty three chromosomes. The forty six chromosomes contain two sets of genes.[2] One set of genes is inherited from the biological mother and the other set is inherited from the biological father. The germ cells responsible for the development of sperms and eggs carry only one set of chromosomes. The single set of chromosomes in the egg or sperm is not an identical copy of one of the sets found in the individual's other cells but it is a mixture of genes from the two sets. Therefore, the genetic material in each germ cell has a unique combination. When the sperm fertilises the egg the forty six chromosomes and the two sets of genes are restored, resulting in a random and equal contribution of genes from each biological parent.

Inheriting the genes from the biological parents explains the cause of genetic diseases. When genetic material is passed on to the next generation errors can occur in the process, which may alter the structure of the genes. These alterations, known as *mutations*, may be harmful and may cause serious disorders.[3] In many cases the effect of the mutation is so severe that the embryo is unable to survive a full term of pregnancy. In other cases a child may be born with a disability, or may develop it during his or her lifetime. In yet other cases the individual may not suffer from a genetic disorder but may carry one mutative copy (out of the two he

---

[1]   The text in this part is based on: Harper P., *Practical Genetic Counselling*, Oxford, Butterworth–Heinemann (5th edn., 1999); Lenaghan J., *Brave New NHS?* London, IPPR (1998), Ch. 1; Fauci A., et al., (eds.), *Harrison's Principles of Internal Medicine*, New York, McGraw–Hill (14th edn., 1998), 365–395; British Medical Association, *Human Genetics: Choice and Responsibility*, Oxford, Oxford University Press (1998), Ch. 2; The Nuffield Council on Bioethics, *Genetic Screening: Ethical Issues* (1993), Ch. 2; Laurie G., *Genetic Privacy*, Cambridge, Cambridge University Press (2002), Ch. 3.

[2]   It is estimated that 30,000 human genes exist in these chromosomes. See: Collins F., et al., "A vision for the future of genomics research" (2003) 422 *Nature* 835.

[3]   Mutation generally refers to any genetic change. Not all of these genetic modifications are harmful.

or she has) and thus may pose a risk to a future offspring.

When determining a genetic risk, it is important to know that genetic disorders are caused in three different ways. First, patients may develop a disorder due to a fault in a single gene (known as *single–gene disorders*). Second, patients may suffer from a genetic disease because of faults in several genes (known as *polygenic disorders*); and finally, they may be disposed to a disease owing to a combination of genetic and environmental factors, such as smoking and diet (known *as multifactorial disorders*). However, a patient who has a mutation for a genetic disorder is not necessarily affected by it. The proportion of people with the mutation who will be affected is called the 'penetrance' of the condition. A condition has complete penetrance if clinical symptoms are present in all individuals who have the disease–causing mutation. Having reduced or incomplete penetrance is when clinical symptoms are not always present in individuals who have the disease–causing mutation.

2.1.1.1 Single–gene disorders. As noted above, each individual inherits two sets of genes, one from each parent. So with any particular gene an individual may inherit two mutative copies, two healthy copies, or one mutative copy and one healthy copy. Those who receive two healthy copies from their parents will not suffer from the particular disorder. If the individual receives two defective copies of the gene he or she will develop the disorder. However, whether an individual with one faulty copy develops the disorder depends on the mode of inheritance of that particular disorder. In single gene disorders there are three common types of inheritance patterns: dominant, recessive, and X–linked.

(1) Autosomal dominant disorders – In this subcategory the individual will develop the disease by inheriting one healthy copy and one mutative copy. Since the transference of genes from the parents to their offspring is random (the affected parent may pass either the healthy or the mutative copy) the risk of having an affected child is 1 in 2 (50%) in every pregnancy. The fact that the other parent transfers a healthy copy is irrelevant because the mutative gene prevails. The question of whether the offspring will develop the disorder depends also on the proportion of people carrying the mutation, i.e., the penetrance of the disorder. An example of a dominant disorder is Huntington's disease, a terminal and incurable neurological disorder, which is manifested when people reach their forties or fifties.[4]

(2) Autosomal recessive disorders – A patient will suffer from a recessive disorder, such as cystic fibrosis, by inheriting two mutative copies of the gene. Those who inherit only one mutative copy will not be affected because the healthy copy overrides the fault on the other copy. Those with one mutative copy and

---

[4] Ball D., Tyler A., Harper P., "Predictive testing and children: Lessons from Huntington's disease" in Clark A. (Ed)., *Genetic Counselling: Practice and Principles*, London, Routledge (1994), 63–94.

one normal copy are carriers. When one carrier reproduces with another carrier, the chance of a child inheriting two mutative copies and so develop the disorder is 1 in 4 (25%) in every pregnancy. The chance of the child inheriting one mutative copy and one healthy copy and thus being a carrier is 1 in 2 (50%). There is 1 in 4 (25%) chance that the child will inherit two healthy copies, and thus be neither affected nor a carrier. Since these types of disorders can be passed on only when two carriers reproduce (and even then there is only a 25% chance) they tend to affect siblings within a single family because they may skip several generations and often occur without forewarning.

(3) X–linked disorders – In this subcategory the mutative gene is on the X chromosome (the sex chromosome).[5] Most X–linked disorders are recessive and a healthy copy overrides the mutative one. These disorders usually affect only males as they have only one copy of the X chromosome, while females have two. Therefore, if a male child inherits a mutative X chromosome there is no other healthy chromosome to compensate for it. Females who inherit a mutative chromosome will be carriers and are usually unaffected because of the existence of a second healthy X chromosome. Affected fathers do not pass the disorder onto their sons (because they pass on a Y chromosome and not an X chromosome to produce a boy) but all their daughters will be carriers, putting their grandchildren at risk. A carrier mother and a non–carrier father have a 1 in 2 (50%) chance of passing on the mutative gene to their children in every pregnancy, but usually only boys will be affected.

2.1.1.2 Polygenic and multifactorial disorders. Many common diseases, such as cancer, have a genetic component. These diseases are caused by mutations on a number of different genes and the interactions between them. Frequently, disorders are caused by a combination of genetic and environmental factors. These are called *multifactorial.* For example, it is estimated that 5–10% of all cases of breast cancer are due to mutations in one of two genes, known as BRCA1 and BRCA2. When the patient carries a mutation in one of these two genes her or his risk of developing breast cancer is higher than the risk in the general population. When a tested individual carries a mutation in one of these genes he or she can take preventive measures, such as undergoing prophylactic surgery to reduce the risk.

Yet the results of genetic testing for such disorders will generally be less straightforward than for single gene disorders, because of their mixed nature. Though carriers of the BRCA1/2 genes are at high risk of developing breast cancer, it is very difficult to predict whether or not they will develop it. The prevalence of the mutative gene does not guarantee the onset of breast cancer, but the risk is high: inherited breast cancer has a high penetrance, of up to 85%.[6]

---

[5] Males have one X chromosome and one Y chromosome, while females have two X chromosomes. Thus, the biological father may transfer either an X or a Y chromosome to his offspring, while the mother will always transfer an X chromosome.

[6] Morrow M., Gradishar W., "Recent Developments: Breast Cancer" (2002) 324 *BMJ* 410.

2.1.1.3 Genetic testing. Common to many single–gene disorders and multifactorial ones is the availability of genetic tests to determine whether the person is a carrier, or a potential sufferer. There are number of different techniques used for genetic testing, but the primary aim is to identify the presence or absence of a particular mutation. This is not an easy task. The particular mutation associated with the disorder must first be identified and its interaction with other genes has to be assessed. In addition, in many single gene disorders a number of different mutations are often found for each disorder. For example, since the gene responsible for cystic fibrosis was identified, over 600 different mutations have been found. Most are very rare. The twelve common mutations, however, which account for around 85% of the total incidence, can be detected by genetic testing. A negative test result means that the individual is at a significantly reduced risk of being a carrier, but there remains a small chance of being a carrier of an unidentified mutation.

In some disorders this type of direct genetic testing is not possible because the particular mutation associated with them has not been identified. Sometimes a *family linkage study* will be necessary to determine whether an individual has inherited the same chromosome region as an affected family member. Although these results are not as conclusive as direct testing, this method can be conducted before the identification of the gene mutation. However, unlike direct genetic testing, a linkage study requires the participation of other family members, those who are affected and those who are not. In this respect genetic testing has a unique familial characteristic which does not exist in other medical tests and requires the patient to relinquish his or her right to keep the information in confidence.

This unique feature of genetic testing has relevant implications for the context of this book. it positions the patient as a member of a community of blood relatives. This means that the doctor may include the family in the unit of medical care. This can carry legal and ethical implications in respect of the duties of doctors and patients to family members in this area. These implications will be discussed in the next two chapters.

In the context of this chapter, the need for relatives' knowledge and cooperation is relevant to the formulation of a definition of family in genetics. Though it is clear that having blood ties is essential here, the requirement of asking family members to participate in the patient's diagnostic procedure indicates that the nature of the relationship is important as well. The agreement of a family member to participate in a family linkage study depends to a large extent on the relationship he or she has with the patient prior to testing. When the relationship is close the affected relative may be more willing to cooperate, and it makes it easier for the patient to approach him or her and ask for help. To conclude, a family linkage study depends not only on the existence of blood relations, as it may seem at first glance, but also on the nature of the relationship.

Genetic testing can be usefully performed in a wide range of circumstances and for various purposes. First, people may have diagnostic tests if they suffer from a particular disorder, or if their family history indicates that they are at risk. The aim of this testing is to initiate pre-symptomatic surveillance, change the patient's lifestyle, and commence treatment if any exists. Second, carrier screening is available to learn whether a particular individual carries a mutation which may be passed on to the offspring. This testing can be offered to the general population, to members of an ethnic group known to be in a higher risk, or to couples who plan to have a child. One example is Tay-Sachs which is common among Ashkenazi Jews.[7] Thirdly, when one or both parents are known to be carriers of a genetic disease, pre-implantation diagnosis together with an IVF treatment may be undertaken. This procedure may help to select an unaffected embryo for implantation. Fourthly, prenatal testing may be undertaken, which may result in carrying the pregnancy to term or terminating it.[8] Fifthly, neonatal screening is undertaken soon after birth. Some routine tests are performed on all newborn infants. These tests facilitate early treatment or close monitoring for symptoms.

The decision to take a genetic test often depends on whether it concerns an early–onset or a late–onset disorder. Genetic diseases develop soon after birth or during adult life. For example, cystic fibrosis (CF) is an early–onset recessive disease, which develops when the child is young. Although nowadays CF patients reach an average age of 30, many parents prefer not to have an affected child. The same applies to other rare genetic disorders, where the child does not reach his or her teens. In contrast, Huntington's disease and breast cancer are late–onset disorders.[9]

The distinction between early–onset and late–onset disorders is not trivial. Ethical and legal issues arise when parents want to submit their children to genetic tests for genetic disorders. Though a majority of commentators do not oppose neonatal screening for early–onset disorders,[10] many would oppose the right of parents to submit their children to genetic tests for late–onset disorders. It is argued that submitting the newborn to genetic tests for late–onset disorders may expose the child to discrimination and stigmatisation throughout his or her life if he or she is diagnosed as a carrier or potential sufferer. Additionally, it is argued that the child's autonomy to decide independently in adult life whether or not to take the test is compromised. While in early–onset disorders these considerations are often overridden by the parents' wish to avoid financial and psychological adverse consequences if they have to raise a disabled child, this factor is absent in late–onset disorders. Giving the authority to parents to screen their children for late–

---

7   The Nuffield Council on Bioethics, *Genetic Screening: Ethical Issues*, (1993), pp. 110–114.

8   Cameron C., Williamson R., "Is there an ethical difference between preimplantation genetic diagnosis and abortion?" (2003) 29 *Journal of Medical Ethics* 90.

9   The Advisory Committee on Genetic Testing, *Report on Genetic Testing for Later Onset Disorders,* London, Department of Health (July, 1998), 10.

10 The Nuffield Council indicates that screening for early–onset recessive disorders does not result in discrimination. The report provides information about neonatal screening programmes in the UK. See: The Nuffield Council on Bioethics, supra n. 1, Ch. 8.

onset disorders is paternalistic, for it contests patient autonomy. Indeed, in some Western countries advisory bodies recommend that children not be submitted for testing for late–onset disorders.[11]

However, the focus of this book is on diagnostic testing, either predictive or pre-symptomatic.[12] In this context the definitions suggested by the *Advisory Committee on Genetic Testing*[13] are adopted. The Committee holds that diagnostic testing is used to assist in the diagnosis, treatment, and management of asymptomatic individuals.[14] Pre-symptomatic or predictive genetic testing is used to provide healthy people with information about their future health in the context of specific inherited diseases.[15] The focus in this book, then, is on genetic testing which assists doctors in making an accurate diagnosis, or predicting whether a healthy individual is a carrier or a potential sufferer. This includes susceptibility testing which provides information about the genetic component in a multifactorial disease.

The predictive characteristic of genetic testing must be appreciated. One of the most prominent aspects of genetic testing is its ability to predict future ill health. This tool helps genetic counsellors and doctors to provide the patient with a risk assessment and to take preventive measures to avoid the onset of a genetic disease when possible. When there is no cure for the relevant disorder, whether it is a single–gene or a multifactorial disorder, genetic information can facilitate informed choice, particularly when people consider marriage, reproduction, or career options. Moreover, knowing their risk status may help potential sufferers to prepare psychologically for the onset of the disease in advance, by seeking early professional help or by joining a support group. They may also be able to avoid unnecessary financial expenditures.

Contrary to these advantages, some commentators emphasise that genetic testing may have adverse consequences.[16] First, they argue, no genetic disorders have a cure (though some are treatable).[17] Hence, knowing that one will develop a

---

[11] In the UK: The Advisory Committee on Genetic Testing, *Report on Genetic Testing for Late Onset Disorders*, London, Health Departments of the United Kingdom (1998), p. 26; in the US: *The Genetic Privacy Act* 1995, which was produced for the Human Genome Project by three academics from Boston University. For content of the Act see www.bumc.bu.edu/sph. Section 16 discusses genetic testing of minors. For commentary see: Annas et al., "Drafting the Genetic Privacy Act: Science, policy and practical considerations" (1995) 23 *Journal of Law, Medicine and Ethics* 360.

[12] However, the results of these tests may help people to make informed reproductive decisions.

[13] See The Advisory Committee of Genetic Testing, supra n. 11.

[14] Ibid., at p. 8.

[15] Ibid.

[16] This argument is advanced by those who promote a right not to know. See further discussion below.

[17] Some genetic conditions are treatable, such as PKU, a rare recessive genetic disorder which may cause brain damage. If the disorder is detected shortly after birth adopting a

terminal disease will provide some certainty but it may also cause mental distress. Therefore, the availability of information without any means to overcome the onset of the disorder may not be beneficial. In addition, in many cases certainty is not guaranteed. In multifactorial diseases, such as inherited breast cancer,[18] there is no certainty that carriers will develop the disease in the future because these disorders are triggered by environmental factors, which cannot be predicted or fully controlled. Furthermore, in some single–gene disorders negative test results cannot ensure that the child will not develop the disease because many tests cannot account for 100% of the cases and therefore there is a small chance that an affected child will be born.

In addition, the efficacy of genetic tests may be limited.[19] Tests cannot predict either the particular likelihood of the onset of a disorder, the date of its onset, or its severity. Furthermore, tests cannot be fully effective especially when they concern long genes, which are more likely to carry mutations. For example, the BRCA1 gene is unusually long and contains over a hundred common mutations.[20] This means that it is not sufficient for unaffected individuals to know that they are at risk; they also need to know the details of the particular mutation. This means that information from an affected family member should be available to an unaffected one before he or she takes a test.[21]

Consequently, it is argued that genetic testing yields ambiguous information. Graeme Laurie argues that the foregoing factors, and others, weaken the effectiveness of genetic tests; they yields probable and not certain information.[22]

2.1.1.4 Genetic information. Following this brief account on genetic disorders and genetic testing, the next step is to define what genetic information is. Graeme Laurie argues that genetic information concerns the family, not just the individual patient.[23] It helps to determine which of the family members is at risk to develop the disease, and can help assess the possibility of family members developing the disease they are prone to. Laurie notes that genetic information can predict which currently healthy people will suffer from a genetic disease in the future, and that genetic information can assist in determining the risks of the foetus.[24]

This definition of genetic information can be seen as a summary of the

---

strict diet can lead to a normal mental development. See The Nuffield Council, supra n. 1, at p. 112.

18   Inherited breast cancer accounts only for 5–10% of all cases of this disease.

19   Laurie G., *Genetic Privacy: A Challenge to Medico–Legal Norms*, Cambridge, Cambridge University Press (2002), pp. 101–102.

20   Eeles R., "Testing for breast cancer predisposition BRCA1" (1996) 313 *BMJ* 572.

21   Ibid.

22   See Laurie, supra n. 19, at pp.103–104.

23   Ibid.

24   Ibid., at p. 104; note that genetic information is not only about health, although in this study this is the primary focus.

foregoing discussion. However, in the context of this book the most important component is that genetic information concerns the family and not just the individual patient. This is the main challenge that the area of genetics poses to doctors, patients, and relatives. When the interests of the patient collide with those of the relatives, policy–makers, lawyers, and ethicists struggle to form a suitable mechanism owing to reliance on the liberal tradition. The fact that medical information may not be controlled exclusively by the individual patient confronts well–established moral principles of autonomy, confidentiality, and consent. The question of how English law and medical ethics deal with these moral principles in light of the familial characteristic of genetic information will be examined in detail in the next two chapters.

Concentrating on the main theme of this chapter, the brief account of genetics highlights the importance of blood ties when searching for a clear definition of the family. It can be argued that defining a family member according to blood ties would undoubtedly achieve objectivity and clarity.[25] Such a definition (with the exception of the patient's partner when a reproductive decision is concerned), would help the courts and the parties to know to whom the duty – if one exists – is owed. In addition, it would assist doctors in formulating clear professional guidelines.

Loane Skene promotes such an approach.[26] She argues that genetic material (DNA) creates a community of blood relatives who are all members of the same gene pool. This leads Skene to argue that genetic information is familial and accessible to all blood relatives (and the spouse where reproduction is concerned). However, as the discussion about the family linkage test indicates, it is argued that blood ties are necessary but insufficient in the definition of a family member or relatives in genetics. Skene is correct in arguing that genetic information is relevant to family members because they are all part of the same gene pool. However, from a moral perspective relying solely on blood relations is insufficient in respect of the moral duties of doctors and patients because the decision *to whom* the doctor or the patient should disclose the information is determined also by the nature of the relationship the parties have. For example, questions arise as to whether patients owe a moral duty to disclose information to a distant cousin whom they have never met. As Rhodes correctly argues, the existence of this duty will depend – at least morally if not legally – on whether patients and relatives have a relationship which is based on friendship and mutual responsibility.[27]

Furthermore, Skene seems to ignore that any definition of the family leads to

---

[25] The Israeli *Genetic Information Act* 2000, which deals, inter alia, with the issue of communication to third parties, defines a family member as one who has blood ties with the tested individual.

[26] Skene L., "Genetic secrets and the family: A response to Bell and Bennett" (2001) 9 *Medical Law Review* 162, 169.

[27] Rhodes R., "Genetic links, family ties, and social bonds: rights and responsibilities in the face of genetic knowledge" (1998) 23 (1) *Journal of Medicine and Philosophy* 10.

different legal implications. First, a definition of the family will have a significant role in determining the scope of the legal duty that doctors may owe to family members; for that reason it is necessary to take into account the social aspects of familial relationships. Promoting a pure biological definition may result in giving distant blood relatives the possibility of bringing claims against the patient's doctor when it is unreasonable to do so, while rejecting a claim by non-blood relatives who are closely involved in the patient's lives. For example, the interest of adopted children or unmarried partners in knowing whether they will have to provide daily care to the patient when his or her condition deteriorates may not be legally recognised because they are not blood related and the information does not concern reproduction.[28]

However, one can still object and argue that a pure biological definition should be promoted because it is compatible with the legal position.[29] Since English law is based on prevention of harm and respect for patient autonomy, defining a family in genetics according to blood relations (with the exception of the spouse in reproduction) will accord with this legal approach, which by and large ignores the relevance of social relationships in one's identity and autonomy.

Still, in the search for a satisfactory definition of a family in genetics a fundamental question arises: what role should the law have in English society? If law has to reflect public attitudes and practice, in the specific context of this study it is not possible to ignore research that suggests that genetic information has a psychological impact on patients and their relationships with both blood and non-blood relatives. However, if law has an independent role in shaping social policy and changing social behaviour, a purely biological definition can be adopted, even at the expense of contradicting current social behaviour and practices in this area. Yet, before deciding between the two it is necessary to examine the research available on the psychosocial impact genetic information has in this area. This will be discussed next.

2.1.2 Psychological Implications of Genetic Information

Genetic information has considerable psychological impact on patients and their relationships with their relatives. Lori Andrews comments that genetic information challenges the patient's self–image and his or her relationships with family members, making them think about their responsibilities differently.[30] Andrews stresses that people approach genetic testing with a particular perception of their identity and of morality but end up re-evaluating their view of their personality as well as their relationships with family members. This argument reflects a

---

[28]   Whether relatives can bring a claim when they suffer harm to their right to make informed decisions is a complicated question; it is discussed in Chapter 3.

[29]   The legal and ethical positions will be discussed in the next two chapters.

[30]   Andrews L., *Future Perfect: Confronting Decisions about Genetics*, New York, Columbia University Press (2001), 31.

communitarian perception of the individual as socially embedded. Furthermore, if genetic information does affect individuals, their identity, and their relationships with others, autonomy in this area is more relational than individualistic.

In examining the psychological impact of genetic information the purpose of this section is to determine whether genetic information affects patients and family members simply because they are blood relatives or also because they have an interdependent relationship. This will help arriving at a definition of a family. An additional aim of this section is to explain why patients and relatives have an interest in receiving genetic information and controlling its access. Discussing the impact genetic information has on familial relationship may help understand the underlying interests of patients and family members in this area. The discussion in this section will be divided into two subsections: one will analyse the effect genetic information has on the individual patient and the other will focus on the effect it has on his or her relationships with relatives.

2.1.2.1 Effect on patients. Genetic information has a considerable effect on the individual patient. Research on patients who discover that they are carriers of a genetic disorder indicates that they change their view about themselves and may feel damaged.[31] This reinforces Andrews's argument about the effect genetic information has on patients' perception of their self–image. When the individual receives negative, but more especially positive test results the perception of himself or herself changes.

In addition, a study discovered that receiving positive test results can cause mental distress and anxiety. In a study of BRCA1 testing, carrier patients experienced more psychological distress than non-carriers.[32] However, the level of anxiety is influenced by the availability of preventive measures. Research suggests that individuals at risk for incurable disorders such as Huntington's disease suffer from higher anxiety levels than those at risk for colon cancer, which is treatable if detected at an early stage.[33] However, the difference between these two disorders may also be attributed to the nature of the disorder. Those who have the mutation for Huntington's disease (HD), a neurological degenerative disorder, may fear for loss of their identity and self, while carriers of other disorders may not. In the specific case of HD, the nature of the disease, coupled with lack of any measures to prevent it, may have a devastating effect on carriers. One study indicated that the

---

[31] Watson E., et al., "Psychological and social consequences of community carrier screening programme for Cystic Fibrosis" (1992) 340 *Lancet* 217.

[32] Croyle R., et al., "Psychological responses to BRCA1 mutation testing: preliminary findings" (1997) 16 *Health Psychology* 63.

[33] Dudoke De Wit, et al., "Psychological distress in applications for predictive DNA testing for autosomal dominant, heritable late onset disorders" (1997) 34 *American Journal of Medical Genetics* 382.

suicide rate among HD carriers is significantly higher than among the general population.[34]

The effect genetic information has on patients' self–image suggests that they view themselves as socially embedded. Perceiving oneself as 'marked' or 'damaged' is a relative concept: the individual sees himself or herself 'damaged' in comparison with others who, in his or her view, are not. If all other family members, friends and acquaintances had been carriers of the same genetic disorder the patient would probably not have felt that way.

However, patients' psychological reactions to genetic information are not as straightforward as they may first appear. Studies cited below show that patients react unexpectedly to genetic test results. The assumption that positive test results always stimulate an adverse emotional reaction or that negative results always bring relief should be empirically examined and confirmed.

(1) The effect of negative test results – While negative test results usually provide relief to patients this is not always the case;[35] they may create an adverse emotional reaction. In one study 10% of those who took genetic tests for Huntington's disease and discovered that they do not have the mutation experienced psychological problems as a result.[36] Another study indicated that people without the mutation for Huntington's disease felt initial relief when they received the results but felt helpless three years later.[37] By contrast, a different study revealed that in many cases negative results relieve mental distress. A study on CF testing shows that those who were diagnosed as non-carriers described themselves as 'happy' and 'relieved', while those who were diagnosed as carriers were more anxious.[38] The same applies to incurable disorders, such as HD.[39]

(2) The effect of positive test results – Genetic testing is often thought to be beneficial even for those who test positive. It can motivate carriers to stay under close surveillance and to cope better if the disease does become manifest later. However, research has indicated that these benefits do not always prevail.

---

[34]   Almqvist el al., "A worldwide assessment of the frequency of suicide, suicide attempts, or psychiatric hospitalization after predictive testing for Huntington disease" (1999) 64 *American Journal of Human Genetics* 1293.

[35]   Trock B., et al., "Psychological side effects of breast cancer screening" (1991) 10 *Health Psychology* 259; Lynch H. T., Watson P., "Genetic counselling and hereditary breast/ovarian cancer (1992) 339 *Lancet* 1181.

[36]   Huggins M., et al., "Predictive testing for Huntington's disease in Canada: Adverse effects and unexpected results in those receiving a decreased risk" (1992) 42 *American Journal of Medical Genetics* 508.

[37]   Tibben A., et al., "Three–year follow–up after presymptomatic testing for Huntington's disease in tested individuals in partners" (1997) 16 *Health Psychology* 20.

[38]   Bekker H. et al, "The impact of population based screening for carriers of Cystic Fibrosis" (1994) 31 *Journal of Medical Genetics* 364.

[39]   See Tibben, supra n. 37, at p. 32.

In fact, research suggests that the distress suffered when genetic test results are received may reduce the likelihood that carriers will engage in surveillance and monitor themselves for early signs of the disease.[40] However, even if carriers are willing to undertake preventive measures the physical and psychological harm from increased stress may outweigh any benefit of increased surveillance.[41]

As noted, receiving positive test results may cause anxiety.[42] Contrary to this, studies show that positive results can also relieve mental distress, especially in individuals who suspected but were not sure that they were carriers. Research suggests that following an initial period of anxiety the level of mental distress among CF carriers decreases to the level experienced by the general population.[43] Not only does this occur among carriers of recessive disorders, such as CF, it also prevails among carriers of dominant incurable late–onset disorders such as Huntington's.[44] This is explained partly by the sense of certainty that the information provides to people who already suspect they are affected, enabling them to make informed decision about their lives.

The variety in patients' reactions to genetic information can be explained – at least partly – by the social relationships the individual has. For example, as some of the above studies suggest, the reason for different reactions to genetic information are associated with personal experience. While those who do not have an affected relative may be devastated when diagnosed as carriers, those who have one may be less anxious because they might already suspect that they are carriers. Consequently, the influence of the social relationship on the individual who receives the information highlights its significance when disclosure to family members is considered.

Furthermore, these studies indicate that genetic information can yield various and unexpected reactions that could not be predicted because they derive from the specific social circumstances of the tested individual. It is not possible to make clear distinctions and argue that disclosure to family members is always beneficial

---

40 Lerman C., et al., "Mammography adherence and psychological distress among women at risk for breast cancer" (1993) 85 (13) *Journal of the National Cancer Institute* 1074, 1079.

41 Baum et al., "Stress and genetic testing for disease risk" (1997) 16 *Health Psychology* 8, 10.

42 See Croyle, supra n. 32, at p. 69; Marteau T., et al., "Long–term cognitive and emotional impact of genetic testing for carriers of Cystic Fibrosis: The effects of test result and gender" (1997) 16 (1) *Health Psychology* 51, 55; see in the context of breast cancer: Tercyak K., et al., "Effects of coping style and BRCA1 and BRCA2 test results on anxiety among women participating in genetic counselling and testing for breast and ovarian cancer risk" (2001) 20 (3) *Health Psychology* 217.

43 See Watson, supra n. 31.

44 Lawson et al., "Adverse psychological events occurring in the first year after predictive testing for Huntington's disease" (1996) 33 *Journal of Medical Genetics* 856.

when preventive measures are available; or that disclosure is always harmful when cures are not available. Patients' various reactions to genetic information suggest that in practice the dilemma doctors face is complex. Not knowing how the relatives will react to the information communicated to them, the doctor faces a real difficulty in deciding whether or not to disclose the information to them. This may suggest that doctors and patients should seriously consider the reaction relatives are likely to express when they are informed. However, as we shall see in Chapters 3 and 4, the law ignores this aspect.[45]

2.1.2.2 The effect of genetic information on the familial relationship. Genetic information affects familial relationships. The availability of information within a family can establish or destroy social relationships between relatives. Learning that they are carriers makes some patients feel responsible for transmitting a genetic mutation to their offspring. Non-carriers experience 'survivor's guilt', wondering why they do not carry the mutation while other relatives develop the disorder.[46]

The existence of survivor's guilt among carriers and non-carriers emphasises the relevance of social relationships in this area, especially in the search for a definition of a family. It is argued that feelings of guilt emerge because family members *care* about those who have inherited their mutative genes. This aspect would most probably be absent if they did not have any social relationship with the affected relative. One can assume, for example, that a sperm donor who discovers that he is a carrier of a genetic disorder may feel less guilty – if at all – about his biological child than a biological father who brings up his child.

The importance of blood ties and social relationships prevail when the relationship between siblings is examined. Studies indicate that siblings who have the same chances of inheriting a genetic disorder changed their relationships following testing. When one sibling is found to be a carrier other siblings may direct anger towards him or her.[47] In addition, those tested negative may avoid their carrier siblings, believing they will develop resentment.[48] The impact on a relationship can be profound when one sibling is affected with the disorder for which another is undergoing prenatal diagnosis. Learning that her foetus is affected with a disorder may adversely affect the woman's relationship with her affected

---

[45]   Ethicists, however, recognise this factor. See: Laurie G., "Challenging medical–legal norms: The role of autonomy, confidentiality and privacy in protecting individual and familial group rights in genetic information" (2001) 22 *The Journal of Legal Medicine* 1; and also: Genetic Interest Group, *Confidentiality and Medical Genetics* (1998), www.gig.org.uk/policy.

[46]   Quaid K., et al., "Knowledge, attitude, and the decision to be tested for Huntington's Disease" (1989) 36 *Clinical Genetics* 431.

[47]   Fanos J., Johnson J., "Perception of carrier status by Cystic Fibrosis siblings" (1995) 57 *American Journal of Human Genetics* 431, 434.

[48]   Ibid., at p. 435.

brother, who may view her decision to terminate the pregnancy as a moral judgement of his condition.[49]

The significance of blood ties in the formulation of a definition of a family may be reduced by studies which indicate that genetic information creates new decisions for the family as a social unit. Andrews describes a case where a couple learned that their unborn child was affected with CF. When the couple asked their relatives whether they would receive their support if they decided to have the child, a few family members opposed the birth of that child, worrying that he or she would receive an excessive share of the grandparents' time.[50] When approaching their relatives the couple did not make any distinction between blood and non-blood relatives. They turned to all who would be affected by it. Furthermore, the couple's conduct implies that the social and biological components of a family definition are interwoven and sometimes cannot be separated.

Undoubtedly, Andrews's case highlights the liberal–communitarian debate about patient autonomy. The couple's decision to consult their family members before having a child stresses that autonomy in the family is often more relational than individualistic: even if the couple decided to have the child – despite the reluctance of some relatives, in their decision they let their relatives express their concerns and they considered their views. This case, therefore, stresses the gap between practice and law: while in practice patients take the views and interests of their family members into account, the courts either do not deal with this aspect of the decision–making process or perceive it as undue influence.

Furthermore, the effect of genetic information on familial relationships is manifested in an examination of the patient–spouse relationship. Research indicates that genetic information has a considerable effect on this relationship. For example, when spouses are informed about the condition of their loved ones, they will obviously worry about their children. Partners of those who have the mutation for Huntington's disease may become resentful and hostile over the fact that the disease may have been transmitted to their children.[51] However, when the disorder was less life–threatening spouses stated that the experience of genetic testing strengthened their relationship with the patient.[52]

Furthermore, studies indicate that the individual is greatly influenced by the conduct and condition (both physical and mental) of his or her relatives. More specifically, when genetic information becomes available, the ability of the patient to cope emotionally with bad news depends, inter alia, on the reaction of his or her

---

[49]   Fanos J., Johnson J., "CF carrier status: The importance of not knowing" (1994) 55 (3) *American Journal of Human Genetics* A292.

[50]   See Andrews, supra n. 30, at p. 48.

[51]   Hans M., et al., "Huntington's Chorea: Its impact on the spouse" (1980) 168 (4) *Journal of Nervous and Mental Disease* 209.

[52]   Metcalfe K.A., et al. "Evaluation of the needs of spouses of female carriers of mutations in BRCA1 and BRCA2" (2002) 62 *Clinical Genetics* 464, 469.

partner.[53] This supports the conclusion that genetic information affects the familial relationship because it is based on a close social relationship and not simply on blood ties.

Conclusion.

2.1.2.3 The importance of biological and social components. The empirical data reviewed in this part leads to the following observations. First, it reinforces Laurie's statement that genetic information concerns the family and not just the individual patient. It also implies that genetic information has various social and psychological implications: it affects (1) the self–image of the patient; (2) his or her mental health; (3) his or her relationships with other family members (whether blood or non-blood relatives); and (4) the family member's mental health.

More importantly, the studies cited above support the argument that any definition of family in this context cannot overlook the social relations between patients and their family members. However, the central question is whether a purely social definition of the family in genetics is comprehensive and sufficient. It was suggested, in a different legal context, that a family member can be the one whom the patient feels intimately close to.[54] This implies that a group of individuals is considered family not because they share the same genetic material but because they have intimate and mutual relationships. If this is applied to genetics, blood relations will not be relevant in the consideration of whether or not to disclose information.

Nevertheless, the legal implications of letting people decide who their relatives are should be carefully considered. First, as the studies cited above indicate genetic information is more relevant to blood relatives than to their friends or extended non-blood relatives. Genetic information first and foremost refers to the physical health of the individual and can in some circumstances prevent physical harm to adults, minors, and the unborn. If a purely social definition is adopted, patients

---

[53] Quaid K.A., Wesson M.K., "The effect of predictive testing for Huntington's disease on intimate relationship" (1994) 55 (3) *American Journal of Human Genetics* A294; this is also true for other close relatives who report 'worrying a great deal' when the patient is diagnosed with breast cancer. See: Chalmers K., et al., "Reports of information and supports needs of daughters and sisters of women with breast cancer" (2003) 12 *European Journal of Cancer* 81, 84; the significance of family support in this context will be investigated in detail in Chapter 5. However, when the relationship between parents and young children is examined, one study on women who undergo BRCA tests suggests that there is no difference in parent–child daily functioning whether or not the parents disclose the results to their children. See: Tercyak K., et al., "Parent–child and their effect on communicating BRCA1/2 test results to children" (2002) 47 *Patient Education and Counselling* 145, 150.

[54] Buchanan A., Brock D., *Deciding for Others: The Ethics of Surrogate Decision Making*, Cambridge, Cambridge University Press (1989), 146.

may disclose genetic information to their best friends, whom they consider family, but not to their biological children, to whom the information is critical.

Moreover, giving patients the authority to decide who their family members are may require doctors to allocate valuable resources to become familiar with the social world of the patient. Furthermore, such a definition would create uncertainty and confusion because lawyers would have to abandon well–established legal concepts, such as marriage, adoption, and the like, and instead struggle to know who is a family member and who is not. Undoubtedly, the legal system would be ineffective if fundamental concepts were not clearly articulated. Therefore, defining a family in genetics based solely on social relations and emotional closeness seems to be inappropriate.

To conclude, if the previous section emphasised the importance of the biological component when defining a family in genetics, this section has indicated that a social component is essential though insufficient. Hence, with none of the definitions suggested above being satisfactory in this context, the next step is to examine what is the view of English law on this issue.

2.2 Searching for a legal definition of the family

2.2.1 The Family in English Law

At the outset, it should be stressed that neither the courts nor Parliament provide an explicit definition of the family in the context of genetics. The question is why this is so. There are several possible answers. First, there is no direct case or statute that discusses the issue of communication of genetic information to family members. Second, when the status of family members is discussed in other areas of medical law a clear definition of the family is not always provided. A good example is the area of organ donation and transplantation. Section 1 (2) of the *Human Tissue Act* 1961, in force until April 2006, gives the relatives the authority to object to cadaver donation. Yet it fails to identify the relatives in this context. When donation is requested both distant and close relatives, if present at the hospital, possess equal discretion to object to donation. However, as regards living donors, section 2 of the *Human Organ Transplant Act* 1989, in force until April 2006, permits live donation between those who are 'genetically related'. They are natural parents and children, whole or half siblings, uncles and aunts, natural children of whole or half siblings, and natural children of whole or half uncles and aunts. Partners (either married or not) are not included, and their motivation to donate is considered by the Unrelated Live Transplant Regulatory Authority.[55]

A single and clear definition of the family in the area of organ donation and transplantation will be made in April 2006 when the *Human Tissue Act 2004*,

---

[55] *Human Organ Transplants (Unrelated Persons) Regulation* 1989, section 2, (SI 1989, No. 2480).

which received the Royal Assent in November 2004, comes into force. The lack of clear definition of relatives in the *Human Tissue Act* 1961 and the somewhat unsatisfactory definition of the family in the *Human Organ Transplants Act* 1989 are clarified in the new *Human Tissue Act* 2004. This Act repeals and replaces the two Acts.[56] Section 27(4) provides that spouse or partner,[57] parent or child, brother or sister, grandparent or grandchild, child of a brother or sister, stepfather or stepmother, half–brother or half–sister, and friend of longstanding is defined as having 'qualified relationship' to give consent when it is medically possible to use organs or tissues from the deceased patient to transplantation (in this ranking).[58] Similarly, in another area, the government recently introduced a *Civil Partnership Act* 2004, which came into force in December 2004. The new Act is aimed at giving legal recognition to same–sex couples and rights in several areas, such as pensions, inheritance tax, property, social security benefits, adoption as a couple, and parental responsibility in the event of a relationship breakdown. The government explicitly stated that it hoped that the new Act would help same–sex partners to face the difficulties when one of them became ill.[59] But the new Act does not refer specifically to medical issues.[60]

Currently, however, as regards genetic information there is no clear definition of the family. This lack of definition may reflect the attitude of English medical law to the patient's family members. One may argue that if the status of family members were fully recognised – at least in the context of communication of medical information, there would have to be a clear definition of the family. However, it must be admitted that an explicit definition of a family may not be essential because even without it the interest of family members in medical information can be recognised. Such a possibility will be discussed in the following chapters.

An answer to the question 'who is the family?' may be found in the area of family law. It will be convenient to examine this issue in light of two approaches, which prevail in the socio–legal literature. The first approach is *formal* and it

---

[56] Department of Health, *The Human Tissue Act 2004: New legislation on human organs and tissue*,
     http://www.dh.gov.uk/PolicyAndGuidance/HealthAndSocialCareTopics/Tissue/TissueG
     eneralInformation/TissueGeneralArticle.

[57] Following the *Civil Partnership Act* 2004 a same–sex partner is included as well.

[58] http://www.legislation.hmso.gov.uk/acts/acts2004/40030. The Act was in published in 17/11/ 2004. See also section 6 in part 3 of Schedule 4 of the *Mental Capacity Act* 2005.

[59] The Department of Trade and Industry, Women & Equality Unit, Civil Partnership: A framework for the legal recognition of same–sex couples (June, 2003), p. 39. www.womenandequalityunit.gov.uk. For the new Act:
     http://www.legislation.hmso.gov.uk/acts/acts2004/20040033.htm.

[60] For a critique of the difficulties lesbians face in accessing assisted reproduction services under English law even after the enactment of the *Civil Partnership Act* 2004 see: Wallband J., "Reconstructing the HFEA 1990: Is blood really thicker than water?" (2004) 16 (4) *Child and Family Law Quarterly* 387.

examines whether a group of individuals satisfy objective criteria or a familial structure. A group of individuals will be regarded as a family if related by blood or marriage and engage in reproduction. This approach is more concerned with the format and set–up of the social unit, and less with its function or the relationships among its members. The second approach is *functional*, and it examines whether the group as a whole act as a family. It observes the day–to–day functions of the group and monitors the kind of relationships its members have.[61]

Undoubtedly, the first approach presents a more traditional form of the family, and is less open to other alternatives that do not satisfy the objective criteria of blood ties, marriage, or reproduction. For example, same–sex partners may not be regarded as family because they cannot produce children naturally. The functional approach is indeed more open to accepting new family forms as long as the members express close familial relationship. However, in every case this approach requires an indication that such a unit functions as a family. In this formal– functional debate the biological definition of a family in genetics will accord with the formal approach, whereas the social definition will be compatible with the functional one.

Searching for a definition of family involves the purposes the law is set to promote. For many years family policy in the UK encouraged a traditional family form, namely a married heterosexual couple who live with their biological children.[62] Believing that this form could yield a more productive society,[63] policy–makers utilised the legal system to fulfil this aim, recognising parental rights and responsibilities of married parents while ignoring those of single parents. As Hale LJ explicitly stated in 1997, family law was developed to support traditional marriage.[64]

The preference given to the traditional family form has been subject to continuous criticism. Liberal feminists, such as Susan Okin, argued that the traditional family was an unjust social institution for it oppressed women and children especially when marriage broke down and women were left to care for the children by themselves.[65] In addition, supporters of gay and lesbian rights argued that the attitude to same–sex cohabitation, as expressed in courts, was hostile.[66] This feminist critique was directed at liberals and communitarians who ignored the

---

[61] Herring J., *Family Law*, Harlow, Longman (2nd edn., 2004), 2–3.

[62] O'Donovan K., *Family Law Matters*, London, Pluto Press (1993), 31.

[63] Muncie J., Wetherell M., "Family policy and political discourse" in Muncie J., Wetherell M., et al., (eds.), *Understanding the Family*, London, Sage (2nd edn., 2000), 39–80.

[64] As stated in Sclater S.D., et al., "Introduction", in Bainham A., Sclater S.D., Richards M. (eds.), *What is a Parent? A Socio–Legal Analysis*, Oxford, Hart Publishing (1999), 6.

[65] Okin S., *Justice, Gender and the Family*, New York, Basic Books (1989).

[66] Boyd S.B., "What is a normal family? C v C (A Minor) (Custody: Appeal)" (1992) 55 *MLR* 269.

injustices and inequalities prevalent in a society mainly dominated by white middle–class men.

Whether or not academic criticism had any effect, the legal approach to alternative family forms has gradually been changing. Recently statutes and courts' decisions have recognised legal rights that once were given exclusively to the members of the traditional family.[67] This development challenges the definition and the perception of the family: it is not characterised solely by blood ties, marriage, or reproduction but also by close intimate relationships. The fact that unmarried couples or same–sex partners are treated as the heterosexual married couple in several areas of law shows that these alternative forms are gradually considered family.[68] In the context of this book, the shift from a formal to a functional approach must make an impact on the perception of the family in genetics. It implies that in this context family members will not be solely those who have blood relations with the patient, but also those who are emotionally close to the patient such as the biological children of his or her partner.

The shift in the legal perception of the family is reflected in several areas, such as adoption,[69] assisted reproduction,[70] and parental responsibility.[71] The most obvious change may be found in the area of housing. Traditionally, the law adopted a formal approach and provided statutory rights only to heterosexual married couples. For many years the courts limited the right of unmarried partners to inherit a statutory tenancy under Schedule 1 of the *Rent Act* 1977.[72] Addressing the case of an unmarried couple one judge expressed moral disapproval of such a form of relationship and refused to treat the couple as 'husband and wife'.[73]

---

[67] Recently Parliament recognised transsexuals' right to marry in their adopted gender. See: The *Gender Recognition Act* 2004, Schedule 4 (Effect of Marriage). The Act received the Royal Assent on 1 July 2004; the Department for Constitutional Affairs is working to implement the Act by early 2005. The Act was published in July 2004. www.legislation.hmso.gov.uk/acts/acts2004/20040007.htm.

[68] Bainham argues that this shift in the legal approach has 'monumental significance for the development of English family law in the twenty–first century'. See: Bainham A., "Homosexuality and the Lords: Shifting definitions of marriage and the family" (2000) *Cambridge Law Journal* 39.

[69] The new *Adoption and Children Act* 2002 (sections 49–51 and 144 (4) (b)) allows same–sex partners to adopt.

[70] The *Human Fertilisation and Embryology Act* 1990 allows unmarried couples to become parents of a child with whom the father has no blood ties. See section 28.

[71] The *Children Act* 1989 increased the circumstances in which people who are not biologically related to the child can obtain parental responsibility through section 8 orders. The new *Civil Partnership Act* 2004 provides same–sex partners rights in several areas including adoption and parental responsibility.

[72] Only in the 1988 amendment of the *Rent Act* 1977 was it held that 'a person who was living with the original tenant *as* his or her wife or husband shall be treated as the spouse of the original tenant'.

[73] *Gammans v Ekins* [1950] 2 All ER 140; however, even before the landmark case of

Gradually, though, the courts recognised that heterosexual unmarried couples can be regarded not only as 'family members' but also as 'husband and wife', and were thus eligible, like married couples, to inherit a right to occupy a property.[74] Yet the courts refused to hold that other forms of social relations, such as same–sex partnerships, could satisfy either the definition of 'husband and wife' or of 'family members'.[75]

However, recently the House of Lords in *Fitzpatrick v. Sterling Housing Association*[76] changed its attitude, holding that although same–sex partners cannot be considered 'husband and wife' they are perceived as 'family members' for the purpose of the *Rent Act* 1977. In this decision the House of Lords abandoned its formal approach and adopted a functional one. When examining whether a gay couple, who have been living together for almost twenty years, could be defined as 'family members', Lord Slynn stated that essentially in a familial relationship 'there should be a degree of mutual interdependence, of the sharing of lives, of caring and love, of commitment and support'.[77] Subsequently, following the incorporation of the *Human Rights Act* 1998, the Court of Appeal went farther, holding that same–sex partners can be considered 'husband and wife'.[78] This decision equalised the right of same–sex couples and of heterosexual married couples in this particular area of law.

The majority in *Fitzpatrick* expressed a view based on an ethics–of–care perspective. Care, love, commitment, and support, which were explicitly stated, are, as discussed in Chapter 1, prominent values in this feminist–based philosophy. More generally, this view indicated that English family law perceives the individual as one who is closely attached to his or her family members by mutual interrelationships of intimacy, sharing and commitment.

Progressive as this position may be, not all lawyers welcomed it. It was argued that the majority in the House of Lords did not base the decision upon strict interpretation of law, which should have resulted in an opposite outcome, but relied on recent changes in public opinion.[79] It was further argued that such a legal

---

Dyson v Fox and the 1988 amendment the right of an unmarried partner was recognised as a 'family member' and not as 'husband' or 'wife'. See *Hawes v Evenden* [1953] 2 All ER 737. Classifying partners as a family member and not as a spouse limits their legal tenancy right.

[74] *Dyson Holdings Ltd v Fox* [1975] 3 All ER 1030.

[75] *Harrogate BC v Simpson* (1984) 17 HLR 205; however, in this case the court had no real discretion to hold differently since the relevant statute provides a list of those considered family members.

[76] [1999] 4 All ER 705 (Hereafter: *Fitzpatrick*).

[77] Ibid.

[78] *Mendoza v Ghaidan* [2003] 1 FLR 468; the decision was recently affirmed by the House of Lords in *Ghaidan v Godin–Mendoza* [2004] UKHL 30.

[79] Since most of commentators welcomed this decision, the main legal criticism came from the minority judges. Lord Hutton, for example, was reluctant to abandon the formal approach.

development might encourage people to escape marriage as well as the responsibility and commitment it involved; and this might result in a decline in the status of the family as a social institution.[80] It was argued that same–sex partners could not be considered family because the essence of family life, that of reproduction, was absent.[81]

The majority judges did explicitly admit that they relied on public views about the family. They stated that public opinion is constantly changing regarding the family, and that the courts must be attuned to these changes.[82] This position was criticised because it perceived the role of law as a means to reflect the moral values of the society in which it operates. This line of reasoning was difficult for lawyers to accept because they viewed the law as having a central role in shaping public opinion. In contrast, the majority judges attempted to harmonise the law with public views and not to force its formal and out–of–date approach on the public.

Both supporters and opponents of such a functional definition of the family refer to recent trends in British society. Sociologists have been arguing for some time that the traditional form of the family is losing its exclusive place.[83] They argue that many people currently live in alternative family forms. For example, surveys show that the number of single–parent families has increased significantly in the last several years and at present constitutes a significant proportion of all families.[84] In addition, people prefer to live long periods of time in cohabitation before their first or second marriage.[85] Yet despite these tendencies, surveys also reveal that the majority of children (about 80%) live with their two biological married parents, and that the traditional family is still the most widespread family form in English society.[86]

The shift in the position of English law may lead to the conclusion that family law adopts liberal, communitarian and ethics–of–care conceptions. On the one

---

[80] Duckworth P., "What is a family? – A personal view" [2002] *Family Law* 367; for other commentaries. see: Diduck A., "A family by any other name ... or Starbucks comes to England" (2001) 28 (2) *Journal of Law and Society* 290; Glennon L., "Fitzpatrick v Sterling Housing Association Ltd – An endorsement of the functional family" (2000) 14 *International Journal of Law, Policy and the Family* 226.

[81] See Duckworth, ibid., at p. 371.

[82] See, *Fitzpatrick*, supra n. 76, per Lord Nicholls.

[83] Lewis J., "Debates and issues regarding marriage and cohabitation in the British and American Literature" (2001) 15 *International Journal of Law, Policy and the Family* 159.

[84] McRae S., "Introduction: family and household change in Britain" in McRae S. (ed.), *Changing Britain: Families and Households in the 1990s*, Oxford, Oxford University Press (1999), 1–35.

[85] Haskey J., "Demographic aspects of cohabitation in Great Britain" (2001) 15 *International Journal of Law, Policy and the Family* 51.

[86] Gibson C., "Changing family patterns in England and Wales over the last fifty years" in Katz S., Eekelaar J., MacLean M. (eds.), *Cross Currents: Family Law and Policy in the United States and England*, Oxford, Oxford University Press (2000), 31–55, 38.

hand, the recognition of alternative family forms, which are based on care, commitment, and mutual support, indicates that the law appreciates the existence of close *social* relationships in their own right. Family law accommodates these values when required to define a family for legal purposes. On the other hand, the assistance given to unmarried individuals in reproduction, the recognition of the right of gay and lesbian couples to adopt, and of the parental rights given to those who are not biologically related to the child – all aim to secure the fundamental rights of the individual. This reflects recognition of the individual's right to make free choices with little intervention from the state and emphasis on principles of equality and tolerance. The conclusion is that the family is an important institution both for liberals who promote individual rights and for communitarians who promote group or family rights. Yet while the liberal emphasis on rights promotes the interests of family members as individuals, communitarians and proponents of ethics–of–care concentrate on the promotion of the interests of family members as a social unit. The recent trend in English family law attests that both exist.

Consequently, if it is accepted that English family law reflects liberal, communitarian, and ethics–of–care perspectives it is argued that such an approach should be adopted in medical law as well. In the definition of a family in the context of genetics, this should result in a *biosocial* definition, which relies on universal and objective criteria of blood ties and marriage and on context–bound and subjective conceptions of care, commitment, mutual responsibility, and accountability. The adoption of a biosocial definition of the family will accord with the conclusion arrived at the end of the previous section, namely that relying solely on one component, either the biological or the social, is insufficient. The question of how such a definition is applied to the area of genetics is discussed next.

2.2.2 A Biosocial Definition of the Family

So far, the discussion in this chapter has resulted in the conclusion that the definition of the family in genetics ought to include both biological and social components. However, before formulating such a definition it is necessary to examine whether one already exists. As argued above, law and ethics do not discuss this issue explicitly. Graeme Laurie identifies the parties whom he considers to be family members.[87] However, he does not specifically define a family member but instead discusses those relatives with the strongest interest in either knowing or not knowing genetic information. In his discussion Laurie mentions parents, children, and siblings as relatives because they have the closest blood ties with the patient and thus can avoid physical harm if informed in advance. Laurie also mentions spouses, for they have an interest in making informed reproductive decisions, a factor which can affect their decision to stay in the relationship. Laurie seems to adhere to a formal definition of the family, based on marriage, blood ties, and reproduction.

---

[87] See Laurie, supra n. 19, at pp. 113–129.

Defining family members according to their interests is understandable if it is accepted that the question 'who is the family in genetics?' involves the scope of the legal duty to family members. Limiting this concept to a small, identifiable group of people provides coherence, especially if such a definition is adopted by law. However, the ground of Laurie's definition is narrow as it ignores other familial relations recognised in law, such as adoption and permanent cohabitation. If by omitting these relationships Laurie implies that the interests of adopted children in genetic information should not be recognised, his approach may not accord with recent developments in English law or with socio–medical research. If, however, Laurie intends to include the interests of these relatives, this should be articulated.

In the absence of an explicit definition of family in genetics, it is thus argued that it ought to include both biological and social components. On the one hand, the importance of a social component is self–evident. A sense of love, intimacy, and mutual responsibility turns a group of blood relatives to a family unit. On the other hand, in the context of genetics 'biology seems to be the foundation of social obligation'.[88] In a slightly different context, Andrew Bainham supports the view that social and biological components are both essential in the definition of a parent.[89] Bainham's underlying argument is that children benefit from both biological and social parents, even when only one pair has parental responsibility. Bainham links the question of 'who is a parent?' to the legal implications that any answer entails.

Applying this to the context of this work, it is inevitable that by preferring one particular definition to the other we do not simply discuss terminology but also express a view about the scope of duties and interests, which law and ethics should recognise in this area. Hence, adopting a biosocial definition of the family would suggest that a duty – if one exists – would include not only close blood relatives but also close non-blood relatives. By implication, promoting such a definition would mean that various interests, which currently may not be discussed by the courts,[90] would be considered, even if not fully recognised. Since in the case of non-blood relatives the patient's genetic information has no relevance for their physical health, other interests they have would be considered as well. One example is the interest of adult adopted children in knowing whether they would need to provide daily care to their parents so as to order their lives accordingly.

So who is a family member in the context of genetics? Parents, children, siblings, spouses, and other first–degree blood relatives are recognised in the academic literature.[91] But is it necessary to specify verbatim, as the law sometimes does, who is and who is not a family member? Surely, such an explicit definition

---

[88]   Finch J., *Family Obligations and Social Change*, Cambridge, Polity Press (1989), 36.

[89]   Bainham A., "Parentage, parenthood and parental responsibility" in Bainham et al., *What Is a Parent? A Socio–Legal Analysis*, Oxford, Hart Publishing (1999), 25–46.

[90]   For example, the right to make informed choices; for a detailed discussion see Chapters 3 and 4.

[91]   See Laurie, supra n. 19; and Andrews, supra n. 30.

would help patients and doctors when they are involved in legal claims. However, it is argued that this may not be necessary as it would be possible to rely on current conceptions of the family in English law, with its recognition of both formal and functional approaches. As we have seen, English law recognises the traditional form, based on marriage and blood ties, and social forms, such as same–sex partnerships, without specifically stating who is a family member and who is not.

Nevertheless, how broad is the biosocial definition? Is a distant blood relative a family member in genetics? It is suggested that the main consideration is the overall *effect* the information has on the relatives' lives. This characteristic combines the two biological and psychosocial aspects discussed above. Obviously, blood and non-blood relatives who are closely involved in the patient's life would be considered family members because the impact genetic information has on their lives is considerable whether or not they share the same DNA. When it comes to distant blood relatives the biological aspect of the definition prevails. Although the realisation that the patient suffers from a genetic disorder would not affect the life of extended family members as it may affect the patient's closest relatives, this information may have implications for their physical health. Statistically, there is a risk of 12.5% that the patient's first–degree cousin will suffer from the patient's dominant single gene disorder. Since this biological risk is significant the social requirement becomes less influential.

According to this test the biological and social components complete each other. When the family member is closely involved in the patient's life then blood ties will not be necessary; however, when the relatives are less close to the patient, the biological component will prevail. Yet even in the case where there are no strong social relations but only blood ties, a minimum level of social connection must exit. Distant cousins cannot be considered family if they have never met or interacted in any way, and the same applies to a sperm donor who does not know the identity of his biological child, even if there is a 50% chance that he passes a genetic disorder to his offspring. The mere fact that the biological father suffers from a genetic disorder cannot be used as a sufficient reason to perceive the father and the child as family.

Still, an argument against a biosocial definition is that not all families have close and intimate relationships, and when this is the case relatives may not be informed and thus unnecessary physical harm may occur. A possible answer may be that in circumstances where intimacy and sense of mutual commitment do not exist at all the familial relationship is on the verge of breakdown. When the family does break down blood ties are insufficient to maintain a free flow of information among its members. As noted earlier, the courts support such a view, holding that the hallmark of a familial relationship is the expression of a certain degree of love and commitment.[92]

This definition is admittedly more social than biological: while blood relatives may not be considered family members if they do not have a social relationship,

---

[92] See *Fitzpatrick*, supra n. 76.

non-blood relatives may be considered family members if they share close and mutual relationship. It should be stressed that reliance is also placed on existing family relations recognised by law, such as adoption and registered partnerships, so close friends cannot be regarded as relatives.

The biosocial definition relies on a subjective concept of *effect*. If a family member is defined according to the effect the information has on his or her life, this simply substitutes one incoherent definition with another. To know who a family member is it might be necessary to describe the level of effect or the circumstances that would justify defining the person as a relative. However, in most cases it will not be difficult to determine the level of effect that genetic information has for the relatives. As the medical account of genetics indicates, the effect of genetic information on family members' physical health and financial condition can be assessed. In addition, as the socio–medical research presented above reveals, the effect of genetic information on the relatives' psychological health can be determined.

However, one can still argue that defining a family member according to the effect made by the information on his or her life may raise a difficulty in cases, say, where the structure of the family is not traditional. For example, when a child living with his mother and stepfather has a poor relationship with his biological father the question arises whether the latter is defined as a family member in circumstances when the child is diagnosed as a carrier or a sufferer of a genetic disorder. How does the bad relationship affect the definition of the family? How does this affect the involvement the biological father in the decision–making process? And how will it affect his interests in the information?

In such a hypothetical case, the application of the biosocial definition with its underlying test of effect may not be of much help. If the mother and child refuse to perceive the biological father as a family member, the fact that the child's genetic condition may affect the biological father's physical as well as psychological health has little meaning unless the law requires either the doctor or the mother and child to see the father as a family member who is involved in the decision–making process. This, however, may seem like the state's interference in the patient's autonomy. Yet by not interfering in this preliminary issue, the state may compromise the biological father's health and personal interests. Hence, the application of the test is problematic. It assumes that family members want to involve each other in the decision–making process. However, when the social relationships between the parties are negative, the patient and his mother may leave the biological father outside the medical decision–making process even when the information has serious implications for him.

Such a hypothetical case raises a practical difficulty. It will require allocating extra resources to deal with a preliminary question of the definition of the family. It will leave courts, lawyers, doctors, patients, and family members in a similar state of uncertainty as they currently are.

Nevertheless, this test reflects the fact that blood ties and social relations are interwoven and interdependent. It may also lead one to realise that patient individuality is not the sole consideration in this area but that values, such as care, commitment, and principles, such as accountability and mutual responsibility, are also important. They all imply that familial relationships in themselves have added value even in an area ruled primarily by blood ties. The view taken in this book is that adopting a biosocial definition would present a more balanced approach than the one that currently does (not) exist in medical law.

However, defining a family member and a relative in this area is not the end of this introductory discussion. Before dealing with the legal and ethical position of the tensions between patients and family members over genetic information it is necessary to understand their interests that underlie their moral and legal claims. Therefore, the next part, which analyses these interests, can be seen as a link in a chain. First, disclosure and non–disclosure of genetic information affect patients and family members in various aspects. This effect then shapes their interest in the information. Finally, these interests are formulated in law and ethics as rights and duties. The first part of this chapter was dedicated to the effect genetic information has on patients and relatives; the next part will discuss the interests they have in it. In Chapters 3 and 4 the legal and ethical position will be analysed.

2.3 Identifying the Parties' Interests

The physical and psychological implications of genetic information for patients and relatives demonstrate how significant it is for both parties.[93] Consequently, patients and relatives have various interests in this information and sometimes these interests collide. In this context, Laurie's definition of an interest is adopted: it is a claim that a benefit can be gained by any party (in our context patients and family members) by recognising that he or she has existing or potential rapport to genetic information.[94] In the following paragraphs these interests will be specified and analysed.

2.3.1 The Patient

The vast majority of legal and bioethical commentators concentrate on two interests, which patients have. First, they argue, patients are interested in receiving available information about their susceptibility to genetic diseases.[95] Receiving information enables the patient to avoid harm and to make informed choices. In genetics the interest in receiving information can help patients to avoid physical harm or begetting a disabled child.[96] In addition, genetic information can facilitate

---

[93] Obviously, genetic information has implications for other parties such as employers and insurers. See Laurie G., supra n. 19, pp. 129–150 (insurance), and pp. 150–165 (employment).

[94] See Laurie, supra n. 19, at p. 114.

[95] Ibid.

[96] Research suggests that about 25% of people who take genetic tests for Huntington's

free and informed choices, whether these concern reproduction or any other major life decision.

Second, once patients receive the information they may have an interest in keeping it in confidence.[97] As noted earlier, the considerable psychological impact of genetic information on their self–image and relationship with others leads patients to regard genetic information as sensitive. The fear that their new genetic status may adversely affect their relationship with their family members underlies their interest to keep the information in confidence. Therefore, they want to control its access.

With these two interests combined, patients seemingly have an interest in receiving genetic information *alone*, without the presence or knowledge of others. As we shall see in Chapter 4, professional codes of ethics perceive genetic information like any other type of medical information: it is personal and controlled exclusively by the patient, even when it affects others. Obviously, this conclusion reflects a patient–centred approach where the individual patient exercises autonomy individualistically rather than relationally.

The focus on prevention of harm and informed choices as the underlying interests of the patient raises the question of whether he or she has other interests. Some commentators argue that patients have an interest in not knowing genetic information. This interest will be dealt with below. However, if it is accepted that some patients may have an interest in knowing genetic information whereas others have not, the conclusion is that two opposite interests can co-exist in this area. As much as people may have an interest in obtaining genetic information, depending on the characteristics of the disease and their personal views about it, so may they have an interest in not knowing genetic information, when they suspect that it may cause them harm. By the same token it can be argued that the two opposite interests of keeping genetic information in confidence and sharing it with others can co-exist as well, depending, of course, on the circumstances.

An interest in sharing genetic information can be identified and based on a communitarian perception of the individual and his or her relationships with others. This perception led commentators on both sides of the Atlantic[98] to argue that entering into familial relationships entails not only rights but also responsibilities. Applying this to the genetic context, patients have an interest in sharing genetic information with their relatives because they want to maintain their relationship with them. This leads patients to feel responsible for their relatives. This moral responsibility results in exchange of valuable information within the family. The mutual aspect of the familial relationship leads many patients to disclose

---

disease state that their motive is reproduction; Spijker A., et al., "Psychological aspects of genetic counselling: A review of the experience with Huntington's disease" (1997) 32 *Patient Education and Counselling* 33.

[97] See Laurie, supra n. 19, at p. 119.

[98] See Rhodes, supra n. 27, at p. 18; Sommerville A., English V., "Genetic privacy: orthodoxy or oxymoron" (1999) 25 *Journal of Medical Ethics* 144.

information to their relatives, assuming that if they do so on one occasion the family members will reciprocate in the future. This mutual communication of information may improve the relationship with the relatives provided they wish to know. In addition, it may also benefit the family as a group, helping it to cope in difficult times and to maximise its common good.

Yet personal accounts of patients who struggle over whether or not to disclose genetic information to their relatives suggest that such an interest in sharing information does not always prevail. For example, an account given by a breast cancer patient who ponders whether or not to disclose the BRCA1 test results to her two adult daughters indicates that parents' desire to protect their children from receiving bad news often overrides considerations of moral responsibility.[99]

One possible response is to argue that the interest in sharing information with family members is strong because it does not derive exclusively from a sense of moral responsibility to others, which some people have and some do not. It also stems from a personal *need* to share distressful information with close relatives. As will be discussed thoroughly in Chapter 5, patients who receive medical information need to share the information they gain with at least one close relative or friend. Doing so helps them to relieve mental distress and anxiety, to cope with the bad news, and ultimately to survive.[100] Returning to the breast cancer patient mentioned above, though she was reluctant to disclose the test results to her daughters she did ask her husband to accompany her to the clinic so that they might receive the results together, for she needed his support in that crucial time when the information was communicated to her.

Unlike the interests discussed above, acknowledging that patients have an interest in sharing information with others reflects a relational perception of autonomy. It suggests that any decision patients make affects those with whom they share their lives; and that their capacity to make decisions is nurtured by the relatives. The interest in sharing the information helps patients to maximise their individuality and to maintain their identity and freedom during the difficult times of receiving genetic information.

---

[99] Robertson J., et al., "BRCA1 screening in woman with breast cancer: A patient's perspective with commentary" (2001) 11 (2) *Women's Health Issues* 63; For other personal accounts see Marteau T., Richards M., (eds.), *The Troubled Helix: Social and Psychological Implications of the New Human Genetics*, Cambridge, Cambridge University Press (1996), Ch. 1.

[100] Bloom J., "The role of family support in cancer control" in Baider L., Cooper C., Kaplan De-Nour A., (eds.), *Cancer and the Family*, Chichester, Wiley (2nd edn., 2000), 53–71, 60; The need to share information to relieve stress and anxiety is also true for family members. See, for example, Beeson R., et al., "Loneliness and depression in caregivers of persons with Alzheimer's disease or related disorders" (2000) 21 *Issues in Mental Health Nursing* 779.

2.3.2 The Relatives

The interests discussed with regard to patients apply to family members also. They may have an interest in knowing genetic information, and when gaining the information they may want to keep it in confidence. However, family members are not an indistinguishable entity and they may not share similar interests with regard to genetic information: whereas some may wish to know and share information, others may wish to keep it in confidence or to remain ignorant.[101] Therefore, an extreme communitarian view, which highlights the common good of the family as a whole, is not promoted in this book. As explained in Chapter 1, focusing on the common good of the family will compromise the interests of its weaker members, mainly women and children. It will also mitigate the importance of principles such as autonomy, confidentiality, and privacy, which help the individual patient at the difficult time of receiving genetic information.

Focusing on the interest in confidentiality, a distinction is made between the patient and his or her relatives because the former have made a conscious decision to acquire the information, whereas the relatives in most cases have not. This distinction led to the recognition of the patient's legal right to confidentiality, which bars relatives from accessing the information. Yet such a distinction between patients and relatives does not exist in practice in many cases. Research suggests that patients often approach doctors only after consulting their close relatives on whether to seek professional medical advice.[102] The relatives' view in this regard is very influential. They may either encourage the patient to approach the doctor or convince him or her that medical advice is not necessary. The decision to take a genetic test is often shared and not taken by the patient alone. By contrast, emphasising the difference between the patient, who decides to take a test, and the relatives, who are unaware of that decision, reflects a liberal approach which ignores the value of social relationship in decision–making. Hence, it is argued that a gap may exist between law and the medical practice in this context.

Another difference between patients and relatives, which is rarely discussed, is that the relatives' interest in keeping genetic information in confidence can be compromised by the patient even without the relatives' knowledge. Such a situation may occur when the patient who receives genetic information decides to communicate it to other third parties, such as the doctor, thus revealing information about the relatives as well. Whether or not the relatives are aware of these circumstances they may be unable to control the flow of information if their interest in controlling the information is not legally recognised. Promoting only the patient's interest in confidentiality, but not the relatives', may be unjust, for it is based on mere chance, as the patient was the first to approach the doctor and gain

---

[101] McGowan R., "Beyond the disorder: One parent's reflection on genetic counselling" (1999) 25 *Journal of Medical Ethics* 195.

[102] See, for example, Bloom, supra n. 100.

the information. Injustice prevails if it is accepted that patients and family members share genetic material but could not share control over genetic information. Furthermore, if the interests of family members are not protected in this situation it could be argued that the patient's personal interests receive higher priority than the relatives'. Recently the Human Genetics Commission supported such an unbalanced approach, arguing that patients have a right to disclose genetic information about their relatives to their doctor.[103] Undoubtedly, this point emphasises the challenge genetic information (with its familial characteristic) poses to law and ethics. In this context it may be asked if implementation of a communitarian approach would not be more just.

2.3.3 The Interest in Not Knowing

A recent trend in the academic literature is to discuss whether patients and relatives have an interest in not knowing genetic information, and if they do, whether it should be legally[104] and ethically[105] recognised. The discussion about this interest is usually conducted in circumstances where genetic disorders are incurable or when it is impossible to determine that the carrier will develop the disease in the future (these are indeed the more common situations). The assumption that patients and relatives may have an interest in not knowing relies on research, suggesting that provision of genetic information may cause psychological harm. As noted, a study on Huntington's disease, for example, showed that suicide rates among those with the mutation for it are significantly higher than those among the general population.[106] Research on breast cancer indicates that carriers of BRCA1/2 mutations suffer greater mental distress than non-carriers.[107] Therefore, if it is impossible to avoid the onset of a disease the benefit in disclosing the information is in doubt.

The argument that patients and relatives have an interest in not knowing genetic information is based, inter alia, on the assumption that people act *rationally*: people would like to receive genetic information if there are available cures or measures to avoid the onset of the disease, but they would prefer not to know if there are no preventive measures, because they fear they would suffer from mental distress as a result. Yet the counter–argument, which suggests that people are entitled to act irrationally,[108] is confirmed in practice. As indicated in the previous part, research

---

[103] Human Genetics Commission, *Inside Information: Balancing interests in the use of personal genetic data*, London, Department of Health (2002), para 4.1, at p. 69.

[104] Laurie G., "Obligations arising from genetic information– negligence and the protection of familial interests" (1999) 11 (2) *Child and Family Law Quarterly* 109, 116.

[105] Raikka J., "Freedom and a right (not) to know" (1998) 12 (1) *Bioethics* 49.

[106] See Almqvist, supra n. 34.

[107] Meiser B., et al., "Psychological impact of genetic testing in women from high–risk breast cancer families" (2002) 38 *European Journal of Cancer* 2025, 2029.

[108] Takala T., "The right to genetic ignorance confirmed" (1999) 13 (3/4) *Bioethics* 288;

suggests that people *react* unexpectedly when they receive genetic test results. Non-carriers may still suffer an adverse reaction, whereas carriers of terminal disorders may react positively. However, it should be stressed that the above research concerns patient's *reactions* and not actions. But if these unreasonable reactions may lead to irrational decisions, the question arises whether individual autonomy includes the right to act irrationally. Studies suggest that people may *act* contrary to what may seem to doctors as their best interests. For example, women who discover that they are BRCA carriers and at risk of developing breast cancer may refuse mastectomy, which would significantly reduce their risk and relieve mental distress post operation. This is because they fear that undergoing mastectomy will affect their femininity and self–image.[109] Moreover, a recent study, which examined whether or not patients prefer to know distressful information, suggested that the vast majority preferred to receive a diagnosis of degenerative neurological disease, rejecting the opportunity to live in blissful ignorance.[110]

Although it is true that receiving genetic information about a terminal disease may be distressful this should not lead automatically to the conclusion that people may prefer not to know. On the contrary, researchers conclude that even in incurable disorders such as Huntington's disease those who have tested positive gain psychological benefits from knowing their genetic status regardless of the initial mental distress from which they may suffer.[111] As one researcher concludes, genetic testing for Huntington's disease has been a success, and its few adverse consequences are minor as against the large number of people who have been relieved of the anxiety of not knowing whether or not they will develop the disease.[112] The only conclusion one can draw from this research is that the influence of predictive genetic testing is more complex than previously assumed, as carriers potentially gain psychological benefits and suffer emotional costs when receiving the results.[113]

This insightful observation implies that when the interests of patients and family members in disclosure are considered, the question of whether harm can be avoided is not crucial. This is because genetic information is associated with both psychological costs and benefits in any given situation regardless of whether there

---

legally, the House of Lords held in several occasions that autonomy include the right to make irrational decisions.

[109] Hatcher M., et al., "The psychosocial impact of bilateral prophylactic mastectomy: Prospective study using questionnaires and semi-structured interviews" (2001) 322 *BMJ* 76.

[110] Schattner A., Tal M., "Truth telling and patient autonomy: The patient's point of view" (2002) 113 (1) *The American Journal of Medicine* 66.

[111] See Lawson, supra n. 44, at p. 859.

[112] Bundey S., "Few psychological consequences of presymptomatic testing for Huntington disease" (1997) 349 *The Lancet* 4; see also Spijker, supra n. 96, at p. 38.

[113] See Meiser, supra n. 107, at p. 2030; see also: Spijker, supra n. 96.

are preventive measures to avoid the disease. As indicated above, many patients prefer to know medical information even when physical harm cannot be avoided. Consequently, the issue of whether or not to inform patients and family members when their preference is unknown must be based on other considerations which do not concern prevention of harm. However, if the law concentrates on the harm principle – and this will be examined in the next two chapters – a gap between law and practice once again prevails.

Laurie founds the interest in not knowing on the principle of privacy.[114] First, he argues that imposing information on patients and relatives without asking them about their preferences may be considered disrespectful. This immediately raises the question of whether it is disrespectful to disclose information when the one who discloses the information does not know whether the other would like to receive it. It is argued that in these circumstances approaching the patient or the relative and finding out considerately whether they would like to receive genetic information is considered a respectful conduct. The focus is on the method of disclosure, not the content of the information. In light of the research outlined above, the method of disclosure is what makes it either considerate or disrespectful.

Second, Laurie argues that imposing genetic information on patients or relatives – notwithstanding that this may not cause physical or psychological harm – invades people's privacy and forces them to change their self–image and re-evaluate their identity.[115] Although this argument shifts the focus away from the harm principle, taking it one step farther it implies that receiving unsolicited information about oneself is invasion of privacy, which leads one to re-evaluate one's selfhood, while receiving unexpected information about one's closest relative is not. One can argue that the distinction between the two is very delicate. Consider, for example, the difference between a mother who tells her daughter that she (the mother) has breast cancer and a mother who tells her daughter that since she is a BRCA1 carrier the daughter should take the test as well. According to Laurie's view, the first statement may be allowed while the second one may be considered as invasion of privacy. Many would agree with Laurie that information about one's physical health has a considerably greater effect on his or her privacy, identity and self–image than information about the physical health of his or her family member. Yet it can be argued that although the second statement directly concerns the health of the daughter and is communicated to her unexpectedly the first statement may have an equally adverse effect on the daughter's life for she may worry that her mother is at great risk. This may lead Laurie to assume that the first statement may also be considered invasion of privacy, thus forbidding the

---

[114] Laurie argues that people live in a sphere of spatial privacy, which is 'a bubble of privateness around the individual that cannot and should not be invaded without due cause'. See Laurie "Challenging Medical–Legal Norms" (2001) 22 *Journal of Legal Medicine* 1, 30.

[115] See Laurie, supra n. 19, at p. 126.

mother to communicate the information to her daughter. Yet if, according to Laurie, the first statement is not regarded as invasion of the daughter's privacy, while the second one is, one must admit that the difference between the two is very fine, especially if the relationship between them is close. In the specific example of breast cancer, one has to admit that the two statements by the mother may impel the daughter to the same inference, namely that she might be at risk for the disease as well. If the mother's two statements are considered distinct in their emotional effect on the daughter, the starting point or core belief is admittedly that even in the family the individual is fundamentally separate from his or her closest relatives. But if the two statements are deemed to have almost the same psychological effect on the daughter, the influence family members have on each other has to be appreciated. As the research described in this book suggests, the reaction of close relatives (especially partners) to genetic test results is often fiercer than the patient's.

Finally, the view taken in this book is that Laurie walks on a slippery slope. If people have to be constantly considerate, and careful not to invade the private sphere of their loved ones, this will impose restrictions on the flow of information within the family, for the underlying rule is that information should not be disclosed unless the circumstances justify it.[116] Respecting one's right to privacy within the family, as Laurie suggests, may limit the flow of information in the family and will question the existence of the family as a social institution. It may also estrange close family members. Yet unlike other forms of relationships the family is based on free flow of information among its members. However, if non-disclosure is the rule and not the exception, it may turn the family into a group of individuals rather than a social unit which provides support to its members.

2.4 Conclusion

This chapter concludes the introductory part of this book. It aimed to set out its contextual framework. A practicable definition of family and relatives has been formulated in light of the medical characteristics of genetic information and its psychological impact on patients and relatives. The final part of this chapter attempted to lay down the foundations for the next two chapters by identifying the interests that patients and relatives have. Whether these interests are legally and ethically recognised will be examined in the next chapters.

---

[116] See Laurie, supra n. 114, at p. 39.

Chapter 3

English Tort Law and the Patient's Family Members

3.1 Introduction

In Chapter 1 it was assumed that English law and medical ethics reflect a patient–centred approach. It was argued that this approach might be based on liberal conceptions which perceived patient autonomy as free from social constraints and influences. The individual's background and his or her community did not receive significant attention. In this and the following chapter these assumptions will be examined with regard to communication of genetic information in the family. Therefore, these two chapters should be read together for they specify and analyse the legal and ethical positions of family members in this area. While this chapter focuses on principles of tort law, the next chapter concentrates on medical confidentiality.

The position of law and medical ethics regarding the status of family members will be examined in two possible scenarios: in the first, the patient receives medical genetic information from his or her doctor but refuses to disclose it to the family members. In the second scenario, the patient is willing to share the information with his or her relatives but they are reluctant to receive it. In the first scenario, the doctor faces the serious dilemma of whether to respect the patient's decision not to disclose the information or to inform the relatives. In the second scenario, the doctor considers whether to respect the relatives' right to remain ignorant especially when the information can help them avoid harm. In these scenarios, attention is given to two situations: where the relatives are registered as the doctor's patients and where they are not. As we shall see, legally, this distinction may be significant.

These two scenarios reflect the various interests which patients and family members have when medical genetic information becomes available. As was discussed in Chapter 2, the first scenario reflects the interest in receiving genetic information and keeping it in confidence whereas the second scenario reflects the interest in sharing the information with the relatives as well as the interest in not knowing it. Therefore, these scenarios raise legal and ethical tensions between patients and their relatives. First, there is a tension between patients' right to keep medical information in confidence and relatives' right to know; and second there is a tension between patients' right to communicate information and relatives' right not to know. Concerning these tensions the focus will be on tort law. This is because professional obligations and moral responsibilities are translated in law into a tortious duty of care which one person owes to another.

However, addressing the status of family members more generally, it can be argued that the wider context of this study is medical decision–making and the entitlement of family members to participate in this process. In other words, the question is whether the interests of family members are legally recognised when the patient receives medical information and has to make a decision whether to disclose it to others. As was specified in Chapter 1, the question is whether the law in this area perceives patient autonomy individualistically or relationally. Therefore, one can argue that this chapter should focus on the patient's right to self–determination.

Legally, however, the issue of communication of medical information is examined in the context of a tortious duty of care.[1] The patient's inability to exercise the right to autonomous choice is dealt with in tort law for two reasons. First, failure to provide relevant information to the patient is perceived in law as failure to provide reasonable medical care, which may amount to negligent conduct. In addition, failure to respect the patient's interests (in disclosure or in non–disclosure) may be regarded as breach of his or her rights, which may result in a claim in negligence for the harm he or she suffers.[2] Therefore, a claim in negligence against the doctor or the patient is the legal device available to relatives when their interests are compromised and they cannot exercise their autonomy. In other words, the legal status of family members can be examined through their entitlement to receive compensation for their damage in courts.

Another option available for relatives who wish to be informed is to make an application to a court to order doctor's or patient's disclosure of information.[3] As the discussion in Chapter 4 reveals the courts usually weigh two competing interests: the public interest in protecting medical confidentiality and the public interest in promoting public health.[4] Thus, the court may justify such an application if the relatives can prove that the information can help them avoid serious physical harm. However, as Ngwena and Chadwick argue, this may not be sufficient to

---

1   Derek Morgan asks 'what is medical law?' and argues that it encompasses various areas
     of law, including in our context tort law. See Morgan D., *Issues in Medical Law and
     Ethics*, London, Cavendish (2001), pp. 3–6.

2   Stern K., "Confidentiality and medical records" in Kennedy I., Grubb A. (eds.),
     Principles of Medical Law, Oxford, Oxford University Press (1998), pp. 514–518.

3   See, for example: *Frankson and others v Home Office* [2003] EWCA Civ 655, [2003] 1
     WLR 1952.

4   *W v Egdell* [1990] 1 All ER 835 (Hereafter: *W v Egdell*), at p. 846 per Sir Stephen
     Brown P.

justify disclosure of information[5] as the courts emphasised that only exceptional and compelling circumstances will justify it.[6] In addition, the possibility of such an application depends on whether the relatives know that relevant familial genetic information is available, or alternatively, whether they know that the patient is seeking genetic advice from the doctor. If this is not the case, the relatives' only option is to apply for a legal remedy through a claim in negligence after the damage has occurred.

Focusing on English tort law, the structure of this chapter will be as follows. Following this introduction the basic principles of English tort law will be specified with emphasis on the legal requirements essential to establish a duty of care (between the doctor or the patient as the defendant and the family member as the claimant). Since *proximity* between the claimant and the defendant is the most problematic component in this regard, the following three parts will examine this issue in the context of the three categories of damage recognised in English law: physical injury, psychological harm, and economic loss. In the last part the third component of the duty of care will be examined, namely whether it is *fair, just and reasonable* to impose a duty of care. Consequently, the first task is to specify the basic principles of English tort law. This will provide an insightful look at its underlying philosophical approach.

3.2 The Basic Principles of Negligence Law

Any claim in negligence should satisfy the following requirements: (1) the defendant owes the claimant a duty of care; (2) the defendant breaches the duty of care; (3) the defendant's breach of duty causes damage to the claimant (hereafter: duty of care, breach and causation). However, the essence of the claim is determined by the type of damage. Although some of the principles applied by the courts are similar for all categories of damages specified below, as will be shown in this chapter specific mechanisms exist for each of them. Recently the courts tried to present a uniform approach and apply principles employed in one category of damage to the others. In the medical context, for example, the notion 'assumption of responsibility', which was first developed in the area of economic loss,[7] was adopted in the other two categories of damage.[8]

---

[5] Ngwena C., Chadwick R., "Genetic diagnostic information and the duty of confidentiality: Ethics and law" (1993) 1 *Medical Law International* 73, 81.

[6] See *W v Egdell*, supra n. 4, at p. 851.

[7] *Hedley Byrne v Heller* [1964] AC 465 (HL).

[8] *Palmer v Tees HA* [1999] Lloyd's Rep Med 351 (CA) (hereafter: *Palmer*).

The courts recognise three categories of damage.[9] The first is *physical injury*, where bodily harm or damage to one's property occurs. In this category the claimant sues for the consequential costs of the injury. In genetics, patients sue when they suffer from a disease which could have been prevented if the doctor had warned them about it in advance. The second category is *psychological harm*, where a recognised mental illness is caused to the claimant after experiencing a traumatic event. In genetics, patients may suffer from psychological harm after being informed carelessly or inaccurately that they suffer from a genetic disorder. The third and final category is *economic loss*, where the claimant suffers loss of profit or gain without suffering physical or psychological harm. In genetics, patients may claim that a failure to detect a genetic defect in the foetus caused them additional costs of rearing a disabled child.

Obviously, relatives can suffer damage in each category. For example, when relatives are not informed about the possibility that their children may develop a genetic disease they may wish to sue those who could have warned them about it, namely the doctor or the patient. Yet it can be argued that the three categories of damage are not comprehensive for they do not reflect the various interests of patients and relatives. The relatives' right to make an informed decision whether or not to embark upon a demanding career may not be recognised if it cannot be classified into one of the three categories of damage specified above. As will be discussed further below, harm to choice receives limited recognition in law. However, the discussion in this chapter will concentrate on these three categories.[10]

3.2.1 Can the Relative Sue the Patient?

Stating that the relatives may wish to sue either the doctor or the patient, the first question is whether they can sue the patient in negligence. In the genetic context the relatives may wish to sue the patient if his or her failure to inform them prevents them from taking preventive measures against harm. As will be discussed below, English law does not bar such a claim against the patient. Where the patient refuses to communicate genetic information received from the doctor to the relatives the courts see the patient as the party responsible for the relatives' harm.

---

9   Recently the House of Lords in a claim in negligence against doctors for failure to perform a sterilisation operation, which resulted pregnancy and the birth of a healthy child, held that when the mother is disabled she is entitled to a limited amount of compensation for the loss of the 'opportunity to live in the way she planned'. See: *Rees v Darlington Memorial Hospital NHS Trust* [2003] 3 WLR 1091. In a broader perspective this 'conventional award' can be viewed as compensation for harm to choice, thus leading in the future to the recognition of a fourth category of damage which unlike the other three is intangible.

10   For a brief account on the right to damages under the *Human Rights Act* 1998 see Giliker P., Beckwith S., *Tort*, London, Sweet & Maxwell (2nd edn., 2004), pp. 451–452.

However, no reported case was found where relatives sued patients for failure to warn about a genetic risk. An analogy can be drawn to cases where patients did not warn their partners about their sexually transmitted disease (STD). In these cases, when the patient failed to inform that they were at risk the partners brought a claim in negligence once they discovered that they had not been informed.[11] The patient's legal duty to the partner has been recognised in some parts of the US. In one case the court upheld a claim brought by a man against a woman who did not inform him she had herpes before having sexual relations with him.[12] In another case the court held that 'one who knows, or should know, that he or she is infected with genital herpes is under a duty to either abstain from sexual contact with others or, at least, to warn others of the infection prior to having contact with them'.[13] In addition, some states in the US have imposed a statutory duty on HIV patients to inform their partners.[14]

English law's position in this area of STD has not yet been determined. Although Lord Brandon stated extra–judicially that such a duty exists,[15] there is no English authority on this. Mason, McCall–Smith and Laurie agree with Lord Brandon's statement, arguing that English courts will establish such a legal duty.[16] However, they appreciate that claimants will face other legal difficulties, such as establishing causation between the patient's conduct and the partner's damage, especially in AIDS cases, owing to the long incubation period.

However, one can argue that the legal position in the area of STD has limited relevance to the legal position in genetics. While in STD cases the imposition of a duty on the patient is considerably affected by the fact that he or she causes the risk of physical harm, in genetics the patient does not cause the genetic risk to the relatives but merely fails to warn them about it.[17] As will be discussed thoroughly below, this distinction between these two categories reflects the different attitude in tort law to acts and omissions. While the courts tend to impose a legal duty in the former they do not in the latter. However, this distinction loses its force when the

---

[11] However, there are several other heads under which a claim for damage can lie.

[12] *Long v Adams* (1985) 333 SE. 2d 852 (Ga Ct App).

[13] *Berner v Caldwell* (1989) 543 So. 2d 686, 689 (Ala Sup Ct); see in the context of AIDS: *Doe v Johnson* (1993) 817 F. Supp. 1382 (W.D. Mich.); for a comprehensive discussion regarding the position in the US see: Gostin L., Hodge J., "Piercing the veil of secrecy in HIV/AIDS and other sexually transmitted diseases: Theories of privacy and disclosure in partner notification" (1998) 5 *Duke Journal of Gender Law & Policy* 9.

[14] For a recent review of the statutory position see: Rose JW., "To tell or not to tell: Legislative imposition of partner notification duties for HIV patients" (2001) 22 *Journal of Legal Medicine* 107.

[15] Litton K., James R., "Civil liability for communication of AIDS–a moot point" (1987) 137 *NLJ* 755.

[16] See Mason JK., McCall–Smith RA., Laurie GT., *Law and Medical Ethics*, London, Butterworths, (6th edn., 2002), 65.

[17] Suter S., "Whose genes are these anyway?: Familial conflicts over access to genetic information" (1993) 91 *Michigan Law Review* 1854, 1855.

parties have a close relationship.[18] Indeed, one cannot think of a closer relationship than that between family members. So when the genetic patient fails to warn about a risk of harm which can be avoided, a legal duty may be imposed on him or her.[19]

However, many of the decisions in STD concern two individuals who have no intention of becoming a family. Furthermore, in other cases where the parties were married or lived as partners the claimant brought the claim when the marriage was on the verge of a breakdown or the parties were already divorced.[20] This highlights a possible distinction between a case of STD and a case in genetics. While in the former the patient voluntarily and knowingly endangers the partner's welfare, in the latter the intention of the patient who does not inform the relatives may be sincere (usually to protect them from receiving bad news). Though the patient's reasons may not be accepted by the relatives and may be considered paternalistic, the relatives may find it difficult to cast doubt on the patient's good intentions. This distinction perhaps explains the gap between the existence of caselaw in STD and its absence in genetics. However, in both types of cases, when the relationship is good and the patient does not know about his or her health status the relatives will argue that had the patient been asked by the doctor to inform them he or she would have done so.[21] (This argument, however, is not always supported by the facts.[22])

The lack of case law in genetics may lead us to review other intrafamilial claims. For example, In the American case of *McFall v Shimp* the court held that an individual could not be forced to donate bone marrow to his cousin, despite the low risk involved in such a procedure.[23] The court explicitly held that one is under no legal obligation to provide assistance or to rescue another. The court explained: 'our society, contrary to many others, has as its first principle, the respect for the individual, and that society and government exist to protect the individual from being invaded and hurt by another'.[24] Thus, when individuals have to put themselves at risk of physical harm their autonomy outweighs any altruistic principle of beneficence or solidarity.

In *McFall v Shimp* the court made an explicit distinction between law and ethics. While it held that the cousin's refusal to donate was morally 'indefensible', it also admitted that it could not adhere to legal measures to force him to donate. This distinction brings us back to the argument made in Chapter 1, namely that

---

[18]　See the discussion in part 3.3.1.2 below.

[19]　As we saw in Chapter 1, doctors owe an affirmative duty to warn patients for potential risks of the proposed treatment. See also the discussion below and the discussion in Chapter 4.

[20]　*Beller v Tilbrook* (2002) 571 SE. 2d 735 (Ga Sup Ct); *McPherson v McPherson* (1998) 712 A. 2d 1043 (Me Sup Ct); Stafford v. Stafford (1987) 726 S.W.2d 14 (Tex Sup Ct).

[21]　*Reisner v Regents of the University of California* (1995) 37 Cal. Rptr. 2d 518 (Cal App 2nd Dist), pp. 519, 523 (Hereafter: *Reisner*).

[22]　*Safer v Pack* (1996) 677 A. 2d 1188 (NJ Super A. D.), pp. 1189–1190 (Hereafter: *Safer v Pack*).

[23]　*McFall v Shimp* (1978) 10 Pa. D & C 3d 90 (Pa Com Pl).

[24]　Ibid., at p. 91.

law and ethics sometimes reflect different attitudes. This is also true in genetics. As we shall see in Chapter 4, ethicists and professional codes of ethics do make the distinction between patients' moral duty to disclose genetic information and the legal duty. While they recognise the former, many do not promote the latter.

Another relevant factor, which may affect the legal position at least in the context of communicating genetic information between parents and children,[25] is the courts' reluctance to intervene in parents' decisions regarding rearing their children. Commenting on the American legal position, Clayton argues that the courts do not perceive the parents as legally responsible for not communicating genetic information to their at–risk children. The parents' reply that the time was not right, or that the child was likely to be distressed by the information, would probably be accepted by the court.[26]

However, even when the courts allow an intra–familial claim the willingness of family members to sue the patient may be affected by a practical financial aspect. People usually do not insure themselves for such claims, and even when relatives wish to sue the patient, they will realise that the patient's pocket is not as deep as the doctor's.

To conclude, family members can legally bring claims against patients. The courts will uphold such a claim when the patient can prevent a serious risk of harm to the relatives' health. However, the lack of caselaw narrows the perspective taken by English law. Since no claims have yet been brought by relatives against patients the courts focus on the *doctor–relatives* relationship, overlooking the *patient–relatives* one. Therefore, the discussion in this chapter will concentrate on the doctor–patient and the doctor–relatives relationships.

3.2.2 The Doctor's Duty of Care

The first hurdle claimants face is proving that the defendant owes them a duty of care. The claimants have to prove that a special relationship with the defendant exists, from which the courts can conclude that the defendant was legally responsible to them. In the medical context, the existence of a doctor–patient relationship implies that the doctor owes a duty of care to the patient.

Doctors owe a *common law duty of care* to the patient. This duty includes provision of reasonable care in diagnosis, treatment, and advice.[27] In the context of provision of medical information the doctor has to inform the patient about the

---

[25] The issue of state intervention in parents' medical decisions is a wide–ranging and complex matter, and beyond the scope of this book. Here I concentrate only on communication of medical information.

[26] Clayton E., "What should the law say about disclosure of genetic information to relatives" (1998) *Journal of Health Care Law & Policy* 373, 381.

[27] Grubb A., "Duties in contract and tort" in Grubb A., (ed.), *Principles of Medical Law*, Oxford, Oxford University Press (2nd edn., 2004), 323.

nature, the purpose, the risks, and the consequences of the proposed treatment.[28] For example, when a patient undergoes a sterilisation operation the doctor should inform him that there is a possibility that he may become fertile again.[29] Failure to do so may prevent the patient from taking contraceptive measures to avert the birth of an unwanted or disabled child. Hence, the doctor has a *duty to warn* the patient. This aspect of the doctor's duty will be the central theme in this chapter.

When a patient visits a general practitioner (GP) a *statutory duty of care* emerges.[30] The *National Health Service (Choice of Medical Practitioner) Regulations* 1998[31] apply. The regulations set out the procedure whereby the patient applies to register at the doctor's clinic, and the doctor adds him or her to the clinic's list of patients. Once the patient is registered the *National Health Service (General Medical Services) Regulations* 1992 impose on the doctor a range of duties to the patient.[32]

The nature of the doctor's duty was analysed in Chapter 1. It was stated that doctors owe a duty of care to patients because they undertake the responsibility to treat them. This undertaking led the courts to describe the relationship as a doctor's 'assumption of responsibility' to the patient,[33] which reflects the general attitude to the imposition of a duty of care on professionals.[34] Furthermore, as was argued in Chapter 1, the doctor's duty of care is owed exclusively to the patient. This implies that the relatives are excluded from this relationship. The duty is directed to the person who turns to the doctor for medical advice. As the courts held, the fact that family members were adversely affected by the doctor's conduct does not mean that the doctor assumed responsibility to them; on the contrary, in many cases mere contact between them does not amount to an imposition of a duty on the doctor.

Undoubtedly, this position reflects a patient–centred approach. Stating that the doctor assumes responsibility only to the individual who turns to him or her for medical advice is to describe the unit of medical care as consisting of a single member, that of the individual patient. The doctor's undertaking is not directed to the patient who has relationships with close family members but is focused on the individual patient alone. This perception of the doctor–patient relationship creates a gap between law and medical practice. It also overlooks the fact that doctors operate in a social environment that leads to the imposition of involuntary duties to family members.[35]

---

[28] Jones M., "Breach of Duty" in Grubb, ibid, at p. 413.

[29] *Thake v Maurice* [1986] QB 644.

[30] When the patient is in hospital, the consultant owes a common law duty of care. See: *Capital and Counties plc v Hampshire CC* [1997] 2 All ER 865 (CA), 883.

[31] SI 1998/668, as amended by SI 1999/3179.

[32] SI 1992/635.

[33] See Grubb, supra n. 27, at p. 324.

[34] *White v Jones* [1995] 2 AC 207; *Henderson v Merrett* [1995] 2 AC 145.

[35] For example, Christie and Hoffmaster argue that providing support to relatives in difficult times is part of the doctor's work. See: Christie R., Hoffmaster B., *Ethical*

So when claimants wish to prove that doctors owe them a duty of care they must satisfy three different requirements: *foreseeability* of the damage; *proximity* of the relationship between the claimant and the defendant; and that the imposition of a duty of care is *'fair, just and reasonable'*.[36] However, usually when the courts deal with claims between doctors and patients they do not examine these requirements. The existence of a doctor–patient relationship assumes that the doctor owes a duty to the patient. Hence, the courts begin the discussion from the breach level, examining whether the doctor has acted below his or her professional standards. However, when they discuss claims against doctors where a doctor–patient relationship does not exist they examine whether a duty of care can be imposed.

Hence, when a relative sues a doctor, the three components have to be established. *Foreseeability* is unlikely to be a problem because any reasonable doctor can foresee that withholding medical genetic information from relatives can cause them harm. The two problematic requirements are *proximity* and *policy* (or whether it is *'fair, just and reasonable'* to impose a duty of care on the doctor). Although the courts argue that proximity and policy are sometimes facets of the same thing[37] they address them separately when they examine third parties' claims against doctors.[38] Therefore, the remainder of this chapter will examine whether doctors and relatives can establish a proximate relationship with the doctor and whether it is *'fair just and reasonable'* to impose a duty of care on them. While proximity will be examined in each of the categories of damage specified above the discussion about policy will apply to all.

3.3 Physical injury

3.3.1 Limitations in Establishing Proximity between the Doctor and the Relatives

In light of the exclusivity of the doctor–patient relationship the next step is to examine whether there are exceptional circumstances where doctors owe the relatives a duty of care. Therefore, the focus in this part will be on the following issues: (1) the limitations of tort law with regard to proximity between doctors and relatives; (2) the application of these limitations to the area of genetics; (3) the exceptional circumstances where doctors are proximate to relatives; (4) the

---

    Issues in Family Medicine, New York, Oxford University Press (1986), 73.

[36] *Caparo v Dickman* [1990] 2 AC 605.

[37] Ibid., per Lord Oliver at p. 633; and see also *Marc Rich v Bishop Ltd* [1996] 1 AC 211, per Lord Steyn at p. 235, and *Stovin v Wise* [1996] AC 923 per Lord Nicholls at p. 932.

[38] See *Palmer*, supra n. 8, per Stuart–Smith LJ at p. 357; see also, in general, Lunney, M., Oliphant K., *Tort Law: Text and Materials*, Oxford, Oxford University Press (2nd edn., 2003), 123–124.

potential developments which may lead to the establishment of proximity between doctors and relatives in the area of genetics.

Concerning the first issue, it is possible to identify four limitations with regard to proximity between doctors and relatives.[39] First, the doctor has to identify the relative, as a particular person at risk, or as a member of a small group of people.[40] Next, the courts are reluctant to impose a duty of care on professionals for their omissions;[41] they usually do not impose a duty to act affirmatively. Indeed, the doctor's failure to warn the relatives is perceived as an omission and not as a negligent act.[42] Third, doctors usually do not owe a legal duty to prevent patients from harming relatives. English law usually holds the patients themselves responsible for the relatives' harm.[43] Finally, the courts decline to impose a duty of care when the doctor does not cause the damage but only increases the risk or allows it to continue.[44] Stating these limitations, the next step is to examine how they apply to the specific context of genetics.

3.3.1.1 Identification. Recalling that people inherit their susceptibility to genetic disorders from their biological parents at conception, the doctor can identify the relatives who are at risk when he or she interacts with the patient. Professionally, the doctor has to ascertain the patient's family medical history. Doing so involves questions about the relatives, such as if they are alive or if they suffer or have suffered from serious illnesses. The answers will assist the doctor to determine the identity of the relatives at risk. Peter Harper, a leading expert in genetics,[45] argues that learning a family's medical history is a fundamental part of the doctor's professional duties. When the doctor takes these details he or she discovers the identity of the relatives at risk and to a limited extent their risk status. An alternative view is taken by Graeme Laurie, who argues that when a patient and his or her two relatives are treated by the same doctor, *proximity* could be established.[46] If this not the case, then establishing a duty of is more problematic.

The view taken in this book is that the relatives can be identified whether they are registered in the doctor's clinic or not. In this regard, the prominent characteristics of genetics should be taken into account. The doctor can identify the relatives at risk not just because they are registered as patients but also because

---

[39]   See Grubb, supra n. 27, at pp. 344–345.

[40]   *Hill v Chief Constable of West Yorkshire* [1989] 1 AC 53, 62; See also, *Palmer v Tees HA* [1998] Lloyd's Rep Med 447, 459.

[41]   *Smith v Littlewoods Organisation Ltd* [1987] 1 AC 241, 270–271.

[42]   Kennedy I., Grubb A., *Medical Law*, London, Butterworths (3rd edn., 2000), 677–678.

[43]   See *Smith v Littlewoods*, supra 41.

[44]   *Goodwill v BPAS* [1996] 1 WLR 1397, [1996] 2 All ER 161, 167; This distinction was made by Grubb supra, n. 27, at p. 345.

[45]   Harper P. S., *Practical Genetic Counselling*, Oxford, Butterworth–Heinemann (5th edn., 1999), 5.

[46]   Ibid.

they share the same DNA with him or her. Being registered as the doctor's patients is important when establishing proximity but it may not be sufficient to make the relatives identifiable. In the existing NHS system, where GPs have over 2,000 patients,[47] they surely do not know or remember all the familial ties of their patients even when all of them are registered in their clinic. Instead, doctors can identify the relatives by asking the patients about their family, which constitutes part of their work. In the American case of *Safer v Pack*, where a relative sued the doctor for not disclosing genetic information, the court held that the doctor could have identified the family members at risk.[48] Finally, Laurie's position can be challenged from an opposite perspective. The fact that the relatives are registered at the doctor's clinic does not automatically lead to the conclusion that proximity is satisfied. The courts held that the doctor's duty is owed to the individual patient even when the relatives are registered as patients too.[49] Thus, one can argue that the conflict the doctor faces between the patient's interests and the relatives' is greater when both sides are registered as patients.

Examining the identification requirement more closely, it replaces the exclusive doctor–patient relationship: while doctors undertake a responsibility to a specific individual patient, they may owe a duty to another individual who is not their patient provided they can identify him or her. Still, the legal position indicates that the doctor does not position himself or herself in a community of people where a sense of mutual commitment and responsibility exists; he or she is situated in a society of individuals where contractual notions take precedence.

3.3.1.2 Liability for a failure to act. English courts usually do not impose a duty to act affirmatively.[50] Basil Markesinis argues that the roots for this position come from 'an era in which private selfishness was elevated to the rank of a public virtue'.[51] In *Stovin v Wise* the House of Lords provided some justifications for the lack of liability for omissions. Focusing on the moral perspective, it was argued that a duty to rescue could be applied to a large group of people, but 'why should one be held liable rather than another?'[52] The court discussed the example of a child drowning in a shallow pool who could be saved by a bystander. The court agreed that the benefit in saving the child outweighed the costs but held that the bystander had no duty to rescue him or her. 'Something more' was required to

---

47 Department of Health, General and Personal Medical Services Statistics: England and Wales, 30/9/2001, www.doh.gov.uk/public/gpcensus2001.htm.

48 See *Safer v Pack*, supra n. 22, at p. 1192.

49 *Powell v Boldaz* [1998] Lloyd's Rep. Med. 116; *RK and MK v Oldham NHS Trust and Dr B* [2003] Lloyd's Rep Med 1.

50 *Smith v Littlewoods Organisation Ltd* [1987] 1 AC 241, 270–271.

51 Markesinis, B., "Negligence, nuisance and affirmative duties of action" (1989) 105 *LQR* 104, 112; Williams K., "Medical Samaritans: Is there a duty to treat?" (2001) 21 (3) *Oxford Journal of Legal Studies* 393.

52 [1996] AC 923; [1996] 3 All ER 801, per Lord Hoffmann at p. 819.

impose a duty.[53]   The courts, however, did not explain what would satisfy this requirement. Commentators argued that a prior relationship, such a doctor–patient relationship, has to exist to fulfil this requirement.[54]

The view in *Stovin v Wise* reflects a liberal discourse. First, recalling the distinction made by Beauchamp and Childress between general and specific beneficence, this legal position implies that there is no *general* duty of beneficence in English tort law. However, as was discussed in Chapter 1, medical ethics recognises a general moral duty of beneficence between a doctor and a stranger provided there is no danger posed to the doctor and that the benefit to the stranger outweighs the costs to the doctor.[55]   The law lacks this beneficent duty to act and in this regard it reflects a more individualistic approach than medical ethics.   In addition, Lord Hoffmann's question, 'why should one be held liable rather than another?', expresses preference for the view that no individual will be found liable over the possibility that a random individual will have to bear the responsibility of all bystanders. Furthermore, this position presents an atomistic perception, where each individual should take care of his or her own affairs. It seems that the courts are less interested in promoting society's common good, and more attracted to the right of the individual to act freely. This view does not correspond with an overriding utilitarian principle, which would encourage the bystander to save the drowning child so long as he or she faces no risk.

Concentrating on the status of the relatives, the relationship they have with doctors in genetics cannot be compared with that of a doctor and a stranger. This is because doctors are required by their professional obligations to present the patient with the implications of his or her medical condition for the health of the relatives.[56]   Furthermore, as Williams recently commented, the moral justification in *Stovin v Wise* does not apply when it is possible to identify specifically the person who has to act.[57]   In the context of genetics it is possible to identify the doctor, who can positively act for the benefit of the relatives. Therefore, although doctors do not have a doctor–patient relationship with the relatives their professional obligations may constitute a legal relationship between them. Although there is no case that directly supports this argument, *White v Jones* may provide some help.[58]   In this case the defendant solicitor did not have any professional relationship with the claimants, his client's two daughters, when he

---

[53]   Ibid., per Lord Nicholls, at p. 807.

[54]   Deakin S., Johnston A., Markesinis, B., *Tort Law*, Oxford, Oxford University Press (5th edn., 2003), 149–167; See also: Lunney and Oliphant, supra n. 38, at pp. 424–441.

[55]   See Chapter 1; Beauchamp and Childress address the hypothetical case of a person who is drowning in a shallow pool. They accept that in these circumstances a moral duty arises.

[56]   Ngwena C., Chadwick R., "Genetic information and the duty of confidentiality: Ethics and law" (1993) *Medical law International* 73, at p. 79.

[57]   See Williams, supra n. 51, at p. 398.

[58]   *White v Jones* [1995] 2 AC 207.

failed to draft a new will for him. However, the court held that the solicitor had to take the claimant's interests into account.[59] This implies that the solicitor should have conferred a benefit to the client's daughters of whose interests he was aware.

However, *White v Jones* was a case of economic loss and not of physical injury so its relevance is limited. In addition, in the majority of cases doctors do not owe an affirmative or a beneficent duty to third parties.[60] As Williams argues, the courts only begin to impose a legal duty on health care professionals to act affirmatively in limited circumstances of emergency.[61] However, in the context of genetics the risk is not immediate or imminent so as to impose on the doctor to act and to warn the relatives.

3.3.1.3 Doctors' liability for intervening conduct of a patient. This issue is relevant where the doctor informs the patient but the latter does not inform the relatives. In these circumstances the question is whether the doctor is liable for the patient's intervening conduct. In English tort law the general rule is that 'one man is under no duty of controlling another to prevent his doing damage to a third.'[62] This rule is grounded in the traditional approach of English law that people should not interfere in other people's matters. The courts have difficulty abandoning this approach and adopting one which reflects the change in public attitude. The fact that other European jurisdictions set a general rule of liability in this situation has not led English law, as yet, to change its approach.[63]

Obviously, this legal position reflects individualistic conceptions. Legally, it accords with the principle of non–liability for omissions. The fact that people are not obliged to intervene to prevent harm to others implies that English tort law perceives society as a group of atomised individuals separate and distinct from each other. The view that by helping others one may improve the social environment one lives in is invisible to this position. Although the law does not prohibit the doctor from intervening it does not impose a duty on him or her to do so and leaves the decision to his or her discretion. The law prefers the individual's rights to the common good.

An attempt to change this attitude was presented in *Smith v Littlewoods*.[64] Lord Mackay did not rely on the act–omission distinction but argued that in the

---

[59] However, in this case the interests of the client and the beneficiaries could readily be assumed to be identical. For an ethical analysis of the case see below, at para 3.5.2.

[60] See Grubb, supra n. 27, at p. 344.

[61] See Williams, supra n. 51, at p. 395; Williams refers to the recent decision in *Kent v Griffiths* [2001] QB 36 where the Court of Appeal held that an ambulance service was liable when it failed to respond promptly to a rescue call from an identifiable member of the public.

[62] *Smith v Leurs* (1945) 70 CLR 256, at pp. 261–262.

[63] See, Markesinis, supra n. 51, at p. 112; Howarth, D., "My brother's keeper? Liability for acts of third parties" (1994) 14 *Legal Studies* 88.

[64] [1987] 1 AC 241 (hereafter: *Littlewoods*).

particular circumstances of the case the defendants had not acted unreasonably. Examining whether the defendants were careless in not preventing hooligans who invaded their estate from harming the adjacent properties, he stated: '...what the reasonable man is bound to foresee in a case involving injury or damage by independent human agency, just as in cases where such agency plays no part, is the probable consequences of his own act or omission.'[65] This led Markesinis and Deakin to argue that Lord Mackay would have imposed a duty of care on the defendants had the risk to the third parties been more obvious in advance.[66] They argued that Lord Mackay assumed the possibility of a duty of care in that case by concentrating on the separate issue of the breach of the duty. This could lead to the conclusion that once professionals foresee the implications of their conduct (acts or omissions) they may be legally responsible for the damage inflicted on a third party they know.

Lord Mackay's approach was supported by two other members of the House of Lords as well as by legal commentators.[67] However, the courts prefer the conservative approach taken by Lord Goff, who held that there was no duty on A to prevent B from harming C.[68] The choice of the courts to follow Lord Goff's approach[69] suggests that English law fails to impose a beneficent duty especially in circumstances where professionals can help a third party. Applying this to the context of genetics it seems that the relatives' claim against the doctor for non-disclosure will probably fail. Yet as Lord Goff noted, circumstances arise where a duty of care may be imposed. Among these circumstances a mechanism of *control* may establish *proximity* between the doctor and the relatives.

A salient characteristic in cases where the courts imposed a duty on professionals to prevent an intermediary from harming a third party was control over the source of the danger. For example, the officers in *Dorset Yacht v Home Office* owed a duty of care because they had control over the boys who harmed the third parties' boats.[70] The schoolteacher in *Carmarthenshire CC v Lewis* had control over the child who ran onto the main road and caused a car accident.[71]

However, these cases are not applicable to a situation where a doctor reveals information to a patient who refuses to share it with the relatives. This is because the subject of the doctor's control is not the information but the patient. Since the doctor cannot force the patient to inform the relatives he or she cannot fully control the relatives' risk. Unlike the *Dorset Yacht* type of cases, doctors in the area of genetics do not have similar control over their patients. The patients are not held in secure institutions and do not have to follow doctors' orders. Instead, they have the

---

65 Ibid., at p. 261.
66 See Deakin, Johnston, and Markesinis, supra n. 54, at p. 151.
67 See Markesinis, supra n. 51 and Howarth, supra n. 63.
68 See *Littlewoods*, n. 64, at pp. 270–271.
69 See, for example, *Topp v London Country Bus Ltd* [1993] 1 WLR 977 (CA).
70 [1970] AC 1004 (hereafter: *Dorset Yacht*).
71 [1956] AC 549.

freedom to act as they choose: they can decide to disclose or not to disclose genetic information to their relatives. The doctors do not have control over the patients' conduct and they do not always know if their patients are following their advice.

In addition, the doctors face legal and practical difficulties when they want to exercise their decision. First, not only do they have no control over the patient and his or her relationships with the relatives, they are also legally prohibited from disclosing information without the patient's consent. If they decide to approach the relatives directly they expose themselves to the possibility that the patient will sue them for breach of confidentiality. As the discussion in Chapter 4 indicates, confidentiality is a high barrier in these circumstances. Second, in many disorders doctors cannot manipulate the genetic risk; they can merely provide an assessment. Therefore, the *control* mechanism is not applicable.

3.3.1.4 The doctor does not cause the damage. This is the fourth limitation in establishing proximity between the doctor and the relatives. The courts limit the liability of doctors when they do not cause the damage. This prevailed in *Goodwill v BPAS*.[72] In that case the patient underwent a sterilisation operation. The doctor failed to warn the patient that there was a remote risk, which in fact materialised, that he might become fertile again. After the operation the patient met the claimant and commenced a sexual relationship with her. Relying on the doctor's advice, they did not take any contraceptive measures. Subsequently, the claimant found out that she was pregnant. She sued the doctor for the costs of rearing a healthy but unwanted child.[73] Perceiving the damages as purely economic, the Court of Appeal held that since the doctor could not know that that particular claimant would rely on his advice, he owed her no duty of care. Furthermore, the court held that the claimant did not rely upon the doctor's advice because she consulted her own GP. Therefore, the court struck out the claim. The decision in that case suggests that a duty of care is imposed when the doctor can identify the particular third party and when he or she relies on the advice. However, as we shall see in the next part, these two requirements are more prominent in the area of economic loss than in the area of physical injury.

Commenting on this decision, Andrew Grubb argues[74] that doctors who create a risk by infecting patients with HIV might be held liable for harm caused to the

---

[72] *Goodwill v BPAS* [1996] 1 WLR 1397 (hereafter: *Goodwill*).

[73] Following *McFarlane v Tayside Health Board* [2000] 2 AC 59 parents of a healthy but unwanted child cannot claim these costs. However, the doctor is liable when the child is born disabled; see: *Rand v East Dorset HA* [2000] Lloyd's Rep Med 181, *Hardman v Amin* [2000] Lloyd's Rep Med 498. But when the mother is disabled she is entitled to a limited amount of compensation for the loss of the 'opportunity to live in the way she planned'. See: *Rees v Darlington Memorial Hospital NHS Trust* [2003] 3 WLR 1091.

[74] Grubb, A., "HIV transmission: doctor's liability to future partner" (1997) 5 *Medical Law Review* 250.

patient's sexual partner,[75] but those who fail to prevent a risk by not warning the partner of the danger will not. In genetics, when the harm is the genetic disorder, it is obvious that the doctor does not cause it. For example, when the relatives consider reproduction the doctor only allows the disease to pass on to their unborn child. Grubb criticises this distinction as being too fine.[76] Indeed, this argument did not prevent the courts from establishing *proximity* between doctors and those who considered reproduction.[77] In those cases, the doctors did not create the risk but their failure to detect it and inform the prospective parents resulted in their begetting a disabled child.[78] However, the claimants in these cases were the doctor's patients, a factor which is absent in the doctor–relatives relationship. The conclusion is that family members will face serious difficulties in establishing proximity with the doctor in the context of genetics where the doctor did not create the risk but merely failed to warn of its existence.[79]

The analysis so far indicates that the relatives will probably fail in bringing a claim against the doctors because they cannot establish *proximity* with them.[80] Despite this legal position, it is possible to point out some recent developments which may change the attitude to family members. This is the subject of the next section.

3.3.2 Developments in Establishing Proximity between Doctors and Relatives

To state that relatives will never succeed in establishing *proximity* is inaccurate. Two developments may signal a change in the legal attitude to family members.

---

[75] See *Reisner*, supra n. 21.

[76] See Grubb, supra n. 27, at p. 315.

[77] See *Rand v East Dorset HA* and *Hardman v Amin*, supra n. 69; *Lee v Taunton & Somerset NHS Trust* [2001] 1 FLR 419.

[78] In *Parkinson v St James & Seacroft University Hospital* [2002] QB 266, the doctor failed to perform a sterilisation operation adequately; ten months later the woman claimant conceived a child, who was born disabled. Despite the doctor's warning that the child might be born disabled she preferred not to terminate the pregnancy. Upholding the mother's claim for the extra costs of rearing a disabled child Hale LJ concluded at para. 92 that 'any disability arising from genetic causes or foreseeable events during pregnancy (such as rubella, spina bifida, or oxygen deprivation during pregnancy or childbirth) up until the child is born alive, and which are not *novus actus interveniens*, will suffice to found a claim'.

[79] See, however, the *obiter* of Hale LJ in *Parkinson v St James & Seacroft University Hospital* [2002] QB 266, at para 93 where she argues that a doctor may owe a duty to a father who does not live with the claimant's mother but meets 'his parental responsibility to care for the [disabled] child'.

[80] However, when the relatives approach the doctor together with the patient and are present during the consultation the courts may view them as the doctor's patient. See: *Thake v Maurice* [1986] QB 644.

3.3.2.1 The Human Rights Act *1998.* Leading commentators argue that English courts have to consider the *Human Rights Act* 1998 with regard to third parties' claims in medical negligence. Andrew Grubb asserts that the courts will have to impose an affirmative duty on doctors when they can prevent an imminent danger to third parties such as the patient's relatives.[81] Grubb relies on the decision in *Osman v UK*[82] where the European Court of Human Rights held that the right to life (Article 2 of the European Convention on Human Rights) requires public authorities to take affirmative actions when they are aware that one person poses a real and imminent risk to an identifiable third party.[83] Genetic disease is not a criminal act, nor is the patient's conduct when he or she refuses to disclose the information to the relatives. Still, Grubb suggests that doctors who work in the public sector should have the same responsibilities that the European Court imposed on the police in *Osman v UK*. Lunney and Oliphant support this view.[84] They argue that Section 6(1) of the Act creates a new cause of action when public authorities violate human rights. These rights include, inter alia, the right to life. Although Section 6 of the Act speaks in terms of 'act', in view of *Osman v UK* English courts will have to consider seriously whether to interpret 'act' as including omissions when public authorities fulfil their responsibilities.

The commentators' view received further support in the European Court. In *Z v UK*[85] the European Court of Human Rights partly reversed the House of Lords' decision in *X v Bedfordshire*[86] holding that public authorities owe a positive duty to protect children who suffer from domestic abuse (Article 3 of the European Convention on Human Rights). Recently, the European Court followed this decision in yet another domestic abuse case, holding that public authorities were required to ensure that one individual was not subjected to inhuman and degrading treatment by another individual.[87] Accordingly, the public authorities should provide effective protection to vulnerable people when they know or ought to know about a possible harmful behaviour.

Furthermore, the European Court held that failure to take reasonable steps that could probably change the outcome or mitigate the harm is sufficient for imposition of the responsibility on the relevant public authority. In that case the court held that the lack of investigation, communication, and co-operation by the relevant public authorities contributed significantly to the harm caused to the children, and that if the authorities had fulfilled their responsibilities properly and effectively this would have probably prevented or at least minimised the risk or the

---

[81] Grubb, A., "Medical Negligence: Duty to third party" (1999) 7 *Medical Law Review* 331, 335.
[82] (1998) 5 BHRC 293.
[83] Ibid.
[84] See Lunney and Oliphant, supra n. 38, at pp. 493, 497–98.
[85] [2001] 2 FCR 246.
[86] [1995] 2 AC 633.
[87] *E v United Kingdom* [2002] 3 FCR 700.

damage suffered by the children. Therefore, the Court held, there had been a breach of Article 3 of the European Convention.

If English courts accept this approach the relatives will be able to pass the two major obstacles in establishing *proximity*, namely the issues of non-liability for omissions and non-liability for the intervening conduct of the patient. Adopting the approach suggested above will require doctors to be legally aware of the implications of their omissions when they can foresee that a relative may suffer harm as a result of the patient's conduct. Analysis of *Osman v UK* does not immediately impose a duty of care, but it does raise the question whether the danger to the relatives in the context of genetics is imminent enough to impose a duty on the doctor to warn the relatives. This will be discussed in detail in the next chapter.

3.3.2.2 Awareness. Though the test of assumption of responsibility is often used by the courts when examining proximity in cases of physical injury[88] it is possible to deduce a conception of professional *awareness* from recent cases where intervening conduct of an intermediary was involved. In *Palmer v Tees* a mentally ill patient told his doctors that he would kill a child after his release from the hospital.[89] Indeed, several months after his release the patient carried out his threat, killing the daughter of the claimant, who sued the doctors for failure to warn. The Court of Appeal struck out the claim, holding that at the time of the homicide the psychiatrist had no control over the patient and that there was no close relationship between the doctor and the victim. Stuart–Smith LJ pointed out that in order to establish *proximity* the doctor should have identified the victim because the most effective way of protection would be to warn her.[90] In addition, he asked himself what the defendant could have done to avoid the danger.

Several conclusions can be drawn from the speech of Stuart–Smith LJ in *Palmer*. First, identification is clearly the most dominant factor in establishing proximity between doctors and family members. In some cases identifying the relatives may suffice. Gage J at first instance stated explicitly that if the victim was identifiable he would have held that proximity was satisfied.[91] Grubb suggests that the Court of Appeal would have ruled the same.[92] Second, the consideration of 'what the doctor could have done to avoid the danger' replaces the control

---

88　*X (Minors) v Bedfordshire CC* [1995] 2 A.C. 633, 752–753. The test of assumption of responsibility is explained in Chapter 1 part 1.3.2.3. See further analysis of this test at part 3.5.
89　*Palmer v Tees HA* [1998] Lloyd's Rep Med 447 (QBD); [1999] Lloyd's Rep Med 351 (CA) (hereafter: *Palmer*).
90　[1999] Lloyd's Rep Med 351, 359; *Palmer* was applied in *Surry CC v M (a minor)* [2001] EWCA CIV 691.
91　[1998] Lloyd's Rep Med 447, 461.
92　Grubb, A., "Medical negligence: Duty to third party" (1999) 7 *Medical Law Review* 331, 335.

mechanism with a less strict means of warning the victim or the family members. Hence, it is not necessary to control the patient if it is possible to warn the relatives. Moreover, one may argue that this approach accords with Lord Mackay's speech in *Littlewoods*. When asking what the doctor could have done to prevent the harm, Stuart–Smith LJ brought breach–of–a–duty considerations into the discussion about proximity. Finally, replacing control with warning implies that if the doctor can identify the relatives and warn them, proximity may be established. This suggests that in order to establish proximity the doctor must be aware of the danger posed to an *identifiable* relative. In the context of genetics, this *awareness* may establish proximity because the doctor, according to his or her professional standards, can identify the relatives at risk.

This characteristic of awareness was applied in other cases where professionals had no control over the intermediary. In *Osman v Ferguson*[93] the claimants (a family) sued the police alleging a failure to prevent a schoolteacher from killing the father and injuring the son. Although the Court of Appeal struck out the claim against the police,[94] it was held that the claimants established a proximate relationship with the police.[95] This decision demonstrates the different elements of the duty of care. While the court recognised that there was *proximity* between the defendant police and the claimants, it nevertheless held that the third element of the duty of care (whether it is fair, just and reasonable to impose a duty of care) was not satisfied.[96] In this case the police identified the teacher but had no control over him. In addition, it failed to stop the teacher from harassing the family and failed to arrest him. Proximity was established since the police were aware that the claimants were at risk. This was explicitly identified in *K v Secretary of State for the Home Office* where Smith J stressed that the claimants in *Osman* were 'able to show a close degree of proximity with the police, who were aware that P [the teacher] was obsessed with the plaintiff's son and knew that the family was at risk of serious harm'.[97] To conclude, the notion of awareness as derived from the cases just analysed implies that proximity can be established if doctors are aware of the implications of their conduct for identifiable at–risk third parties. In *Palmer* the

---

[93]   [1993] All ER 344 (hereafter: *Osman*).

[94]   This decision was overruled by *Osman v UK* (1998) 5 BHRC 293.

[95]   See *Osman*, supra n. 92, at p. 350.

[96]   The decision, however, was overturned in *Osman v UK* (1998) 5 BHRC 293. For a detailed discussion about this third element see the discussion below.

[97]   [2001] C.P. Rep. 39; this was an application for a pre-action disclosure by the claimant who sued the Home Office for psychological damage she suffered after having been raped by an illegal asylum seeker. The claimant argued that the Home Office knew that the offender was dangerous but failed to deport or detain him. In her application the claimant sought disclosure of documents which might have shown that the Home Office had known about the offender's criminal behaviour. This application was rejected. However, the claimant brought a claim in tort against the Home Office, but the Court of Appeal rejected it, holding that there was no proximity between the parties. See: *K v Secretary of State for the Home Department* [2002] EWCA Civ 775.

doctors were unquestionably aware that the patient was dangerous and that he posed a risk to others.[98] In addition, from Stuart–Smith LJ's main consideration of what the doctor could have done to prevent the danger, one can conclude that both the doctors and the courts where aware of the implications for third parties of the doctors' conduct when treating the psychiatric patient.[99] The main difficulty was that the doctors could not identify the victim.

The conception of awareness must be examined in view of the unique features of genetics. Unlike the circumstances in *Palmer*, the doctor can identify the relatives who might be at risk. As noted earlier, not only can doctors be aware of the existence of the relatives when treating the patient, they are also required by their professional standards to explain to the patient the effect of his or her condition on the relatives.[100] The doctor's duty of care derives from his or her awareness that his or her professional conduct can affect the health of identifiable relatives in the patient's family when facing the decision whether or not to inform them. Furthermore, in some cases when a genetic linkage study is required to confirm the patient's diagnosis, the co-operation of the relatives is needed. In these circumstances doctors must be aware of the relatives who can be tested because they depend on their help to provide the patient with an accurate diagnosis.[101] If proximity is interpreted as awareness it will mitigate the strict limitations the courts apply with regard to the patient's relatives. Although this will not guarantee that the relatives will be able to establish a duty of care it can be considered a major step towards its recognition.

Theoretically, the two potential developments mentioned above reflect an approach, which is less individualistic than the existing one. First, the *Human Rights Act* 1998 may force English law to recognise, to a limited extent, a legal duty of beneficence, because it will require doctors to benefit others with whom they have no close or prior relationship. Second, the conception of *awareness* will pay attention to the relatives who are closely involved in the patient's life. In the medical context, the doctor will be aware that the patient is a person with a particular social background, life story, and relationships with close others who may be affected by the medical decision. For doctors, it will indicate that they can choose their responsibilities to others but that they also have other responsibilities

---

[98]   The doctors admitted this in court. See Pill LJ's speech, mentioning that the defendant's counsellor 'fairly includes amongst the facts relevant to proximity the fact that the defendants were aware that Armstrong [the patient] had said that a child would be murdered after he was discharged from hospital'.

[99]   Stuart–Smith LJ mentioned the difficulties the doctors face when wishing restrain psychiatric patients.

[100] See, Harper, supra n. 45, Ch. 1, and also Chadwick R., Ngwena C., "The development of a normative standard in counselling for genetic disease: Ethics and law" (1992) 3 *Journal of Social Welfare and Family Law* 276, 290–291.

[101] See Ngwena and Chadwick, supra n. 56, at p. 89 when they pointed out that in genetics the doctor and the relatives have a proximate relationship because the doctor can identify the at-risk relatives through his contact with the patient.

that are not freely chosen. Requiring doctors to be aware of other individuals will lead them to perceive themselves as situated in their community. Finally, by adopting the notion of *awareness* and recognising a beneficent duty to others the gap between law and ethics will be narrowed.

Nevertheless, the discussion about the developments in tort law still takes place from a utilitarian perspective. In *Palmer*, for example, the prominent consideration stated by Stuart–Smith LJ is providing the victim with 'the most effective way of protection' by investigating what the doctor could have done to avoid the danger.[102] The development of a beneficent legal duty is not based on a communitarian perspective, where each member has a moral responsibility to improve the common good. It relies on the utilitarian notion of taking the one step that can prevent the greatest harm. Furthermore, the *Human Rights Act* 1998 promotes fundamental individual rights, especially the right to choose and to take informed decisions. The recent applications to the European Court of Human Rights show that individuals employ the European Convention in their conflict with public authorities, adopting a language and terminology of rights. Claimants' recent tendency to appeal to the European Court stresses the confrontational aspects of the relationship between the individual and the state, and not the shared aims which may promote the common good of society as well as the particular good of each one of its members. This tendency, however, is understandable: after all, the system of tort law is inevitably confrontational: it exists to resolve conflicts and compensate individuals for their damage. The promotion of common good is incidental.

Reviewing the current position of English tort law in the category of physical injury does not conclude the discussion. Another category of damage which constantly develops is psychological harm. Undoubtedly, concern about physical health may also affect people's mental health. Hence it is essential to discuss this issue with regard to genetics. The central question posed in this context is whether doctors have a proximate legal relationship with relatives who suffered psychological harm due to non–disclosure, late disclosure, or unsolicited disclosure of genetic information.

3.4 Psychological harm

As was argued in Chapter 2, research indicates that receiving genetic information can cause mental distress and lead to an increase in suicide rates and hospitalisation.[103] Psychological harm may occur by disclosure or by non–disclosure. When the relatives are not informed in advance that they may develop a

---

[102] [1999] Lloyd's Rep Med 351, 359.

[103] Almqvist E., "A worldwide assessment of the frequency of suicide, suicide attempts or psychological hospitalisation after predictive testing for Huntington disease" (1999) 64 *American Journal of Human Genetics* 1293.

genetic disorder they may experience an adverse psychological reaction when first diagnosed. This can be prevented if information is communicated to them when the patient is diagnosed. The information can afford the relatives the opportunity to prepare psychologically for the onset of the disease by seeking early counselling. Furthermore, psychological harm to the relatives may occur when they are informed – despite their wishes not to know – that they may develop a disorder in the future. This possibility stresses the distinction between psychological harm and physical injury. Where in the latter case only non–disclosure may cause damage to the relatives, in the former, disclosure of information may be harmful as well. Therefore, in this area the doctor faces a dilemma, whether the relatives do or do not wish to receive genetic information.

The discussion about proximity in the previous part may apply to this category of psychological harm, as well as to the next category of economic loss. However, there are other legal conceptions that reflect a different attitude to the patient's family members. These conceptions in these two areas have to be examined.

3.4.1 Alcock's Criteria in Establishing Proximity between Doctors and Relatives

Unlike physical injury, English law has been slow to recognise that psychological harm, as a head of damage, merited compensation. The reasons for this include the difficulty of assessing this damage in monetary terms, the burden of excessive litigation, and the problem of proving causation between the negligent act and the injury[104]. Despite Lord Bridge's explicit words that a physical injury can cause a psychological illness in a wide range of people[105] it is accepted that English law poses restrictions in this area. As Deakin, Johnson, and Markesinis argue, psychological harm does not receive equal treatment as physical injury.[106]

The first distinction made by English law in this area is that a claim for psychological harm which does not involve physical injury can succeed only if the claimant suffers a recognised psychiatric illness.[107] If the claimant does not suffer any personal injury he or she may not recover damages for mere distress or mental anguish.[108] In the majority of cases the courts have dealt with the medically recognised condition of post–traumatic stress disorder, which may occur as a reaction to an unexpected violent death of a close relative or friend.[109]

Another distinction is between primary and secondary victims of psychological harm. A primary victim is one who suffers psychological harm after being involved in an accident and either suffers physical injury or experiences fear of

---

[104] Murphy J., *Street on Torts*, London, Butterworths (11th edn., 2003), 219.
[105] *McLoughlin v O'Brian* [1983] 1 AC 410, 433.
[106] See Deakin, Johnston and Markesinis, supra n. 54, at p. 96.
[107] *Grieve v Salford HA* [1991] 2 Med LR 295.
[108] *Reilly v Merseyside HA* [1995] 6 Med LR 246.
[109] For example see *Alcock v Chief Constable of South Yorkshire* [1992] 1 AC 310, [1991] 4 All ER 907 (hereafter: *Alcock*).

physical injury.[110] A secondary victim is not exposed to risk of physical injury but suffers psychological harm as a result of witnessing or being informed about an accident which involved another.[111] Recently Hale LJ coherently summarised the distinction between the two classes of victims. She held that primary victims are those within a foreseeable scope of physical injury, or those identified in advance at risk of foreseeable psychological harm as a result of breaches of contractual duty of care towards them. Secondary victims are those outside that scope who suffer harm as a result of harm to others, such as the witnesses in the Hillsborough disaster or when they have contractual relations with the defendant, such as the officers in *Frost*.[112]

In the health care context, the patient who suffers physical as well as psychological harm does not raise any serious difficulty. As Grubb argues, once physical injury to patients as primary victims is foreseeable they can recover for any recognised psychiatric illness suffered as a result of the doctor's breach of duty even when they do not suffer physical injury.[113]

The law imposes restrictions when the claimant is a secondary victim. In this category foreseeability of psychological harm is necessary but not sufficient for establishing a duty of care. The courts require a claimant to show that: (1) the psychiatric illness was caused by shock; (2) he or she was proximate in time and place to the accident or its immediate aftermath; (3) and he or she had a close relationship (personal or familial) with the primary victim. These requirements were established in *McLoughlin v O'Brian*[114] and reasserted in *Alcock v Chief Constable of South Yorkshire*.[115]

The criteria for establishing proximity between doctors and relatives that were formulated in *Alcock* may not suit the situation in genetics. First, under the *Alcock* criteria the first presumption is that the professional breaches the duty to the 'primary victim', namely the patient. For example, in *Alcock* the police admitted that they breached their duty of care to the spectators who were killed and injured in the stadium. Following this admission, the court examined whether the police owed a duty of care to their relatives who saw the horrific event on the television. In the medical context, however, the doctor does not always breach the duty to the patient. Doctors may inform the patients but rely on them to communicate the

[110] See Deakin, Johnston and Markesinis, supra n. 54, at p. 97.
[111] *Page v Smith* [1996] AC 155, 183–184; See also the discussion in Deakin, Johnston and Markesinis, supra n. 54, at pp. 97–98 and Murphy, supra n. 104, pp. 219–220; *Frost v Chief Constable of South Yorkshire Police* [1999] 2 AC 455, per Lord Steyn at pp. 496–497 (hereafter: *Frost*).
[112] *Hatton v Sutherland, Barber v Somerset CC, Jones v Sandwell MBC, Bishop v Baker* [2002] EWCA Civ 76, at para. 21.
[113] Grubb, supra n. 27, at p. 335 relies on the speech of Lord Oliver in *Alcock*, supra n. 109, at pp. 923–24 and on the decision of the House of Lords in *Page v Smith*, supra n. 111.
[114] [1983] 2 AC 410.
[115] [1992] 1 AC 310, [1991] 4 All ER 907; See also *Frost v Chief Constable of South Yorkshire Police* [1999] 1 AC 455.

information to the relatives.[116] Currently, it seems that in these circumstances the doctor's conduct will not be considered negligent.

Second, the court in *Alcock* required that the relatives had to perceive the horrific event or its immediate aftermath with their own senses and to suffer from shock as a result.[117] But in genetics, as well as in other medical cases,[118] not only are the relatives absent when the patient is diagnosed, they also may not be present in the 'immediate aftermath'. Often the relatives do not perceive the communication between the doctor and the patient directly but are informed by one of them some time afterwards. In addition, the harm may not be inflicted by shock but by gradual accumulation of stress.

The attitude to family members prevails in the final criterion, which requires the relatives to have close ties of love and affection with the patient.[119] At first glance, it seems that this requirement accords with a communitarian or an ethics–of–care perspective of the family. The courts seem to realise that familial relationships are based on love, and when the relatives are not close to the patient they cannot claim that they were affected by the bad news. However, the court in *Alcock* treated the members of the nuclear family unequally. On the one hand, it assumes that close ties of love exist between children and parents but on the other hand it requires siblings to prove that they love each other even when the harm they suffered was not in doubt.[120]

The view taken is that the inconsistency in the attitude to close family members derives from a lack of a clear definition of the family. As stated in Chapter 2, English law does not have a clear definition of family members. The result is the expression of different attitudes to different familial relationships. Formulating a clear definition, however, will eliminate these inconsistencies. Undoubtedly, the court's attempt to adopt a *biosocial* definition in *Alcock* should be encouraged. However, it should have been applied to all family members equally. The law could either provide a list of relatives who are considered as family members or require all of them to show that they have a close relationship with the patient. Yet whether the court adopts a clear definition of the family or not,[121] the *Alcock*'s

---

[116] See *Safer v Pack*, supra n. 22, at p. 1192.

[117] *McLoughlin v O'Brian* [1983] 1 AC 410.

[118] *Taylor v Somerset HA* [1993] 4 Med LR 34; *Sion v Hampstead HA* [1994] 5 Med LR 170; *Tan v East London and the City HA* [1999] Lloyds' Rep Med 389.

[119] *Alcock v Chief Constable of the South Yorkshire Police* [1992] 1 AC 310, [1991] 4 All ER 907.

[120] Ibid, [1991] 4 All ER 907, 914, 919–920, 930 and 935.

[121] The Law Commission, *Liability for psychiatric Illness: Item 2 of the 6 programme of law reform*, London, Stationary Office (1998), at p. 123 recommends to 'lay down a fixed list of relationships where close ties of love and affection shall be deemed to exist, while allowing a plaintiff outside the list to prove' that he or she has these ties with the primary victim. The recommended list includes: spouses, parents, children, siblings, and unmarried heterosexual and homosexual permanent partners. See also Giliker P., Beckwith S., *Tort*, London, Sweet & Maxwell (2nd edn., 2004), Chapter 4, para. 4–038.

criteria cannot provide a legal framework in the context of communication of medical information for the reasons specified above.[122] Therefore, other alternatives should be discussed.

3.4.2 Psychological Harm Resulting from Communication of Information

The courts do not rely exclusively on *Alcock* when they discuss the duty of doctors in communicating medical information to patients or to their relatives.[123] There are a few cases which deal with this issue. In *Allin v City & Hackney HA*[124] doctors told the mother of a newborn that her child had died shortly after delivery. The child in fact survived, but the doctors communicated the good news to the mother only several hours afterwards. The court upheld the mother's claim for psychological harm. In *AB v Tameside & Glossop HA*[125] a large group of patients received a letter from their health authorities informing them that their former doctor was diagnosed with HIV and that there was a remote chance that they were infected. The patients claimed that the communication caused them psychological harm. The Court of Appeal dismissed their claim, holding that since the news had to be delivered to several hundreds of patients sending a letter was a reasonable method of communication. In *Powell v Boldaz*[126] the parents discovered following their son's death that the doctors who treated him misled them. The court rejected their claim for psychological harm.

Apart from *Powell*, the court in these cases did not have to apply the criteria held in *Alcock* because it was plain that the parties had a doctor–patient relationship.[127] In *Allin* the courts established proximity because the doctors provided medical treatment to the claimant, and in *AB* the defendant doctors did not challenge this assumption. By contrast, in *Powell v Boldaz* the court explicitly stated that the parents did not establish a doctor–patient relationship with the doctors.[128]

Consequently, the conclusion one may reach is that the notion of assumption of responsibility explains the different attitude to patients and relatives in this area. While doctors assume responsibility to their patients, they do not undertake such responsibility to family members. Despite this position leading commentators, such

---

[122] The House of Lords tried to relax the *Alcock*'s criteria in *W v Essex CC* [2000] 2 All ER 237.

[123] See Deakin, Johnston, and Markesinis, supra n. 54, at pp. 109–110; Lunney and Oliphant, supra n. 38, at p. 313.

[124] [1996] 7 Med LR 167 (hereafter: *Allin*).

[125] [1997] 8 Med LR 91 (hereafter: *AB*).

[126] [1998] Lloyd's Rep. Med. 116 (hereafter: *Powell*).

[127] In that regard the claimants were primary and not secondary victims.

[128] See *Powell*, supra n. 114; the claimants' attempt to challenge this decision in the European Court failed on admissibility grounds: *Powell v United Kingdom*, application no. 45305/99, 4/5/2000.

as Mullany and Jones,[129] argue that the mechanism of 'assumption of responsibility' can be applied even when the claimant cannot establish a doctor–patient relationship. Mullany argues that the single meeting between the doctor and the relatives when the bad news is communicated creates the legal relationship between them.[130] Jones argues that there should be no difference between the status of family members when they receive information about the patient and when they see the doctor treating the patient. If relatives can establish proximity with the doctor when they witness the treatment, they should be able to do so when they receive information.

The commentators' view is convincing as it recognises the involvement of family members in the patient's care. It requires doctors to act responsibly when interacting with relatives even though they have not voluntarily undertaken a duty to them. It recognises that relatives can be adversely affected when they receive information from the patient's doctors, whether or not they can establish a doctor–patient relationship with them. Undoubtedly, it reflects awareness of the social environment in any medical situation: it acknowledges that the doctor–patient relationship does not operate in a vacuum but actually influences others.

Yet despite the commentators' suggestion to adopt the 'assumption of responsibility' test the courts in two recent cases applied the primary/secondary distinction.[131] In *The Creutzfeldt–Jakob Disease litigation; Group B Plaintiffs v Medical Research Council and another*[132] clinicians negligently gave to children suffering from dwarfism human growth hormone potentially affected by CJD. The children claimed that once told the distressing news they suffered psychiatric harm because of the gradual fear that they may develop the disease in the future. The court upheld their claim, classifying them as secondary victims despite its recognition that the clinicians–children relationship was 'akin to that of doctor and patient'.[133] Despite Grubb's view that a doctor–patient relationship leads to perceiving the patient as a primary victim,[134] the judge in the *CJD* case

---

[129] Mullany N., "Liability for careless communication of traumatic information" (1998) 114 *LQR* 380, 383; Jones M., "Negligently inflicted psychological harm: Is the word mightier than the deed?" (1997) 13 (4) *Professional Negligence* 111, 113.

[130] See Grubb, supra n. 27 at pp. 356 where Grubb asserts that proximity is satisfied. Grubb, however, does not give any detailed explanation why this is so.

[131] Another unique case of communication of information is *Farrell v Avon HA* [2001] Lloyd's Rep Med 458. The claimant attended the hospital, where he was wrongly informed by the staff that his newborn child had just died and was given the baby's corpse to hold. Subsequently he was informed that there had been a mistake and that his son was in fact alive. F brought a claim for psychological harm. The court upheld the claim, holding that the father was a primary victim.

[132] *The Creutzfeldt-Jakob Disease litigation; Group B Plaintiffs v Medical Research Council and another* (QB) [2000] Lloyd's Rep Med 161, 41 BMLR 157 (Hereafter: the *CJD* case).

[133] Ibid.

[134] Grubb A., (ed.), *Principles of Medical Law*, Oxford, Oxford University Press (2nd edn.,

distinguished its circumstances from those in *Page v Smith*. In the latter, the primary victim's participation in the traumatic event, his shock, and the resultant psychological harm occurred simultaneously; with the children, the trigger for the psychological harm was their awareness of the risk and the nature of the disease, not specifically the medical treatment they received.[135]

In *A v Leeds Teaching Hospital NHS Trust*[136] parents of children whose organs were removed and retained by the hospital without their consent brought a claim against the doctors for psychological harm they suffered when they discovered the doctor's acts. Upholding their claim, the court stated that the parents established a doctor–patient relationship with the doctors, reluctantly holding that the parents were primary victims.

Some conclusions can be drawn from *A*. First, the judge refused to rely on *Powell*, determining that the circumstances in the two cases were different. Yet from a reading of the two decisions the differences which led the judge in *A* to arrive at an opposite conclusion are not clear. The judge did not provide a clear explanation why doctors who misled the parents in these two cases should deserve different attitudes from the courts with regard to proximity. Second, when comparing *A* with the *CJD* case one can see that they contradict. In the *CJD* case the court held that despite a close relationship between the parties (akin to that between doctor and patient) the children were classified as secondary victims; but the judge in *A* held that once there is doctor–patient relationship the parents should be classified as primary victims. Lastly, in the *CJD* case and in *A* the courts applied the primary/secondary distinction and not the assumption of responsibility test.[137] Indeed, as the judge in *A* recognised, this distinction may not be relevant in the medical context. Yet ultimately, as in the area of physical injury, the courts' determination of whether or not a doctor–patient relationship existed between the parties led them to decide whether proximity was established between the parties. This undoubtedly reflects a patient–centred approach as the point of reference is the exclusive doctor–patient relationship.

This legal position notwithstanding, the commentators' view may be taken one step farther and *Allin* and *Powell* can be perceived as familial claims. For example, in *Allin* the family that was affected by the news included the newborn baby, the mother, and the grandmother. Though the judge mentioned that the grandmother was gravely affected by the events he did not treat the claim as familial but as personal. The court viewed the case as the claim of an individual patient against a doctor and not one of a family against the doctor. A similar approach could have been taken in *Powell*, where the parents were greatly affected by the conduct of

---

2004), 335.

[135] But the decision to classify the children as secondary victims was heavily influenced by policy considerations.

[136] [2004] 2 FLR 365, [2004] 3 FCR 324 (Hereafter: *A*).

[137] In *A*, the judge specifically stated that he had no choice but to follow the primary/secondary distinction despite his reluctance to do so. Ibid., at para. 197.

their son's doctor. However, despite the close involvement of the parents in that case, Stuart–Smith LJ rejected the proposition 'that a doctor…who tells relatives what has happened thereby undertakes the doctor–patient relationship towards the relatives'.[138]

The attitude to family members in *Powell* is artificial. If it is accepted that doctors should communicate information professionally, the existence of a doctor–patient relationship may be irrelevant. Whether or not the relatives can establish a doctor–patient relationship, the information communicated should be accurate and conveyed sensitively, taking into account the emotional impact it may have on them. As medical academics confess, communication of information is part of the doctor's professional work, and this task should be performed professionally[139] irrespective of the doctor's duty to the patient. The courts may have to recognise that doctors owe obligations not only to the patient but also to relatives with whom they interact throughout the provision of medical services to the patient.

However, when imposing such a duty on the doctor Mullany relies on the encounter between the doctor and the patient. The question remains whether proximity can be established when the doctor does not communicate information to the relatives and they suffer psychological harm as a result. This may occur when the doctor does not convey the information to the relatives in advance, preventing them thereby from receiving early counselling. If such an interest deserves recognition the model presented by Mullany may not be sufficient.

To conclude, the chances of the relatives succeeding in a claim for psychological harm are slim and depend on his chances to prove a doctor–patient relationship with the defendant doctor. The next stage is to examine whether there are potential developments which may lead to the establishment of proximity. This is the subject of the next section.

3.4.3 A Potential Development in Establishing Proximity in Psychological Harm

It should be recalled that a conception of *awareness* was identified by English courts in recent physical injury cases. Proximity was based on the doctor's awareness of the implications of the patient's medical condition for the relatives. The notion of undertaking of responsibility was expanded to include circumstances where the doctor failed to prevent harm to identifiable third parties. It was argued

---

[138] See *Powell*, supra n. 126, at pp. 123–124; it should be noted, however, that commentators perceive *Powell* as a unique case and not one which accords with the ordinary cases in this area. See: Kennedy I., Negligence: Duty of care; nervous shock; duty of candour" (1998) 6 *Medical Law Review* 112.

[139] Buckman R., Kason Y., *How to Break Bad News: A Guide for Health–Care Professionals*, London, Papermac (1992); Brewin T., *Relating to the Relatives: Breaking Bad News, Communication, and Support*, Oxford, Radcliffe Medical Press (1996); Faulkner A., *When the News is Bad: A Guide for Health Professionals on Breaking Bad News*, Cheltenham, Stanley Thornes (Publishers) Ltd (1998).

that this model can be applied to the context of genetics. When doctors diagnose patients they know that their findings may affect the physical health of their relatives who may develop the condition as well. This factor requires doctors to be more concerned and aware of the relatives' health.

If this notion is accepted, doctors should be aware not only of the relatives' physical health but also of their mental health. As the research provided in Chapters 2 and 5 indicates, genetic information greatly affects the mental state of the relatives as well as their relationship with the patient. The doctor's awareness of the psychological effect of the information on the relatives should lead him or her to realise that he or she should communicate it professionally and with due care.[140]

The situation may become complicated when the *patient* discloses the information to the relatives despite their wishes. Doctors can argue that under English law they have no obligation to prevent the patient from disclosing unwanted information to relatives. Relying on the interpretation of *proximity* as *awareness*, the relatives, in contrast, may assert that the doctor should be aware of the possibility that they may wish not to know, and that the patient may compromise this relatives' wish. The doctor faces the dilemma of how to reconcile the two opposite duties: to be aware of the relatives' interest in knowing the information and to consider their interest in not knowing.

This issue becomes more complex when the doctor has no contact with the relatives. In this situation it is very difficult to establish proximity. However, the mechanism of *awareness* may create the legal relationship between the two parties in these circumstances because it does not require the doctor to contact the patient but merely to be aware that his or her actions or omissions may have an adverse impact on identifiable third parties, namely the relatives. In the context of genetics, family members are closely involved in the patient's lives from the early stage of the diagnosis to the later stage when the illness manifests itself. As the medical literature and socio–medical research demonstrate, doctors are well aware of the interests of the relatives even when they have no interaction with them. Therefore, one may argue that this factor, and not the single meeting between the doctor and the relatives, as Mullany suggests, will create the legal proximity between these two parties. A close legal relationship between the doctor and the relatives may be established when the doctor does not approach the relatives directly but asks the patient to inform them. Undoubtedly, adopting this conception will make the current legal position less patient–centred and more family–based. It will recognise that the doctor's conduct affects not only the patient who requests medical help but also the family members. In addition, it will require the doctor to consider whether the relatives do or do not want to receive the information, and how they may react if it is communicated to them.

---

[140] In the *CJD* case the judge did state that 'the defendants were not only aware of the risk of CJD, but also that the risk of CJD might not become a reality for years or even decades'.

A fundamental question remains: if a duty of care is imposed in circumstances of both disclosure and non–disclosure, the doctor will be in an impossible position where he or she will have to determine whether or not to approach the relatives and communicate the information. Yet arguing that doctors face contradicting obligations in this context should not lead automatically to the conclusion that they should not owe any duty to the relatives in this context. Doctors, like other professionals, face conflicts in various aspects of their work. Although it is difficult to reconcile these obligations a mechanism will have to be formulated to assist doctors in this conflict. If the law gives priority to patient autonomy the tendency will be to provide the doctor and the patient with the discretion to decide whether or not to disclose the information to the relatives. The utilitarian mechanism adopted in English law will also suggest that non–disclosure will be the rule. This is because doctors cannot determine in advance whether disclosure will prevent or exacerbate an adverse psychological reaction, especially when the disease is incurable. As the research outlined in Chapter 2 indicates, the reaction of those who receive information is unexpected and unpredictable.

To sum up, the discussion in the first two categories of damage reflects only one interest out of those specified in Chapter 2: the interest in avoiding harm. However, the interest in making informed choices, which is common to patients and relatives, should be dealt with as well. In tort law this interest is translated into a tangible harm, more specifically to economic loss. This may occur when the relatives consider reproduction and suffer loss due to the doctor's failure to warn them that the foetus may carry a genetic disorder. In these circumstances family members may have to bear the extra financial costs of rearing a disabled child. Therefore, the main focus in this category of damage is non–disclosure and not disclosure.

3.5 Economic Loss

At first glance the scope of the doctors' duty in the area of economic loss seems more restricted than in the areas of physical injury and psychological harm, because generally the law is reluctant to impose a duty of care in this area.[141] Recent cases indicate that the courts are not as favourable to the patient's financial interests as they are to the patient's physical health especially in circumstances where a duty of care is not automatically assumed.[142] However, the courts acknowledge that doctors may cause economic loss to their patients. They recognise, for example, that when doctors fail to detect congenital abnormalities in

---

[141]   See Lunney and Oliphant, supra n. 38, at p. 339.
[142]   *Kapfunde v Abbey National* (1998) 45 BMLR 176; *Baker v Kaye* (1996) 39 BMLR 12; See Deakin, Johnston and Markesinis, supra n. 54, at p. 210 where they observe that society 'places a higher value on physical interests than on economic welfare'.

the foetus they may be liable for the parent's extra expenses.[143] Whether or not the doctors owe a duty to the patient's relatives who consider reproduction remains to be examined.

3.5.1 *From* Hedley Byrne *to* White v Jones *via* Caparo v Dickman

The formulation of a duty of care in cases of pure economic loss was developed in *Hedley Byrne v Heller*.[144] The House of Lords held that when professionals provide information or advice to another whom they know (or ought to know) will rely on this information, they owe that person a duty of care in tendering this information or advice. This was labelled 'assumption of responsibility.'[145] However, in subsequent cases the courts limited the effect of this decision. In *Caparo v Dickman* the House of Lords held that the professional should know: (1) the purpose for which the advice is given (purpose); (2) that it will be communicated to an identifiable third party (identification); (3) that he or she will rely on it (reliance).[146] In addition, it was held that in any event the imposition of such duty is limited to provision of statements or advice.[147] However, despite these strict criteria the House of Lords followed *Hedley Byrne*'s notion of 'assumption of responsibility' in situations where professionals provide other services and not just advice.[148] Furthermore, in *White v Jones* the House of Lords upheld a claim brought by intended beneficiaries for the financial loss they suffered due to the failure of their father's solicitor to draft a new will.[149] In that case the court mitigated the significance of the reliance requirement.

The flexible approach presented in *White* was rejected in the medical context. In *Goodwill v BPAS*,[150] the single case so far where a third party directly sued a doctor for economic loss, the Court of Appeal struck out a claim of a patient's sexual partner against a doctor for her financial costs in rearing a healthy but

---

[143] See *Parkinson*, supra n. 78, at para. 92. Giliker and Beckwith, supra n. 121, at pp. 57–58 argue that following the decision in the House of Lords in *Rees v Darlington Memorial Hospital NHS Trust* [2003] 3 WLR 1091 the decision in *Parkinson* was not overruled and that a claim for additional costs of rearing a disabled child was still possible.
[144] [1964] AC 465 (hereafter: *Hedley Byrne*).
[145] Ibid., per Lord Devlin at p. 529.
[146] *Caparo v Dickman* [1990] 2 AC 605, [1990] 1 All ER 568, 589–594.
[147] Ibid., at p. 587.
[148] *Spring v Guardian Assurances* [1995] 2 AC 296, 318 (hereafter: *Spring*); *Henderson v Merrett* [1995] 2 AC 145 (hereafter: *Henderson*).
[149] *White v Jones* [1995] 1 All ER 691 (hereafter: *White*); in *Gorham v BT* [2000] 1 WLR 2129 the Court of Appeal was willing to accept that the principle held in *Hedley Byrne* could lead to the imposition of a duty of care on a provider of services to the dependants of a deceased person who had been given negligent financial advice.
[150] [1996] 2 All ER 161 (CA) (Hereafter: *Goodwill*).

unwanted child.[151]   In rejecting the claim the court was greatly influenced by two factors. First, the doctor could not identify the claimant because the patient did not have any relationship with her when the doctor treated him. Second, the claimant consulted her own GP about the remote possibility that the patient would become fertile again and thus did not rely on the doctor's advice.

The court in *Goodwill* did not follow the decision in *White* but rejected the claim.[152]   Yet at least part of the court's arguments may be challenged. First, as for reliance, Lord Browne–Wilkinson in *White* argued that this was not always essential for the establishment of a duty of care.[153]   In addition, as Jonathan Griffiths pointed out, though the claimant in *Goodwill* turned to her own GP, clearly she relied partly on the doctor's advice as communicated to her by the patient. Thus, instead of denying the existence of the duty of care altogether the court could have held that although the claimant contributed to her loss she also relied partly on the doctor's advice.[154]   Furthermore, the fact that the claimant consulted her own doctor goes to causation (*novus actus*) and not to the duty of care because in approaching her GP the claimant broke the chain of causation between the doctor's conduct and her loss. Second, the distinction made in *Goodwill* between provision of services and advice was dismissed by the House of Lords in other cases.[155]   Finally, Peter Gibson LJ's argument that the doctor did not owe a duty to the claimant because the patient did not tell him that he would communicate the advice to future partners can be contested by arguing that the doctor could appreciate it himself, without the patient's explicit statement.

If it is accepted that the decision in *Goodwill* is based primarily on lack of identification, this is not problematic in the context of genetics. While in *Goodwill* the doctor could not identify the claimant when he treated the patient, in the genetic context the doctor can identify the relatives. When the doctor fails to advise the patient that future children in the family may suffer from a genetic disorder, the doctor knows that other close family members, such as the patient's sister or brother, may be affected by this lack of information. Nevertheless, a significant limitation in this context is reliance. When the doctor communicates the information to the patient, but the patient is reluctant to inform the relatives, they are then unaware of the information and do not rely on it. The relatives' awareness of the interaction between the doctor and the patient is essential before proximity can be established.

---

[151]   For a detailed description of the facts see para 3.3.1.4. Following *McFarlane v Tayside Health Board* [2000] 2 AC 59 such claims are no longer possible in any event.

[152]   See *Goodwill*, supra n. 150, at p. 167.

[153]   See *White*, supra n. 149, per Lord Browne–Wilkinson at p. 714.

[154]   Griffiths J., "The duty of care in cases of wrongful conception" (1996) *Nottingham Law Journal* 56.

[155]   See *Spring* and *Henderson*, supra n. 148.

3.5.2 White *and* Goodwill – *An Ethical Analysis*

When examining the attitude this legal position reflects with regard to family members it is essential to analyse the decision in *White* and *Goodwill* closely. The decision in *White* is considered exceptional,[156] and as *Goodwill* proves, the courts have been trying to distinguish the cases before them from that of *White*.[157] A possible explanation for this is that in *White* the House of Lords accepted that a beneficent legal duty could be owed to family members, whereas the general view is that such a duty does not exist. In *White* there was no prior and close relationship between the solicitor and the client's daughters.[158] In addition, the court imposed a duty on the solicitor to act despite the lack of liability for omissions. However, it is possible to argue that although the solicitor had not met the claimants he could identify them as the intended beneficiaries, and he knew that his conduct in drafting a new will would affect their financial interests. In particular, the court stated that the client told his two daughters about his wish to include them in his new will and the solicitor knew about this communication.

However, the House of Lords could not conclude that the daughters relied on the solicitor's conduct. They did not act upon their expectation to receive a large sum of money when their father died. Lord Goff held, 'the loss suffered by the disappointed beneficiary is not in reality a loss at all; it is, more accurately *a failure to obtain a benefit*'.[159] Therefore, the decision in *White* implies that the solicitor should have acted for the benefit of others whether or not they rely upon it. In his not drafting a new will the solicitor failed to confer a benefit, and this was perceived as a negligent conduct. It was not a question of helping a drowning child in a shallow pool, which reflects a moral duty to rescue; it was more than that: it was conferring a benefit which, if not fulfilled, causes no harm. But as the case of *Stovin v Wise* suggests, imposing a duty of care in these circumstances is exceptional in English law.[160]

Consequently, in the absence of a duty to benefit it is not difficult to understand why the court in *Goodwill* was reluctant to follow *White*. In ethical terms, the court in *Goodwill* dismissed the argument that the doctor should have acted to benefit the patient's partner. For that purposes, the judge argued that preventing pregnancy

---

[156] Weir T., "A Damnosa Hereditas" (1995) 111 *LQR* 357; Witting C., "Justifying liability to third parties for negligent misstatements" (2000) 20 *Oxford Journal of Legal Studies* 615; Lunney and Oliphant, supra n. 38, at p. 412 state that if *White* was widely applied it would be something English tort law has never recognised. Yet in *Gorham v BT*, supra n. 149 the judges expressed the view that the circumstances of the case were similar to those in *White*.

[157] See Giliker and Beckwith, supra n. 121, at pp. 84–85.

[158] Murphy J., "Expectation losses, negligent omissions and the tortious duty of care" (1996) 55 (1) *The Cambridge Law Journal* 43.

[159] See *White*, supra n. 149, at pp. 694, 700, 717 (my emphasis).

[160] [1996] AC 923, 931–932.

could not be regarded as conferring a benefit to others or as prevention of physical harm, because producing children cannot be considered as a curse but as a blessing. But is this statement accurate? Until recently the courts did not present a united front but disagreed as to whether or not pregnancy is a blessing. In some cases the courts argued that pregnancy could be regarded as personal injury.[161] However, following *McFarlane v Tayside HB*[162] a healthy pregnancy is now considered a blessing.

Taking a less individualistic approach in *Goodwill* might have led to a different outcome, requiring the doctor to be aware of the interests of the patient's potential partners. Lord Nolan's speech in *White* reflects such an approach. The judge indicated that the solicitor owed a duty of care to the client's daughters because he was the *family*'s lawyer. Practically, the solicitor did not provide services only to his client, but also to his two daughters. Lord Nolan argued, 'as is commonly the case the contract was with the head of the family, but it would be astonishing if, as a result, they owed a duty of care to him alone, to the exclusion of the other members of the family'.[163] This implies that for Lord Nolan the claim was familial and not personal. He realised that the duty of the solicitor was to consider the interests of all family members involved (the father and his two daughters). Lord Nolan appreciated that examining separately the solicitor–client relationship and the solicitor–beneficiaries relationship would not reflect the facts of this case.

Consequently, Lord Nolan apparently saw the client as a person with close familial relationships. This perception led the judge to note that the common good of the family could not be promoted if the court were to break the familial relations into several components and perceive the client and his family members as separate individuals. The father and his two daughters had a common interest, so the traditional rule that solicitors owe a duty of care only to their individual clients could not reflect such an interest. The human intuition to do justice in this case[164] could be delivered only by taking a family–based approach. This attitude was not followed in *Goodwill* probably because the claimant was not the patient's relative but his lover. There the court examined separately the doctor–patient relationship and the doctor–partner relationship. The view taken in this context is that incorporating some communitarian insights into the legal position might have resulted in the doctor's realisation that his failure to warn the patient could adversely affect the interest of a third party.

To sum up, following *Goodwill* the prospects of the relatives succeeding in a claim against doctors for economic loss are not promising, especially when they are unaware of the communication between the doctor and the patient. The right of

---

[161]   *Thake v Maurice* (1986) 1 QB 644; *Emeh v Kensington and Chelsea and Westminster AHA* [1985] 1 QB 1012; Mullis A., "Wrongful conception unravelled" (1993) 1 *Medical Law Review* 320.

[162]   *McFarlane v Tayside HB* [2000] 2 AC 59 (HL).

[163]   See *White*, supra n. 149, at p. 736.

[164]   Ibid., at p. 702.

family members to make informed choices seems limited. However, recent developments in this area may change this position.

3.5.3 Reconsidering the 'Assumption of Responsibility'

As noted earlier, recently the House of Lords returned to the more pragmatic notion of 'assumption of responsibility'. This notion was heavily criticised by the commentators for its incoherence.[165] The current tendency is to perceive this notion as a judgement reflecting the court's view as to whether or not the defendant should owe a duty to the claimant in the particular circumstances of the case.[166] Yet relying on recent cases, such as *Spring, Henderson,* and *White,* a different interpretation of this conception may be suggested. The argument put forward in this chapter is that when professionals are *aware* that an identified third party may be *affected* by their conduct, proximity is established. *Reliance* is replaced with causal notions of *awareness* and *effect.* Accordingly, doctors are legally proximate to relatives not because they assume responsibility to them or undertake to treat them but because they are *aware* of the *effect* their conduct has on them as identifiable third parties. Choice and agreement, which are reflected in the notion of assumption of responsibility and are fundamental to the establishment of a duty of care, are substituted by social awareness, which reflects the view that professionals owe compulsory duties when they decide how to act.

This mechanism of awareness that the courts have begun to develop in the area of physical injury can be applied to this area of economic loss. If it is accepted that awareness and effect replace reliance, proximity can be established between doctors and relatives whether or not the relatives are aware of the doctor–patient communication and rely upon it. Furthermore, this analysis may relax the artificial distinction between liability to commissions and omissions. The doctors, like the solicitor in *White,* know that when they fail to verify that the relatives receive genetic information financial harm may occur. Ultimately, promoting a conception of awareness will provide more recognition of family members' interests for it may enable them to make informed reproductive decisions. The doctor will be aware that his or her conduct has implications not only for the patient but for various interests of other relatives who are closely involved in and affected by the patient's life.

---

[165] Barker K., "Unreliable assumptions in the modern law of negligence" (1993) 109 *LQR* 461, 464; McBride N., Hughes A., "Hedley Byrne in the House of Lords: An interpretation" (1995) 15 *Legal Studies* 376; Hepple B., "Negligence: The search for coherence" (1997) 50 *CLP* 69.

[166] See Lunney and Oliphant, supra n. 38, at p. 400; *Phelps v London Borough of Hillingdon* [2000] 4 All ER 504, per Lord Slynn at p. 518.

3.6 *Proximity* between Doctors and Relatives – Conclusion

The examination of *proximity* in tort law leads to the conclusion that the scope of the doctor's duty to the relatives is limited. The discussion in this chapter has indicated that whether it is physical injury, economic loss, or psychological harm,[167] the legal attitude to proximity derives from the involvement of a third party. Recently Laws LJ confirmed this saying that:

> ...in the common law's present maturity we have very broadly arrived at a position in which liability for damage carelessly occasioned to another's person or property is, as a matter not of legal principle but of pragmatic reality, the rule not the exception where there is no third agency which constitutes the immediate cause of the damage; but *where there is such a third agency, liability is the exception not the rule.*[168]

Although, this part of Law LJ's speech was *obiter*, the current position of English tort law reflects a reluctance to impose a duty of care on professionals who cannot specifically identify the third parties, no matter how grave the risk is. As we have seen, this derives from the courts' tendency, in the area of professional liability in all categories of damage, to apply the assumption of responsibility test, which reflects obligations the professional chooses to undertake. In the medical context the question of proximity is examined in light of the exclusivity of the doctor–patient relationship. In the few cases where the courts held that proximity between the relatives and the doctor was established, the courts held that the claimant had a doctor–patient relationship with the defendant doctor, determining that the doctor assumed responsibility to the relatives.[169] Still, adopting such a mechanism to impose a duty of care to third parties in general or to family members in particular seems artificial.

Furthermore, when dealing with the first hurdle the relatives face, this discussion indicates that *proximity* does not mirror the involvement of family members in the patient's care. To argue that doctors are not legally *proximate* to the relatives is to overlook the reality that doctors interact with them, and in the

---

[167] The decision in *Rees v Darlington*, supra n.143 to award a blind mother of an unwanted but healthy child a 'conventional award' for the lost of her right to limit the size of her family can be seen as creating a new category of damage, namely harm to choice and to the individual's right to autonomy. Nevertheless, relationship between the mother and the doctor was close and legally proximate.

[168] *K v Secretary of State for the Home Department* [2002] EWCA Civ 775, para 16 (my italics).

[169] In *A v Leeds Teaching NHS Hospital* [2004] 2 FLR 365, [2004] 3 FCR 324, a case of psychological harm, Gage J held in para. 200: '... this issue depends on the question of whether or not there existed a doctor–patient relationship between the clinicians and the parents...If it did, there can be no real difficulty in satisfying the tests of proximity... Further, in my opinion, the purpose and the assumption of responsibility tests will be satisfied'.

area of genetics he or she even depends on their co-operation. The conclusion one can draw is that English law reflects an individualistic patient–centred approach.

This position leads one to argue that the law does not fully recognise the various interests of family members in genetic information. The interest in avoiding physical harm is recognised to a limited extent, but the interest in making informed choices, as represented in the area of economic loss, is not, even when the doctor can identify the relatives. In this area reliance is still a prominent requirement.

However, the limitations of this legal position may be mitigated if the unit of medical care includes the family and not the individual patient alone. As the following chapters reveal, this will more accurately reflect medical practices especially in the area of genetics, where information affects both patients and family members. Ultimately, such an approach will result in taking the interests of family members into account when making a decision. As stated, English tort law is beginning to shift its approach in this direction. The courts realise that in some circumstances doctors owe duties not only to their patients but also to other identifiable third parties. Therefore, in genetics, where the doctor can identify the relatives at risk, proximity may be established. However, this change requires further development, moving away from the current patient–centred towards a family–based approach. Yet the legal discussion does not end at this point. As noted earlier, proximity is only the second element when establishing a duty of care. The third element, namely whether the imposition of a duty is 'fair just and reasonable', is not free from dispute either. The next part deals with this issue.

3.7 *'Fair, Just and Reasonable'* – Policy Considerations in Genetics

Discussing the doctor–relatives relationship with regard to communication of genetic information the question arises whether it is *'fair, just and reasonable'* to impose on the doctor a duty of care. Dealing with this question, the courts discuss *policy* considerations. These are regarded as a set of arguments 'undefined in nature and unlimited in number' that are invoked by the courts to dismiss claims even when proximity is satisfied.[170] They are usually discussed when the defendant is a public body (the police, local authorities, etc.) as the courts are reluctant to impose a duty on authorities whose role it to protect the public. Since doctors provide services within the NHS, policy considerations are relevant to the discussion in this context.

Obviously, policy arguments can go either way. They can justify a particular conduct but at the same time they can point to its possible adverse outcomes. This is a potential weakness in the search for 'policy' approval. However, in this context this is not a vice but a virtue, because the examination of policy considerations

---

[170] See Lunney and Oliphant, supra n. 38, at p. 124.

taken by the courts may enlighten us about their underlying philosophical approach.

Policy will be examined in the context of a physical injury claim. The law perceives public health as a paramount interest that requires protection, and if the courts adopt a policy which limits the interests of the relatives in this area it is likely to restrict them when the claim is for psychological harm or economic loss. Moreover, the courts have already accepted that policy considerations are applied to all categories of damage.[171]

3.7.1 Formulating the Traditional Considerations: From Hill to X v Bedfordshire

Policy was first argued as a separate element even before *Caparo*.[172] In *Hill v Chief Constable of West Yorkshire*[173] the House of Lords articulated its *policy* arguments.[174] When striking out a claim against the police, Lord Keith asserted that imposition of a duty of care would not promote the professional standards in suppressing crime. Furthermore, he argued that it might inhibit police work and lead to professional defensive conduct. In addition, he stressed that public bodies have the discretion to take professional decisions and it would be inappropriate to challenge this discretion in courts. Finally, he argued that imposing a duty of care might lead to a significant diversion of human resources from the important task of suppression of crime because the police would have to devote extra efforts to face third parties' claims.[175] Lord Templeman added that if duty is imposed on the police it might open the floodgate, allowing any individual to challenge police work in court.[176]

Other *policy* arguments were formulated where local authorities were involved. *X v Bedfordshire CC* concerned two different groups of cases. One group, known as the child abuse cases, addressed on the one hand the failure of local authorities to take children into care, which caused them to suffer from abuse at home, and on the other hand the negligent decision of the authority to take a child into care, causing psychological harm to the mother and the child. The second group concerned the failure of local authorities to provide adequate education for children

---

[171] *X v Bedfordshire* [1995] 2 AC 633, [1995] 3 All ER 353, 380 where the contention that these considerations apply only to economic loss cases was rejected.

[172] In *Yuen Kun Yeu v A-G of Hong Kong* [1988] 1 AC 175 the court treated policy as a different and separate element. This was fundamental to the test formulated in *Anns v Merton LBC* [1978] AC 728 where Lord Wilberforce established a two stage test applied to the imposition of a duty of care which was later replaced by the three limb test of *Caparo*.

[173] [1989] 1 AC 53 (hereafter: *Hill*).

[174] Monti G., "*Osman v UK*–transforming English negligence law into French administrative law?" (1999) 48 *International & Comparative Law Quarterly* 757, 759.

[175] See *Hill*, supra, n. 173, at p. 63; however, this part of Lord Keith's speech was *obiter*.

[176] *Hill* was applied in subsequent police cases. See: *Osman v Ferguson* [1993] 4 All ER 344 (CA).

with special needs.[177] To the arguments discussed in *Hill*, the House of Lords added that professionals in public bodies were required to perform a delicate task and that the claimants in these cases had an alternative remedy. In addition, it was argued that the courts have to be careful when they impose liability on public bodies which have the statutory responsibility to protect society from wrongdoers.[178] Stuart–Smith LJ followed this approach in *W v Essex CC*.[179] In that case the local authority placed a child known to be abusive in a foster family. The foster parents sued the authority when they discovered that the boy had abused their biological children. The Court of Appeal struck out the parents' claim for psychological harm, preferring the authority's view to the parents' interests. Stuart–Smith LJ rejected the argument that striking out the parents' claim would send an adverse and deterrent message to people who wish to contribute to society by becoming foster parents.[180]

Obviously, these arguments can be applied to the doctor–relatives relation–ships.[181] First, imposing a duty of care on doctors would overburden them with numerous claims out of a single encounter with the patient. Furthermore, it may be unreasonable to expose doctors, who do not cause the disease and often can do nothing to prevent it, to liability disproportionate to their conduct. Second, if a duty of care is imposed doctors may adopt a defensive practice, by warning relatives even when it is not required. This may lead to an unnecessary breach of patients' right to confidentiality, which may deter patients from approaching doctors.[182] Third, imposing a duty may not contribute to the improvement of medical standards, for it can be argued that doctors are not motivated by the legal liability cast on them but by their sense of professional responsibility. Fourth, imposing a duty may lead to a diversion of resources, requiring extra time to find out whether patients have disclosed the information, and if not, to locate the relatives and inform them directly. Finally, relatives have an alternative remedy: they can apply to the GMC and complain.

These *policy* considerations reflect a paternalistic approach. The above cases being perceived as a conflict between the individual and the state, the interests of the latter are protected even in circumstances where the damage was serious and the negligence was self–evident (*X* and *W*). The courts seemed to prefer the

---

[177] [1995] 2 AC 633; [1995] 3 All ER 353 (HL) (hereafter: *X*).

[178] [1995] 3 All ER 353, 382; however, the House of Lords' decision was recently reversed (on different grounds) in the European Court of Human Rights: *Z v UK* [2001] 2 FCR 246.

[179] [1998] 3 WLR 534 (CA) (hereafter: *W*).

[180] The parents' appeal was upheld in the House of Lords: *W v Essex CC* [2000] 2 All ER 237. The position taken in the House of Lords was more sensitive to family members. See discussion below.

[181] In *Palmer v Tees* [1998] Lloyd's Rep Med 447 where Gage J was convinced by these arguments.

[182] See Ngwena and Chadwick, supra n. 56, at p. 88.

discretion of the authority over the interest of the individual. In so doing the courts ignore the communitarian message that people have to contribute to society's common good. The speech of Stuart–Smith LJ in *W* implies that the desire of people to foster children and contribute to the community should be outweighed by the interest of the state that its work will not be challenged in courts. This highlights the confrontational aspects of the relationship between the individual and the state and not their shared goals and aims.

These policy considerations also reflect a utilitarian approach. Arguing that doctors might adopt a defensive practice which would result in unnecessary disclosure of information implies that patients would be deterred from approaching geneticists because they may fear that doctors would invade their privacy and breach their confidentiality. If patients need counselling but are reluctant to approach doctors, public health may not be improved.

The decisions in *X* and *W* were reversed in higher courts[183] but the European Court of Human Rights in *Z v UK* and the House of Lords in *W* upheld the claims on different grounds. In *W* the court focused on the question whether the parents satisfied *Alcock*'s proximity criteria; and in *Z v UK* the European Court held that the claimant's right not to be tortured (Article 3) was breached. Despite the different grounds of these decisions a change in the courts' attitude could be observed.

3.7.2 A Change of Attitude: From Osman v UK to D v East Berkshire NHS Trust

A change in the courts' attitude began in *Osman v UK*,[184] although even before this case some judges presented a balanced view.[185] In this case the European Court of Human Rights held that *policy* considerations could not give immunity to the police against claims regarding suppression of crimes.[186] This decision led the House of Lords to reduce the influence of this requirement when the defendant was a public body. In *Barrett v Enfield LBC* Lord Slynn stated that the arguments of defensive conduct and diversion of resources had 'little, if any, weight.'[187] Furthermore, he rejected the proposition that imposing a duty of care would not

---

[183] *W v Essex CC* [2000] 2 All ER 237; *Z v UK* [2001] 2 FCR 246, at para 69.

[184] (1998) 5 BHRC 293.

[185] *Swinney v Chief Constable of Northumbria Police Force* [1997] QB 464 (CA); see the speech of Judge LJ in *W*, supra n. 179, at p. 556; *Capital & Counties v Hampshire CC* [1997] 2 All ER 865, 891.

[186] However, in *Z v UK* [2001] 2 FCR 246 the European Court acknowledged that the policy element does not provide immunity to public bodies but is 'an intrinsic element of the duty of care'. For possible interpretations of *Osman v UK* see: Monti, supra n. 174; Rt Hon Lord Hoffmann, "Human Rights and the House of Lords" (1999) 62 *Modern Law Review* 159; Hoyano L., "Policing flawed police investigations: unravelling the blanket" (1999) 62 *Modern Law Review* 912; Giliker P., "Osman and police immunity in the English law of torts" (2000) 20 (3) *Legal Studies* 372.

[187] [1999] 3 All ER 193, 208 (hereafter: *Barrett*).

improve professional standards. Sharing the same views, Lord Hutton added that the existence of an alternative remedy did not prevent the court from discussing a claim for compensation.[188] The decision in *Osman v UK* led Lord Browne–Wilkinson in *Barrett* to not strike out the claim in that case due to his suspicion that the claimant would apply to the European Court of Human Rights if it was rejected.[189] Following his speech the courts were reluctant to strike out claims on policy grounds alone.[190]

Lord Browne–Wilkinson's call to the European Court to reconsider its position was listened to, and in *Z v UK* the European Court accepted the legal mechanism exercised in English law where negligent claims are stricken out on grounds of policy.[191] But despite the European Court's change of mind, the English courts did not resort to their methods that existed before *Osman v UK* and were careful not to strike out a claim on the basis of policy.[192] For example, in *D v Berkshire Community Health NHS Trust*,[193] which was held after the decision in *Z v UK*, the court did not strike out several claims, holding that the traditional policy considerations raised to reject the existence of a duty of care had to accommodate the Human Rights Act 1998. The court held that in child abuse cases the question of whether the local authority owes a duty of care to the child[194] cannot be decided without a full trial. These led Giliker and Beckwith to argue that currently the courts shifted their focus from the traditional policy arguments, which had lost their primacy, to consideration of violations of fundamental human rights as recognised in the Convention. The two commentators also observed that following the developments in the law in this area the courts were reluctant to narrow the extent of the duty of care by the traditional policy considerations.[195]

Mitigating the influence of the traditional *policy* arguments reflects a shift from a paternalistic to a liberal approach. Following the decisions in *Osman v UK*, *Barrett*, and *Phelps*, the courts began to treat the fundamental rights of individuals and the interest of the state equally. These decisions enabled claimants who suffered from the conduct of state authorities to use all available remedies provided by law. In dismissing the traditional policy considerations the courts recognised that people should be free to choose how to exercise their legal rights.

---

[188] Ibid., at p. 228; see also *Phelps v London Borough of Hillingdon* [2000] 4 All ER 504 (hereafter: *Phelps*), at p. 535, where Lord Clyde referred to the floodgate and the defensive conduct arguments.

[189] See *Barrett*, supra, n. 187, at pp. 199–200.

[190] *Palmer v Tees* [1999] Lloyd's Rep Med 351, 360; *S v Gloucester CC* [2001] Fam 313.

[191] See also in this context *TP v UK* [2001] 2 FCR 289.

[192] As Giliker and Beckwith, supra n. 121 point, out *Osman v UK* had a 'lasting mark' on the attitude of the courts in this area of law.

[193] [2004] 2 WLR 58.

[194] The court held once again that doctors in these circumstances do not owe a duty of care to the parents of the children involved. This was upheld in *D v Berkshire Community Health NHS Trust* [2005] 2 FLR 284. See Chapter 1, part 1.3.2.3 for analysis.

[195] See Giliker and Beckwith, supra n. 121, at pp. 50 and 66.

Applied to the medical context, this change may provide more recognition of the interests of family members. First, imposing a duty of care on doctors to relatives may lead to improvement in professional standards. For example, if relatives are informed about the patient's medical condition they may be willing to help to diagnose the patient more accurately by submitting themselves to genetic tests. Second, it may improve public health. For example, warning a daughter of a breast cancer patient that she should undergo genetic testing to know whether she is at risk may lead to the prevention of the disease if she decided to undergo prophylactic mastectomy or to submit to frequent and close surveillance. Third, although imposing a duty on doctors to relatives may cause additional financial costs (genetic tests, doctor appointments, etc.) it may avert extra expenses, such as rearing a disabled child, which may be inflicted if the relatives are not informed. The costs in informing and testing the relatives may be inexpensive comparing with those needed to support a disabled child. As for the contention that imposing a duty may lead to a flood of claims and to professional defensive conduct, these arguments are yet to be empirically tested.[196]   But even if a duty of care is recognised the courts will still have other means to control the flow of claims. Passing the duty level does not promise the relatives success in their claim. They will still have to prove breach and causation.

Furthermore, recognition of the interests of the individual vis-à-vis the state is reflected by positive arguments which promote the imposition of a duty of care. These arguments may provide the ground for the change in attitude to family members.

3.7.3 Positive Policy Arguments in Establishing a Duty of Care

Not only have the courts mitigated the influence of the traditional policy arguments, they have also provided other considerations in favour of the imposition of a duty of care. First, the courts held that the starting point in any discussion about policy is that wrongs should be remedied and that only strong counter–arguments can override it.[197] Next, *Osman v UK* highlights that the seriousness of the harm and the gravity of the breach are valid arguments in consideration of the imposition of a duty of care.[198]   A duty could be imposed on doctors when the relatives suffered a genetic disorder (serious harm) due to their

---

[196]   See Deakin, Johnston and Markesinis, supra n. 54, at p. 148; Markesinis B., "Plaintiff's tort law or defendant's tort law? Is the House of Lords moving towards a synthesis?" (2001) 9 *Tort Law Journal* 168. Hartshorne J., Smith N., Everton R., "*Caparo* under fire: A study into the effects upon the fire service of liability in negligence" (2000) 61 *MLR* 502, indicate that the courts rely upon prediction and that they should shift their approach and rely on empirical data.

[197]   *X v Bedfordshire* [1995] 2 AC 633, [1995] 3 All ER 355, 380.

[198]   See Monti, supra n. 174, at p. 759; and *Phelps v Hillingdon LBC* [2000] 4 All ER 504, 534.

failure to inform them (gravity of breach). Undoubtedly, this reflects a wider perspective that takes into account not only the doctor's undertaking of responsibility but the particular circumstances of each case. It implies that if doctors are grossly negligent they should bear the responsibility whether or not they assume responsibility to the relatives. Finally, the argument that non–liability would send an adverse message to society can be applied to the area of genetics. Taking as an example the situation where the co-operation of the relatives is required to confirm the patient's diagnosis, their willingness to help the patient may be discouraged if they know that they will not be entitled to receive the information gained about the patient.

Yet the argument that the seriousness of the harm and the gravity of the risk should be taken into account is based on a narrow ground. It immediately brings to mind the utilitarian principle of prevention of harm to others. If the courts' primary concern is avoiding a situation where people are seriously harmed by the negligent conduct of professionals, prevention of harm is indeed the most important policy consideration of all. However, as the next two chapters will indicate, doctors and patients may have other considerations than those discussed in the courts when deciding whether or not to disclose information to family members.

To sum up, the discussion about policy considerations does not support entirely the assumption that the courts rely on liberal–individualistic conceptions. Rather, it presents a shift from a paternalistic approach, where the courts upheld the authorities' conduct, to a utilitarian model, where prevention of harm to others is prominent. A liberal discourse has come to prevail only recently, when the courts began to realise that individuals are entitled to choose freely how to exercise their rights, and that those rights are at least as powerful as the authorities' discretion to take decision. However, the trend in the courts to examine violations of fundamental human rights as recognised in the European Convention is limited to the patient alone. As the Court of Appeal recently held, the parents could not win a claim against their child's doctor owing to the possibility of conflict of interests, which led the court to hold that the doctors in such cases owe a duty only to the individual patient.[199] From a reading of the decisions of the courts which examine whether there was interference with the rights recognised in the Convention (especially articles 3 and 8) the impression is that the courts perceived the children (patients) and their parents (relatives) as separate individuals with conflicting rights and interests, and not as a community concerned to safeguard its unity and to promote its common good.

In any event, whether the courts' approach is paternalistic, utilitarian, or liberal, they focus on a limited range of *legal* arguments. However, as Jones suggests,[200] the discussion in this context is not confined to its legal aspects. There are other considerations set in social dimensions that should be considered as well. Such considerations may include, for example, the influence of the social background in

---

[199] *D v East Berkshire Community Health NHS Trust* [2004] 2 WLR 58 (hereafter: "*D*").
[200] Jones M., *Textbook on Torts*, London, Blackstone Press (7th edn., 2000), 43.

which the individual lives: it is difficult to ignore the horrific familial circumstances under which the claimants had to live in the cases of W and X. Still, the Court of Appeal in W and the House of Lords in X could not find a way to rectify the social injustices that those claimants had to face. Instead, they focused on artificial legal conceptions, failing to consider the significance of the relationship within the families and its implications for the authorities' legal liability to the claimants.

Alternatively, the House of Lords in W attempted to present a family–based approach. In that case the court apparently saw the children and their parents as one family that suffered from the abuse of a fostered child. Imposing a duty of care on the local authority to the children but not to their parents (as the Court of Appeal held) seemed artificial and arbitrary. In addition, it sent a clear message to family members that their interests were not fully valued and appreciated. By contrast, the decision of the House of Lords appreciated the influence of the close relationship between parents and children and the trauma parents experienced when their children are treated unfairly by the state. The House of Lords was right in perceiving W as a familial case and not as two separate individual claims. We will have to wait and see whether the courts follow this approach in future cases. The decision in D is not encouraging in this respect. Yet the view taken in this chapter is that the approach expressed in the House of Lords in W should be applied to other child abuse cases, especially those where the child is negligently taken into care. English law should find a mechanism whereby the harm caused to the parents is recognised when the professional is negligent. The flow of claims in this regard in the last few years teaches us that professionals in this area could be more cautious when intervening in the family's life.

However, one may ask what a family–based approach implies in the context of genetics. Does it mean that the doctor will be reluctant to respect the decision of the individual patient not to inform the relatives because it undermines the interests of the family? Does it promote the interests of the family as a whole, and not those of the individuals who comprise it? After all, if doctors are required to be legally aware of the interests of family members when genetic information is communicated to the patient, the interests of the family may be preferred to those of the patient.

It should be stressed that the purpose of emphasising relationships when the imposition of a duty of care is considered is not to promote the interests of the family as a whole at the expense of the individual's right, but to integrate into English law a social dimension that is currently absent. This does not imply rejecting altogether patient's rights, but to add that patient autonomy is reciprocal and collaborative. Thus, when the interests of both the patient and family members are compromised by professionals or public bodies, promoting a communitarian approach will facilitate a just solution. However, when familial tension arises, and the doctor faces a serious dilemma, the task is to find a mechanism that combines the attractive liberal and communitarian conceptions while rejecting their pitfalls.

The questions of whether and how the law can formulate such a mechanism will be discussed in Chapter 6.

3.8 Conclusion

In this chapter the state of English tort law was examined. As indicated, the circumstances where a duty of care is imposed on doctors or patients to family members are limited. A closer look revealed that future developments in the legal position may change its existing attitude to family members. Be that as it may, the central argument advanced in this chapter was that the law has to look at the doctor–patient relationship through communitarian eyes. If this is accepted other arguments beyond the legal will become relevant, most prominently the views of doctors, patients, and the public at large.

However, another principal issue the courts discuss in the context of genetics (as well as in other medical law cases) is the doctor's duty of confidentiality. This issue, at least potentially, is the most powerful barrier in determining the scope of doctors' *legal* and *ethical* duties to the relatives; and it provides patients with the discretion to decide who will have access to their medical information. This important issue deserves a separate discussion, to be conducted in the next chapter.

Chapter 4

Medical Confidentiality and Genetic Privacy

4.1 Introduction

The issue of the flow of genetic information from doctors and patients to relatives involves, as was mentioned earlier, two possible conflicts: first, there is the tension between the patient's refusal to disclose information to others and the relatives' interest to be informed; second, there is a tension between the patient's desire to share information and the relatives' interest in not knowing it.[1] In the literature the first conflict is labelled the *right to know*, the second the *right not to know*.

A principal issue in the conflict of the *right to know* is medical confidentiality. It is well–established that doctors owe a duty of confidentiality to their patients and that only exceptional circumstances justify breach of the patient's right and disclosure to other third parties. This right enables patients to decide who will have access to their medical information, and it prohibits doctors from revealing it without consent. Confidentiality affects both the doctor–relatives and the patient–relatives relationships for it bars relatives from fulfilling their interest in gaining medical information.

Confidentiality, however, is less prominent in the second conflict of the *right not to know*. The relatives who refuse to know genetic information cannot rely on this principle because it does not help them not to receive information. It gives the relatives means to control the information they gain but it cannot bar others, such as the doctor or the patient, from communicating it to them without their consent. In this context, other conceptions, such as autonomy and privacy, are more relevant.

The existence of these two conflicts divides this chapter into two parts. In the first part the conflict of the right to know will be examined. It begins with a description of the legal and ethical sources of the right to confidentiality. This is followed by an analysis of the circumstances in which breach of confidentiality

---

[1]   Certain other conflicts are not discussed thoroughly in this book, for example, the tension between the patient's right not to know genetic information and the relatives' interest in obtaining genetic information, and the patient's interest to communicate to the doctor his or her family's medical history which may reveal details about the relatives they do not want others to know.

may be justified especially in the area of genetics. Next, the question of whether doctors and patients owe a duty to warn relatives will be dealt with. This examination of medical confidentiality in the area of genetics will be viewed within the theoretical framework presented in Chapter 1. Hence, the existing approach to medical confidentiality will be reviewed in light of the assumption that English law and ethics are based on liberal–individualistic conceptions and express a patient–centred approach. This will be followed by the provision of a different perspective to confidentiality.

The second part of this chapter will deal with the conflict of the right not to know. First, the question of whether there is such a right will be discussed; and second, if such a right does exist what are the mechanisms to protect it. Finally, it will be argued that other considerations should be taken into account when dealing with the relatives' right not to know.

4.2 The Right to Know

4.2.1 Respect for Medical Confidentiality

The grounds for the doctor's duty of confidentiality are set in the areas of medical law and medical ethics. Legally, the courts do not question that doctors owe a duty of confidence to their patients. In *W v Egdell* Scott J states that the question is not whether the doctor owes a duty of confidentiality to the patient but what is its scope.[2] Hence, the courts do not pay great attention to the moral ground of this duty.

Ethically, it is possible to identify four different grounds for this duty. The first is based on a utilitarian principle. Confidentiality encourages patients to approach doctors and communicate to them the information needed to obtain an accurate diagnosis. It enables patients to seek medical help without the suspicion that their most intimate secrets will be revealed.[3] By contrast, if a confidential environment is not provided patients may be deterred from approaching doctors and this will threaten the promotion of public health. Second, this duty enables patients to exercise their autonomy. The entitlement of patients to decide who will have access to their medical information reflects their ability to lead their lives according to their personal choice.[4] Third, confidentiality is part of the principle of

---

[2]   *W v Egdell* [1989] 1 All ER 1089, 1102; *X v Y* [1988] 2 All ER 648.

[3]   Stern K., "Confidentiality and medical records" in Kennedy I., Grubb A. (eds.) *Principles of Medical Law*, Oxford, Oxford University Press (1998), 496; Montgomery J., *Health Care Law*, Oxford, Oxford University Press (2nd edn., 2003), 252; Beauchamp T., Childress J., *Principles of Biomedical Ethics*, New York, Oxford University Press (5th edn. 2001), 304.

[4]   Mason J., McCall Smith R., Laurie G., *Law and Medical Ethics*, London, Butterworths (6th edn., 2002), 239.

privacy, which may be different from autonomy. In this context confidentiality protects the patients' privacy from invasion, preventing exposure of their personal matters to others.[5]   Fourth, medical confidentiality is based on the close relationship between the doctor and the patient. In this relationship patients trust doctors and expect them to keep the information in confidence. A failure to do so implies not only a breach of the agreement that the information will be kept in secret but also a violation of the patient's trust which is the foundation on which the doctor–patient relationship is built.[6]

When English courts discuss the importance of medical confidentiality they rely on these moral arguments. First, a utilitarian ground is explicitly adopted.[7]   In *X v Y* Rose J stated that preservation of confidentiality is the only way of protecting public health, enabling patients to come forward and be counselled.[8]   Next, the trust between doctors and patients was pointed out in *A–G v Guardian Newspapers (No 2)*.[9]   In that case Lord Griffith stated that the right to confidentiality was based on a moral principle of loyalty and Lord Goff added that it arises when the parties *agree* that information disclosed will be kept in confidence.[10]   When dealing with medical issues the patient's interest in privacy emerges.[11]   A possible explanation is the incorporation of the European Convention on Human Rights into English law. The courts began to examine the implications of the right to privacy (Article 8) when claimants argued for non–disclosure of personal information to others.[12]

The terminology used in the courts when dealing with confidentiality leads to the conclusion that they emphasise two liberal conceptions: the patient's autonomous right to self–determination and a utilitarian principle which aims to promote public health. The emphasis on these two aspects reflects an individualistic perception of patient autonomy. The patient is as an individual who has to assert his or her rights vis–à–vis others.

However, although the courts and professional codes of ethics underscore the importance of medical confidentiality they accept that it is not absolute. There are circumstances which justify the breach of the patient's right to confidentiality. Examining these justifications especially in the area of genetics will provide an insight into the extent that the relatives' interests in genetic information are recognised.

---

[5]   See Beauchamp and Childress, supra n. 3, at p. 304; Montgomery, supra n. 3, at p. 252.

[6]   Stern, supra n. 3, at p. 497; and Jones M., *Medical Negligence*, London, Blackstone Press (1996), 80.

[7]   The General Medical Council, *Confidentiality: Protecting and Providing Information*, London, General Medical Council (2000), para 1 (hereafter: the GMC).

[8]   *X v Y* [1988] 2 All ER 648, 653; see also *R v Department of Health* [1999] 4 All ER 196.

[9]   *A–G v Guardian Newspapers (No 2)* [1988] 3 WLR 776.

[10]   Ibid., at pp. 794 and 805.

[11]   *R v Department of Health* [2000] 1 All ER 786, at p. 796.

[12]   *Re R (a child) (adoption: disclosure)* [2001] 1 FCR 238; *R v Chief Constable of the North Wales Police* [1999] QB 396; *Woolgar v Chief Constable of Sussex Police* [1999] 3 All ER 604.

4.2.2 The Limitations of Medical Confidentiality

Both law and medical ethics employ the term 'public interest' when examining whether or not to justify breach of medical confidentiality.[13] However, as Graeme Laurie argues this term can be used for opposite purposes: either to protect medical confidentiality or to justify its breach.[14] Nevertheless, analysing the 'public interest' exception as expressed in courts and in professional codes of ethics can enlighten us as to the philosophical perception that underlies decisions in the area of genetics.

A useful starting point in this context is the guidance of the General Medical Council.[15] The courts rely on it when discussing issues of medical confidentiality.[16] The GMC allows doctors to reveal to other third parties the patient's medical information when it can avert a serious harm or injury to them.[17] Information can be disclosed after doctors 'weigh the possible harm (both to the patient and the overall trust between doctors and patients) against the benefits which are likely to arise from the release of information.'[18] When the costs and benefits are being weighed, two considerations should be taken into account: first, the third party must be exposed 'to risk of death or serious harm', and second, disclosure cannot be made to the public at large but only to 'an appropriate person or authority.'[19] The GMC makes it clear that preventing a risk of serious harm to others is the paramount consideration that would justify breach of the patient's right to confidentiality. However, the question of how serious the harm must be to justify disclosure emerges in this context. Reviewing courts' decisions may provide an answer.[20]

---

[13]   The patient's common law right to confidentiality can be lawfully breached. See section 60 of the *Health and Social Care Act* 2001.

[14]   Laurie G., "Challenging the medical–legal norms: The role of autonomy, confidentiality, and privacy in protecting individual and familial group rights in genetic information" (2001) 22 *Journal of Legal Medicine* 1, 16 (hereafter: Challenging the medical–legal norms).

[15]   See GMC, supra n. 7.

[16]   In *W v Egdell* [1989] 1 All ER 1089 Scott J starts his discussion by examining the GMC guidance.

[17]   See GMC, supra n. 7, at para 14, 18.

[18]   Ibid., at para 19.

[19]   Ibid., at para 36.

[20]   Regarding the 'public interest' consideration, which justifies disclosure of confidential information, the NHS code of practice on confidentiality does not address genetic information specifically but states that in the medical context, prevention of serious harm justifies disclosure. See: Department of Health, *Confidentiality: NHS Code of Practice* (2003), www.doh.gov.uk/ipu/confiden. Yet as argued by Laing J., Grubb A., "Confidentiality and Data Protection", in Grubb A. (ed.), *Principles of Medical Law*, Oxford, Oxford University Press (2nd edn., 2004) at p. 573, the particular circumstances

The decisions in the few cases on this subject may shape the scope of the doctor's legal duty. In *W v Egdell* the claimant, who was detained in a secure hospital, appointed a psychiatrist to produce a report supporting his application to obtain a conditional discharge.[21] Since the psychiatrist opposed the transfer to a less secure hospital the claimant withdrew his application. After learning that the application had been withdrawn and that the hospital had not received the report the psychiatrist sent the report to the hospital, which forwarded it to the Home Office. The claimant sued the psychiatrist for breach of confidentiality.

Scott J at first instance held that doctors have two separate duties: one of confidentiality to the patient, the other to protect public health.[22] He held that the duty to the public required doctors to disclose to the authorities the result of their examination if public safety so required regardless of the patient's wishes. The Court of Appeal upheld Scott J's decision.[23] Bingham LJ held that decisions regarding release from a secure hospital should not be made unless the authorities are properly able to make an informed judgment. Therefore, if a psychiatrist becomes aware of information that leads him or her to fear that the authority's decision may be made on the basis of inadequate information and with a real risk to the public, he or she is entitled to take reasonable steps to inform the authority of his or her concern.

This decision was applied in *R v Crozier*.[24] In this case the appellant pleaded guilty to attempted murder of his sister following a dispute with her over the management of his dead wife's trust fund. He instructed a psychiatrist to examine his mental condition and to produce a report for the sentencing hearing. The psychiatrist took the view that the appellant should be put in a secure hospital for unlimited time. Therefore, the appellant did not give the report to the judge, and was sentenced to nine years in prison. During the sentencing hearing the psychiatrist learnt that his report was not forwarded to the judge and so he handed it to him. As a result the judge changed the sentence and ordered that the appellant should be put in a secure hospital for unlimited time. The appellant argued that in revealing the report the psychiatrist breached his confidence. The Court of Appeal upheld the psychiatrist's decision to disclose the report by applying the decision in *W v Egdell*.

In *Re C*[25] a mother withdrew her consent to give her child to adoption. The prospective adopters added to their application an affidavit sworn by the mother's GP describing her medical condition. The mother claimed that the doctor breached

---

in which the patient's right to confidentiality can be breached by the doctor are a question for the courts.

21 [1989] 1 All ER 1089 (CH D); [1990] 1 All ER 835 (CA) (hereafter: *W v Egdell*).

22 [1989] 1 All ER 1089, 1104–105.

23 [1990] 1 All ER 835; However, the Court of Appeal held that the doctor's conflicting duties are both situated in the public interest. See Sir Stephen Brown P, at p. 846.

24 [1991] Crim LR 138; (1990) 8 BMLR 128 (hereafter: *R v Crozier*).

25 [1991] 2 FLR 478; [1991] 7 BMLR 138 (hereafter: *Re C*).

her confidence and therefore this evidence should not be admitted. The Court of Appeal rejected her claim relying on two legal grounds. First, it followed *W v Egdell* holding that the court should receive all relevant information that is helpful for its decision. Since the affidavit was highly relevant it was held that the judge at first instance was right to admit it. Second, the court held that children's welfare is a matter of great public interest, which outweighs the public interest in maintaining confidentiality.

The decisions in these cases can lead to the following observations. First, they indicate that the most prominent justification for breaching the patient's right to confidentiality is the prevention of risk of *physical* harm to others.[26] The risk to the public in *W v Egdell* and *R v Crozier* and the risk to the child in *Re C* concerned physical health. Therefore, when doctors disclose confidential information to prevent risk of serious physical harm to others the courts are likely to justify such a conduct. However, these cases show that the risk of physical harm to others should be real but not imminent. Though the risk that the two mentally–ill patients posed to others in *W v Egdell* and in *R v Crozier* was, according to the medical evaluation, real, the danger to the public was not immediate because they both were held in a secure institutions and a full discharge was not automatic.

Furthermore, these decisions emphasise that state authorities can acquire the most adequate and updated information available. Bingham LJ established this principle in *W v Egdell* and it was applied in *R v Crozier* and *Re C*. Recently, the courts reiterated this point.[27] This leads to the conclusion that the courts prefer a free flow of information between governmental bodies to an effective duty of confidentiality. It seems that the balance the courts strike is withholding the information from the public at large but informing those who monitor public health and safety.[28]

The combination of these observations reflects a paternalistic approach, where the patient's right to confidentiality can be considerably compromised by state authorities. *W v Egdell*, *R v Crozier*, and *Re C* present a conflict not between a patient and another individual who needs to know material information but between individual patients and state authorities whose role is to protect the public. In this conflict, the interest of state authorities prevails. They interfere in the individual's rights not to prevent an imminent and grave risk to others, but simply to gain more relevant information before making a decision. For example, the public in *W v Egdell* did not face immediate and serious danger. The patient would

---

[26] The risk is only to physical harm and not to any other tangible harm. See Stern, supra n. 2, at p. 504; Brazier M., *Medicine, Patients and the Law*, London, Penguin (3rd edn., 2003), 68; Laing and Grubb, supra n. 20, at p. 572.

[27] *Woolgar v Chief Constable of Sussex Police* [1999] 3 All ER 604 and *R v Chief Constable of North Wales Police* [1999] QB 396.

[28] It is possible to apply this analysis to *X v Y* [1988] 2 All ER 648 as well, where the hospital as the doctors' employer knew the information but was not allowed to disclose it to the public.

have had to undergo a careful inspection including additional tests before he could have been fully discharged. The risk to the public in *R v Crozier* was even less imminent because the patient was sentenced to nine years in prison even before the doctor breached his duty of confidence. Consequently, it seems that patients' right to confidentiality is not a 'trump' card when they endanger others, but a low barrier to those who are responsible for the protection of public health.

In addition, this position expresses a utilitarian approach, which focuses on the individual patient. It is utilitarian because in a conflict between the patient's right to confidentiality and the relatives' right to know the courts and the GMC justify disclosure only when the benefits to the relatives outweigh the advantages in protecting the patient's right to confidentiality. In addition, the courts see only two parties, the individual patient and the public, as if the public is a uniform entity, not composed of individuals, communities, and social relationships. For example, in *R v Crozier* the court employed a 'public' terminology, holding that the patient was a threat to the public, while the psychiatrist who examined him stated that he was a threat to his family.[29] Thus, from the relatives' perspective the principle of prevention of harm is limited because their interests can be recognised only when they are at risk of real and serious physical harm. According to this position, other interests, such as the entitlement to make informed decisions, may not be considered.

Still, the approach taken in the European Court of Human Rights may improve the chances of family members to receive medical information in the future. The question in the English courts following the *Human Rights Act* 1998 is whether it changes the scope of the common law duty of confidentiality and whether it changes the legal attitude to disclosure to third parties. The most relevant Convention article, which deals with the protection of medical confidential information, is Article 8 which protects the individual's 'right to respect for his private and family life'. Yet as English law recognises, this right is not absolute and disclosure can be justified if it complies with the terms set in Article 8 (2), which holds that disclosure will be justified if it is in accordance with the law, necessary in a democratic society, and for the following public interests: public safety, the economic interests of the country, the prevention of crime, the protection of public health or morals, or the protection of rights and freedoms of others. As Laing and Grubb observe in the medical context, Article 8 requires a balance between the interest of the patient in confidentiality and the public interest in health.[30]

The guiding decision of the European Court in the context of medical confidential information is *Z v Finland*.[31] In that case the police took hold of medical records of an HIV patient when investigating her husband on several

---

[29] *R v Crozier* [1991] Crim LR 138; (1990) 8 BMLR 128; this contrast is observed in the headnote.

[30] See Laing and Grubb, supra n. 20, at p. 599.

[31] (1997) 25 EHRR 371; see also *MS v Sweden* (1997) 45 BMLR 133.

charges. At the husband's trial the patient's doctor was asked to present the patient's medical records. The European Court held that there was no breach of Article 8 as the breach of the patient's right was justified under the terms of Article 8 (2). In this case the European Court had to strike a balance between the patient's right to medical confidentiality and the public interest in prevention of crime and protection of freedoms of others. Commenting on this decision, Laing and Grubb argue that the European Court limits the scope of the patient's right to confidentiality substantially.[32] They argue that the justification to breach the patient's right to confidentiality under the Convention is wider than the justification to breach under English law.[33]

How do the English courts treat Article 8? In *W v Egdell* Bingham LJ admitted that Article 8 (2) raises the possibility where a public authority may legitimately breach the patient's right to confidentiality, holding that in the particular circumstances of the case before him the doctor acted in accordance with the law, and his conduct was necessary to protect public safety and to prevent crime.[34] Other cases express an approach which is compatible with the decision in *Z v Finland*. For example, the Court of Appeal recently justified disclosure to the patient's mother to enable her to seek legal advice.[35] In this case, Hale LJ expressed a familial approach, stating:

> There is a clear distinction between disclosure to the media with a view to publication to all and sundry and disclosure in confidence to those with a proper interest in having the information in question. We are concerned here only with the latter. The issue is only whether the circle should be widened from those professionals with whom this information has already been shared... to include the person who is probably closest to him in fact as well as in law and who has a statutory role in his future and to those professionally advising her.[36]

In the next chapters we shall deal with the distinction Hale LJ made between the attitude to family members and to other third parties in the context of confidentiality, but at this point suffice it to say that this decision enables family members to receive legal recognition in the decision–making process they are involved in, especially, as in this case, where the patient cannot make a decision independently. However, this decision does not address the particular context of disclosure of medical or genetic information of a competent adult patient to his or her relatives to enable them to make decisions about their health and general well–being.

---

32   See Laing and Grubb, supra n. 20, at p. 600, referring to Brazier, supra n. 26, at p. 80.
33   Ibid, at p. 600.
34   [1990] 1 All ER 835, 853.
35   *R (on the application of S) v Plymouth CC* [2002] 1 FLR 1177; *R v Chief Constable of the North Wales Police* [1998] 3 All ER 310; *Woolgar v Chief Constable of Sussex Police* [1999] 3 All ER 604.
36   Ibid, at para. 49.

Returning to the context of this study, stating that the patient's right to confidentiality 'ends where the public peril begins'[37] is not the end of the discussion. The next question is how this position applies to the area of genetics. In this context, there are differences between law and ethics. First, ethicists are not confined as the courts are to deal with circumstances of a particular case but they can consider other relevant factors. For example, ethicists and policy–makers are not limited to deal only with the doctor–relatives relationship, they can address the patient–relatives relationship as well. Second, unlike the courts, they do not restrict the discussion to the legal aspects of the issue but consider its social and moral implications as well.

Following these differences, the next section is divided into three categories. First, the application of the legal position to the area of genetics will be dealt with. Second, the position of ethical codes that specifically deal with confidentiality in genetics will be examined. This will be followed by an analysis of the view of leading commentators in this area. The discussion in the next section will help determine the attitude to family members when genetic information is available.

4.2.3 Preventing Harm to Others in the Area of Genetics

4.2.3.1 The law. How does the principle of prevention of harm to others apply to genetics? First, when the onset of a genetic disease can be avoided or an effective treatment is available a breach of confidence will most probably be justified.[38] There is no English case which directly deals with this issue. The only two American cases that discuss the relatives' right to know genetic information examine whether or not the doctor owes a duty to the relatives to breach the patient's right to confidentiality, but not whether the doctor is justified in breaching it.[39] Yet these two categories are distinct. While in the English cases mentioned above the patients sued the doctors because they disclosed the information, in the American cases the relatives sued the doctors for their failure to disclose. In the English cases the doctors had to explain why they breached confidentiality whereas in the American cases they had to explain why they did not.

As yet, many genetic diseases are not effectively treatable. Therefore, the principle of prevention of harm to others may be applied to multifactorial disorders where the potential causes of the disorder are not solely genetic but also environmental. As was mentioned in Chapter 2, changing a lifestyle may

---

[37] *Tarasoff v Regents of the University of California* (1976) 551 P 2d 334 (Cal Sup Ct), 345.

[38] Laurie G., "The most personal information of all: An appraisal of genetic privacy in the shadow of the human genome project" (1996) 10 *International Journal of Law, Policy & the Family* 74, 85.

[39] *Pate v Threlkel* (1995) 661 So.2d 278 (Fla Sup Ct) (hereafter: *Pate*); *Safer v The Estate of Pack* (1996) 677 A.2d 1188 (NJ Super A. D.) (hereafter: *Safer v Pack*).

minimise the risk of developing such a disorder.[40] Yet it is not clear whether disclosure of information in these circumstances is justifiable. Graeme Laurie argues that although changing a lifestyle may be beneficial, genetic tests that predict the patient's predisposition to these disorders are less reliable.[41] As a result, it is necessary to test a few relatives so as to obtain an accurate diagnosis, hence to breach the patient's right to confidentiality several times without knowing whether this will prevent the onset of the disease.

By arguing that the predictability of genetic tests does not justify breach of confidentiality Laurie overlooks another important aspect. This position bars the relatives from deciding whether they are willing to take the risk of having a genetic disorder or whether they wish to try to prevent it even when the chances are slim. In this respect, the relatives lose their ability to make free choices. Although disclosure of confidential information to relatives in multifactorial diseases may be ineffective medically, it will reflect respect for their autonomy. In addition, any decision which favours patients' right to confidentiality over the relatives' right to be informed will have to face a possible adverse impact on the familial relationship once the relatives discover that they had a possibility – even a remote one – to avoid a genetic disease.

To conclude, the law limits the possibilities of relatives receiving genetic information even in the narrow context of physical harm as numerous genetic diseases have no effective treatment.[42] Since in many cases the information does not enable the relatives to avert the onset of the disease completely breach of confidentiality will not be justified. Yet the question remains whether other interests of family members justify breach of confidentiality. The courts have not as yet dealt with this question. An answer may be found in professional codes of ethics or medical guidance, which play an important part in formulating doctors' and patients' conduct. The next section will focus on these codes.

4.2.3.2 Professional guidance. Confidentiality in the area of genetics yielded several reports. Unlike the courts, these reports take a wider perspective, referring to the patient–relatives relationship and to the various interests the relatives have in genetic information beyond that of physical harm. Although these reports do not impose any legal duty on doctors or patients they shed light on the ethical approach to relatives.

---

[40] Suter S., "Whose genes are these anyway?: Familial conflicts over access to genetic information" (1993) 91 *Michigan Law Journal* 1854, 1903.

[41] See Laurie, supra n. 38, at pp. 86–87.

[42] However, medical intervention is available in some genetic disorders. Examples are: childhood screening for familial adenomatous polyposis (FAP); prophylactic mastectomy for inherited breast cancer; prescription of beta blockers for Long QT syndrome which may cause cardiac arrest.

The Nuffield Council addresses the issue of confidentiality in genetics.[43] The Council sees the patient as responsible for the relatives' interests. It holds that a responsible patient would always wish to disclose genetic information to the relatives.[44] Although the Council does not discuss it specifically, it seems not to confine the relevance of the information to the relatives' interest in avoiding physical harm but to extend it to any decision that the relatives may have to take in the future.[45] Furthermore, the Council takes a familial approach, suggesting that patients should consider the relatives' position. For example, patients should take into account the possibility that relatives are unaware that they have taken genetic tests and therefore they have to consider whether the relatives may wish to know this information and in what manner it should be communicated to them.

This view is more family–based than the legal position, for it requires the patient to be aware of the relatives' psychological state when he or she communicates information to them. Despite this approach the Council does not impose any duty on patients to disclose but leaves the decision to their discretion. Ultimately, though, it seems to prefer the patient's interests to the relatives'. The Council argues that since patients are those who approach the doctor first, they win exclusive control over the information. Undoubtedly, this view presents a patient–centred approach, for it maintains the autonomy of the individual patient while overlooking the autonomy of the relatives.

The Council's view manifests itself when examining the doctor's duty of confidentiality. First, the Council recommends that in the area of genetics medical confidentiality should be protected 'as far as possible'.[46] Second, it justifies breach of confidentiality without the patient's consent only in exceptional circumstances. When specifying these circumstances the Council is inconsistent. On the one hand it employs a utilitarian principle of prevention of harm to the relatives, but on the other hand it takes into account the impact of the information on the familial relationship when the father discovers that he is not the biological parent. In this context, the Council takes an ethics–of–care perspective protecting the mother and the child from a possibly angry father. Thus, it attempts to secure the rights and position of the weaker parties in the family.[47]

---

[43] Nuffield Council on Bioethics, *Genetic Screening*, London, Nuffield Council on Bioethics (1993) (hereafter: the Nuffield Council).
[44] Ibid., at p. 49, para 5.25.
[45] Ibid.
[46] Ibid., at p. 43, para 5.7; see also: The Advisory Committee on Genetic Testing, *Report on Genetic Testing for Late Onset Disorders*, Department of Health (1998), at p. 12.
[47] See the Nuffield Council, supra n. 43, at pp. 50–51; yet the House of Commons Science and Technology Committee, Third Report, Human Genetics: The Science and its Consequence, Vol. 1, Report and Minutes, London, HMSO (1995) saw the patient's right to confidentiality as 'paramount', stating, at para. 227: 'If genetic tests are desirable for individual or public health reasons people should be able to take them without the fear that their genetic constitution would be revealed to others'.

The British Medical Association addresses the issue of genetic information too.[48] From the outset it seems to presents a wider view as it considers harm to choice and not only physical harm.[49] More importantly, when discussing patient–relatives relationships the BMA recognises both the significance of familial relationships and the autonomy of the patient.[50] It acknowledges that patients need support from their relatives, but at the same time it holds that the final decision whether or not to disclose medical confidential information belongs to the patient.[51] This appreciation of the patient's right on the one hand and of the involvement of family members on the other leads to the conclusion that the BMA strikes the right balance between patient autonomy and relatives' interests.

Therefore, the perception of patient autonomy taken by the BMA is relational. On the one hand the BMA stresses that medical information is controlled by the individual patient, who can decide whether or not to inform the relatives. On the other hand it also states that patients have to consider seriously the interests of the relatives, as disclosure within the family can improve the familial relationship.[52] Compared to the other interpretations of relational autonomy, as expressed by Hardwig or the Lindemann–Nelsons in Chapter 1, the BMA's perception is closer to that of the Lindemann–Nelsons, who believe that although family members should be involved in the decision–making process, the decision is that of the individual patient.[53]

However, the tendency of the BMA to prefer the patient's interests to the relatives' emerges when it discusses the doctor's duty of confidentiality. Though the BMA admits that some geneticists see the family as the unit of care, it nevertheless asserts that the doctor's duty of confidentiality *to the individual patient* is very important and can be breached only when this is legally required or there is an *overriding public interest* in such a step.[54] Considering the justifications for breaching patients' right to confidentiality, the BMA states that disclosure would be allowed in exceptional circumstances when serious harm or death to others can be avoided. When formulating the criteria for breaching the patient's right to confidentiality the BMA instructs the doctor to consider the severity of the disorder, the availability of preventative measures, the ability of genetic testing to predict the onset of the disease, the level of harm caused by withholding the information, and the patient's reason for refusing to disclose. Undoubtedly, by this

[48] British Medical Association, *Human Genetics: Choice and Responsibility*, Oxford, Oxford University Press (1998) (hereafter: BMA).
[49] Ibid., at p. 15.
[50] Ibid., at p. 21.
[51] Ibid., at p. 22.
[52] Ibid., at p. 24.
[53] Lindemann-Nelson H., Lindemann-Nelson J., *The Patient in the Family*, New York, Routledge (1995), 151.
[54] See the BMA, supra n. 48., at p. 69 (my emphasis).

approach the relatives' status is limited because other interests, which do not concern avoidance of physical harm, are not fully recognised.[55]

Finally, it is important to examine the view of patients and their families. The Genetic Interest Group, a national alliance of organisations that supports families and individuals affected by genetic disorders, published a report on confidentiality.[56] The report discusses the patient–relatives relationship only briefly, concentrating instead on the doctor–relatives relationship. Here the GIG adopts a cost–benefit evaluation, considering the nature and the seriousness of the disorder and whether it is treatable or not. However, it reflects a perspective wider than the legal position, requiring doctors to think about the anxiety genetic information may cause to the relatives.[57] The GIG goes beyond the limited interest of prevention of physical harm, considering the psychological impact disclosure may have on the relatives.

To conclude, it can be argued that the majority of professional guidelines in this area take a wider perspective than the courts. However, at core the ethical view remains patient–centred, as it furnishes the patient the ability to control exclusively the information received from the doctor. This was recently reiterated by the Human Genetics Commission, which concluded that disclosure of genetic information to family members may occasionally be justified where a patient refuses to give consent and *'the benefit of disclosure substantially outweighs the patient's claim to confidentiality'*.[58]

4.2.3.3 Academic commentary. The review so far indicates that neither the courts nor the professional guidelines discuss the various interests of the relatives in genetic information. However, a wider discussion is conducted in the legal and bioethical academic literature.[59] Examining this literature will indicate whether other arguments beyond the legal ones are employed. This examination will be best conducted in light of relatives' interests in knowing genetic information. Recall that patients and relatives have two central interests in this context. First, they want to avoid any kind of tangible harm (physical, psychological, and financial); second, they want to make informed choices in light of as much information as possible.

---

[55] Consideration of the patient's reason for refusal to disclose may involve the social relationship in the background of his or her decision not to disclose. Nevertheless, the impact of the decision on the various interests of the family members is not explicitly recognised.

[56] Genetic Interest Group, *Confidentiality and Medical Genetics* (1998); www.gig.org.uk/policy (hereafter: the GIG).

[57] Ibid., at p. 14.

[58] Human Genetics Commission, *Inside Information: Balancing the Interests in the Use of Personal Genetic Data*, London, Department of Health (2002), Ch. 3, para. 3.68 (my italics).

[59] See for example the discussion conducted in (2001) 1 (3) *The American Journal of Bioethics* 1–35.

As for physical harm, consensus exists among commentators that if disclosure can avert the physical harm caused by a genetic disorder it is legally and morally justified.[60] With psychological harm the position is more complicated. It was already argued in Chapter 3 that relatives may want to receive genetic information so to be prepared mentally for the onset of the disease. But as Laurie argues, an adverse psychological reaction can also occur when the relatives wish not to know the information but are informed nevertheless. Studies noted in Chapter 2 indicate that suicide rates among people who know they have a terminal and incurable genetic disease are higher than among the general population.[61] Therefore, it is necessary to know in advance whether or not the relatives wish to know genetic information. However, if the relatives do not express any views about it the doctor cannot ask them whether or not they wish to know. Approaching them will immediately negate the relatives' potential wish not to be informed.[62] Since the doctor cannot ask the relatives whether or not they wish to know, he or she cannot be certain that disclosure will prevent psychological harm. The conclusion that commentators such as Laurie draw from this is that breaching a patient's right to confidentiality is not always justified.[63]

However, the view that prevention of psychological harm does not justify breach of confidentiality indicates that commentators focus on narrow conceptions and are not open to other considerations. The research that will be discussed in Chapter 5[64] indicates that, despite the adverse psychological impact genetic information may have on people, the majority of patients prefer to receive information and not to remain ignorant[65] because they take into account other considerations, such as the relatives' interest in the information and their responsibility to their family members as well as the effect on their relationship with family members even when disclosure cannot prevent the disease.[66]

---

[60] Stern, supra n. 3, at p. 504 and 516; Beauchamp and Childress, supra n. 3, at p. 312; Mason, McCall-Smith and Laurie, supra n. 4, at p. 214.

[61] See Chapter 2, at para 2.1.2.1.

[62] This is a fundamental point in the discussion whether relatives have a *right not to know* and I will address this issue in detail in section 4.3.

[63] Laurie G., "Protecting and promoting privacy in an uncertain world: further defences of ignorance and the right not to know", (2000) 7 *European Journal of Health Law* 185; Laurie G., supra n. 14, at p. 40; but see: Bottis M., "Comment on a view favouring ignorance of genetic information: confidentiality, autonomy, beneficence and the right not to know" (2000) 7 *European Journal of Health Law* 173, 180.

[64] See Chapter 5, part 5.5.2.2.

[65] Schattner A., Tal M., "Truth telling and patient autonomy: The patient's point of view" (2002) 113 (1) *The American Journal of Medicine* 66.

[66] See, for example: Hallowell N., "Doing the right thing: Genetic risk and responsibility" (1999) 21 (5) *Sociology of Health & Illness* 597; Hallowell N. et al., "Surveillance or surgery? A description of the factors that influence high risk premenopausal women's decisions about prophylactic oophorectomy" (2001) 38 *Journal of Medical Genetics* 683.

Furthermore, as indicated in Chapter 2, by undergoing genetic testing patients can have positive as well as negative experiences, and it is difficult to predict, even in patients who seem emotionally vulnerable, the circumstances where one kind exceeds the other.[67] Yet, the commentators seem to express a narrow approach, concentrating on the utilitarian mechanism of prevention of harm. They are reluctant to abandon this view, which is too crude to deal with the complex issues emerged when genetic information becomes available.

If prevention of psychological harm cannot justify breach of confidentiality, does prevention of economic loss justify it? Sonia Suter seemingly answers this question in the affirmative when disclosure can prevent begetting a disabled child.[68] Other commentators answer this question in the negative even when the doctor considers communication of information to the patient's spouse. Ngwena and Chadwick stress that in these circumstances disclosure is not the only means to avoid financial loss so it would not be justifiable to breach confidentiality. Although the costs of rearing a disabled child can be prevented by disclosure before a reproductive decision is made,[69] they can also be avoided by other means, such as terminating pregnancy or undergoing antenatal testing.[70] In addition, as Laurie suggests, disclosure will not assure prevention of the extra financial costs in all cases for there may be people who prefer to keep a pregnancy even when the risk to the foetus is highly probable.[71]

Undoubtedly, the approach taken by these commentators is individualistic. It does not grant sufficient consideration to the social relationship between the patient and his or her partner but perceives them as separate individuals whose life together is ruled primarily by their personal interests and not by their shared goals. By this position the patient can withhold from his or her partner relevant information when they both are contemplating one of the most important decisions in life, that of reproduction.

Lastly, the commentators refer to the possibility that protecting the patient's right to confidentiality will harm the relatives' right to make informed choices. Although withholding genetic information from the relatives may not result in tangible damage, it may be as important because it will enable them to lead their lives as they choose. However, ethicists are sceptical whether harm to choice can

---

[67] Meiser B., et al., "Psychological impact of genetic testing in women from high–risk breast cancer families" (2002) 38 *European Journal of Cancer* 2025, 2029, See also Chapter 2, part 2.1.2.

[68] See Suter, supra, n. 40, at p. 1883.

[69] For recent cases, which discuss the doctors' failures to detect a congenital abnormality see: *Hardman v Amin* [2000], Lloyd's Rep Med 487; *Rand v East Dorset HA* [2000] Lloyd's Rep Med 181; and for a failure to detect a genetic disorder in Scotland see: *Anderson v Forth Valley HA* 1998 SCLR 97.

[70] Ngwena C., Chadwick R., "Genetic information and the duty of confidentiality: Ethics and law" (1993) 1 *Medical Law International* 73, 86.

[71] See Laurie, supra n. 38, at p. 87; such a case was *Parkinson v St James & Seacroft University Hospital* [2002] QB 266.

justify breach of confidentiality. Ngwena and Chadwick argue that it is not clear why the relatives' interest in making informed decisions should enjoy higher priority than patients' entitlement to choose who will have access to their personal medical information.[72] Undoubtedly, this view reflects a patient–centred approach. Ngwena and Chadwick acknowledge the interests of both parties but they favour those of the patients because they have already approached the doctor and thus possess the right to confidentiality, which the relatives do not.

The conclusion one can draw so far is that leading commentators in the UK adopt a liberal approach. Neither Laurie nor Ngwena and Chadwick hide their personal view.[73] They rely on a liberal perception of the individual and on a utilitarian mechanism of prevention of harm to others.

Even in this liberal discourse it is possible to hold conversely that the interest in making informed decisions dictates a presumption of disclosure in the area of genetics. Rosamond Rhodes, for example, argues that gaining information is essential for people's ability to choose, because relevant information can change their decision and lead them to act differently from the way they might have acted without it.[74] Rhodes relies on Kant, arguing that since individuals rule themselves they have an obligation to make informed and careful decisions. She argues that people must receive information that a reasonable person would wish to have in the situation.[75] It follows that if patients withhold information from the relatives they obstruct the relatives from fulfilling their obligation to know.

However, this Kantian argument does not lead Rhodes to qualify the doctor's duty of confidentiality; on the contrary: Rhodes argues that this duty should be rigorously maintained because it helps promote public health.[76] Rhodes is not willing to qualify the patient's right to confidentiality. She simply divides the discussion into two parts: the patient–relatives relationship and the doctor–patient relationship. While in the former Rhodes imposes a moral duty on the patient to disclose genetic information to family members, in the latter she argues that doctors' disclosure without patients' consent can be conducted only in exceptional

---

[72] See Ngwena and Chadwick, supra n. 70, at p. 86.

[73] Ngwena and Chadwick, ibid., at p. 89 advocate this position explicitly, while Laurie does not conceal his ethical preference either. See: Laurie G., supra n. 14, at p. 15.

[74] Rhodes R., "Genetic links, family ties and social bonds: Rights and responsibilities in the face of genetic knowledge" (1998) 23 (1) *Journal of Medicine and Philosophy* (1998) 10, 17.

[75] Ibid., at p. 18; For the opposite view see: Takala T., Hayry M., "Genetic ignorance, moral obligations and social duties" (2000) 25 (1) *Journal of Medicine and Philosophy* 107; For a reply see: Rhodes R., "Autonomy, Respect and Genetic Information Policy: A reply to Tuija Takala and Matti Hayry" (2000) 25 (1) *Journal of Medicine and Philosophy* 114.

[76] Rhodes R., "Confidentiality, genetic information and the physician–patient relationship" (2001) 1 (3) *The American Journal of Bioethics* 26; see further discussion in Chapter 6.

circumstances.[77]

To conclude, a review of courts' decision, professional codes of ethics and the academic literature reflects a discourse which gives limited room to family members. But in the narrow circumstances where law and ethics do justify breach of confidentiality, the next stage is to examine whether a duty to warn the relatives is imposed on doctors and patients or whether they have discretion to disclose. Providing doctors and patients with discretion will be seen as another sign of the patient–centred approach taken by the courts. Imposing a duty to disclose may express a different view, where relatives' interests are as important as those of the patient when genetic diseases can be prevented or cured.

4.2.4 Imposing a Duty or Providing Discretion

4.2.4.1 Doctors. As yet no English court has held that doctors owe a duty to breach patients' right to confidentiality and warn relatives. However, the California Supreme Court in the case of *Tarasoff v Regents of the University of California* imposed a duty on a psychiatrist who failed to warn the victim that his patient threatened to kill her.[78] The court accepted that the confidential dialogue between doctors and patients promotes public health but it held that confidentiality ends 'where public peril begins'.[79] The court stressed that society cannot tolerate exposure to danger resulting from concealed knowledge doctors possess.[80]

Subsequent cases involving psychiatric patients express different attitudes to this decision. Some courts impose on the doctors a duty to warn whenever they can foresee that people will be exposed to danger by the patient.[81] Others limited the boundaries of *Tarasoff*, requiring that the doctors will be able to identify a particular victim.[82]

---

[77] Ibid., at p. 27; Rhodes, supra n. 74, at p. 119 where she argues that while doctors owe a duty to protect patient confidentiality as it enables patients to trust them, their duty to benefit third parties is weaker.

[78] *Tarasoff v Regents of the University of California* (1976) 551 P 2d 334 (Cal Sup Ct). Tobriner J held: 'When a therapist determines, or pursuant to the standards of his profession should determine, that his patient presents a serious danger of violence to another, he incurs an obligation to use reasonable care to protect the intended victim against such danger. The discharge of this duty may require the therapist to take one or more of various steps, depending upon the nature of the case. Thus it may call for him to warn the intended victim or others likely to apprise the victim of the danger, to notify the police, or to take whatever other steps are reasonably necessary under the circumstances'.

[79] Ibid., at p. 347.

[80] Ibid.

[81] *Lipari v Sears, Roebuck & Co.* (1980) 497 F Supp 185 (Neb D Ct); *Williams v United States* (1978) 450 F Supp 1040 (SD D Ct); *Petersen v State* (1983) 671 P.2d 230 (Wash Sup Ct).

[82] *Thompson v County of Alabama* (1980) 614 P 2d 728 (Cal Sup Ct); *Mavroudis v*

In cases concerning sexually transmitted diseases, such as *Reisner*[83] and *DiMarco v Lynch Homes–Chester County*,[84] the court held that the doctor should have warned the patient about the risk she was exposed to. This could have prevented the claimant, the patient's partner, from having unprotected sexual relations with the patient and consequently being infected with the disease.[85] The court in *Reisner* held that the doctor could fulfil his duty to third parties by warning the patient.[86]

The question arises how the decision in *Tarasoff* was applied to the genetics context. A more specific question is whether doctors owe a duty to breach patient's right to confidentiality and communicate genetic information directly to the relatives. Only two American cases have addressed these questions. In *Pate v Threlkel*, the patient's daughter sued the doctor for not warning the patient that the daughter should be tested. The claimant argued that had she been warned in time she could have taken preventive measures. The court held that though the doctors owed a duty of care to the patient's children they were not required to breach the patient's right to confidentiality. Doctors should warn their patients, and they may expect them to warn the relatives.[87] The court in *Safer v Pack* was less decisive.[88] It held that there might be circumstances where doctors will have to approach the relatives directly when the patient refuses to inform them.[89] Unlike *Tarasoff*, in genetics doctors are not obliged to breach the patient's right to confidentiality. Since the requirements of English tort law are stricter than those of the American, it is unlikely that the courts will impose an affirmative duty on doctors to breach confidentiality without the patient's consent.

A few commentators, however, argue that a duty to warn can be imposed in some circumstances.[90] Lori Andrews confines the scope of this duty to circumstances where disclosure can prevent physical harm to the relatives.[91] In addition, Ngwena and Chadwick point out that if the decision is left to the

---

Superior Court of California (1980) 162 Cal Rptr 724 (Cal Ct App); *Brady v Hopper* (1984) 751 F 2d 329 (Colo Ct App).

[83] *Reisner v Regents of the University of California* (1995) 37 Cal Rptr 2d 518 (Cal Ct App).

[84] (1990) 525 Pa 558 (Pa Sup Ct).

[85] Ibid., at pp. 521–523.

[86] For a comprehensive discussion about the US position see: Gostin L., Hodge J., "Piercing the Veil of Secrecy in HIV/AIDS and Other Sexually Transmitted Diseases: Theories of Privacy and Disclosure in Partner Notification" (1998) 5 *Duke Journal of Gender, Law & Policy* 9.

[87] See *Pate v Threlkel*, supra n. 39, at p. 282

[88] See Chapter 1, p. 1 for a description of the facts.

[89] See *Safer v Pack*, supra n. 39, at pp. 1192–1193.

[90] Capron A., "Tort liability in genetic counselling" (1979) 79 *Colombia Law Review* 618, 677–8.

[91] Andrews L., "Torts and the double helix: Malpractice liability for failure to warn of genetic risks" (1992) 29 (1) *Houston Law Review* 149, 180.

discretion of the doctor it may result in discrimination because disclosure will depend on the doctor's personal view and not on an objective legal test.[92] Finally, Burnett relies on the biological connection between the patients and their blood relatives, arguing that this should lead to the recognition of a doctor's duty to warn the relatives.[93]

Admittedly, however, the majority of commentators agree that discretion is the preferable option.[94] Laurie argues that lack of prior relationship with the relatives undermines the doctor's duty to warn them.[95] Suter asserts that doctors should never be compelled to disclose confidential information to relatives. She distinguishes between the *Tarasoff* line of cases and cases in genetics. Whereas in *Tarasoff* the patient threatened to harm a third party, in the genetics cases the patient does not. Instead, the genetic risk is created by the mutative gene and the relatives' ignorance of their genetic risk.[96]

Ngwena and Chadwick stress that imposing a duty on doctors to warn relatives may lead to defensive medical practice, which may result in frequent and unnecessary breach of confidentiality.[97] Furthermore, Andrews asserts that imposing a duty on doctors to approach the relatives directly is time–consuming and impractical. Doctors would have to try to locate and contact[98] the at–risk relatives and this may be difficult, especially when they live abroad or in another part of the country.[99]

To conclude, the legal discourse indicates that the relatives' interests in receiving genetic information are not fully recognised. Not only are family members informed in limited and exceptional circumstances (when they face a risk of *physical* harm), but also the decision whether they will be informed is not obligatory but discretionary. The courts and legal commentators set the balance point on prevention of physical harm. This, however, stands in contrast to the empirical studies provided in Chapters 2 and 5 which reflect the considerable effect genetic information has on patients and their familial relationship. Adopting an overriding mechanism of prevention of harm overlooks this research. The law is reluctant to cast an extra burden on doctors or is oblivious to the socio–medical research regarding the impact of genetic information. Whatever the explanation, a gap between law and practice emerges. While the doctor's duty in

---

[92] See Ngwena and Chadwick, supra n. 70, at p. 88.
[93] Burnett J., "A physician's duty to warn a patient's relatives of a patient's genetically inheritable disease" (1999) 36 *Houston Law Review* 559, 578–582.
[94] See Laurie, supra n. 63, at p. 188.
[95] See Laurie, supra, n. 38, at pp. 83–84.
[96] See Suter, supra n. 40, at pp. 1882–4; for a full analysis of the distinction between *Tarasoff* and the genetic context see Laurie, supra n. 38, at pp. 82–84.
[97] See Ngwena and Chadwick, supra n. 70, at p. 90.
[98] For the difficulties of patients and doctors to remain in contact see Fitzpatrick et al., "The duty to recontact: Attitudes of genetic service providers" (1999) 64 *American Journal of Human Genetics* 852.
[99] See Andrews supra n. 91, at p. 181.

practice may include consideration of family members who are closely involved in the patient's care and life, the legal duty is narrow and focused on the individual patient. This last observation, however, requires elaboration and it will be discussed in Chapter 5 where the medical position of family members is analysed.

4.2.4.2 Patients. As stated above, professional codes impose a moral duty on patients to warn their relatives. Hence, a question arises whether this duty is enforceable. In this respect consensus seems to prevail among policy–makers that a legal duty should not be imposed on the patient. The Nuffield Council admits that there may be good reasons for patients not to inform their relatives.[100] The BMA view is similar. Although it encourages patients to share genetic information with their relatives it does not impose on them a duty to disclose.[101]

The vast majority of commentators support this view. Suter, for example, accepts that patients owe a moral duty to warn their relatives, but argues that such a moral duty does not entail a legal one.[102] She distinguishes between cases in AIDS, where patients who fail to warn their sexual partners can be regarded as criminals, and cases in genetics, where patients do not cause harm to the relatives but merely fail to notify them about it.[103] Suter thereby highlights the legal distinction between commissions and omissions. Patients in the context of genetics do not put the relatives at risk of harm owing to their negligent act; they simply refrain from alerting them to the possibility that they may develop a disease in the future. Suter's argument accords with the position of English law of non–liability for omissions.[104] As the discussion in Chapter 3 indicated, doctors (like other professionals) are not liable for their failure to act when it concerns individuals with whom they have no prior relationships.[105]

Suter's view deserves close examination. The position taken in this book is that this distinction does not accord with the nature of the familial relationship. For many family members the distinction between acts and omissions is irrelevant when they have a close familial relationship based on intimacy, commitment, and moral responsibility. Relatives who ask patients why they did not inform them about the genetic disorder would not accept the patients' reply that they did not have to because they did not cause the disease. Suter admits that a legal duty to warn the relatives may be imposed only when there is a 'special relationship'

---

[100] See the Nuffield Council, supra n. 43, at p. 49.

[101] See the BMA, supra n. 48, at p. 22.

[102] See Suter, supra n. 40, at p. 1886.

[103] Ibid., at p. 1885.

[104] See Chapter 3, section 3.3.1.2.

[105] As Grubb argues, the omission–commission distinction has less relevance in the doctor–patient relationship where a pre–tort relationship exits. See Grubb A., "Consent to treatment: The competent patient" in Grubb A., (ed.), Principles of Medical Law, Oxford, Oxford University Press (2nd edn., 2004), at pp. 179–180.

between them. She distinguishes a parents–children relationship, which satisfies such a legal requirement, from a siblings' relationship, which may not. She argues that while parents and children have a dependent relationship, other familial relationships are not dependent.

Clayton agrees with Suter that generally patients do not have to act affirmatively.[106] However, Clayton does not agree that the children's dependency on parents can lead to the imposition of a parental duty of care. Clayton argues that in the United States parents are immune from liability for decisions involved caring and rearing children. Hence parents will not owe a duty to disclose genetic information when they can argue that they did not inform their children because the child was likely to be emotionally distressed at the news.[107] Considering whether a moral duty to warn the relatives can be enforceable, Laurie is sceptical about the likelihood of recognition of liability in tort reflecting the familial attitude to communication of genetic information in the family.[108]

On the liberal–communitarian spectrum, the views expressed above are situated in the middle. Arguing that patients owe a moral duty to disclose information reflects the relationship many families have. The argument that individuals are entitled to rights, but also have some responsibilities when entering into a relationship, relies on communitarian conceptions. The reluctance of policy–makers to intervene in familial relationships and impose a duty on one relative to another reflects the belief that state intervention should be minimal and that patient autonomy in the family is important.

Nevertheless, the legal debate presented above is patient–centred in essence. The starting point is that the patient controls exclusively the information received from the doctor. Had the information been accessible to all family members this debate would have been irrelevant: the relatives would have gained unconditional access to the information and questions of duty or discretion would not have been discussed. Such a model is presented by Loane Skene. In her model, when undertaking genetic tests, the patient accepts that the information received will be common to all family members and that he or she will not object if they want access.[109]

As discussed in Chapter 1, other academics express an approach that

---

[106] Clayton E., "What should the law say about disclosure of genetic information to relatives?" (1998) 1 *Journal of Health Care, Law & Policy* 373, 374–382.

[107] Ibid., at p. 381.

[108] Laurie G., "Obligations arising from genetic information–negligence and the protection of familial interests" (1999) 11 (2) *Child and Family Law Quarterly* 109, 117; see also Annas et al., "Drafting the Genetic Privacy Act: Science, policy and practical considerations", (1995) 23 *Journal of Law, Medicine and Ethics* 360 who argues that patient should have the ability to decide whether to inform the relatives.

[109] Skene L., "Patients' rights or family responsibilities?" (1998) 6 *Medical Law Review* 1, 32.

incorporates communitarian conceptions.[110] Not all of them address the question of whether the patient owes a legal duty to disclose information to the relatives. Sommerville and English, who argue that the patient owes a moral obligation to the relatives,[111] imply that the patient does not owe a legal duty to warn the relatives. When the patient refuses to disclose information the doctors are those who face the legal dilemma of whether or not to warn the relatives. The view taken by Sommerville and English therefore reflects a distinction between ethics and law. While there seems to be consensus that patients owe a moral duty to disclose information to relatives (whether it is based on liberal or communitarian conceptions), imposing a legal duty on them to disclose is difficult. This position accords with the general approach to parental responsibilities to children's health. The courts do not intervene in this aspect of the familial relationship.[112] Although the law requires parents to ensure that their children receive effective medical treatment, this duty does not include, as yet, an obligation to discuss with the children familial genetic risks.[113]

4.2.5 Formulating a Different Perspective to Medical Confidentiality

The discussion so far has stressed two points: first, medical confidentiality is highly valued in law and ethics as it promotes public health and enhances individual's autonomy. Doctors have a duty to preserve the patient's right to confidentiality. Breach is justified only in exceptional circumstances. Second, patients should disclose genetic information to relatives but they are not compelled to do so. This moral responsibility derives from the utilitarian principle of prevention of harm to others as well as from the social bonds that patients share with their relatives.

One can argue that the first point does not fully accord with the second. If doctors should respect patients' moral right to confidentiality as much as possible,[114] and if patients are entitled to refuse disclosure, how does this accord with their moral duty to share information with the relatives? A possible starting point to understand this inconsistency is to examine *why* patients tend to keep medical information in confidence and *whether* patients conceal medical information from their relatives as they withhold it from other third parties.

As regards the first question, it can be argued that the patients' motives for insisting on their right to confidentiality are not based solely on their wish to be autonomous and to take informed choices; it also derives from *fear*, which

---

[110] See Chapter 1, part 1.5.2.

[111] Sommerville A., English V., "Genetic privacy: orthodoxy or oxymoron?" (1999) 25 *Journal of Medical Ethics* 144, 148.

[112] Lunney M., Oliphant K., *Tort Law: Text and Materials*, Oxford, Oxford University Press (2000), 402

[113] See Clayton, supra n. 106, at pp. 380–1.

[114] See the Nuffield Council, supra n. 43, at p. 53.

comprises of two aspects. First, there is *fear* of discrimination.[115] Patients suspect that if genetic information is revealed they may suffer discrimination, for example, in their workplace,[116] and in obtaining insurance.[117] Those who have the mutation for Huntington's disease may suspect that if this condition is disclosed to their insurer they will be refused a policy.[118] Second, as was indicated in Chapter 2, patients may *fear* that revealing information to their relatives will have an adverse effect on their familial relationship. One study shows that relatives may direct anger and resentment against them.[119] This may intensify the guilt the patient feel in any event.[120]

It follows that a distinction should be made between disclosure to relatives and to other third parties, such as employers and insurers. While the core reason for withholding information from relatives is subjective and based on the nature of the patient–relatives relationship, the reasons for concealing information from other third parties are objective and based primarily on economic interests. This subjective–objective distinction can be described as the difference in the relationships patients have with relatives and other third parties. The relationship that patients have with their insurers is commercial, as between a consumer and a supplier. They are not attached to them as they are to their close relatives, with whom they share an intimate and close relationship. Therefore, it is understandable that patients are reluctant to disclose genetic information to these third parties, while they are more willing to share information with relatives. Put it differently, although patients may refuse to disclose information to relatives their decision is based not on economic interests but on the level of attachment they have with them. Whether patients have an intimate or a hostile relationship with their relatives, their decision–making process is not guided solely by objective reasons or by a cost–benefit evaluation; it also involves an emotional level, which reflects the nature of their relationship.[121]

---

[115] McLean S., "Intervention in the human genome" (1998) 61 *MLR* 681, 684–5.

[116] See the Nuffield Council, supra n. 43, chapter 6; Rothstein M., Gelb B., Craig S., "Protecting genetic privacy by permitting employer access only to job–related employee medical information: Analysis of a unique Minnesota Law" (1998) 24 *American Journal of Law & Medicine* 399.

[117] See the Nuffield Council, supra n. 43, chapter 7; Cook D., "Genetics and the British insurance industry" (1999) 25 *Journal of Medical Ethics* 157.

[118] Low et al., "Genetic discrimination in life insurance: Empirical evidence from a cross sectional survey of genetic support groups in the United Kingdom" (1998) 317 *BMJ* 1632.

[119] Fanos J., Johnson J., "Perception of carrier status by cystic fibrosis siblings" (1995) 57 *American Journal of Human Genetics* 431.

[120] McGowan R., "Beyond the disorder: One parent's reflection on genetic counselling" (1999) 25 *Journal of Medical Ethics* 195, 197.

[121] The distinction between disclosure to family members and to other third parties, which should lead to different attitudes, is recognised by Hale LJ. in *R (on the application of S) v Plymouth CC*. There she holds that 'there is a clear distinction between disclosure to

Another factor distinguishing relatives from other third parties is that patients can hide their medical condition from their employers and insurers till a relatively progressive stage of their illness, but they face difficulties in concealing it from their relatives. When relatives are closely involved in the patient's life they may notice changes in his or her daily routine and health. In addition, as argued in Chapter Two, patients need to share medical information with at least one close relative to relieve the stress they experience throughout their illness. Keeping their medical condition to themselves will in some circumstances be almost impossible.[122]

This analysis should lead us to reconsider the issue of medical confidentiality and its purposes within families. While this principle should be almost absolute in relation to employers and insurers, it should be more pragmatic when patients interact with their families. The patients' right to confidentiality within the family cannot be protected 'as far as possible' but it should be qualified. This qualification does not mean that patients will have to waive their right to confidentiality altogether when they interact with their relatives, but it ought to reflect the reality that there is information patients share with close relatives but not with others.

What are the grounds of this qualified perception of confidentiality? It was argued in Chapter 1 that the familial relationship is largely based on intimacy and mutual responsibility, which is grounded in the notion that the individual is not only separate from others but also has social relationships that constitute part of his or her identity. These conceptions alter the perception of patient autonomy. Autonomy is perceived less individualistically and more relationally where it is recognised that the individual's ability to make personal choices is nurtured by his or her interaction with close others. Consequently, confidentiality within the family cannot be an end in itself but should be considered together with the principles of beneficence and justice, which give serious consideration to the well–being of others.

Accepting that medical confidentiality should be qualified revives the liberal–communitarian debate about the perception of an individual's identity with its constant tension between the sense of being separate and the sense of belonging. Stressing only one aspect of this tension, either the commonality of the information (as argued by Skene) or the exclusive control of the patient over the information (as advanced by the majority of commentators) does not accord with the two aspects of one's personhood. Therefore, a more sensible approach is to consider

---

the media ... and disclosure in confidence to those with a proper interest in having the information in question. We are concerned here only with the latter. The issue is only whether the circle should be widened... to include the person who is probably closest to him in fact as well as in law...'.

[122] Labrecque et al., "The impact of family presence on the physician–cancer patient interaction" (1991) 33 (11) *Social Science & Medicine* 1253; Benson J., Britten N., "Respecting the autonomy of cancer patient when talking with their families: Qualitative analysis of semi–structured interviews with patients" (1996) 313 *BMJ* 729.

these two aspects into account. Decisions whether or not to disclose information to the relatives will depend not only on the objective features of the disorder but also on the subjective characteristics of the familial relationship. Such a mechanism will have to accommodate the interest of patients in controlling the flow of information in the family to the interest of the relatives in accessing it.

Admittedly, though, it is difficult to set a general mechanism providing a proper balance between the principle of confidentiality, which highlights the patient's interest to make an independent decision, and communitarian principles such as solidarity and mutual responsibility, which promote the interests of the family members. At times the patient's insistence on protecting his or her confidentiality will be understood while at others it will not. A possible solution is to balance the competing principles according to the specific circumstances of each case. As the discussion in Chapters 5 and 6 will indicate, in most cases, the decision is not between disclosure and non–disclosure or between disclosure to no one and disclosure to everyone. It is more a decision between immediate or future disclosure, and between disclosure to one relative and to several.

For the doctors, the qualification of confidentiality means that their duty to the patient with reference to family members should be less strict than it is with regard to other third parties. The decision whether or not to disclose should be based on knowledge and understanding of the particular familial relationship and background. Familiarity with these aspects will help doctors understand (even if not accept) the patient's decision, which often accords with the specific life–story of his or her family. In addition, it will assist doctors to decide whether or not to respect the patient's decision.

Accepting this argument does not end the discussion. The next questions are whether such a qualified principle of confidentiality accords with medical practices and public views, and how the law can accommodate it in practice. While the first question will be dealt with in Chapter 5 the last question will be discussed in Chapter 6.

4.3 The *Right Not to Know*

A recent debate in the literature is whether the relatives' interest in not knowing genetic information should be respected. International conventions address this issue, recognising that the individual has a right not to receive genetic information.[123]

English courts have not been required to deal with such a claim. The discussion in this part, as opposed to those conducted in previous chapters, will deal with the

---

[123] Council of Europe, *Convention for the Protection of Human Rights and Dignity of the Human Being with regard to the Application of Biology and Medicine: Convention on Human Rights and Medicine* (1997), 10 (2); UNESCO, *Universal Declaration on the Human Genome and Human Rights* (1997), 5c.

question whether a legal right not to receive information should be recognised. In this context the available mechanisms which may assist the relatives to exercise this interest will be analysed.

The issue of the right not to know genetic information arises in situations where disclosure cannot prevent physical harm to the relatives.[124] More especially, when the patient is diagnosed as a carrier or a sufferer of an incurable disorder, a question arises whether the relatives want to know that they may be disposed to a terminal disease.[125] Knowing that nothing can be done to avert the onset of the disease can be devastating because it deprives the relatives from the blessed ignorance of when and how they will die. In addition, being diagnosed with a disposition to a genetic disorder may result in constant fear of its onset. Obviously, some people may be reluctant to live in such a fear and refuse to undergo testing for incurable disorders, such as Huntington's.[126] Moreover, as the studies reviewed in Chapter 2 revealed, the availability of genetic information which cannot prevent physical harm may lead to unexpected and sometimes unpredictable reactions. In these circumstances people perceive genetic information as beneficial in some respects but as harmful in others. Therefore, a question arises whether the relatives wish to be informed.[127]

4.3.1 Should There Be a Legal Right Not to Know?

The determination that knowledge may be harmful leads to the question whether a right not to know should be legally recognised. Commentators disagree about the answer. While some argue that such a right should not be recognised, others stress that relatives[128] should have the right not to receive genetic information. This debate relates to the role information plays in autonomy. As was argued in the previous part, some commentators, such as Rhodes, argue that information is

---

[124] For a detailed discussion about the interest in not knowing see Chapter 2, para 2.3.3.

[125] Another conflict, not thoroughly discussed here, is between the patient's right not to know and the relatives' interest in being informed of the patient's test results and diagnosis.

[126] Chadwick R., Levitt M., Shickle D. (eds.), *The Right to Know and the Right Not to Know*, Aldershot, Avebury (1997), 2.

[127] Angus Clarke is known for asking the question whether people have a right not to know especially in the context of children. See Clarke A., "The genetic testing of children" in Harper P., Clarke A., Genetics, Society and Clinical Practice, Oxford, Bios Scientific (1997), pp. 15–28, and Clarke A., "Challenges to Genetic Privacy: The control of personal genetic information" in Harper & Clarke, pp. 149–164.

[128] Obviously, patients too have the right not to receive diagnostic medical information from their doctors. Yet the familial characteristic of genetic information and its implications for the patient's family members raises the question of whether they have the right not to know once the patient is informed.

fundamental in making decisions,[129] and its lack compromises the individual's right to act autonomously.

Undoubtedly, arguing that the individual has a moral duty to receive information overlooks the psychological and social aspects of an individual's identity, especially when making important decisions. These aspects can lead the relatives to prefer ignorance to knowledge when the disorder is terminal and incurable.[130] For example, it can be argued that informing a woman who is prone to depression (but still mentally competent) that she is likely to develop Huntington's disease may not be beneficial. The effect of this news on this woman's emotional stability may outweigh her will to make informed decisions about her life.

In addition, it is possible to challenge Rhodes's position by analysing the principle of autonomy from a different perspective. Referring to the patient's decision whether or not to receive information from the doctor, Beauchamp and Childress argue that patients have a right to be ignorant because doctors cannot force them to receive information.[131] Furthermore, the patients' decision not to receive information but to allow a third party to make a decision on their behalf reflects their autonomy because they choose between two options: to receive information and decide by themselves, or not to obtain information and to appoint a proxy as a decision–maker. These two options require an autonomous decision. If patients are competent and free from undue influence, choosing between these two alternatives will express their autonomy. Applied to the context of the relatives' right not to know, their voluntary decision to remain ignorant does not imply that they waive their ability to control their lives but that they *choose* not to receive information.

Some commentators argue that there should be a right not to know. They argue that this right is based on notions of liberty and freedom. Laurie, for example, argues that the individual must have the freedom to choose to be autonomous, which requires the possibility to act under minimal external influences.[132] This leads Laurie to adopt a notion of privacy which is defined as a state of separateness from others.[133] The existence of the individual's private sphere should prevent others from invading it, for example, by communicating unsolicited information. In Laurie's view less significance should be given to information that enables individuals to choose and more to their ability to act free from external

---

[129] See Rhodes, supra n. 74; Ost D., "The 'right' not to know" (1984) 9 *Journal of Medicine and Philosophy* 301.

[130] Surely there is a practical difficulty because in the majority of cases the relatives do not know that the patient has knowledge which may or may not be disclosed to them. I will address this issue below.

[131] See Beauchamp and Childress, supra n. 3, at p. 63.

[132] See Laurie, supra n. 38, at p. 90.

[133] However, Laurie argues that privacy is not similar to freedom but it protects only some aspects of it; see: Laurie G., "Challenging medical–legal norms" (2001) 22 *Journal of Legal Medicine* 1, 35.

interference. Takala also contests the view of those who argue that ignoring a relevant and significant piece of information is irrational, hence not autonomous. Takala stresses that in liberal and democratic societies individuals are allowed to act unreasonably and foolishly so long as they do not harm others.[134]

Ruth Chadwick takes a similar approach, suggesting that the right not to know may be based on the right to self–determination.[135] Raikka elaborates this, arguing that when individuals make decisions they should be competent, have authentic desires, and have the power to implement them.[136] In exercising this right to self–determination the individual's conduct can be justified so long as it does not harm others.[137] In the context of genetics the right not to know can be perceived as a right to self–determination. In the familial relationship the patient is justified in respecting a relative's right not to know when this decision does not harm other relatives.

Analysing the views of Laurie and Raikka, it seems that they do not see eye to eye. While Laurie accepts that privacy as freedom from interference leads to a presumption of non–disclosure,[138] Raikka emphasises that the relatives are free to be ignorant as long as non–disclosure does not harm others.[139] So while Laurie sees the individual as primarily separate from others Raikka appreciates the implication for others of the decision not to know. The moral ground for these two views is similar, namely autonomy as freedom, and they both attempt to secure the relatives' right not to know. However, Raikka emphasises a point that Laurie does not fully appreciate, namely the influence on others of the decision not to know.

Analysing the literature on the right to know, one can detect a similar approach to the one existing with regard to the right to know. The principle of prevention of harm to others is evident, as the above review indicates, in the debate about this right. This, it is argued, is a narrow perspective because measuring the tripartite doctor–patient–relatives relationship by harm neglects other important principles, especially in small and intimate communities such as the family. As the research set forth in Chapter 5 will indicate, a sense of responsibility and accountability guides many patients when they consider whether or not to approach their relatives, pondering whether their right (but not necessarily wish) to remain ignorant should be respected.

---

[134] Takala T., "The right to genetic ignorance confirmed" (1999) 13 *Bioethics* 288, 292; Takala T., Hayry M., "Genetic ignorance, moral obligations and social duties" (2000) 25 (1) *Journal of Medicine and Philosophy* 107, 112.

[135] Chadwick R., "The philosophy of the right to know and the right not to know" in Chadwick R., Levitt M., Shickle D. (eds.), *The Right to Know and the Right Not to Know* (1997), 19.

[136] Raikka J., "Freedom and a right (not) to know" (1998) 12 *Bioethics* 49, 52.

[137] Ibid., at p. 59.

[138] See Laurie supra n. 133, at pp. 36 and 39.

[139] See Raikka, supra, n. 136, at p. 59.

A fundamental difficulty for those who support recognition of the right not to know is the usage of the term *right* when the relatives are unaware of its existence. This occurs when the patient possesses material genetic information but the relatives do not know that and therefore cannot choose not to receive it. As Wertz and Fletcher recognise, when the relatives are asked whether they want to know the risk for a particular genetic disease the geneticist has already communicated the essence of the information.[140]   More importantly, in these circumstances the relatives are deprived from their right to choose whether or not they want to know. Bottis argues that the relatives do not have a *right* not to know but instead they *are not obliged* to receive genetic information.[141]

The view taken in this context is that if we want to promote the relatives' right not to know we can argue that they may be aware that they possess a *general* right not to know,[142] and that this right can be exercised before doctors or patients approach them. It is general because the relatives do not know the content of the information but they are aware of their right to refuse to receive it. The refusal of relatives to receive information may be defined as a choice or as a right only when they are aware in advance of that option.[143]   This is reflected in some of the commentaries. Rhodes, for example, assumes that the relatives know that there is genetic information that can affect their future lives when they consider whether or not to obtain it; she does not address the more difficult situation where the relatives are unaware that genetic information is available.

As the discussion between Laurie, Bottis, Wertz, and Fletcher suggests, it is difficult to define the situation where the relatives are unaware of the possibility to refuse information as a right.[144]   Furthermore, in some conditions, such as Huntington's disease, when the onset of the disease is inevitable, it is difficult to argue that people have the right not to know. The symptoms of the disease will reveal to those who have the mutation that they will suffer from the disease, and there is nothing they can do about it. Thus, a more accurate definition of the right not to know, if the usage of rights is accurate in this context, is the right not to be informed about one's health status against one's wishes by others, usually doctors.[145]

---

[140] Wertz D., Fletcher J., "Privacy and disclosure in medical genetics examined in an ethics of care" (1991) 5 (3) *Bioethics* 212, 221.

[141] See Bottis, supra n. 63, at p. 179.

[142] Andorno R., "The right not to know: an autonomy based approach" (2004) 30 *Journal of Medical Ethics* 435, 437, seems to agree.

[143] See Laurie, supra n. 63 at p. 190.

[144] Recently Laurie agreed that using the terminology of rights in this context is questionable, preferring to speak about interests instead of rights. See Laurie, "Commentary: A Response to Andorno" (2004) 30 *Journal of Medical Ethics* 439, 440, commenting on Andorno R., "The right not to know: an autonomy based approach" (2004) 30 *Journal of Medical Ethics* 435.

[145] I would like to thank Professor Michael Parker who made this observation when reading an earlier version of this book.

Concluding, like some commentators, that an interest in not knowing genetic information should be ethically recognised, raises the next question, namely whether doctors and patients should owe a legal duty not to communicate information to family members. As we saw in Chapter 3, imposing such a duty would put the doctor in a dilemma if a legal duty to disclose were recognised as well. Although we shall deal with this difficulty thoroughly in Chapter 6, it should be stressed at this point that those who advocate a right not to know believe nevertheless that a legal duty not to inform should not be imposed. Despite their differences, Andorno and Laurie both believe that family members should not be able to enforce this right in courts and sue patients for not respecting their right. But they seem to differ with regard to doctors. While Andorno refuses to impose a duty on the doctor, Laurie argues that the doctor may owe a duty to draw the patient's attention to the factors which indicate the relatives' interest in not knowing.[146]

Whether or not it is accepted that there is a right not to know, the current debate focuses on the principle of autonomy. Some commentators, such as Rhodes and Ost,[147] perceive autonomy as comprised of informed choices and rational decisions, a perception which leads them to reject the notion of a right not to know. Others, such as Laurie and Takala, view it as freedom to take decisions without controlling interferences, which leads to recognition of a right not to know. However, this discourse leaves outside the debate the following considerations: (1) whether it is possible to respect within a family a relative's right not to know when other family members do know or wish to know: (2) whether the recognition of such a right contradicts the essence of the family as a social unit: (3) whether the interests of the family as a whole and the desire of its members to live in harmony are compatible with recognition of this right. Before dealing with these issues it is necessary to examine whether and how the relatives' right not to know is protected.

4.3.2 The Available Mechanisms to Protect the Right Not to Know

There are some mechanisms that protect the relatives' right not to know. First, there is the principle of medical confidentiality. The Genetic Interest Group provides similar guidelines concerning the relatives' right to know and their right not to know.[148] According to this approach, when considering whether or not to disclose genetic information to the relatives a cost–benefit evaluation should be conducted, where 'as with the issue of confidentiality, discretion to disclose should

---

[146] See Andorno, supra n. 142, at p. 438, and Laurie G., *Genetic Privacy*, Cambridge, Cambridge University Press (2002), at pp. 265–266.

[147] See Ost, supra n. 129.

[148] See Genetic Interest Group, supra n. 56, at pp. 15–16; see also: Brownrigg A., "Mother still knows best: Cancer–related gene mutation, familial privacy and a physician's duty to warn" (1999) 26 *Fordham Urban Law Journal* 247, 272–3; Bell D., Bennett B., "Genetic secrets and the family" (2001) 9 *Medical Law Review* 130, 156.

be based on the principle of maximising benefit and minimising harm'.[149] Patients and doctors should take into account the severity of the disease, the availability of preventive measures, the accuracy of genetic tests, whether the relatives know that they are disposed to the condition, and most importantly the anxiety they are likely to experience when they are informed. The realisation that the relatives might suffer from distress led the GIG to the conclusion that the relatives' interests in not knowing should be respected.

However, the attempt to protect the relatives' right not to receive genetic information by adhering to the principle of confidentiality is misplaced because it does not put the relatives' interests in the centre. Confidentiality aims to protect patients when they wish the doctor, who lawfully gains access to their medical information, not to reveal it to others. It does not aim to protect those who do not wish to receive information. This is reflected in the GIG's guidelines, where they look at the issue from the doctor's viewpoint and not from the relatives'. Confidentiality cannot adequately protect the relatives' right not to know because it provides the discretion to the doctor and the patient and not to the relatives in this context.[150]

The right not to know can be protected by the principle of respect for autonomy. Beauchamp and Childress argue that people generally respect others by respecting their wishes not to be intruded upon. The two authors assert that the individual is entitled to prevent unauthorised access and that such an entitlement is based on the right to allow or refuse access.[151] The authors hold that the principle of respect for autonomy includes the individual's right to decide what will happen to information about his or her life.[152] It follows that the relatives' decision not to be informed should be respected because they can decide that any relevant information about their lives will not be conveyed to them.

Not everyone takes this view. As some commentators assert, knowledge is fundamental in the exercise of autonomy. As Laurie puts it, the individual cannot have a meaningful choice if he or she does not receive information regarding the relevant factors which affect his or her choice.[153] In addition, Wertz and Fletcher argue that the autonomy–based model is problematic when the relatives are unaware that they can refuse information.[154] When patients inform the relatives because they want to provide the relatives with the possibility to exercise their right to make informed decisions, they negate the relatives' right not to receive genetic information. Whether the patients decide to inform the relatives or respect their right not to know, they act paternalistically to enable the relatives to act autonomously and this is self–contradictory. Laurie adds another aspect.

[149] See GIG, ibid., at p. 15, para 5.2.4.
[150] See Laurie, supra n. 133, at p. 24–26.
[151] See Beauchamp and Childress, supra, n. 3, at p. 296.
[152] Ibid., at p. 297.
[153] See Laurie, supra, n. 133, at p. 21.
[154] See Wertz and Fletcher, supra n. 140 at p. 221.

Comparing the status of the relatives with that of the incompetent patient, they both cannot choose for themselves and must have choices made for them. The incompetent patient cannot decide whether or not to receive a particular medical treatment and the relatives cannot independently decide whether or not they wish to receive genetic information. Taking this argument one step further, it is legally accepted that when making a decision for incompetent patients the doctor has to consider the patient's best interests. However, it may be difficult to determine the relatives' best interests in genetics because, as was demonstrated in Chapter 2, one's reaction when receiving the information is unpredictable. Thus, autonomy cannot be properly used to protect the right not to know.[155]

Despite this criticism Andorno advocates an autonomy–based approach.[156] Well aware of the criticism levelled against recognition of a right not to know,[157] Andorno argues that the interest in not knowing is part of the individual's right to self–determination. However, Andorno limits the right not to know to patients' not being informed by doctors, assuming that the patient has a general knowledge of the genetic risk. Andorno correctly argues that to exercise autonomy in this context the patient has explicitly to express his interest in not receiving the information about his or her condition.

As for relatives, Andorno admits that it is difficult to talk about a right not to know because, as mentioned, they cannot exercise this right when they do not know that familial genetic information is available.[158] Andorno adds another practical difficulty: how might the doctor know that the relatives have an interest in not being informed? These as well as other problems lead Andorno to conclude that the right not to know can only be exercised in the doctor–patient relationship.[159]

The third model proposed for the protection of the relatives' right not to know is based on privacy as a state of separateness from others.[160] In his model Laurie divides this notion into two categories. First, he identifies a conception of *informational privacy*, which reflects the patient's interest in preventing access to the information by, or disclosure to, other third parties.[161] Second is the conception of *spatial privacy*, which completes the notion of informational privacy. The notion of spatial privacy is defined as a private sphere around the individual that cannot and should not be intruded upon without a justifiable cause.[162]   The

---

[155]   See Laurie, supra n. 133, at p. 21.

[156]   See Andorno, supra n. 142.

[157]   Andorno, supra n. 142, mentions the argument that recognition of the right to not to know contradicts the principle of solidarity that exists in the family. See above for further discussion.

[158]   Ibid, at p. 438.

[159]   Ibid, at pp. 438–439.

[160]   A comprehensive discussion about privacy and its application to genetics is beyond the scope of this book. For a detailed account see Laurie G., *Genetic Privacy: A Challenge to Medico–Legal Norms*, Cambridge, Cambridge University Press (2002).

[161]   See Laurie, supra n. 133, at pp. 29–30.

[162]   Ibid.

relatives' special privacy is unjustifiably invaded either by unsolicited physical contact or by unwanted intrusion into the sphere of their psychological integrity. In the context of genetics, the relatives' spatial privacy is unjustly invaded if genetic information is communicated to them when there is no indication that they would wish to have such information.

It follows from this account that spatial privacy underlines the relatives' right not to know genetic information. At first glance, Laurie seems to argue that the general rule in this model is non–disclosure; disclosure is the exception.[163] However, replying to one critic[164] he argues that in this model he merely challenges people's wishes but does not assume that generally people have an interest in not knowing.[165] Yet even in his most recent commentary Laurie appears to imply that when doctors and patients do not know exactly the relatives' expressed wishes non–disclosure should be the rule. In these circumstances, he argues, those who communicate the information should be careful when deciding to disclose genetic information. They should pay attention to the availability of cures, the severity of the condition, the nature of the disease, and the genetic tests. Most important in this context are the questions of how the individual might be affected and react if subjected to unsolicited information, and whether he or she has expressed any views regarding the possibility to receive such information.[166] When the disorder is incurable the primary consideration is the relatives' potential reaction. Ultimately, Laurie argues, the assumption is that the psychological integrity of the individual (either the patient or the relative) should be respected unless it is justifiable to invade it.[167]

Undoubtedly, this account of spatial privacy takes the interests of the relatives more seriously than the models suggested above. Taking the question of how the relatives may react to the information as a significant factor undoubtedly presents a family–based approach, which Laurie tries to develop within the English liberal–individualistic society.[168] Not only should doctors and patients consider whether there is a cure for the disease before they inform the relatives, they also have to consider other factors, such as whether the relatives will undertake preventive treatment, or if they wish to receive information when nothing can be done to prevent the onset of the disease.

A closer look at Laurie's model leads to the conclusion that it is more individualistic than family–based. First, as Laurie admits,[169] while the patient, who lacks medical knowledge about the nature of the disease, will focus on the possible

---

[163] Ibid., at p. 39.

[164] See Andorno, supra n. 142.

[165] See Laurie, supra n. 144, at p. 440.

[166] See Laurie, supra n. 133, at p. 49.

[167] See Laurie, supra n. 144, at p. 440.

[168] See Laurie, supra n. 133, at p. 51 where Laurie states that his model is based on ethics–of–care conceptions.

[169] Ibid., at p. 50.

The Status of the Family in Law and Bioethics

emotional reactions of the relatives when they are informed, the doctor, who is influenced by the ethics of his or her profession, will focus on *objective* factors, such as the nature of the disorder, its severity, and the like. In many cases doctors will engage in an objective cost–benefit evaluation, giving insufficient consideration to the psychological impact of the disclosure on the relatives. If this model aims to protect the relatives' right, practically patients and doctors will have to share the decision whether or not to approach the relatives; otherwise the relatives' right not to know may be compromised.

Second, when patients consider whether or not to invade the relatives' spatial privacy they have to rely on their appreciation of what the relatives' best interests are.[170] For example, Laurie argues that the patient may be driven not to invade the relative's privacy because he or she knows that the relative is prone to depression, or has a needle phobia.[171] Laurie asks the patient to stand apart from the relatives and evaluate the relevant aspects of the issue according to *his or her* knowledge of the relatives' interests. Therefore, Laurie overlooks the effect of the intimate relationship between the patient and the relative, which makes it difficult to view the situation objectively. Laurie seems to ignore the fact that when the patient considers whether or not to disclose genetic information he or she considers the implications this would have on the relationship with the relatives. The patient does not simply make a decision for the relatives according to his or her knowledge of their wishes but is also affected by the nature of the relationship in the family. As communitarians and proponents of ethics–of–care argue, this is inevitable because the patient is part of the relatives' life and they are part of his or her identity. Thus, another factor should be added to Laurie's criteria, that of the influence of the decision on the familial relationship.

Third, Laurie's failure to consider the effect the patient's decision has on the familial relationship prevails in another aspect. As argued above, Laurie does not deal with the consequences of the relatives' right to remain ignorant. He ignores the possibility that in respecting a relative's right not to know, the patient may compromise the interests of other relatives who wish to receive this information. Consider, for example, a patient who respects her brother's privacy and refrains from informing him that she carries the mutative gene for Huntington's disease. The brother's wife may wish to know whether her husband is a HD carrier for making an informed reproductive decision. How does the patient can resolve such a conflict? The patient is in a difficult position, not knowing which of the interests to prefer. It is not clear how Laurie deals with this dilemma.

Fourth, Laurie argues that the patient should respect the relatives' right not to know as he or she respects the relatives' right not to be watched clandestinely.[172]

---

[170] Berry R., "The genetic revolution and the physician's duty of confidentiality" (1997) 18 *Journal of Legal Medicine* 401 explicitly calls on doctors to consider the best interests of the relatives.

[171] See Laurie, supra n. 133, at pp. 19 and 40.

[172] See Laurie, supra n. 63, at p. 190.

But is this an accurate analogy? It is possible to argue that there is a distinction between the two. While people who do not want others to invade their privacy can take active measures to prevent it, the relatives cannot take any measures to bar others from invading their genetic privacy. While individuals can prevent a passer-by from looking into their home, or hide their feelings and thoughts from others, thus protecting their psychological integrity, the relatives in genetics cannot prevent patients from knowing genetic information about them because when patients receive genetic information from the doctor they immediately know material information about the relatives. In addition, the relatives cannot bar the patient from communicating genetic information they do not want to know; they depend on the conduct of the patient or the doctor.

In sum, Laurie's account still reflects a patient–centred approach. Although he agrees that doctors and patients have to take the interests of the relatives into account, ultimately the relatives do not participate in the process. In the sense that relational autonomy is both collaborative and reciprocal,[173] Laurie does not fully acknowledge that making a decision is not solely an individual enterprise but a dynamic balance among people who are closely involved in each other's lives. As Laurie himself admits, the decision is made for the relatives paternalistically. Furthermore, although Laurie realises that the relatives depend on the patient's decision, he does not fully appreciate that the relationship is mutual and that the patient depends on the relatives as well. In this sense his model is not fully collaborative as proponents of relational autonomy believe it should be. However, as Laurie himself argues, since information is the essence of the familial conflict, it is difficult to involve relatives in the decision whether or not to disclose it to them.

To conclude, although some of the commentators attempted to offer a more familial approach to the right not to know, at core they still perceive the patient as being separate from the relatives. One may ask whether it is possible to suggest another alternative based on different conceptions. This will be discussed next.

4.3.3 Family Privacy and the Interest in not Receiving Genetic Information

In the previous part it was asserted that the nature of the relationship within families qualifies the principle of medical confidentiality and may result in recognition of the relatives' right to know. Similarly, in the context of the right not to know the nature of familial relationships may lead to the acknowledgement of the relatives' interest in not receiving genetic information.

A distinction was made in the previous part between family members and other third parties. If it is accepted that the interests of the relatives in not knowing should be protected, the above distinction will apply to this context as well. As was argued throughout this work, family members are not entirely outside the private

---

[173] Donchin A., "Autonomy and interdependence: Quandaries in genetic decision–making" in Mackenzie C., Stoljar N. (eds.), *Relational Autonomy: Feminist Perspectives on Autonomy, Agency and the Social Self*, New York, Oxford University Press (2000), 236.

sphere of the patient. To a certain extent they share with each other thoughts, desires, and feelings that they do not share with others and that in some circumstances they do not want to share with others. Those who are not family members cannot have access to this familial information because the communication within the family is based mainly on intimacy, a sense of commitment, and a need for mutual support. Sharing information in the family is private as others are barred from accessing it freely, but at the same time it is common to the family members involved. Consequently, it is possible to identify a conception of *familial privacy*, where all relatives have access to information that is communicated in the family.

This conception of familial privacy implies that when the patient considers whether or not to disclose genetic information to family members he or she can rely on their close familial relationship. Knowing the relatives as no one else does, patients can reach a decision after a careful process based on the sharing of thoughts, beliefs, and desires in the family. When the patient cannot determine what the relatives would wish in a specific situation he or she can discover it by approaching the relatives and asking them indirectly what is their general view about receiving distressful information. The relatives' view regarding genetic information can be taken into account because it can be considered within the family, privately, before genetic information becomes available. Obviously, sometimes the patient does not have any difficulty knowing the view of the relatives. On other occasions a family discussion can be conducted with no specific reference to the patient's or relatives' health. The patient will be able to respect the relatives' wish based on the communication within the family and not on his or her personal beliefs of what is best for the relatives. This can be conducted when the relationship is intimate and a sense of mutual responsibility exists in the family. When this is not the case the decision of the patient will be more personal and autonomy will be less relational.

In this process the relatives' desire to protect their privacy may not be fully exercised: when the patient initiates the discussion the relatives will have to share their thoughts and views about genetic information despite their reluctance to do so. Such a discussion will raise their awareness of the implications of exercising their interest in not knowing. Their sense of belonging may override their desire not to know genetic information. They will become aware that fulfilling their interest in not knowing may adversely affect the well–being of other members of the family, such as unborn children. This sense of responsibility to others will ultimately lead them to compromise their right not to know. Nevertheless, the decision not to exercise this right will be theirs and will not be made by the doctor or the patient.

The distinction between relatives and other third parties and the notions of qualified confidentiality and familial privacy will provide the doctor legal and ethical justifications to act more freely when family members are closely involved in the patient's care. As will be argued in Chapter 5, doctors perceive the relatives as active participants in the patient's care, relying on them when treating the patient. As Doherty and Baird observe, in the vast majority of cases the relatives are involved in the communication between the patient and the doctor.[174] If law and ethics perceive confidentiality and privacy as qualified principles within the family, doctors will not constantly have to try to reconcile their duties to the patients with the interests of their families because the family and not the patient will be seen by all disciplines as the unit of care.[175]

Furthermore, the two qualified conceptions of confidentiality and privacy may lead to the recognition of the relational perception of autonomy. As the discussion in this chapter indicates, the liberal perception of autonomy does not give a comprehensive answer to the specific conflict between the patient and the relatives. When doctors wish to respect patients' choices as well as the relatives' interests they face a serious dilemma. In this context, the liberal perception of patient autonomy cannot help the doctor because it highlights only the confrontational aspects of social relationships and the narrow utilitarian mechanism to solve conflicts.

A relational approach may seem more helpful. Adopting such an approach will reflect the patient's decision–making process where he or she considers the interests of others. Respecting patient autonomy will require the doctor to perceive patients not as individuals who govern themselves alone but as people with social relationships that define who they are. The emphasis in this perception of autonomy is not information but a mutual discourse with close others who affect and can be affected by the patient's illness and decisions. From the relatives' perspective a mutual discourse will assist them to discover whether the patient and the doctor possess material information they need and would like to know.

The arguments advanced in this chapter regarding confidentiality and privacy may reflect a romantic perception of the family. Arguing that familial relationships are based on intimacy and good communication may not accord with the reality of many families, whose relationships are fraught with resentment, anger, and disputes. The dynamics in some families can be destructive, so patients may want to keep the information to themselves and not share it with their relatives. In these circumstances patients and family members may not be able to conduct an informative discussion about genetic information; on the contrary, in the heat of an argument they may disclose information to the relative who does not want to know. Moreover, some people may feel more attached to close friends or other non–family members and rely on them when support is needed. How can a health care system cope with patients who prefer to share their thoughts and views with their friends and not with relatives? Is it possible to promote the interests of family members in either knowing or not knowing genetic information in such circumstances?

---

[174] Doherty W., Baird M., "Developmental levels in family–centred medical care" (1983) 18 (3) *Family Medicine* 153.

[175] This argument is discussed here briefly and will be discussed in detail in the next chapter.

A hypothetical example discussed by several ethicists, lawyers, geneticists and counsellors in this context is of a pregnant woman who wants to have a prenatal test of her eight–week old foetus for Huntington's disease, as she recently found out that there is a history of the disease in her husband's family.[176] The father, however, does not wish to know his genetic status and feels anxious that he might develop the disease in the future. The couple fight a great deal and are currently separated, but seeing a marriage counsellor. The woman does not want to discuss the issue with her husband and wants to take the test so as to make an informed decision about her pregnancy. In such a situation it is very difficult to embark on a perception of confidentiality and privacy presented above. How can the doctor deal with such a situation? Obviously, the couple do not want a family discussion of the matter, and to reach an agreed solution, especially if the husband does not know about the pregnancy, is a difficult task. Angus Clarke wonders whether the mother would be able to keep the test result from her partner, asking whether the information would be revealed, most hurtfully, when the couple were arguing and she thought he was behaving irrationally. Would this information, asks Clarke, not damage their relationship permanently?[177]

A possible answer is to admit, as was argued in Chapter 1, that communitarian and ethics–of–care principles cannot furnish a comprehensive solution to the doctor–patient–relatives relationship. In some families, liberal conceptions of justice, equality and autonomy as a state of non–interference should be favoured, as they will be able to settle serious confrontations and disputes. They will help the weakest parties in the family to promote their interests even when family members do not recognise their mutual moral responsibilities. However, in the scenario presented here it must be admitted that a sensible solution is difficult to achieve whatever moral approach one takes.

Tassicker et al. conclude their ethical discussion on this scenario by arguing that the adverse effect genetic information has on other relatives does not justify withholding information from the patient especially when he or she may benefit from it. As a general principle, these researchers assert, doctors should offer patients a test regardless of what other family members may think about it. They conclude that information that might be relevant to the relatives should seldom (if ever) be withheld from the patient in order to protect the family members.[178] It is difficult to accept this view as it gives little consideration to the interests of the relatives. The view taken in this book is that family members who are affected by the patient's decision should be involved as well. The patient cannot ignore their interests completely even when hostility dominates the familial relationship.

---

[176] Parker M., Lucassen A., "Concern for families and individuals in clinical genetics" (2003) 29 *Journal of Medical Ethics* 70, box 3; Tassicker R., at al., "Prenatal diagnosis requests for Huntington's disease when the father is at risk and does not want to know his genetic status: clinical, legal, and ethical viewpoints" (2003) 326 *BMJ* 331.

[177] Clarke A., "Commentary" (2003) 29 *Journal of Medical Ethics* 80, 81.

[178] See Tassicker, supra n. 176, at p. 333.

4.4 Conclusion

The last two chapters discussed the legal and ethical positions of family members in genetics. The discussion indicates that legally the relatives' interests in genetic information are limited. These limitations are the result of an individualistic perspective, which is expressed by the lack of an affirmative duty to act, and a strict rule of medical confidentiality. Furthermore, although the leading approach in *medical ethics* is more sympathetic to the relatives it nevertheless prefers the patient's interests to those of the relatives.

Despite the similarities one can identify distinctions in the approaches of medical law and medical ethics. While the law seems to take a patient–centred approach medical ethics provides some family–based models. However, as analysed in Chapter 1, these models fail to present a comprehensive account in this context. It was argued that greater emphasis should be given to a relational perception of autonomy, which might represent more adequately the various interests of the relatives in genetic information.

Several questions remain open. They result directly from the discussion in the last two chapters. One can still ask whether the current legal and ethical approach to genetic information accords with the day–to–day medical practice in which patients, relatives, and doctors interact and exchange information. A few signs were observed throughout the previous chapters, suggesting that the answer is negative. A serious examination will be made as to whether the legal and ethical position accords with doctors' and relatives' views. Arriving at a well–researched answer will help to reach a conclusion as to whether the balance struck by the law between the interests of patient and relatives is adequate, or whether a change in this area is needed.

Chapter 5

Who is the Patient? The Medical Perception of the Family

5.1 Introduction

It is not possible to discuss comprehensively the status of family members in health care in general, or in the area of genetics in particular, without examining medical models and practices. Such an examination will help in reaching a conclusion whether the legal and ethical positions accord with the views of doctors and patients.

At the outset it should be stressed that medical academics and socio–medical researchers concur that illness affects the entire family, especially when the disease is chronic or terminal. This derives partly from the perception that illness is one of the most stressful life events.[1] In the context of genetics, genetic information has considerable psychological effects on the patient and it may cause mental distress especially when a mutative gene is passed on to the next generation. As the discussion in this chapter will demonstrate, genetic information, like many illnesses, affects the entire family and not only the individual patient.

The doctors' belief that family members have an important role in health care led them to speculate whether the doctor should provide care to family members to improve the patient's condition, or whether the relatives deserve medical help in their own right. In the context of medical information the question is whether information should be disclosed to family members to help them provide daily care to the patient who needs their assistance to recover, or whether they should receive information so that they will be able to make informed decisions about their life. This debate, which concerns the scope of the doctor's obligations to family members, emphasises the difference between the legal position and the medical approach. While in medical law the question is whether or not to recognise the relatives' involvement in patient's care, in the medical literature the issue is how far this involvement should be recognised.

In considering these issues this chapter will focus, inter alia, on the involvement of family members in the medical decision–making process and on the

---

[1] Cole S. et al., "The biopsychosocial model in medical practice" in Stoudemire A. (ed.), *Human Behaviour: An Introduction for Medical Students*, New York, Lippincott-Raven (3rd edn., 1998), 36–84, 49.

attitudes of doctors and patients regarding the communication of medical information to family members. It is divided into five parts. Following this introduction, the second part describes the *biomedical model*, which was practised by doctors for many decades. The third part specifies the shift from the *biomedical model* to the *biopsychosocial model*, which encourages doctors to consider the psychological and social aspects of the patient's illness. Since the involvement of the family is appreciated in this model, the fourth part discusses the place of family members in the biopsychosocial model. The involvement of family members in the patient's care will be examined when the patient receives genetic information from the doctor. The conclusion is reached that it may adversely affect family members, so the fifth part concentrates on doctors' and patients' views when they need to decide whether or not to inform the relatives.

For the examination of the socio–medical literature the terms disease, illness, and sickness should be defined. Disease is an objective definition, which describes a condition of physical or mental ill–health. It is usually defined by its biological aspects, which are independent of the person who suffers from it.[2] Diagnosis of a disease is based on findings of physiological and anatomical abnormalities in the patient's body. By contrast, illness is a subjective definition that describes the patient's personal experience of the disease. This experience depends not only on physiological symptoms of the disease but also on environmental and psychological factors, such as the patient's mental and emotional state.[3] Finally, sickness is defined as a social role, or as a status society provides to the patient. Being sick is associated with a clear set of exemptions as well as obligations. The sick are exempt from normal social activities such as going to work. They are not blamed for their medical condition but have an obligation to try to get well and to cooperate with the doctors.[4] As Marinker cynically argued, sickness provides reassurance to the patient if he is fortunate enough to suffer from a disease.[5]

5.2 The *Biomedical Model*

For many decades, at least until the late 1970s, doctors practised the *biomedical model*. Within it, disease was categorised in the same way as other natural phenomena. Each disease had a specific cause and the doctor's task was to detect and diagnose it, and provide the patient with available medication which either removed its cause or eased the symptoms.[6] Mental and physical diseases were

---

[2]   Ibid., at p. 50.
[3]   Ibid., at pp. 83–85; and also: Eisenberg L., "What makes persons 'patients' and patients 'well'?" (1980) 69 *The American Journal of Medicine* 277.
[4]   Cole et al., supra n. 1, at p. 76.
[5]   Marinker M., "The family in medicine" (1976) 69 *Proceedings of the Royal Society of Medicine* 115, 122.
[6]   McWhinney I., *A Textbook of Family Medicine*, New York, Oxford University Press

considered separately, with provision for a group of psychosomatic diseases where the patient's mind appears to act on the body.[7]

As George Engel points out, this biomedical model is based on a 'reductionistic' approach, namely that one principle is responsible for a complicated phenomenon.[8] According to the biomedical model biological and anatomical changes in the human body are the causes of a disease.[9] This reductionist approach is in its core similar to the underlying principles of causation in tort law where the damage is a consequence of one or a few provable causes.[10]

In an examination of the doctor–patient relationship under this biomedical model, the doctor is perceived as an observer, detached from the patient, who is usually a passive recipient. The doctor has little or almost no interest in the patient's feelings, thoughts, or preferences, and he or she perceives the disease as a separate entity distinct from the patient.[11] This distinction between the disease and the person reflects a debate which is not unique to medicine, known as the mind–body dualism. Descartes was among the first to distinguish the thinking mind from the physical body, a distinction that fundamentally influenced the way doctors think to date.[12] Under this approach the body was perceived as a machine, the disease as a breakdown in the machine, and the doctor as having the job of repairing it. The principal approach in medicine was to concentrate analytically on the biological processes of the disease, and to ignore its psychological, and social aspects.[13]

Predictably, this approach, where the doctor focuses on the disease and not on the patient, went well with the paternalistic approach adopted by many doctors. The biomedical model, which provided patients with little room to articulate their preferences, suited the doctors, who thought they knew what was best for the patient. Patients' consent, their entitlement to receive medical information, and their right to make informed choices were not appreciated, and the imbalance in power between the doctor and the patient was self–evident. Obviously, if the patient had little or no say, the family in these settings was almost invisible in the medical decision–making process.

(2nd edn., 1997), 50.

[7]   This distinction still exists today.

[8]   Engel G., "The need for a new medical model: A challenge for biomedicine" (1977) 196 *Science* 129.

[9]   Ibid., at p. 130.

[10] Lunney K., Oliphant M., *Tort Law: Text and Materials*, Oxford, Oxford University Press (2nd edn., 2003), pp. 188–236, 183; Deakin S., Johnston A., Markesinis B., *Tort Law*, Oxford, Clarendon Press (5th edn., 2003), pp. 185–201.

[11] See Engel, supra n. 8, at p. 131.

[12] Walker E., Katon W., "Psychological factors affecting medical conditions and stress responses" in Stoudemire, supra n. 1, pp. 85–109.

[13] See Engel, supra n. 8, at p. 131.

For many decades patients were willing to accept the practice and implications of the biomedical model. Even nowadays, when several patient–centred models exist, this approach is followed in emergency medicine when it is impossible to wait for the patient's informed decision. This acceptance derived from the novel and rapid advances in medicine. Doctors and researchers, who focused on the biological aspects of diseases, discovered, invented, and developed new and improved treatments to help combat many acute and terminal disease.[14] Their success changed the daily work of doctors both in general practice and in areas of specialisation. In recent years doctors have been dealing mostly with the management of chronic diseases, developmental disorders and accidents, as fewer patients suffer from infections and contagious diseases. It is appreciated that this improvement was largely due to the practice of the biomedical model in both treatment and research.[15]

5.3 The *Biopsychosocial Model*

The biomedical model began to lose its dominance during the late 1970s when George Engel, a psychiatrist and internist, published a seminal article[16] challenging the practice of the biomedical model. The change in the medical approach had begun before that. In the 1950s Michael Balint, a British psychiatrist, gathered groups of GPs in an attempt to draw their attention to the social factors patients bring to the medical encounter.[17] Balint developed the conceptions of 'attentive listening' and 'patient's offers' to provide doctors with the means to understand patients and their illnesses better. Balint was among the first to distinguish between the search for the biological causes of a disease and an overall diagnosis, which included knowledge about the patient's personality and social background.[18]

In addition, the academic discourse among general practitioners in the early 1970s highlighted the social aspects of the doctor–patient relationship. In dealing with the most fundamental issue of their profession, namely the definition of family medicine as a separate discipline, GPs discussed the importance of non–biological factors. Family medicine was defined as a rising medical discipline concerning the attitude of small social groups to health and illness. It focused on the ecology of relationships in the family and between the family and its surroundings.[19] General practitioners acknowledged as long ago as the early 1970s

---

[14]   See McWhinney, supra n. 6, pp. 3–9.

[15]   Ibid.

[16]   See Engel, supra n. 8.

[17]   Balint M., *The Doctor, His Patient and the Illness*, London, Churchill–Livingstone (2nd edn., 1964).

[18]   Ibid., p. 39.

[19]   Ransom D., Vandervoot H., "The development of family medicine" (1973) 225 (9) *JAMA* 1098, 1099.

that family members had an important role in the patient's care.[20]

The attempts to change the perceptions of doctors when interacting with patients were formulated into a scientific model developed by Engel, who relied primarily on a systems theory.[21] The systems theory sees nature as a hierarchy of arranged continuous systems.[22] Each system consists of the less complex and smaller systems in the hierarchy. The hierarchy of living systems is cells, tissues, organs, nervous system, person, two persons, family, culture, and society. For example, the 'organ' system consists of the 'tissue' system, which consists of the 'cell' system. In addition, each level in the hierarchy represents a system of its own. 'Cell', 'tissue', 'organ', 'person', and 'family' – to name just a few – indicate a distinct level of a complex system. Most importantly, each system has a unique set of relationships of its own, with its specific criteria of study and explanation. For example, the 'family' system cannot be explained in biological terms, which explain the operation of the 'cell' system. Each system is simultaneously a whole and a part.[23]

Another characteristic of the systems theory is that none of the systems exists in isolation. Whether it is a cell or a person, each system is influenced by the other systems in the hierarchy. As Engel observed, the person cannot be fully characterised as a dynamic system without reference to the larger systems of which it is a part.[24] The person (as a separate system) is affected by the changes in the cell system and in the family system.

Relying on the systems theory led Engel to argue that the biomedical model was unsatisfactory because it focused only on specific aspects of the illness, failing to consider the influence of other aspects. He asserted that the presence of a biochemical defect was necessary for the definition of a disease but not sufficient for the occurrence of the illness. While the diagnosis of a disease was first suggested by certain core clinical manifestations, the way the patient experienced them, and the effect they had on him or her required consideration of psychological, social, and cultural factors.[25] According to Engel the patient was not separate from the disease but a person who experienced illness.

---

[20] Curry H., "The family as our patient" (1974) 1 *Journal of Family Practice* 70; for an historical review in the area of family medicine see Smilkstein G., "The family in family medicine revisited, again" (1994) 39 (6) *Journal of Family Medicine* 527.

[21] Engel mentioned Weiss P., "The living system: Determinism stratified", in Koestler A., Smythies J.R. (eds.), *Beyond Reductionism*, New York, Macmillan (1969), 3–55; and von Bertalanffy L., *General Systems Theory*, New York, Braziller (1968).

[22] Engel G., "The clinical application of the biopsychosocial Model" (1981) 6 *Journal of Medicine & Philosophy* 101, 103.

[23] Ibid., at p. 106.

[24] Ibid.

[25] See Engel, supra n. 8, at p. 132.

Consequently, for Engel the patient is an individual in a larger social system.[26] Therefore, when a medical decision is made a medical model must take into consideration not only the biological aspects of the disease but also the social context in which the patient lives. Hence, not only biological systems, such as cells, tissues and organs are involved in the diagnosis of the patient but also other systems such as the two–persons unit and the family.[27] In Engel's view, the medical model has moved from biomedical to *biopsychosocial*.

Applying the notion that each system is part of a higher system in the hierarchy led Engel and his followers to see patients as part of the family system. From the first stages of this model the important role of the family was acknowledged. Engel himself argues that the systems–oriented doctor is aware of his or her responsibilities to the patients, their families, and close others.[28] For the doctor who practises the biomedical model decisions regarding interpersonal and social aspects of patients' lives are made in light of minimal information about the people, relationships, and circumstances involved. But the biopsychosocially–trained doctor, who recognizes the importance of patients' social environment, identifies and considers the patient's relationships with his or her significant others.[29]

Engel's systems theory shares many of its features with the communitarian philosophical approach. Like many communitarians, Engel valued not only individuals but also relationships and communities. He acknowledged that in order to understand the patient, doctors and other health care professionals had to become familiar with the communities of which the patient was a member. He recognised that part of the patient system (or identity, in the eyes of philosophers) contains social and psychological variables, such as the effect of close intimates on him or her.

Yet one of the prominent implications in the shift from the biomedical to the biopsychosocial model was the perception of the patient as a person whose wishes should be respected. This is reflected in an examination of the doctor–patient relationship. In this regard, doctors must have good communication skills.[30] First, they have to acquire a sense of empathy with their patients, having the ability to experience the patient's feelings or putting themselves in his or her place.[31] Second, according to the biopsychosocial model doctors should reassure and support patients to let them know that they are there for them.[32] This will enhance mutual trust and maximise the effect of the medical treatment. In addition, the

---

[26] Ibid.

[27] Ibid.

[28] See Engel, supra n. 22, at p. 120.

[29] Ibid., at pp. 120–121.

[30] Cole S., Bird J. (eds.), *The Medical Interview: The Three–Function Approach*, London, Mosby (2nd edn., 2000), 3.

[31] Shelton S., "The doctor–patient relationship" in Stoudemire, supra n. 1, at p. 6.

[32] Ibid., at p. 19.

doctor–patient relationship should be reciprocal.[33] A patient is unlikely to open his or her heart to a doctor who is detached and objective. If doctors need patients to communicate information to them they have to show that they too are vulnerable. This mutuality creates a sense of partnership between patients and doctors and leads patients to adhere to treatment recommendations.

This change in the perception of the doctor–patient relationship may have various causes. A possible explanation accepted by many commentators is the growing and continuing involvement of behavioural sciences, such as sociology and psychology, in medicine.[34] The contribution of these disciplines is the provision of empirical studies suggesting that social factors, such as the familial relationship and social support, affect patients' ability to cope with illness and disease.[35] This contribution has made doctors and other health care professionals realise that they need to know not only the disease but also the patient's inner and social world.

Another possible explanation for the change in the medical approach may be found in the influence of the liberal discourse in political philosophy and of the autonomy–based approach in medical ethics. Interestingly, the liberal approach in political philosophy attracted attention at the same time as the appearance of Engel's work.[36] This philosophy stressed the individual's primacy, his or her independence and rights vis-à-vis the state. This approach had considerable influence on the development of medical ethics that established the concept of respect for patient autonomy as its most important principle.[37]

Undoubtedly, this ethical principle of respect for patient autonomy and dignity prevails in the biopsychosocial model. Within this model doctors give their patients their undivided attention. This tells the patients that their doctors are interested and concerned, and most importantly it sends the patients a message of respect.[38] The insistence on respect suggests that the practical implication of the biopsychosocial model reflects the principle of patient autonomy. After all, respecting patients' decisions is easier when the doctor is familiar with their inner and social world.[39]

---

[33]   See McWhinney, supra n. 6, at p. 120.

[34]   Ibid., at p. 8; Cole et al., supra n. 1, at p. 78.

[35]   See for example, Huygen F.J.A., *Family Medicine: The Family Life History of Families*, London, The Royal College of General Practitioners (1990) who describes the empirical studies he performed on hundreds of families in his general practice clinic. See also: Williams P., *Family Problems*, Oxford, Oxford University Press (1989).

[36]   The influential works of Rawls J., *A Theory of Justice*, Oxford, Oxford University Press (1971), and Dworkin R., *Taking Rights Seriously*, Cambridge, Harvard University Press (1977) were published at about the same time.

[37]   Mason JK., McCall Smith RA., Laurie GT., *Law and Medical Ethics*, London, Butterworth (6th edn., 2002), at p. 8.

[38]   See Cole & Bird, supra n. 30, at p. 20.

[39]   Lindemann-Nelson H., Lindemann-Nelson J., *The Patient in the Family*, New York, Routledge (1995), Ch. 4.

To conclude, in analysing the underlying principles of the biopsychosocial model it is suggested that it relies on the two main characteristics of individual's identity: that of being free and independent self, and that of being part of a network of close intimates. This model reflects both patient–based and family–oriented approaches. On the one hand, it provides more respect for the patient than the biomedical model, but on the other hand, it also recognises the significant role family members play in the patient's care. Unlike medical law, which continues to rely on reductionist and liberal–individualistic philosophies, medicine combines liberal and communitarian conceptions. In this respect medicine has become more attentive to behavioural sciences than has the law.

5.4 The Family in the *Biopsychosocial Model*

The *biopsychosocial* model takes into account the psychological and social aspects of the illness, thereby recognising the importance of family members in the patient's care. Textbooks for medical students began to dedicate at least one chapter to the patient's family.[40] GPs too started concentrating in their writings on the role of the family in health care.[41] The explicit and common statement was clear: *Illness is a family matter.*

As regards genetics, family members' involvement in the patient's care will be observed in this part from two aspects: first, there is the patient's need for family support on receipt of positive test results and diagnosis as a carrier or a sufferer. Second, there is the effect test results have on the patient's family members. Chapter 2 dealt with the impact of genetic information on the *familial relationship*, supporting the argument that the family in genetics is not confined to its biological ties but is defined also by its social relations. In this chapter empirical data will be presented to examine how information affects the individual relative. Dealing with these two aspects of family involvement is aimed to examine whether receipt of genetic information is a family matter. Realising that family members play a central role in genetics will lead to an examination of the doctor's professional duties to family members. This will affect the discussion in the next part, which is dedicated to the involvement of family members in the medical decision–making process and whether their interests are considered by doctors and patients when disclosure of genetic information is considered.

---

[40] See McWhinney, supra n. 6, Ch. 10; Stoudemire A. (ed.), *Human Behaviour: An Introduction for Medical Students*, New York, Lippincott–Raven (3rd edn., 1998), Ch. 9; Cole & Bird, supra n. 30, Ch. 20.

[41] See for example: Huygen, supra n. 35; Williams, supra n. 35; Christie R., Hoffmaster B., *Ethical Issues in Family Medicine*, Oxford, Oxford University Press (1986).

5.4.1 The Family as a Source of Social Support

One of the most influential social variables in a patient's illness is social support. There is abundant evidence suggesting that the social support family members provide to patients affects their ability to cope with the illness.[42] Peter Steinglass in a literature review on cancer care argues that family social support has a powerful role in influencing patients' morbidity, mortality and the course of most chronic illnesses.[43]

But what is social support? Social support is defined as an exchange of resources between two parties (provider and recipient) aiming to improve the recipient's well–being.[44] Social support has two main aspects. One is the *network* of relationships between the patient and the intimates that connects him or her to the community.[45] The other is the *form* of the support, which may be informational, tangible, or emotional. Informational support refers to the provision of knowledge to the patient when he or she seeks it. Tangible support concerns the assistance that others can provide to the patient, such as financial help or transportation. Emotional support is letting the patient know that he or she is loved, appreciated, and cared for, regardless of his or her achievements.[46]

When does the patient need social support? Social support is needed when the patient experiences a stressful or traumatic life event. The receipt of positive genetic test results is considered a psychologically distressing life event.[47] Learning about a serious threat to one's health may have a profound impact on one's future. In this situation the patient's ability to cope with genetic information depends on the social support he or she receives from others. Since the family is the social environment of most patients its members are considered the main

---

[42] Ruberman W. et al., "Psychosocial influences on mortality after myocardial infarction" (1984) 311 *New England Journal of Medicine* 325; Berkman L., "The role of social relations in health promotion" (1995) 57 *Psychosomatic Medicine* 245; Bloom J. et al., "Sources of support and the physical and mental well–being of young women with breast cancer" (2001) 53 *Social Science & Medicine* 1513; Spiegel D. et al., "Effect of psychosocial treatment on survival of patients with metastatic breast cancer" (1989) 2 *The Lancet* 1989; These are just a few examples.

[43] Steinglass P., "Family processes and chronic illness" in Baider L., Cooper C., Kaplan De-Nour A. (eds.), *Cancer and the Family*, Chichester, Wiley (2nd edn., 2000), 3–15, 6; House and his colleagues argued that the influence of social integration on people's morbidity and mortality is stronger than the effect of smoking; see: House J.S. et al., "Social relations and health" (1988) 241 *Science* 540, 543.

[44] Shumaker S., Brownell A., "Toward a theory of social support: Closing conceptual gaps" (1984) 40 *Journal of Social Issues* 11, 17.

[45] See Bloom, supra n. 42, at p. 1513.

[46] Ibid., at p. 1514.

[47] Tibben A. et al., "Three–year follow–up after presymptomatic testing for Huntington's disease in tested individuals and partners" (1997) 16 *Health Psychology* 20, pp. 20–21.

source of support. This form of social support is based on the mutual relationships within the family.

Numerous studies indicate that social support is crucial in all stages of the illness.[48] However, in the context of this work, the focus will be on the first stages, namely when the patient decides to seek testing and advice and has to deal with the results and diagnosis that ensue.

5.4.1.1 Patients' decisions to seek medical advice. Addressing this issue, Bloom indicates that relatives play an important role in encouraging patients first to enter the health care system.[49] She finds that the patient turns to his or her close family members before making the decision to seek professional advice. She reveals that family members provide the patient with the necessary information and guidance to seek medical advice or not. She suggests that when patients have a close relationship they are willing to act for the overall good of the family rather than for their personal interest. Family members succeed in their attempt to encourage patients to seek professional and medical services by appealing to what Bloom calls 'the patient's sense of family membership'.[50]

Bloom arrives at this conclusion following her study on cancer patients. Undoubtedly, this view supports the communitarian message that in some cases one member agrees to relinquish his or her personal interests for the benefit of the family. Yet it can be argued that sometimes patients are reluctant to give up their personal interests for the benefit of close relatives. Whether or not the views of the relatives are dominant, it should be stressed that the patient does consult them. This implies that when the patient exercises his or her autonomy, the relationship with others is important.

Applied to the context of genetics, Bloom's findings indicate that a decision to take a test, especially one requiring the cooperation of other family members, will be most probably influenced by their views. A study on women who considered genetic testing for breast cancer indicates that their spouses fully supported their decision to undergo testing.[51] Sometimes, as Lori Andrews argues, family

---

48   See, for example: Northouse L., "Social support in patients' and husbands' adjustment to breast cancer" (1988) 37 (2) *Nursing Research* 91; Northouse L.L. et al., "Quality of life of women with recurrent breast cancer and their family members" (2002) 20 (19) *Journal of Clinical Oncology* 4050.

49   Bloom J., "The role of family support in cancer control" in Baider L., Cooper C., Kaplan De-Nour A. (eds.), *Cancer and the Family*, Chichester, Wiley (2nd edn., 2000), pp. 53–71, 60.

50   Ibid., at p. 61.

51   Metcalfe K.A. et al. "Evaluation of the needs of spouses of female carriers of mutations in BRCA1 and BRCA2" (2002) 62 *Clinical Genetics* 464; for difference in attitude of different family members as to the patient's intention to undergo testing see Kenen R., Arden–Jones A., Eeles R., "Healthy women from suspected hereditary breast and

members may compel the patient to be tested.[52] Although such family pressure is not recommended, it indicates that very often the decision to undergo testing is a result of a family discussion and not just of personal choice. This stands in contrast to the legal position, which assumes that the patient alone conducts his or her medical affairs. However, the existence of familial pressure highlights the importance of the patient's right to make an independent decision.

5.4.1.2 Coping with bad news. When a patient receives distressing information, such as positive genetic test results, he or she often turns to his or her close relatives for support. In the context of genetics, however, Andrews quotes genetic counsellors who argue that often people do not receive the family support they expect.[53]

Indeed, studies reveal that patients who undergo testing need the support of their family members. Tercyak and his colleagues discovered that parents who disclosed their test results to their young children had experienced higher level of mental distress than those who did not inform their relatives.[54] The researchers found that those who communicated test results to their children did so as means to cope with upsetting thoughts and feelings they experienced. Another study confirmed this, and indicated that one of the main reasons for BRCA carriers communicating their test results to their close sisters was to win their emotional support.[55] In yet another study people with fewer social contacts or less satisfactory relationships were more prone to depression and mental distress when receiving genetic test results than people who had more social contacts or satisfactory relationships.[56]

Researchers who investigate the link between illness and social support argue that social support promotes the patient's wellbeing owing to the intimacy and the sense of belonging that family members share.[57] Regarding spousal support,

---

ovarian cancer families: the significant others in their lives" (2004) 13 *European Journal of Cancer Care*169, 173–178.

[52] Andrews L., *Future Perfect: Confronting Decisions about Genetics*, New York, Columbia University Press (2001), 55.

[53] Ibid.

[54] Tercyak K. et al., "Parental communication of BRAC1/2 genetic test results to children" (2001) 42 *Patient Education and Counselling* 213, 214, 218.

[55] Hughes C. et al., "All in the family: Evaluation of the process and context of sisters' communication about BRCA1 and BRCA2 genetic test results" (2002) 107 (2) *American Journal of Medical Genetics* 143. This was also evident in Claes E. et al., "Communication with close and distant relatives in the context of genetic testing for hereditary breast and ovarian cancer in cancer patients" (2003) 116A *American Journal of Medical Genetics* 11.

[56] Vernon S. et al., "Correlates of psychologic distress in colorectal cancer patients undergoing genetic testing for hereditary colon cancer" (1997) 16 *Health Psychology* 73, 78.

[57] See for example: Berkman, supra n. 42, at p. 251.

researchers explain that this phenomenon derives from the duration of the marital relationship, its intensity, and the interdependence in the relationship.[58] These explanations led some commentators to conclude that the family and not the patient alone should be seen as the unit of care.[59]

The emphasis on intimacy, solidarity, and interdependence as the main explanations for the beneficial influence of social support on the patient is undoubtedly compatible with the communitarian and ethics–of–care perceptions of the individual. As discussed in Chapter 1, communitarians recognise that health promotion depends not only on doctors and individual patients but also on families and other communities. The studies presented above support this view. They indicate that the individual patient cannot survive mentally or spiritually without a network of intimates who encourage him or her to seek medical help and to cope with a serious diagnosis. During this process patients need their family members to maintain their identity especially in these stressful circumstances where they are given information which considerably changes their self–image.[60] The support patients receive from their relatives helps them to protect their identity and restore their individuality.[61] The family is considered a major instrument in helping patients to regain the sense of independence they had prior to their illness.

The research discussed above confirms another communitarian notion. The relatives' willingness to provide support to the patient suggests that intimacy implies mutual responsibility. Family members accept that living together and having an intimate relationship means assuming responsibility to support the patient who receives distressing news. Since family members share other life events, they expect that when the patient receives bad news they will need to assist him or her, and in some cases they will need the patient's support and assistance. Furthermore, a person's willingness to seek medical advice and undergo testing derives from a sense of responsibility to the family. As research suggests, one of the primary reasons for patients' receiving genetic test results is to help other family members avoid developing the relevant disease.[62] As will be discussed below, this is why patients communicate the results to their at–risk relatives. This sense of obligation that leads the patient to choose a specific course of treatment suggests, yet again, that the patient does not exercise autonomy alone.

However, one can argue that family members may not share intimacy even when they live together, or, as some studies indicate, they may express resentment

---

[58]   Manne S. et al., "Spousal negative responses to cancer patients: The role of social restriction, spouse mood and relationship satisfaction" (1999) 67 (3) *Journal of Consulting and Clinical Psychology* 352.

[59]   See Steinglass, supra n. 43, at p. 12.

[60]   See Andrews, supra n. 52, at p. 55.

[61]   See the Lindemann-Nelsons, supra n. 39, pp. 45–46; the authors argue that being diagnosed with illness distances the patient from himself or herself.

[62]   Vernon S. et al., "Intention to learn results of genetic testing for hereditary colon cancer" (1999) (8) Cancer Epidemiology, Biomarkers & Prevention 353, 355.

at the fact that their relative was diagnosed as a carrier. Opponents may argue that family support loses its healing effect when relatives ignore the patient's need for emotional support. Indeed, research suggests that ignoring the patient's needs for support does not have a neutral effect; on the contrary, it has a negative effect on the patient because it may lead to deterioration in his or her physical and mental health.[63] This illustrates yet again the considerable influence family members have on the patient's condition.

The negative influence on the patient constitutes a serious difficulty for communitarians, who perceive the family as a supportive community. This negative impact may harm the patient's self–image. The intimate relationships can become abusive, and the harm to the patient may be serious as he or she is in a vulnerable position and depends on others to cope with bad news. When this is the case the patient's ability to distance himself or herself from the family and to make independent decisions is indispensable for maintaining his or her individuality. Now the communitarian belief in solidarity and promotion of the common good has little meaning.

5.4.2 The Effect of the Illness on Family Members[64]

Research suggests that genetic information may influence the quality of life of family members. Hollman et al. examined the quality of life of carriers' relatives and of people with no susceptibility to a genetic disorder.[65] The researchers discovered that generally carriers' relatives were as satisfied with their life as people with no disposition to the disorder. However, the relatives were worried that the carriers would develop the disease, and this adversely affected their quality of life. Other studies found that carriers' relatives felt that their quality of life was diminished following their realisation that their loved one (usually their child or parent) was a carrier.[66] These findings were confirmed in research on breast cancer that indicated that first–degree relatives of breast cancer patients suffered from

---

[63] Manne S. et al., "Supportive and negative responses in the partner relationship: The association with psychological adjustment among individuals with cancer" (1997) *Journal of Behavioural Medicine* 101.

[64] Several books focus on the impact of chronic and terminal diseases on the family. See: Baider L., Cooper C., Kaplan De-Nour A. (eds.), *Cancer and the Family*, Chichester, Wiley (2nd edn., 2000); Gilbar O., Ben-Zur H., *Cancer and the Family Caregiver: Distress and Coping*, Springfield, Ill., Charles C. Thomas (2002); Altschuler J., *Working with Chronic Illness: A Family Approach*, London, Macmillan (1997); Light E., Niederehe G., Labowitz B. (eds.), *Stress Effects on Family Caregivers of Alzheimer's Patients*, New York, Springer (1994); Biegel D., Sales E., Schulz R., *Family Caregiving in Chronic Illness*, Newbury Park, CA, Sage (1991).

[65] Hollman G. et al., "Familial hypercholesterolemia and quality of life in family members" (2003) 36 *Preventative Medicine* 569.

[66] Ibid., at pp. 572– 573.

mood disturbance more than the patients themselves.[67] In a recent study, first–degree family members reported feelings of worry about the possibility of developing the disease.[68]

The conclusion one can draw from these studies is that the effect of genetic information on family members is not confined to their physical health. Knowing that their loved one is a carrier and he or she may develop the disease in the future affects their emotional state and quality of life. This does not accord with the legal position, which does not take into account the possibility that family members can be adversely affected by the patient's condition even when their physical health is not at risk.

As research suggests, genetic information affects the spouse considerably. Spouses have to face many difficulties when their partners receive positive genetic test results and are diagnosed as carriers or potential sufferers. A study about spouses of patients diagnosed as BRCA1/2 carriers[69] revealed that they feared the effects of the disease, the treatment, and the increased surveillance that their partners would have to undergo. Approximately one third of the respondents stated that their feelings and emotions had changed since the patient had taken the genetic tests.[70] A different study in breast cancer revealed that levels of mental distress in husbands were higher than the level of the general population.[71] These findings prevail with incurable disorders, such Huntington's. Couples with a partner with an increased risk are more depressed and distressed than couples with a partner with a decreased risk.[72]

Having children was identified in current research as an additional stress factor for spouses.[73] Partners of individuals who were about to undergo genetic testing proved significantly more despondent when they had children than when they did not. In addition, partners of carriers who had children scored significantly higher on mental distress than partners without children. This indicates that for partners the threat that their children may develop an incurable disorder, such as Huntington's, is one of the most dramatic aspects of their lives and may cause feelings of anxiety and hopelessness. A growing number of researchers have

---

[67] Lerman C. et al., "Attitudes about genetic testing for breast–ovarian cancer susceptibility" (1994) 12 *Journal of Clinical Oncology* 843.

[68] Chalmers K. et al., "Reports of information and support need of daughters and sisters of women with breast cancer" (2003) 12 *European Journal of Cancer Care* 81, 84.

[69] The offspring of BRCA carriers are at a greater risk of developing than children of non–carriers.

[70] See Metcalfe, supra n. 51, at p. 468.

[71] Northouse L., Swain M., "Adjustment of patients and husbands to the initial impact of breast cancer" (1987) 37 *Nursing Research* 221.

[72] Spijker A. et al., "Psychological aspects of genetic counselling: A review of the experience with Huntington's disease" (1997) 32 *Patient Education and Counselling* 33, 37.

[73] See Tibben, supra n. 47, at p. 21.

become aware of the effect of predictive genetic tests on the patient's partner. They realise that partners also require attention in the process of genetic counselling. In the context of Huntington's disease, partners are called the 'forgotten person in the family'.[74] As research suggests, partners of those who have the mutation for Huntington's disease express more distress than partners of those who do not have the mutation.[75]

These findings demonstrate the interdependence of patients and relatives. They indicate that relatives are greatly influenced by the patient's medical condition. They reflect the aspect of one's identity that is embodied and closely connected. Not only is the individual who lives in a family unable to detach himself or herself from family members but he or she is also affected by their physical and mental well–being.

Nevertheless, one can still argue that doctors should not veer from their main goal, namely treating the individual patient, as he or she is the one seeking medical help. One may accept the empirical evidence specified above, yet argue that it is not the doctor's responsibility to deal with the family members' anxiety. Legal commentators do adopt such a view. They perceive an obligation to attend to the relatives' concerns as being in conflict with their obligation to the patient.[76] This leads them to suggest that since spouses are at no risk of physical harm doctors do not owe them a legal duty.

The medical literature responds to this objection with one voice. Doctors agree that it is imperative to attend to the relatives' needs because it enables them to provide social support to the patient. Many researchers explicitly mention this instrumental justification.[77] For example, Northouse et al. asserted that professional support has to be directed to both the patient and the spouse for two reasons: (1) both need social support, and (2) if the spouse has problems adjusting to the new circumstances it will adversely affect the long–term adjustment of the patient.[78] In the area of family medicine Christie and Hoffmaster argued that the doctor should provide support to the close relatives as it will help them to assist the patient.[79]

However, even by this approach, which encourages doctors to consider the concerns of the family and acknowledges the impact of the familial relationships on the individual patient, doctors seem to perceive the interests of their patients as their primary concern. This may be understandable if the patient is the only family

---

[74] Kessler S., "Forgotten person in the Huntington's family" (1993) 48 *American Journal of Medical Genetics* 145.
[75] See Tibben, supra n. 47, at p. 22.
[76] Ngwena C., Chadwick R., "Genetic information and the duty of confidentiality: Ethics and law" (1993) 1 *Medical Law International* 73, 86.
[77] Ben-Zur H. et al., "Coping with breast cancer: Patient, spouse and dyad models" (2001) 63 (1) *Psychosomatic Medicine* 32, 33.
[78] Northouse L. et al., "Couples' patterns of adjustment to colon cancer" (2000) 50 *Social Science & Medicine* 270, 283.
[79] See Christie and Hoffmaster, supra n. 41, at p. 73.

member seeking their advice. The next question is how this view is reflected in the medical–decision–making model. The fact that doctors recognise their patients' social embeddedness does not necessarily imply that they prefer the interests of the family to those of the individual patient. This will be discussed further below.

In any event, it seems that the medical approach is more family oriented than the legal position as it addresses various concerns of family members. As we saw in Chapter 3 the courts do not always appreciate that the patient's condition affects the well–being of his or her relatives. Still, the position that the doctor should help the relative to help the patient deserves a closer look. It may cause unease among Kantian ethicists, who strongly believe that people are always an end in themselves and should not be treated as means to fulfil others' needs. Examining the relevant literature on the subject will reveal the medical position regarding the doctor's duty to family members.

5.4.3 The Doctor's Professional Obligations to the Family Members

Stating that the patient needs family social support and that the relatives are considerably affected by the patient's genetic status is not the end of the discussion. The next question is how this affects the involvement of family members in the doctor–patient relationship. In this context one may wonder whether doctors attend to family members only to help them to help the patient, or whether they address the relatives' problems because they see 'the family as the patient'. These questions concern doctors' professional obligations to family members and affect the legal and ethical duties owed to them.

Moreover, if family members are closely involved in the doctor–patient relationship another question arises, namely their effect on the medical *decision–making process*. In the area of genetics, doctors and patients have to decide whether or not to disclose information to family members. In this context the concern for family members can be examined through surveys that investigate the views of doctors and patients.

The attitude in the medical literature to family members' involvement varies. As we shall see, this issue is not settled in the medical literature. Some writers favour treating the whole family, but others prefer to leave the family *outside* the examination room.

Christie and Hoffmaster call on doctors to treat 'the family in the patient',[80] recognising that the familial relationship is part of the biopsychosocial model. For example, when the doctor treats a dying patient at home, the authors argue that the doctor should focus on the sick patient. The doctor should attend to the family members because it will help them support the patient's overall condition. Professionally, the doctor should help family members with their 'disease' even

---

[80]   See Christie and Hoffmaster, supra n. 41, at p. 70.

though they are not his or her registered patients.[81]

Christie and Hoffmaster attempt to strike a balance between the doctor's professional duties, the patient's needs, and the family's involvement. On the one hand, they assert that doctors should perceive the family as unit of illness, but on the other they acknowledge that the patient is the primary focus of care and that family members should be approached to help them help the patient.

The attempt to take into account the patient's personal needs as well as the relatives' interests prevails when the two authors discuss a case–study in their book. In that case a native–American female patient refuses medical treatment that could prolong her life. Her refusal would leave her two young granddaughters without familial adult supervision. Christie and Hoffmaster seem to justify a decision not to comply with the patient's request but to insist on providing her with medical treatment in order to give her grandchildren a few more years of stable family environment. The two authors imply that in some cases doctors should compromise the autonomy of the patient and prefer the independent interests of the family members. However, the authors do not go the extra mile and decide whose interests should be preferred. Instead they argue that providing professional medical care for more than one family member can create conflicts of interest for the family doctor.[82] In the end Christie and Hoffmaster grant the doctor the discretion to decide how to resolve familial tension but they do not impose on him or her any legal or ethical obligation to do so.

The scenario discussed by Christie and Hoffmaster was addressed by the American courts on several occasions when they had to decide whether to allow a parent of young children to refuse life–sustaining treatment. In the majority of cases the patients refused administration of blood due to their religious belief (they were Jehovah's Witnesses). In the 1964 case of *the President and Directors of Georgetown College* the patient had a seven–month–old child.[83] The court, overriding the patient's refusal to receive blood, held that the patient had a responsibility to the community to care for her child and that in such circumstances the state could not let her abandon the child.[84]

Subsequent cases allowed parents to refuse life–sustaining treatment. In *Norwood Hospital v Munoz* the court held that the interests of the state in saving the patient's life and in protecting the child's well–being did not override the

---

[81] Ibid.; see also: Kubler–Ross E., *On Death and Dying*, New York, Routledge (1970), arguing at p. 139 that professionals cannot help the patient who suffers from a terminal disease in a meaningful way if they do not include the family in the management of treatment.

[82] See Christie and Hoffmaster, supra n. 41, p. 82.

[83] *Application of the President and Directors of Georgetown College Inc* (1964) 331 F 2d 1000 and on rehearing (1964) 331 F 2d 1010 (C.A. D C).

[84] Ibid., (1964) 331 F 2d 1000, at p. 1008.

patient's right to refuse life–saving treatment.[85] A similar approach was taken when the patient was a single parent. In *Re Dubreuil*[86] a mother of three minor children refused blood transfusion. She was separated from the father but was married to a man who was not a Jehovah's Witness. The Florida Supreme Court indicated that the biological father did not deny his responsibility to the children. Consequently, the court upheld the patient's right to refuse treatment. Clearly, this many not be the case of all single parent families. When the children are left with no one to care for them the decision of the single parent and of the doctors is much more difficult.

At first glance, this legal position sends a clear message. The balance seems obvious: society should not interfere with the individual's right to make autonomous decisions about his or her health even when other family members depend on him or her. Yet Rosamund Scott suggests another interpretation.[87] Scott argues that the interests of the individual patient and those of his or her children may not be in conflict, and asserts that the patient's freedom to make personal choices may accord with the family's view of life.[88] While parents' choices may reflect their integrity, they may also represent the unity of the family. Scott stresses that autonomy incorporates not only the patient's good but also the family's.[89] When a parent's refusal of treatment is not respected this may compromise both the patient's interest in self–determination and the integrity of the family. However, concerning a single parent's refusal of treatment, Scott admits that it is difficult to reconcile the interests of the parent and those of the child. Undoubtedly, the legal position and Scott's interpretation do not reflect the view taken by Christie and Hoffmaster.

Going back to the medical view of the family, the family–based approach taken by Christie and Hoffmaster is not accepted by all. Marinker, for example, favours a patient–centred approach. Although he admits that the family is inherently involved in the patient's sickness,[90] he holds that to bring family members into the examination room when the doctor thinks it necessary may be to impose a treatment situation on them. Marinker states that in such a situation family members are not helped in their own right because they are not the doctor's patients. Moreover, Marinker holds that doctors are not asked to treat the family as a whole but only the individual patient. In conclusion, he criticises the view that

---

[85] *Norwood Hospital v Munoz* (1991) 564 NE 2d 1017 (Mass Sup Ct); See also: *Re Osborne* (1972) 294 A 2d 372 (D.C. Ct App); *Public Health Trust of Dade County v Wons* (1989) 541 So 2d 96 (Fla Sup Ct); *Re Farrell* (1987) 529 A 2d 404 (NJ Sup Ct); *Fosmire v Nicoleau* (1990) 551 NE 2d 77 (NY Ct App).

[86] *Re Dubreuil* (1993) 629 SO 2d 819 (Fla Sup Ct).

[87] Scott R., "Autonomy and connectedness: A re-evaluation of Georgetown and its progeny" (2000) 28 *Journal of Law, Medicine & Ethics* 55, pp. 61–62.

[88] Ibid., at p. 63.

[89] Ibid.

[90] See Marinker, supra n. 5, at p. 122.

the doctor must shift his focus from the individual patient to the family as a social unit.[91]

Marinker tries to balance two factors: he acknowledges the important role of the family in supporting the patient but on the other hand he is reluctant to impose an additional burden on the doctor. The relatives are approached merely to help the patient cope with his or her condition. The possibility that the illness affects the relatives' wellbeing does not have to concern the doctor, whose aim is to treat the individual patient. Unlike other medical academics, Marinker does not perceive the family as the unit of care; instead his view is close to that of English law, which imposes a duty on the doctor to the patient's family members only in exceptional circumstances.

Concentrating on the means–end debate, one can detect a difference between the approach taken by Christie and Hoffmaster and the one argued by Marinker. While Marinker perceives the family merely as a means to improve the patient's condition, Christie and Hoffmaster argue that in some circumstances the interests and needs of family members require the doctor's attention and in some circumstances may override those of the individual patient.

When these views are compared with the one promoted by Ian McWhinney, a strong family–based approach emerges. McWhinney, a leading authority in family medicine, calls doctors in all disciplines to 'think family'.[92] This suggests that doctors should be attentive to the needs of family members who are affected by the misfortune of their relatives.[93] More particularly, McWhinney loads doctors with several responsibilities to family members. They include: looking out for vulnerable family members and giving them support; providing family members with information at times of serious illness; looking out for vulnerable relatives, who are defined as 'hidden patients'; and convening a family conference at critical times.[94] McWhinney attempts to treat the family and not merely the individual patient. He instructs doctors not to take one side in a familial conflict but to act as a mediator. Like Christie and Hoffmaster, he leaves to the doctor the discretion to decide how to resolve a familial conflict: while in some circumstances the doctor should prefer the interests of the individual patient, in others he or she should favour those of the relatives.[95]

McWhinney's view is decidedly not similar to the legal position. While he evidently admits that doctors owe some obligations to family members when treating the patient, the law does not impose duties to them. For example, McWhinney realises that doctors should communicate information to family members when the patient is seriously ill, but legally a strict duty of confidentiality permits disclosure provided the patient consents. Presumably McWhinney does not

---

[91] Ibid, at p. 123.
[92] See McWhinney, supra n. 6, at p. 235.
[93] Ibid.
[94] Ibid., at p. 254.
[95] Ibid., at p. 230.

mean to impose a *legal* duty on the doctor but refers to the doctor's professional obligations. As demonstrated in Chapter 4, translating an ethical or professional duty into a legal one is something which very few policy–makers and commentators will be willing to do.

The socio–medical literature on the issue of coping with terminal illnesses reflects a position where family members are treated in their own right. Numerous books and articles address the difficulties family members face when their loved one is dying.[96] Socio–medical researchers have developed treatment models for doctors, who have the obligation to help family members to come to terms with the loss of the patient.[97] The main purpose of these models is to assist family members to adjust to the new circumstances even before the patient dies. Research suggests that providing counselling to relatives may help them facilitate normal grief and adjust to living without the patient, and also encourage them to resume a normal life.[98] One study indicates that providing counselling for widows following their husbands' death has a positive impact on their mental health and also on their immunological system.[99]

The conclusion one can draw from these studies is that doctors identify and address the distinctive interests of family members. Yet once again a question arises whether the doctor's duty to arrange counselling for the bereaved amounts to a legal one. Can the relatives sue the doctor for failure to offer them counselling? Whatever the answer, a gap between the legal and the medical attitude to family members prevails.

To conclude, when the approaches to family involvement are evaluated a philosophical debate emerges. Those who perceive the family as means to benefit the patient implicitly argue that the principal goal of medicine is to help the individual patient. If the doctor helps the relatives to relieve distress this is only an incidental good, not a fundamental one. On the other hand, those who address family problems and help family members to come to terms with a diagnosis of terminal illness adopt a family–oriented approach and are aware that ultimately the entire family is affected by the information given to the patient.

Practically, the means–end debate may have implications when a medical decision has to be made. Such a decision in the context of genetics is whether or not to disclose test results to family members. In these circumstances viewing family members as means to benefit the patient may result in ignoring their interests in receiving the results when the patient refuses to inform them. By contrast, taking the relatives' interests into account may result in compromising the

---

[96] For references on this subject see Gilbar and Ben-Zur, supra n. 64, at pp. 242–248.

[97] McWhinney, supra 6, at p. 252.

[98] Freeman S.J., Ward S., "Death and bereavement: What counselors should know" (1998) 20 (3) *Journal of Mental Health Counseling* 216.

[99] Beem E.E. et al., "The immunological and psychological effects of bereavement: Does grief counseling really make a difference? A pilot study" (1999) 85 (1) *Psychiatry Research* 81.

patient's preference to control exclusively the sensitive information he or she receives from the doctor. Doctors too may reflect in their decisions the means–end dichotomy. A doctor who is attentive to the relatives' emotional and informational needs will present a family–oriented approach by frequently overriding the patient's right to confidentiality. A doctor who concentrates on the patient's interests will refer to the relatives only as a means to treat the patient. This doctor may ask the relatives to undergo genetic tests to verify the patient's diagnosis but may be reluctant to disclose the patient's test results to them without the patient's consent.

In legal and ethical eyes the means–end debate seems to reflect a conflict between the patient's interest in exercising autonomy and the relatives' interest in avoiding harm and making informed decisions. When a medical decision has to be made whether to communicate medical information to the relatives or not, law and ethics adhere to principles of consent and confidentiality to help doctors to solve the dilemma. By promoting these principles the family is alienated from the decision–making process, because law and ethics encourage doctors to respect the personal decision of the patient even when little attention is given to the relatives' interests. As it will be discussed in the next part, medical academics do not perceive the involvement of the family as threatening, but they try to resolve familial tensions through models of partnership.

5.5 Family Members and the Medical Decision–Making Process

5.5.1 The Partnership Model

As mentioned earlier, the biopsychosocial model encourages doctors to establish their relationship with their patients in the form of partnership in decision–making. A paternalistic model whereby doctors make decisions without communicating all relevant information to their patients is practised today only in emergency medicine. Furthermore, an extreme informed model, where patients make decisions themselves and doctors only provide the information, is also rarely practised (usually in elective procedures). Instead, a model of shared decision–making is developed where doctors and patients share the responsibility in making decisions.[100]

---

[100]   Charles C. et al., "Decision–making in the physician–patient encounter: What does it mean? (Or it takes at least two to tango)" (1997) 44 *Social Science & Medicine* 681; the shared decision–making model is one among several models discussed in the academic literature. Emanuel EJ., Emanuel LL., "Four models of the physician–patient relationship" (1992) 267 *Journal of the American Medical Association* 2221 identified four models: the paternalistic, the informative, the interpretive and the deliberative. They discuss the values and limitations of each.

In this model both doctors and patients take positive steps to participate in the decision–making process. For doctors this model requires establishing an agreeable atmosphere so that patients feel that their views are appreciated. Second, doctors have to elicit the patient's preferences so that treatment decisions are compatible with his or her social background. Third, in this model doctors have to communicate information to patients clearly and coherently. Finally, doctors can share with the patients their recommendations but should not enforce them on the patients. For the patients, a shared decision–making model requires that they be willing to engage in a decision–making process, to communicate to the doctor their preferences, to ask questions, to consider alternatives, and to formulate a treatment preference.[101]

What does this model mean in practice? Charles and her colleagues describe a meeting between a breast cancer patient and her doctor. At the meeting, the doctor provides the diagnosis again and discusses the patient's concerns with her. Then he specifies the various treatment options, with their advantages and disadvantages, and asks the patient about her preferences, given her lifestyle and values. The patient acknowledges the receipt of the information. After a long discussion the patient chooses one option out of those offered to her. The doctor reminds her that there are some side effects when having this particular treatment but the patient replies that she understands that but still prefers to go ahead with the treatment for the reasons she reiterates. The doctor agrees and says that it is a good choice for her.[102]

Undoubtedly, this model applies to circumstances of chronic and terminal diseases, such as genetic disorders, where decisions are not taken in the emergency room but in the doctor's surgery with the provision of sufficient time to absorb the information and consider its future implications. In their work, Cathy Charles and her colleagues stress that in a shared decision–making model there is a room for family members to participate.[103] They acknowledge that the participation of a family member in this process may be more problematic especially for the doctor (who usually conducts the medical encounter), but they emphasise that making a treatment decision has numerous implications, not all of which are known to the doctor.[104] For example, the treatment of chronic illnesses or the treatment provided in the later stages of a terminal disease requires involvement of family members for they are usually those who provide the daily care to the patient. Undoubtedly, in these circumstances the doctor and the patient need to know the views and concerns of the relatives.

---

[101] See Charles et al., ibid., at p. 687.

[102] See Charles at al., supra n. 100, at p. 691.

[103] Charles C. et al., "Decision–making in the physician–patient encounter: revisiting the shared treatment decision–making model" (1999) 49 *Social Science & Medicine* 651, 657.

[104] American Medical Association, Council on Scientific Affairs, "Physicians and Family Caregivers" (1993) 269 (10) *Journal of American Medical Association* 1282.

When a relative participates in the decision–making process coalitions among the three parties may emerge, especially regarding treatment options. The doctor may face serious opposition from the patient and the relative, or in a different situation the patient may face the coalition of the doctor and the relative. However, the nature of the process depends on the circumstances of each case. While the discussion of long–term treatment for a chronic illness of an elderly patient may be subject to constant tensions between the three parties involved, the discussion of treatment for a breast cancer patient may be subject to fewer coalitions as the decision has to be made rather quickly.[105]

Ultimately, in this model only one party can have the final word.[106] For example, in the genetic context the decision whether or not to disclose can in practice be made by the patient or by the doctor. In their revised model, Charles and her colleagues acknowledge this and argue that the *process* should be shared, thus implicitly admitting that any decision would most probably lead to a compromise.[107] The authors emphasise that a shared decision derives from a *negotiated agreement* between the parties. They stress that this model provides the patient some say without total responsibility, and for the doctor an opportunity to participate in the decision–making process without dominating it.[108]

For family members, the development and incorporation of the shared decision–making model recognises the significant role they play in the doctor–patient relationship. It perceives them as a relevant party with a considerable effect on the decision. In this respect the partnership model does not accord with the legal position. Although the courts recently began to promote the rights of the patient when he or she meets the doctor, they do not provide room for family members to become involved. The review in previous chapters indicates that the interests of family members are not fully considered when the patient is competent to make a decision. Legally, doctors are instructed to think about the best interests of the patient in terms of costs and benefits, risks and chances; they do not have to involve family members in this process or consider their various interests. In this regard, genetics is unique as doctors have to explain to patients the implications of the information for the relatives. But even in this context the doctors have to consider only one interest, namely prevention of physical harm.

How does the partnership model apply to the area of genetics? It is suggested that a decision whether or not to disclose information to family members can be discussed thoroughly between the doctor and the patient, where each party contributes his or her view and expertise on the subject. The doctor will provide the medical aspect, namely the medical implications the decision will have for the patient and for the relatives; the patient will consider the psychosocial implications

---

[105] See, Charles et al., supra n. 100, at p. 685.
[106] See Christie and Hoffmaster, supra n. 41, p. 25.
[107] See Charles et al., supra n. 103, at p. 658.
[108] See Charles et al, supra n. 100, at pp. 689–690.

of the decision for himself or herself, for close family members, and for his or her familial relationship.[109] However, if in this context the doctor or the genetic counsellor tries to persuade the patient to disclose the information to his or her family members, then, as Clarke and his colleagues argue, the professional's attempt cannot be perceived as a shared decision–making process. This is because between the patient and the doctor or the counsellor there is no agreement on this issue, an essential element in this partnership model.[110]

Whether or not a shared decision–making model can be practised when familial tension over genetic information exists, a fundamental question remains as to whether in practice (not just in theory) relatives are involved in the decision–making process and receive medical information from doctors and patients. In this context a reference to empirical surveys may assist reaching a conclusion. This issue will be discussed next.

5.5.2 Disclosing Medical Information to Family Members

Concentrating on the decision whether or not to disclose medical information the principle of confidentiality adds another layer to the tension between patients and relatives. The principle of medical confidentiality reinforces the sense of separateness in the individual's identity. It provides patients the right to bar others from receiving medical information. In its extreme version it perceives the patient as an independent and disinterested individual. For doctors, the principle of confidentiality guides their relationships with patients and other third parties.[111] As was discussed in Chapter 4, legally and ethically doctors are allowed to breach confidentiality only in limited circumstances where serious physical harm to others can be prevented.

In medical practice the preservation of confidentiality is less strict. Patients consider their attitude to this principle before they receive information from their doctors. For example, when bringing a relative into the examination room the patients imply that they are willing to share the information with this person. In addition, when the patient is diagnosed with a serious disorder, keeping this information in confidence is almost impossible because the symptoms appear and the patient becomes dependent on the relatives' assistance and support. In these

---

[109] Hunt and her colleagues indicate that the shared–decision making model can be practised in the area of prenatal genetic diagnosis. See Hunt L., de Voogd K., Castaneda H., "The routine and the traumatic in prenatal genetic diagnosis: does clinical information inform patient decision–making" (2004) 56 (3) *Patient Education and Counseling* 302.

[110] Elwyn G., Gray J., Clarke A., "Shared decision making and non–directiveness in genetic counselling" (2000) 37 *Journal of Medical Genetics* 135, 138.

[111] The General Medical Council, *Confidentiality: Protecting and Providing Information*, London, General Medical Council (2000).

circumstances patients and doctors agree that keeping the diagnosis in confidence is usually impracticable.

In the context of genetics patients may not be ill but may be diagnosed as carriers. Some patients may thereby find it easier to maintain confidentiality. When patients do not suffer from a genetic disease but undergo tests to know whether or not they are carriers, a negative result might in itself reduce mental stress, which will reduce the need for social support. Second, if the patient is tested positive for a late–onset disorder, the symptoms of the disease may only develop in the future, delaying the need to share the information with others to a later stage.

Yet as the studies above suggest, the patient has an interest in sharing the information with others because the receipt of test results (positive or negative) and the revelation that he or she is a carrier or a non–carrier, have considerable effect on his or her life, self–image, identity, and feelings. This leads patients to realise that they *need* to share the information even though they do not suffer from the disorder.

Whether protection of confidentiality is practicable or not, the views of doctors and patients in this regard are not fully compatible with the legal and ethical positions. Generally, these two groups see this principle as more qualified and justify disclosure on different and wider grounds than law and ethics. Obviously, the views of patients and doctors differ. Doctors' views are affected by their contradictory responsibilities and obligations, namely to respect the patient's right to confidentiality on the one hand and to treat the family as the unit of care on the other. Patients value this principle greatly, but tend to disclose owing to their strong sense of moral responsibility to their relatives.

5.5.2.1 Doctors. Doctors do value their duty of confidentiality. Research suggests that the majority of doctors believe that they would not disclose information without the patient's consent.[112] However, a substantial minority of doctors believe that they would breach the patient's right to confidentiality when it concerns the family.

Two studies performed by Lako and his colleagues in the Netherlands and in the US indicated that 20–30% of doctors believed they would disclose medical information to the patient's relatives without consent. In addition, these studies indicated that doctors were more willing to provide medical information to family members than to any other third party. In the Dutch survey, 26% of the respondents believed they would inform the patient's wife without consent whereas only 6% believed they would provide the police with information that could incriminate the patient.[113] Furthermore, while 28% of the respondents stated that they would never

---

[112] Geller G. et al., "Physicians' attitudes toward disclosure of genetic information to third parties" (1993) 21 (2) *The Journal of Law, Medicine & Ethics* 238.

[113] Lako C.J. et al., "Handling of confidentiality in general practice: A survey among general practitioners in the Netherlands" (1990) 7 (1) *Family Practice* 34.

disclose information to family members, 83% stated that they would never inform the police.[114]

In the parallel survey conducted in the US, 25% of doctors believed they would inform the patient's spouse without consent, while half of these doctors (12% of all GPs) stated that they would disclose information provided it benefited the patient.[115] Only 8% of the respondents in this study stated that they would never divulge information to the patient's spouse. By contrast, asked if they would communicate medical information to the police, 20% stated that they would never do so while only 6% would inform without consent.[116]

These findings suggest that despite a strict rule of confidentiality in medical law, doctors express a more pragmatic approach where the family members are concerned. Many doctors do not accept the legal rule as it is and are willing to breach confidentiality if the circumstances so require. Moreover, the distinction doctors make between family members and other third parties accords with the suggested model of confidentiality presented in Chapter 4. There it was suggested that patients distinguish between disclosure to relatives and to other third parties. It was also argued that the principle of confidentiality should accordingly be qualified with regard to family members. Undoubtedly, the findings in these studies support those arguments as many doctors believe this is necessary when providing care to the patient.

This conclusion is confirmed in a UK study conducted by Toon and Southgate. They examined the views of doctors regarding the involvement of family members in the doctor–patient relationship.[117] Of the seventeen doctors interviewed, fifteen agreed that if family members are concerned about the patient's condition the doctor should help them relieve their anxieties. Sixteen doctors agreed that if the family members are involved in the patient's care, the doctor should verify they know the details of the treatment. Fifteen doctors agreed that since patients often absorb information poorly when they are sick doctors should inform someone else who is well.[118]

The doctors disagreed regarding the statement that family members have a right to be informed about the health of their close relative as it concerns them as well as the patient. Only eight out of seventeen doctors agreed with this statement whereas six disagreed. However, eleven out of seveteen doctors agreed with the statement that doctors should attend to the relatives' concerns because it improves the patient's condition.[119]

---

[114] Ibid., at pp. 35–36.

[115] Lako C.J. et al., "Confidentiality in medical practice" (1990) 31(2) *Journal of Family Practice* 167.

[116] Ibid., at p. 169.

[117] Toon P.D., Southgate L.J., "The doctor, the patient and the relative: An exploratory survey of doctor–relatives relationship" (1987) 4 (3) *Family Practice* 207.

[118] Ibid., at p. 209.

[119] Ibid.

These findings reflect the means–end debate discussed above. From their research Toon and Southgate felt that doctors perceive the family member mainly as a means to help the patient or as a party who can help them fulfil their task of treating the patient. Doctors also believe that their role includes dealing with relatives' anxieties as long as this does not conflict with their primary duty of treating the patient.[120] These authors concluded that the doctors did not deem the issue of confidentiality problematic, because the presence of the family in the examination room had been determined by the patient's conduct before the medical encounter began.

Whether British doctors see family members as means to benefit the patient or as an end in themselves, the findings of this study present a family–based approach where the interests of family members to receive information and to relieve stress are considered. Once again, a gap between the legal duties of doctors and their personal views emerges. While doctors believe they should communicate information to family members throughout the patient's illness, legally doctors not only have no responsibility for relieving the relatives' anxiety, they may also not be liable when they cause them mental distress.[121] Moreover, the findings presented above indicate that doctors base their decision to disclose information to family members on a wider ground, namely to relieve mental distress or because the relatives are involved in the patient's care. This does not accord with the legal position, which justifies disclosure without consent to prevent risk of serious physical harm to the family members.

As for genetics, the attitude of family doctors differs (as indicated above) from that of geneticists and counsellors. One study suggests that family doctors are more willing to disclose information than the law currently allows them. Geller and her colleagues examined the views of three groups of health care professionals – geneticists, genetic counsellors, and family doctors – on disclosure of genetic information to the patient's spouse, adult children, siblings, employers, insurers, and the driving licence agency.[122] Among the three groups of doctors examined, family doctors were more willing to disclose information to family members than were the other two groups of specialists.

Geller found that 20% of over 1,100 family doctors believed they would disclose genetic information to the patient's spouse without consent, while almost 30% believed they would disclose it to a healthy adult child.[123] As for geneticists, about 11% believed they would inform the spouse without consent, while 19% believed they would communicate information to a healthy adult child. Genetic counsellors opposed disclosure without consent more than the other two groups of

---

[120] Ibid.
[121] *Powell v Boldaz* [1998] Lloyd's Rep. Med. 116.
[122] See Geller, supra n. 112.
[123] Ibid., at p. 239.

doctors. Only 7% believed they would disclose information without consent to the patient's adult child.

For family doctors the findings accord with the results presented in Lako's studies. Family doctors on both sides of the Atlantic see the relatives as closely involved in the patient's care and are therefore more willing to breach patient's confidentiality. However, it is difficult to explain the attitudes of geneticists and genetic counsellors in Geller's study; after all one of the central aims of genetic counselling is to help *families* and not only individuals to and make informed reproductive choices.[124] A possible explanation for the reluctance of those specialising in genetics to inform without the patient's consent is that they are guided by the principle of non–directiveness, requiring them not to persuade patients to take a particular course of action when providing diagnosis and advice, but to leave it to the patient to decide.[125]

The distinction in doctors' attitude to family members and to other third parties as reflected in the above studies appears in Geller's study as well. No genetic counsellor would disclose information to the patient's employer or insurer, and only 0.5% of family doctors would disclose information to the patient's employer.[126] However, closer analysis reveals that the majority of doctors in all groups would not disclose genetic information to patients' family members without their consent. The proportion of doctors who were willing to disclose information to family members is less than one third. This implies that despite doctors' gradual awareness of the relatives' needs their professional duty of confidentiality does dominate their discretion and practice.

Consequently, the research emphasises the inherent dissonance doctors may have with regard to the interests of relatives in receiving genetic information. Still, two international studies by Wertz and Fletcher in 1984–1986 and 1993–1995 evinced a different trend to that reflected in Geller's study.[127] In their first study, conducted in 19 countries, 60% of British doctors specialising in genetics stated that they would disclose genetic information without consent to the patient's relatives. These findings were in accordance with the views of doctors specialising in genetics in other Western countries. In this study there was no difference between the attitude of doctors with regard to incurable disorder, such as Huntington's disease, and a treatable disorder, such as Haemophilia A. This implies that doctors are not guided primarily by the principle of prevention of

---

[124] British Medical Association, *Human Genetics: Choice and Responsibility*, Oxford, Oxford University Press (1998), 69; Ngwena C., Chadwick R., "Genetic information and the duty of confidentiality: Ethics and law" (1993) 1 *Medical Law International* 73, 79.

[125] Clarke A., "Is non–directive genetic counselling possible?" (1991) 338 *The Lancet* 998; Wertz D., Fletcher J., *Genetics and Ethics in Global Perspective*, Dordrechet, Kluwer (2004), 4.

[126] See Geller, supra n. 112, at p. 239.

[127] Wertz D., Fletcher J., *Ethics and Human Genetics: A Cross–Cultural Perspective*, New York, Springer–Verlag, (1989), 16–17.

harm; other considerations are involved when disclosure to family members is considered.

Wertz and Fletcher's repeat study in 1995 confirmed the tendency of British doctors not to adopt the strict legal rule of confidentiality. Asked whether they would disclose a particular cancer mutation in the patient to at–risk relatives without the patient's consent, 34% believed they would preserve confidentiality while 44% would tell relatives if they were asked and 9% would tell even when unasked (amounting to 53% who would disclose without consent).[128] This led Wertz to conclude that one has to acknowledge that genetics is a family matter requiring solutions for all parties involved.[129] Comparing the finding from the UK with those from other countries the two researchers found no substantial gap between them. In sum, 36% of all respondents stated they would respect patient confidentiality, whereas 32% would tell relatives when asked and 17% would do so when unasked (amounting to 59% who would disclose without consent). Only in five of the 36 countries surveyed in the study (Australia, US (family doctors), Denmark, Germany, Sweden) more than 50% felt they would respect patient's confidentiality.[130] In the remaining 31 countries the rate of doctors who would respect patient confidentiality was below 50%.

However, when looking of any shift in respondents' tendency from the first study to the second, Wertz and Fletcher found that more doctors expressed respect for confidentiality in 1995 than in 1985. In the 1985 study 32% of British respondents believed they would respect patient confidentiality; in the 1995 study 39% of them expressed this view.[131] This trend was evident in all participants in the study.[132]

Research on doctors indicates that the justifications they provide for breaching confidentiality are not restricted to the legal mechanism of prevention of serious physical harm to others. As we saw, many doctors realise that family members have to receive information about the patient's illness as they afford him or her daily care and emotional support.

However, as Wertz and Fletcher conceded, the findings of the studies reviewed above have limited significance as they asked doctors for their views but did not examine what they did in face of a patient's refusal to disclose.[133] The study by Dugan and her colleagues demonstrates that the practice in this context may be very different from the doctors' views. These researchers asked genetic counsellors about their personal experience with this dilemma. Out of 259 respondents only

---

[128] Wertz D., Fletcher J., *Genetics and Ethics in Global Perspective*, Dordrechet, Kluwer (2004), 393.

[129] Wertz D., "No consensus worldwide" (2001) 1 (3) *The American Journal of Bioethics* 14.

[130] See Wertz & Fletcher, supra 128, at p. 393.

[131] Ibid., at p. 394.

[132] Ibid., at p. 395.

[133] Ibid., at pp. 11–12.

119 (46%) had encountered a patient who refused to disclose information to family members. Of these, 24 (21%) told the researchers that they had seriously considered disclosure to relatives without consent but only one respondent actually breached confidentiality.[134] Still, these findings do not wholly contradict those of Fletcher and Wertz, as 63% of all respondents believed they had an obligation to disclose genetic information to family members. Yet when faced with several scenarios only few said they would in fact disclose without consent. For example, only 7% believed they would breach patient confidentiality when the genetic risk to the relatives to develop the disease was high or when changes in the relatives' lifestyle can reduce the risk.

Nevertheless, two doctors argued recently that the legal and ethical duty of confidentiality is impractical as it does not accord with treatment requirements of incompetent patients.[135] The studies reviewed so far revealed that family doctors and specialists in genetics all acknowledge that they have an obligation (moral if not legal) to family members. The difference between the two groups in attitude may be attributed to the particular ethics of their area of expertise: family doctors are educated to 'think family', while geneticists are influenced by the principles of non–directiveness. This does not affect the conclusion that they all treat genetic information as a family matter.[136] The discussion in this part suggests that doctors appreciate the value of the familial relationship and identify it as a factor that mitigates the strict legal rule. As indicated, many see the family not as a separate third party but as part of the unit of care.

5.5.2.2 Patients. Studies suggest that patients value their right to confidentiality and are opposed to disclosure without consent. In a study performed in eight European countries Grol and his colleagues found that all patients agreed that their right to confidentiality was one of the most significant factors when they interacted with doctors.[137] Similar findings were discovered in a UK study by Benson and Britten.[138] All 30 cancer patients interviewed stated that their close family members could receive information about their illness with their consent.[139]

---

[134] Dugan B., et al., "Duty to warn at–risk relatives for genetic disease: Genetic counselors' clinical experience" (2003) 120A (3) *American Journal of Medical Genetics* 374.

[135] Hughes J., Louw S., "Confidentiality and cognitive impairment: Professional and philosophical ethics" (2002) 31 *Age and Ageing* 147.

[136] Dugan et al. found that 97% of the respondents encouraged the patient to inform at–risk relatives. See, Dugan, supra n. 134.

[137] Grol R. et al., "Patients' priorities with respect to general practice care: An international comparison" (1999) 16 (1) *Family Practice* 4.

[138] Benson J., Britten N., "Respecting the autonomy of cancer patients when talking with their families: Qualitative analysis of semistructured interviews with patients" (1996) 313 *BMJ* 729.

[139] Ibid., at p. 730.

Benson and Britten also found that patients would justify doctors' disclosure to relatives without consent. Twenty percent agreed to unconditional disclosure to family members, basing their decision on the close familial relationship and advantages to themselves and to their relatives. The majority of patients (56%) opposed unconditional disclosure but agreed that under specific conditions doctors were allowed to inform the relatives without consent. These conditions were that the relatives were close to the patient or to the doctor and that they could benefit from disclosure. However, 23% of the patients opposed disclosure without consent, stating that they owned the information.

Wertz and Fletcher examined patients' views on confidentiality and disclosure without consent in three Western countries: the US, Germany, and France. The results were similar. About 25% in the US and Germany believed that doctors should maintain confidentiality (compared with 12% in France) when the patient refuses to tell the relatives about the diagnosis of Huntington's disease, but 42–47% believed the doctor should tell the relatives without consent if asked, and 33–42% believed the doctor should locate the relatives and inform them even when unasked.[140]

These findings suggest that patients do consider the implications of medical information for their relatives. Moreover, when disclosure without consent is considered, prevention of harm to the relatives is only one factor, and not a prominent one. The nature of the familial relationship is also relevant in this context. A study conducted on disclosure of genetic information to close and distant relatives revealed that one of the most frequently cited reasons for informing close relatives was good relationship whereas two of the most common reasons for non–disclosure were bad relationship and little contact with them.[141] This was confirmed by other researchers who concluded that unity of the family is among the factors which influence the communication of BRCA test results to relatives.[142]

Moreover, patients want to involve their family members in their care. Botelho et al. found that a majority of patients (about 55%) preferred that a relative or a close friend accompanied them into the examination room.[143] No patient indicated that he or she would never want a family member or friend to go into the examination room. This view stands in contrast with the common legal belief that the examination room is the private sphere of the doctor and the patient.

---

[140] See Wertz and Fletcher, supra n. 128, at p. 444.

[141] Claes E. et al., "Communication with close and distant relatives in the context of genetic testing for hereditary breast and ovarian cancer in cancer patients" (2003) 116A (1) *American Journal of Medical Genetics* 11.

[142] Hughes C. at al., "All in the family: Evaluation of the process and content of sisters' communication about BRCA1 and BRCA2 genetic test results" (2002) 107 *American Journal of Medical Genetics* 143.

[143] Botelho R. et al., "Family involvement in routine health care: A survey of patients' behaviours and preferences" (1996) 42 (6) *The Journal of Family Practice* 572.

Patients' willingness that their relatives will receive genetic information derives from a strong sense of moral responsibility. Hallowell interviewed 40 women with a high risk of breast or ovarian cancer.[144] All the women saw themselves as having the responsibility to take preventive measures to avert or minimise the risk of developing cancer, if possible. Their attendance at the genetic clinics, where they were located for the study, was perceived as the first step in taking responsibility for their risks, and was considerably influenced by their obligations to their relatives.[145] All the respondents stated that they shared the information they received in the clinic with at least one relative,[146] and most of them intended to contact other relatives as well. These findings were confirmed in a study examining parental communication of genetic information to children. Women who communicated information stated that they felt a strong sense of responsibility to provide the child information that was relevant to the child's health.[147]

Nevertheless, the respondents in Hallowell's study were aware of the difficulties genetic information posed for their relatives. They realised that approaching the relatives would compromise their interest in not receiving information. They admitted that disclosing information might cause distress to some relatives. Yet despite these difficulties the respondents stated that they had an obligation not only to communicate this information to their relatives but also to encourage them to seek medical advice.[148]

In the end, though, the respondents' sense of responsibility was apparently the most prominent factor in their decision whether or not to disclose genetic information to their relatives.[149] Since the interviews were conducted before the genetic testing was done many women stated that they would be prepared to undergo such a test because they had a responsibility to provide other relatives with this information. Hallowell herself notes that feelings of 'genetic responsibility' in many of the women in the study led them to compromise their personal need of not knowing their risk for the benefit of others.[150] These results

---

[144] Hallowell N., "Doing the right thing: Genetic risk and responsibility" (1999) 21 (5) *Sociology of Health & Illness* 597.

[145] Ibid., at p. 606.

[146] These were also the results in Green J. et al., "Family communication and genetic counseling: The case of hereditary breast and ovarian cancer" (1997) 6 (1) *Journal of Genetic Counselling* 45, 53.

[147] Tercyak K. et al., "Parent–child factors and their effect on communicating BRCA1/1 test results to children" (2002) 47 *Patient Education and Counselling* 145, 148–9.

[148] See Hallowell, supra n. 144, at p. 607.

[149] Forrest K. et al., "To tell or not to tell: Barriers and facilitators in family communication about genetic risk" (2003) 64 *Clinical Genetics* 317 found that a majority of the respondents believed that responsibility for disclosing information to the relatives rested with the patient and not with the doctor and that only a minority of them decline disclosure to particular relatives.

[150] See Hallowell, supra n. 144, at p. 609.

were confirmed in other studies. Hallowell and her colleagues interviewed women who decided to take preventive measures to minimise the risk of breast cancer. Once again, a strong sense of moral responsibility to their family members was manifested as the common reason for their decision.[151] Another study with women who underwent BRCA testing showed that all informed at least one at–risk family member of the positive result, usually a sister.[152]

These results run counter to the individual's right not to know. As discussed throughout this book, a few legal commentators and ethical codes support the individual's right not to receive medical information. But these findings imply that in practice this right is rarely exercised. In many instances patients waive their right to remain ignorant and submit to testing for the benefit of their children or future offspring.[153] In addition, when received the information they inform vulnerable family members who may be unaware that the patient has undergone testing. Consequently, the relatives' right not to know is compromised because the lives of family members are often interwoven, and respecting such a right may challenge the true nature of their familial relationship.

Wertz and Fletcher confirmed this in their study. They found that the vast majority of US patients (85%) believe they would want to be informed even when the condition was fatal and untreatable; 48% believed that doctors should inform them even when they did not want to know. As regards relatives, 33% of US patients believe that doctors should find the relatives and disclose to them that they were at risk of Huntington's disease, thus compromising their right not to know.[154]

The attitudes of the women interviewed by Hallowell reflect an approach that views autonomy relationally.[155] The respondents' unanimous decision of to inform their relatives implies that autonomy has little meaning outside a social community. The need to make a decision whether or not to disclose information is not based solely on the patient's personal interests but also on the realisation that any decision will affect the lives of the relatives and their familial relationship. This leads patients to involve in their decision–making process altruistic notions of

---

[151] Hallowell N. et al., "Surveillance or surgery? A description of the factors that influence high risk premenopausal women's decisions about prophylactic oophorectomy" (2001) 38 *Journal of Medical Genetics* 683; see also: Julian–Reynier C. et al., "Cancer Genetic clinics: Why do women who already have cancer attend?" (1998) 34 *European Journal of Cancer* 1549.

[152] McGivern B. at el., "Family communication about positive BRCA1 and BRCA2 genetic test results" (2004) 6 (6) *Genetics in Medicine* 503.

[153] Philips K. et al., "Perceptions of Ashkenazi Jewish breast cancer patients on genetic testing for mutations in BRCA1 and BRCA2" (2000) 57 *Clinical Genetics* 376–383 indicate that 96% of the respondents stated that they agreed to undergo testing for the potential benefit of other relatives.

[154] See Wertz and Fletcher, supra n. 128, at p. 444.

[155] Hallowell N. et al., "Balancing autonomy and responsibility: The ethics of generating and disclosing genetic information" (2003) 29 *Journal of Medical Ethics* 74, 78.

care and responsibility.

A study by Lehmann and her colleagues supports this conclusion.[156] The researchers conducted a population–based survey of 200 women to assess attitudes to genetic testing. All the respondents agreed that patients should inform their close relatives when the genetic disease was curable, and 97% preferred disclosure when only *one* preventive measure could be taken. Furthermore, 85% of the respondents believed that patients should disclose genetic information to their relatives when the disease was *incurable* and no preventive measures were available. When asked whether doctors should approach the relatives without consent, the majority of respondents believed they should not. Only 18% of the respondents believed that the doctor could disclose information without consent when it was easy to prevent the disease, and just 16% of the respondents believed the doctors could approach the relatives without permission when the disease could not be prevented.

These findings confirm the argument that in practice prevention of harm to others is not the sole consideration. By providing three different scenarios, the researchers could examine how influential was the 'prevention–of–harm' factor in the respondents' view. The fact that 85% of them believed that patients should communicate information even when there were no available preventive measures reflected a moral approach which was not based primarily on a utilitarian model but on other considerations that acknowledged the mutual relationship within families. In addition, the small gap between those who believed that doctors could disclose information without consent when the disease was preventable and those who believed that they could do so when the disease was not preventable implies that the utilitarian mechanism is not a prominent factor when disclosure to relatives without consent is considered. The nature of the familial relationship carries considerable weight in this context as well.

Another study by Reust and Mattingly supports the conclusion that patients consider the interests of their relatives.[157] Analysing the patients' decision–making process, the two researchers discovered that patients do not weigh medical benefits against possible risks and personal consequences of a given medical option available to them; they balance the treatment option against the effect it will have on their close relatives who will have to adjust to the patient's new medical condition. This stands in contrast with the legal position, which focuses on a cost–benefit evaluation when the doctor explains the treatment options to the patient. While legally doctors must emphasise the risks and the benefits of any available alternative, patients concentrate in their decisions on the effect it will have on their relatives. The fact that one treatment is more dangerous but more effective than

---

[156] Lehmann L. et al., "Disclosure of familial genetic information: Perceptions of the duty to inform" (2000) 109 *American Journal of Medicine* 705.

[157] Reust C., Mattingly S., "Family involvement in medical decision making" (1996) 28 *Family Medicine* 39.

another may have less relevance for the patient who is interested in taking the treatment that family members can adjust to more quickly.

These studies reflect the communitarian contribution to patient autonomy. In contrast to the legal position, the individual is perceived as a social being whose choices are considerably affected by his or her family members.[158] However, the implications of these findings should be restricted. The respondents in Hallowell's and Lehmann's studies were all women, and Hallowell herself suggested that serving the needs of others is so inherent in women's identity that they identify others' needs as their own.[159] The influence of the gender variable was detected in a different study. Ninety male respondents in a study examining attitudes to a future genetic test for prostate cancer mentioned that such a test would help other family members.[160] However, the men also raised concerns about their right to confidentiality in the family, a factor ignored by the women in Hallowell's studies. This led Doukas and his colleagues, who conducted the study, to observe that concern about other family members, which is clearly evident in other studies on genetic testing, were less prominent in this one.[161]

This gender difference[162] elicits discussion on the relevance of the philosophy of ethics–of–care. An accurate analysis of these studies may result in the conclusion that communitarian and ethics–of–care conceptions are not as prominent as perceived at first glance. Instead, they confirm the belief of feminists such as Carol Gilligan regarding the differences in the moral education and ethics of men and women.[163]

A sense of disharmony emerges from the studies reviewed so far. On the one hand, patients value their legal and ethical right to confidentiality, rejecting the possibility that doctors may disclose medical information to the relatives without their consent. On the other hand, they have a strong sense of responsibility to their

---

[158] Hallowell N. et al., "Balancing autonomy and responsibility: The ethics of generating and disclosing genetic information" (2003) 29 *Journal of Medical Ethics* 74, 78.

[159] See Hallowell, supra n. 144, at p. 608; See also Peterson S. et al., "How families communicate about genetic testing: findings from a qualitative study" (2003) 119C (1) *American Journal of Medical Genetics* 78.

[160] Doukas D.J. et al., "How men view genetic testing for prostate cancer risk: Finding from focus group" (2000) 58 (3) *Clinical Genetics* 169, 173.

[161] Ibid., at p. 174.

[162] Dorothy Wertz also drew this conclusion following her international study on the views of doctors and patients on disclosure of genetic information. See: Wertz, supra n. 129.

[163] For an analysis of the moral duty to disclose genetic risk from a gender perspective see: d'Agincourt-Canning L., "Experiences of genetic risk: Disclosure and the gendering of responsibility" (2001) 15 (3) *Bioethics* 231.

relatives, and are willing to share information with them even when physical harm to them cannot be prevented.[164]

A possible response to the ambiguity of these data is to reiterate that the individual's identity is simultaneously interdependent and independent. Patients share information with their relatives out of a sense of independence, namely when they autonomously decide to do so. They incline, however, to disclose information because they realise that it is necessary to maintain good familial relationships especially when they rely on the relatives to cope with distressful bad news. This is compatible with the perception of relational autonomy presented in Chapter 1, namely that autonomy is not solely an individual project but involves a dynamic balance among people who are closely involved in each others' lives and that the individual depends on close intimates when trying to achieve a goal. Consequently, the patient's interest in controlling exclusively the information he or she receives from the doctor does not necessarily have to contradict the interest in sharing it with close family members.[165]

The need to have a network of intimates with whom one can share his thoughts, views, and experiences has been a prominent theme in this chapter. In the context of medical information doctors and patients realise that the individual needs at least one intimate in whom he or she can confide personal information. The importance of having such family confidant is confirmed in practice.[166] In genetics, the need for a family confidant is reflected when patients asked their closest relatives to accompany them to the doctor's clinic when they receive test results as they find it hard to face it by themselves.[167]

Another central theme of this chapter was that contrary to the legal perception of patient autonomy, in medical practice it is relational rather than individualistic. This was reflected in the decision–making process of doctors and patients who take the interests of family members into account. Many patients incline in some circumstances to compromise their personal interests for the benefit of their families. In addition, many doctors are willing to compromise the patient's rights and involve the family to improve his or her condition. This is not based solely on the individual's sense of care for others but on the realisation that the individual exercises autonomy within a community and relies upon it to fulfil his or her goals.

---

[164] Wertz and Fletcher reported that 91% of US patients and 92% of German patients said that they were 'very likely' or 'extremely likely' to inform their sisters of positive test results for breast cancer mutation. See Wertz and Fletcher, supra n. 128, at p. 392.

[165] Sankar P. et al., "Patient perspectives on medical confidentiality" (2003) 18 *Journal of General Internal Medicine* 659, at p. 664 concluded that patients incline to disclose genetic information to their relatives but do not permit their doctors to do so.

[166] Beeson R. et al., "Loneliness and depression in caregivers of persons with Alzheimer's disease or related disorders" (2000) 21 *Issues in Mental Health Nursing* 779.

[167] Robertson J. et al., "BRCA1 screening in woman with breast cancer: A patient's perspective with commentary" (2001) 11 (2) *Women's Health Issues* 63.

5.6 Conclusion

The aim of this chapter was to examine the last hypothesis of this study, namely whether the legal and ethical positions reflect medical practices. Undoubtedly, the discussion in this chapter suggests that illness is a family matter. A gap between law and medicine emerges. While the doctor owes a legal duty of care only to the individual patient, the tendency among medical academics and socio–medical researchers is to accept that the doctor owes some professional responsibilities to the patient's relatives even when they are not his or her patients.

One possible explanation for this gap is the different philosophies that underlie English law on the one hand and the biopsychosocial model on the other. While English law is dominated by a liberal–individualistic approach and a utilitarian mechanism of prevention of harm, the biopsychosocial model relies on a systems theory that evaluates the patient–relatives relationship as an important component.

An intermediate approach may be found in the area of medical ethics, which combines legal and medical conceptions. But as demonstrated in Chapter 4, close examination revealed that the leading ethical approach is more patient–centred than family–based. In the area of genetic information, for example, ethical guidelines in the UK still express preference for the patient's right to confidentiality over the relatives' right to know.[168]

If the observation regarding the gaps between law, ethics and medicine is accurate, the next question is whether it is desirable and possible to bridge them. Some commentators doubt whether this can be done,[169] while others argue that the family is an important social institution and therefore should gain more legal recognition.[170] This debate raises the question of the role the law plays in English society: does it aim to reflect common morality and public attitudes, or does it aspire to formulate social policy and shape professional standards? These questions, which will be dealt with in the final chapter, conclude the discussion in this book.

---

[168] Human Genetics Commission, *Inside Information: Balancing the Interests in the Use of Personal Genetic Data* (May, 2002), Ch. 3, para. 3.68.

[169] Laurie G., "Genetics and patients' rights: Where are the limits?" (2000) 5 *Medical Law International* 25, 41.

[170] Grubb A., "Treatment decisions: Keeping it in the family" in Grubb A. (ed.), *Choices and Decisions in Health Care*, Chichester, Wiley (1993), 37, 41; O'Donovan K., Gilbar R., "The loved ones: families, intimates and patient autonomy" (2003) 23 (2) *Legal Studies* 332.

Chapter 6

The Status of Family Members: Discussion and Conclusions

6.1 Introduction

The status of family members in medical law and medical ethics is the subject of this book. In particular, it has examined whether the interests of family members are legally and ethically recognised when genetic information becomes available. In this context, two familial conflicts have been investigated: first, the conflict between the patient's interest in confidentiality and the relatives' interest in receiving the information; second, the conflict between the patient's interest in sharing information with the relatives and their interest in remaining ignorant. Within these familial tensions two professional obligations have been discussed: the doctor's obligation to respect patient's autonomy, confidentiality, and privacy, and the obligation to assist family members who may not be registered as the doctor's patients.

The discussion in this work has been conducted within the liberal–communitarian debate. In Chapter 1, the main themes of these two philosophies were specified, concentrating on the perception of the individual, his or her identity and autonomy, and the relationship with close family members. It was indicated that while liberals focus on the personal interests and rights of the individual, communitarians emphasise the primacy of the common good over the right. This liberal–communitarian debate has contributed to the discussion about autonomy. Autonomy is often formulated in the liberal discourse as the individual's ability to make free choices so long as he or she does not cause harm to others. Communitarians and feminists add to autonomy a relational dimension. They argue that it is a collaborative and reciprocal project which involves those who are close to the individual. The contribution of these approaches to the moral debate about autonomy is the belief that the individual's social embeddedness nurtures his or her autonomy. Consequently the individual has interests in receiving social support, in maintaining familial relationships, and, for communitarians, in living in a community with which one can identify. This moral view is important as it contributes to the perception of relational autonomy as defined in this book.

However, this perception of relational autonomy is not just communitarian, as it does not aim to promote the interests of the community (in the context of this work, the family) at the expense of the individual's right to lead his or her life as he or she wants. As was argued in Chapter 1, communitarianism has the potential of sustaining injustices in families and hence it has to accept liberal and feminist conceptions which deal better with dysfunctional families. Thus, the starting point is that one's personal interest in making informed and free choices should be valued and appreciated. The promotion of this personal interest is the major vehicle by which individuals can lead their lives as they want, especially when in a disadvantaged position of being ill. Yet this does not exclude the belief that the individual may develop his or her autonomy by engaging with those around him or her.[1]

The first chapter also dealt with the familial relationship. In this context, it is acknowledged that the ethics of families is based considerably on ethics–of–care with its emphasis on care, commitment, and support, which largely characterise the familial relationship. Therefore, it was suggested that communitarian and ethics–of–care conceptions should be taken into account if the interests of family members in the genetic context deserve greater recognition. This does not mean that principles of justice, equality, and the independence of the individual patient are not important. As the Lindemann–Nelsons indicate, it is very difficult to mediate between the various interests of the patient and those of the relatives. In some cases it may require not only promotion of solidarity and mutual responsibility but also recognition that the decision has to be made by the patient alone, who should not be forced to undergo a treatment he or she does not want.[2] Thus, while the view presented in Chapter 1 was that the interests of family members should be recognised, it was also argued that this does not mean that the personal choice of the patient should not be respected.

Regarding the legal status of family members in genetics, it is necessary to define the family. As indicated in Chapter 2, this question has considerable implications for the legal and ethical obligations to family members. The scope of the patient's moral duty to the relatives and the scope of the doctor's legal duty – if such a duty exists – are determined, inter alia, by the definition of the family. The position taken in this study is that such a definition has to correlate with the recent changes in English society's attitudes to this social institution.

Still, some legal commentators concerned with disclosure of genetic information to family members assume a definition of the family in this context by blood ties and marriage. This position pays little attention to the psychosocial effect of genetic information on those who are socially close to the patient. As research indicates, genetic information affects the familial relationship irrespective of blood relations. This effect does not derive solely from the biological fact that

---

[1]   Parker M., "Public deliberation and private choice in genetics and reproduction" (2000) 26 *Journal of Medical Ethics* 160, 162.

[2]   Lindemann-Nelson H., Lindemann-Nelson J., *The Patient in the Family*, New York, Routledge (1995), 117, 151 (hereafter: the Lindemann-Nelsons); however, these authors argue that patients should consider beneficial surgery if it is in the family's interest because an intimate relationship imposes responsibility.

parents pass on to their offspring the susceptibility to genetic disorders; it also derives from the close relationship between them. This leads to the position taken in this study, namely that the family is a *biosocial* unit comprising blood ties and social relations.

Subsequently the position taken in this book was that a biosocial perception of the family accords with the current developments in family law but not with the position of medical law. The examination in Chapters 3 and 4 of the attitude of medical law and ethics to family members indicates that they provide limited access to the patient's medical information. This legal position takes a patient–centred perspective, which arises from several principles. First, the law perceives the doctor–patient relationship as exclusive of everyone except these two parties. The doctor undertakes to provide services to the individual patient who approaches him or her directly.

Second, doctors are not legally responsible to third parties for their omissions. While doctors may owe an affirmative duty to warn their patients, they have no such a duty with regard to family members unless they can identify them as being at a specific risk. The underlying message of this concept is rejection of the moral principle of beneficence, which constitutes one of the four general principles in medical ethics.[3] The impression is that English law promotes individual freedom and liberty over moral principles of mutual responsibility and accountability.

The third legal principle concerns medical confidentiality. Generally, English medical law adheres to a strict rule of confidentiality. The law provides the individual patient the right to control the medical information exchanged with the doctor. Disclosure to family members depends on the patient's consent. Disclosure without consent is justified when doctors can prevent serious physical harm to the relatives. In any event, in the present context of genetics they owe no legal *duty* to warn the patient's family members.

The lack of cure for genetic disorders leads some legal commentators to doubt whether genetic information should be conveyed freely within the family. The adverse psychological impact that genetic test results may have on the individual can be devastating, especially when the disorder is incurable and terminal. Within the liberal discourse patients and relatives ought to have a right *not* to know. For some commentators the interest in being left alone seems to take precedence over the interest in belonging to a close group of intimates.[4] It is implied that the support the individual receives from family members is not as important to his or her ability to survive as the freedom to choose whether or not to receive information.

By contrast, the discussion in Chapter 5 indicated that the involvement of the

---

[3]   As discussed in Chapter 1, although the four principles approach to medical ethics is not the only one, it is certainly considered one of the leading approaches in this area.

[4]   Laurie G., *Genetic Privacy: A Challenge to Medico-Legal Norms*, Cambridge, Cambridge University Press (2002).

family is appreciated in medical practice. The *biopsychosocial* model, which currently dominates the medical literature, recognises that patients are affected by their familial relationship through all stages of illness.[5] The support the family provides to the patient is important.[6] This approach encourages doctors to be attuned to the familial relationship and to involve them in the medical decision-making process.[7]

Consequently, it is suggested that a gap lies between medical practice and the legal position. Concerning communication of medical information, this gap prevails when doctors' and patients' attitudes to disclosure to family members are examined. Research suggests that although these two groups value confidentiality highly, many believe that medical information can, in some circumstances, be disclosed to the relatives without the patient's consent. In the patients' view, disclosure without consent is contingent on a close and intimate relationship,[8] and for doctors it may take place when the relatives' assistance is needed to improve the patient's condition.[9] These findings show that the underlying reasons for breaching confidentiality are not limited to prevention of harm, as emphasised in case law;[10] the breach also derives from a strong sense of moral responsibility to others.

To sum up, the discussion in this dissertation yields the following main findings:

(1) The status of family members in English medical law is limited. In the area of communication of genetic information their interests are not fully recognised.
(2) The limited legal status of the patient's family members derives from an individualistic perception of patient autonomy and from the incompatibility between this perception and the ethics of families.
(3) This legal, and to a certain extent the ethical, position does not accord with the medical model of the doctor–patient relationship and with the views of doctors and patients about autonomy and confidentiality. While there is social and medical consensus that the patient's diagnosis and illness is a family matter, the law focuses on the patient alone.

---

[5]   Engel G., "The need for a new medical model: A challenge for biomedicine" (1977) 196 *Science* 129.

[6]   McWhinney I., *A Textbook of Family Medicine*, New York, Oxford University Press (2nd edn., 1997).

[7]   Charles C., et al, "Decision–making in the physician–patient encounter: What does it mean? (Or it takes at least two to tango)" (1997) 44 *Social Science & Medicine* 681.

[8]   Benson J., Britten N., "Respecting the autonomy of cancer patients when talking with their families: Qualitative analysis of semistructured interviews with patients" (1996) 313 *BMJ* 729, 730.

[9]   Toon PD., Southgate LJ., "The doctor, the patient and the relative: An exploratory survey of doctor–relatives relationship" (1987) 4 (3) *Family Practice* 207, 209.

[10]   *W v Egdell* [1990] Ch. 359.

(4) More specifically, while the law rejects the imposition of a beneficent duty to third parties and adheres to a strict rule of confidentiality, many believe that doctors should offer help to family members who are not their patients,[11] and that in some cases genetic information can be disclosed without the patient's consent to the relatives. As for the *right not to know*, patients and family members communicate medical information to each other rather freely, thus compromising this right in practice.

These findings bring us to the central questions posed in this concluding chapter. These are: (1) whether it is possible and desirable to bridge the gap between law and medical practice; (2) whether a change in the legal position in required; and (3) if a change is needed, what are the alternative models that can deal adequately with familial tensions over genetic information.

6.2 Is it Possible and Desirable to Bridge the Gap between Law and Medicine?

The recognition that a gap exists between law and medical practice may not lead automatically to the conclusion that there is a need for a change in the legal position. Onora O'Neill in her recent work emphasises the significance of trust in the doctor–patient relationship.[12] Trust might indeed be compromised if doctors were to breach their patients' right to confidentiality without consent. Moreover, public health may be threatened if the patient's need for a confidential environment is not provided and guaranteed. Rosamond Rhodes, an American ethicist, argues that in any proposed reform a strict rule of confidentiality should be maintained. In her view confidentiality is so essential for the promotion of public health that society cannot do without it. She is convinced that the moral responsibility of one family member to another does not translate into licence for doctors to breach confidentiality.[13] Other commentators too, such as Richard Ashcroft, doubt whether doctors can act as a moral authority in familial conflicts as they merely possess more genetic knowledge but no high morals.[14]

Ashcroft's argument will be adopted by those, such as Bell and Bennett, who believe that the current common law position – as regards confidentiality – is

---

[11] Williams K., "Doctors as good Samaritans: Some empirical evidence concerning emergency medical treatment in Britain" (2003) 30 (2) *Journal of Law and Society* 258 demonstrates that doctors act as good Samaritans and provide help to strangers irrespective of the legal position.

[12] O'Neill O., *Autonomy and Trust in Bioethics*, Cambridge, Cambridge University Press (2002).

[13] Rhodes R., "Confidentiality, genetic information and the physician–patient relationship" (2001) 1 (3) *The American Journal of Bioethics* 26, at p. 27.

[14] Ashcroft R., "The family: Organic and mechanistic solidarity" (2001) 1(3) *The American Journal of Bioethics* 22, 23.

satisfactory.[15] Indeed, Rhodes's strong support of patient's confidentiality does not remain in the theoretical sphere. Ultimately, patients prefer doctors to obtain their consent before informing family members. They may be willing to disclose information to relatives, but they wish to control the conditions and environment in which disclosure takes place.

The argument about breach of trust should not distract the attention from the conclusion that there is a gap between law and medical practice. The question is whether this gap should be bridged, and whether the law should be changed to reflect public views in this area. The answer depends on the role of law in English society: does it aim to reflect common morality and public attitudes, or does it aspire to formulate social policy and shape professional standards?

Generally, this question is subject to an extensive jurisprudential debate. For many lawyers the law can guide the public when a moral dilemma arises.[16] In a democracy it has the authority morality often lacks. For other legal academics the law is part of a greater social system and therefore has to reflect the norms and fundamental values of society.[17] Roger Cotterrell summarises this position by arguing that a comprehensive analysis of law must include both its existence as an agency of government and its reliance on social and cultural conditions which it cannot control.[18]

In the context of medical law the duality Cotterrell identifies raises two possible arguments. On the one hand, one can argue that medical law *should* reflect medical practices and public views on moral dilemmas, but on the other hand it is also possible to argue that when there is a moral debate the law can guide the practice by stating its moral approach. This latter approach was explicitly taken by Hoffmann LJ in the seminal case of *Airedale NHS Trust v Bland*,[19] where he devoted most of his judgment to a moral debate rather than to a reductionistic legal analysis. The underlying reason for the judge's strategic choice was public concern about the implications of such cases. In his view, the decision of the court should be able to convince the ordinary person, and thus it should be based not only on legal precedent but also on '*acceptable* ethical values'.[20] This statement reflects the duality of law: on the one hand the judge identified the need to guide the public on a moral dilemma, but on the other hand he recognised that the judgment must be

---

15 Bell D., Bennett B., "Genetic secrets and the family" (2001) 9 *Medical Law Review* 130, pp. 159–161.
16 Galanter M., "Law abounding: Legalisation around the North Atlantic" (1992) 55 *Modern Law Review* 1, 15–16.
17 Ibid.
18 Cotterrell R., *The Sociology of Law: An Introduction*, London, Butterworths (2nd edn., 1992), 69.
19 [1993] AC 789; the case concerned a hospital's request to allow the treating doctors lawfully to discontinue the life–sustaining treatment given to the patient, Anthony Bland.
20 *Airedale NHS Trust v Bland* [1993] AC 789, 825 (my italics) (hereafter: *Bland*).

based on acceptable core values. Lord Browne–Wilkinson agreed, stating that the law 'must, to be *acceptable*, reflect a moral attitude which society *accepts*'.[21]

However, in a pluralist society it may be difficult to detect shared values and common morality. This is particularly true in the context of this work where people may have different views and convictions regarding disclosure of information to family members. In this area the position the law expresses can be very influential. If the law aims to influence public moral views the task has to be done sensibly. Formulating a rigorous and inflexible policy may produce the opposite effect, where people may decide either to ignore it or reject it altogether. The emphasis is on public acceptance. Cotterrell argues that the law can effect a change in public views when it derives from a principle deeply rooted in the society. Changes that reflect legal or social revolution are likely to be rejected.[22]

However, when public acceptance is sought, a distinction between Parliament and the courts is made. Courts may not be the most suitable institution to conduct a moral debate or formulate a new law.[23] Judges themselves acknowledge that Parliament is more adequate to offer solutions to issues that involve a moral dilemma or a new policy.[24] The courts, despite their increasing willingness to deal with medical dilemmas, define their role rather narrowly, only as means for dispute resolution.

Practically, in some areas of law the courts and Parliament have recently become more attuned to public attitudes. One example is the provision of legal rights to alternative family forms,[25] which demographically[26] are more widespread today in society than in the past.[27] Another example is the courts' willingness to widen the scope of tortious liability by imposing a duty of care on doctors to identifiable third parties who are not their registered patients.[28] This tendency will undoubtedly affect the relationship between law and medical ethics as it may result in recognition of the doctor's moral obligation of beneficence.[29] However, in other

---

[21] Ibid., at p. 878 (my italics).

[22] See Cotterrell, supra n. 18, at p. 59.

[23] Lee S., *Law and Morals*, Oxford, Oxford University Press (1986), 88.

[24] See, for example, the speech of Lord Browne–Wilkinson in *Bland*, supra n. 20, at p. 878.

[25] See the new *Civil Partnership Act* 2004 and the discussion in Chapter 2, part 2.2.1.

[26] Haskey J., "Demographic aspects of cohabitation in Great Britain" (2001) 15 *International Journal of Law, Policy and the Family* 51.

[27] Bainham A., Sclater S.D., Richards M. (eds.), *What is a Parent? A Socio–Legal Analysis*, Oxford, Hart Publishing (1999), Ch. 1.

[28] Williams K., "Medical Samaritans: Is there a duty to treat?" (2001) 21 (3) *Oxford Journal of Legal Studies* 393, commenting, inter alia, on *Kent v Griffiths* [2001] QB 36.

[29] This is partly due to the incorporation of the European Convention on Human Rights into domestic law. Article 2 (right to life) imposes an affirmative duty on state authorities (hence on NHS doctors) when they can avert an imminent danger to other third parties. See *Osman v UK* (1998) 5 BHRC 293. See also *Z v UK* [2001] 2 FCR 246

areas of medical law Parliament and the courts are slow to react. A possible explanation is that as in the above examples the law adapts itself to social changes only after a lengthy process of public debate.

This conclusion that the law should be willing to change its attitude to family members brings us back to the debate between those such as Andrew Grubb, who argue that the family is an important social institution in English society, and those such as Graeme Laurie, who maintain that English society is based on individualistic conceptions.[30] These two observations are not necessarily contradictory: it can be argued that English law appreciates the significant place of the family, and therefore respects its privacy and freedom from state intervention. When the individual does not physically harm his or her relatives voluntarily, the authorities will not interfere, leaving family members to resolve tensions over medical information. The law is invoked only in exceptional circumstances as a last resort when the familial conflict results in physical harm.

Still, the central argument is that family members' interests are compromised irrespective of the justifications for the current legal position. Various interests of the relatives in this context are not legally recognised, among them the interest in avoiding financial costs and the interest in making informed reproductive decisions. Therefore, both liberals and communitarians should support a change in the legal position. From a communitarian perspective this is obvious. From a liberal perspective the law is unbalanced: it recognises patients' rights but not relatives' rights. If the concern is breach of trust between doctors and patients the answer is that the family is perceived not as a separate third party but to a considerable extent as part of the unit of care.

However, promoting the argument that the family should be part of the unit of care not only has the positive effect of helping the family assist the patient to cope better with the illness, but also runs the risk of compromising the patient's interests. Whether the family is based on loving relationships or not, the patient's preferences may be outweighed by the relatives' insistence on their wishes if they are included in the unit of care. This may occur, for example, when an elderly patient cannot resist the wish of his wife and daughter to treat him at home, despite their difficulties in providing daily care for him. The dilemma for the doctors is to resolve these tensions in a way that does not compromise the interests of either side too much.

The argument that the involvement of family members receives greater recognition in practice than in law raises the following question. In light of the dearth of claims, and the consensus among medical academics and practitioners about the role of the family, one can argue that a change in the current legal

where the European Court held that local authorities owe an affirmative duty to protect individuals within their jurisdiction from 'serious neglect and abuse'.

30　Grubb A., "Treatment decisions: Keeping it in the family" in Grubb A. (ed.), *Choices and Decisions in Health Care*, Chichester, Wiley (1993), 37, 41; Laurie G., "Genetics and patients' rights: where are the limits" (2000) 5 *Medical Law International* 25, 41.

position is not necessary. If in practice doctors and patients do consider the interests of family members and communicate information to them, the overall question is whether a change in the legal position is needed at all. The answer is positive. First, from a narrow legal perspective, a change in the legal position is required to resolve adequately legal conflicts between the three parties involved. Although such disputes over familial access to medical information rarely reach the courts, it nevertheless is essential that when such a claim is dealt with, the court be well equipped to reach a just decision that takes family members' interests into serious consideration. From a wider perspective, law is no longer autonomous and detached from other social systems but operates within society. Therefore, at some level it must reflect public views. Otherwise it may lose its authority or become counterproductive.

Assuming the current legal position is unsatisfactory and that a change is required, any proposed change will have to take into account conflicting considerations. Examples are: patients' insistence on consent before disclosure but their permission to disclose without consent in specific circumstances; patients' willingness to disclose information to some family members who are emotionally close to them but not to other relatives, who may need the information to avert a risk of physical harm; the inability to predict what the relatives want: whether they wish or do not wish to know genetic information. More broadly, any suggested model will have to take into account the conflict between the patient's interest in controlling his or her life and in making free choices and on the other hand his or her interest in being part of a community of close intimates. These contrary considerations lead to the next question, namely the legal changes that are required to promote the interests of family members generally and in genetics particularly.

6.3 What Legal Changes are Required to Promote the Interests of Family Members?

The answer to this question is divided into two parts. The first addresses a situation where the relatives are *aware* of the patient's medical condition or at least aware of the doctor–patient relationship; the second concerns circumstances where they are *unaware* of the communication between the doctor and the patient.

First, when the relatives are aware that the patient seeks medical advice and communicates with the doctor the law should change its patient–centred approach and recognise their involvement. Legally, the courts will have to recognise that doctors owe involuntary duties to the patient's family members when there is no familial conflict. For example, when doctors receive patients' consent and convey information to family members they can appreciate that their contact with the relatives may establish a legal duty even when they do not provide them with medical treatment. This may require a relaxation of the rigid *proximity* requirement, which in many cases limits the possibility of family members' bringing claims in tort against doctors.

Second, a change in the legal position will require abandoning the existing perception of the doctor–patient relationship. Lawyers will have to accept that this relationship is not exclusive. Consequently, the legal position where relatives' claims against doctors are rejected on this ground[31] will not be followed. Whether or not doctors have undertaken the responsibility to treat the relatives they should be aware that their conduct may harm those who are closely involved in the patient's medical care.

Third, as for the medical decision–making process, the doctor's duty cannot be confined to a cost–benefit evaluation where the doctor explains to the patient the medical risks and advantages in any treatment option. The doctor will be required to help the patient understand how any treatment alternative will affect the lives of his or her loved ones. Provided confidentiality is not an issue, family members' interests should be taken into account in the decision–making process.

Doctors may object to this expansion of their legal responsibilities. They may argue that in today's adversarial society the number of legal claims will increase if such a legal duty of care to family members is imposed. They may also argue that they will face conflicting legal duties. However, an increase in the number of claims against doctors is unlikely because in practice many doctors, at least in the area of family medicine, have already taken the interests of the relatives into consideration. Moreover, in the area of genetics, geneticists and counsellors are instructed to consider the implications of genetic information for the relatives and at the very least to discuss with the patient the implications of the information for relatives who may be at risk.[32] In any event, the aim is not to expose the doctor to a conflict of legal duties but to acknowledge that doctors have a legal responsibility to family members.

Yet in the specific area of genetics, patients are treated in the same clinic and by the same professional team. This undoubtedly creates a conflict between the right of one family member to confidentiality and the doctor's duty of care to the other relative. Why should the right to confidentiality override the right to receive adequate medical care? The answer is that even in this case, where there is a possible conflict of interests between the patient and the relatives, the doctor

---

[31] *X v Bedfordshire* [1995] 2 AC 633, 665–666 (although see *Z v UK* [2001] 2 FCR 246); *Powell v Boldaz* [1998] Lloyd's Rep Med 116, 124; and recently *D v East Berkshire Community Health NHS Trust* [2005] 2 FLR 284 where the House of Lords discussed three different claims of parents for misdiagnosis of child abuse.

[32] Harper P., *Practical Genetic Counselling*, Oxford, Butterworth–Heinemann (5th edn., 1999), Ch. 1; Recently the American Society of Clinical Oncology instructed doctors to discuss with their patients the implications of genetic information. See American Society of Clinical Oncology, "Policy Statement Update: Genetic Testing for Cancer Susceptibility" (2003) 21 (12) *Journal of Clinical Oncology* 2397.

should act responsibly and try carefully not to harm the common interest they have in maintaining their familial relationship.[33]

Consequently, when confidentiality is not an issue and family members are involved in the provision of medical care to the patient, the scope of the doctors' legal duty to the relatives will be narrower than the scope of the duty the doctors owe to the patient. After all, the legal duty to family members is involuntary while the one owed to the patient is voluntary. In other words, the duty to the relatives in this context is a by–product of the doctors' duty to the patient. Nevertheless, when there is a familial dispute over a medical treatment the doctors will have to consider seriously the interests of the relatives (though the patient should not be forced to undertake a particular treatment). In addition, the doctors will owe a duty to the relatives if during the provision of treatment to the patient they cause them a tangible harm.[34]

The remainder of this chapter concentrates on the second part of this question, namely the legal changes that are required when the relatives are *unaware* of the communication between the doctor and the patient or of the patient's medical condition. In these circumstances the legal rule of confidentiality should be qualified. Currently, doctors breach the patient's right to confidentiality when they interact with family members without asking the patient's consent. However, the paucity, or lack, of patients' claims suggests that in practice disclosure of information between doctors and family members is not perceived by the patients as a breach of their *legal* rights. Though they prefer the doctor to ask their consent first, they do not feel that their legal rights are severely compromised in this respect.

There are three central justifications for qualifying the strict legal rule of confidentiality. First, there is the practical justification. As some commentators argue, the current legal position restricts doctors' work considerably. It is an impractical rule, which limits the doctors when they want to communicate with family members and others so as to improve the patient's overall condition. It is suggested that the legal rule of confidentiality should be qualified to facilitate this end. A doctor's decision to inform family members may be justified (1) when the

---

[33] This applies to the child abuse cases discussed in Chapter 3. The decision of the courts seems to neglect the argument that when professionals (psychiatrists, psychologists, or social workers) interview and make decisions for children at risk of abuse, they indirectly treat the children's families and thus owe them involuntarily a duty to act with due care. Any decision the professionals take will undoubtedly affect the family members and the family as a social unit. Stating that the professionals owe a legal duty only to the child, as the courts did, reflects once again a patient–centred approach, where the patient's interests are promoted at the expense of family's.

[34] A comprehensive discussion about the doctor's conflicting duties when there is a familial dispute about a medical treatment is beyond the scope of this study. A brief discussion was conducted in Chapter 5 on whether the family is an end in itself or means to improve the patient's condition.

doctor wants to relieve the anxiety of relatives; or (2) when the doctor discloses information to relatives to help them provide the patient with medical care; or (3) when the patient has a difficulty absorbing the information or is not fully competent to make a medical decision.

However, this practical justification may not only qualify the patient's right to confidentiality but also his or her right to make autonomous decisions. The patient may have valid reasons for not disclosing information to family members that the doctor cannot fully appreciate. Despite the relatives' anxiety, the patient may wish to control the situation and decide whether and when to inform them. Therefore, doctors will have to consider carefully and seriously whether or not disclosure should be made when the patient refuses to consent. They will have to justify their decision not only by considering the medical aspect of the patient's condition but more importantly by taking into account the nature of the familial relationship. Thus, if the relationship with family members is not good, and the doctor suspects that the relatives may use the information for the disadvantage of the patient, disclosure without consent will not be justified. This holds especially in the context of genetics, where disclosure cannot prevent physical harm to the relatives.

A second justification for qualifying the doctor's duty of confidentiality is that it will help the patient to maintain his or her individuality through receiving social support from the family. As was argued in previous chapters, when the patient enters the health care system his or her autonomy and identity are compromised. As the Lindemann-Nelsons argue, the process of illness has an effect of estranging the patient from himself or herself.[35] In these circumstances the support given to the patient by family members will help him or her to protect his or her self–image and to remain autonomous. The family can provide the patient with orientation and a point of reference.[36] From this perspective, the concession the patient has to make in qualifying his or her right to confidentiality will, in the end, restore his or her self–confidence when communicating with the doctors about medical decisions.

A third justification for the qualification of confidentiality is that it enables relatives to exercise *their* autonomy and promote *their* interests. This justification is situated in the liberal discourse. As stated above, the promotion of patients' rights should not necessarily bring about the rejection of the relatives' fundamental rights. In this context four questions arise: (1) Should patients owe a legal duty to inform family members? (2) Should doctors be allowed to breach the patient's right to confidentiality when prevention of harm (physical, psychological, or financial) cannot be guaranteed? (3) Should doctors owe a duty to inform family

---

[31]   See the Lindemann-Nelsons, supra n. 2.
[32]   Ibid., at p. 46.
[33]   Ibid.

members in these circumstances? (4) Should doctors owe a duty to respect the relatives' right not to know?

As for the patient–relatives relationship, it must be accepted that the etiquette of families is not based solely on rights and duties but also on care, commitment, and mutual responsibility. Patients' refusal to respect their relatives' interests does not derive from objective but from subjective factors, related to the nature and quality of their familial relationship. Thus, imposing a legal duty on patients to family members will not accord with the nature of the familial relationship. Furthermore, adopting a rights talk may hinder a compromise, highlighting the confrontational aspects of the tensions between the patient and the relatives.

As for the doctors, the discussion throughout this dissertation should lead to the conclusion that it is unreasonable to impose two conflicting legal duties on them. In light of the various consideration involved in genetics, the doctor cannot simultaneously respect the relatives' right to know and not to know. Imposing a duty on doctors to family members will require determining in advance which of these two legal rights is to be preferred. If such a legal regime is adopted the law will be unduly strict and hard pressed to deal with the complicated situations this area of genetic information entails.

Certainly, promoting the interests of family members does not necessarily require the imposition of a legal duty on doctors. The mechanism suggested here is to provide doctors and patients with ethical guidance on how to resolve familial tensions over confidentiality and medical information when prevention of harm cannot be guaranteed. This guidance will encourage doctors and patients to take the interests of family members more seriously. If they follow this guidance their decisions will be justified when challenged in the courts as they will encompass the various considerations involved in this area. Such a mechanism has been recommended by academics and policy makers.[37] As we shall see below, such a mechanism is in harmony with the recent sociological perception of law and with the type and method of solution that the courts and Parliament provide for legal and moral conflicts. The next task is to search for a model that promotes the interests of the relatives more than they are recognised in law at present.

6.4 The Family Covenant

Predictably, not many models can offer an alternative to the unsatisfactory utilitarian mechanism of prevention of physical harm to others. Such a mechanism is dominant in the UK, the US, and other Western countries.[38]

---

[37] Ngwena C., Chadwick R., "Genetic information and the duty of confidentiality: Ethics and law" (1993) 1 *Medical Law International* 73, 90; Nuffield Council on Bioethics, *Genetic Screening: Ethical Issues* (1993), Ch. 5, 53.

[38] In the UK: The General Medical Council, *Confidentiality: Protecting and Providing Information*, London, General Medical Council (2000). In the US: The American

One alternative, briefly discussed in Chapter 1, was developed by David Doukas and Jessica Berg and is called the *family covenant.*[39]   It aims to accommodate conflicting interests of patients and their family members regarding genetic information by reaching an agreement before genetic information becomes available. This requires negotiation and concurrence on the boundaries of confidentiality in the family. The doctor's task is to initiate a discussion about the family covenant as part of the counselling process that usually occurs before testing takes place. Alternatively, the doctor can initiate such a discussion when new patients first register in the surgery or when they come in for a periodic check–up.

Family members can freely decide whether or not they want to be part of the covenant. Those who do must consent to its provisions. Those who decide not to join will not be bound by it. The doctor's professional obligations are also negotiated and articulated to the parties. Before a covenant is established the doctor and the family members discuss how conflicts will be handled and resolved. Essentially, a family covenant is an ongoing, adaptable and voluntary contract in healthcare to which the participating family members consent.[40]   When genetic information becomes available the doctor acts as a mediator, monitoring the communication of genetic information in the family. Doukas and Berg believe that this model facilitates communication by helping patients and their family doctor to understand the interests of the parties involved.

In practice, when the patient receives genetic test results that have implications for the physical health of another family member, these results may be shared with other family members according to the provisions of the covenant. But if the patient does not allow the doctor to disclose the information the doctor will discuss this issue with the patient to find out the reasons for this refusal. The doctor will assess whether the patient's decision accords with the covenant. If the patient insists on his or her refusal he or she may withdraw from the covenant, thereby dissolving it. Alternatively, the doctor may withdraw from the covenant if the decision of one of its members violates its professional integrity. Thus, in extreme cases the doctor can breach the patient's confidentiality and disclose information to other family members.

Undoubtedly, a family covenant model limits the patient's autonomy to act free from social constraints. Moreover, the patient's right to confidentiality is modified. In this model the limits and boundaries of confidentiality are negotiated in the family prior to the formulation of the covenant. If the patient wishes to be part of

---

Society of Human Genetics Social Issues, "Professional disclosure of familial genetic information" (1998) 62 *American Journal of Human Genetics* 474; in Israel: The *Genetic Information Act* 2000. For a brief account on Israeli law see Laurie, supra n. 4, at pp. 284–285.

[39]   Doukas D., Berg J., "The family covenant and genetic testing" (2001) 1 (3) *The American Journal of Bioethics* 2.

[40]   Ibid., at p. 6.

the covenant he or she acknowledges that he or she will have to share genetic information when it becomes available and that the doctor will be able to inform other parties to the covenant. If the patient does not want to disclose information the doctor can dissolve the covenant, an act that may trigger inquiry in the family but will not directly breach the patient's right to confidentiality. In any event, once the covenant is established, confidentiality is maintained within the boundaries agreed by its members.[41]

Examining this model closely, it seems that it balances adequately individual's rights and family's interests. It is a liberal, contract–based model, which incorporates some communitarian insights. It resembles Rawls's original position where the parties have to deal with a hypothetical situation. As in the original position the family members who negotiate a common agreement do not know what will be their position when genetic information becomes available. Realising this, they reach a resolution that suits all family members, whether they will become the patient who undergoes genetic testing or the relatives who do not.

Still, the underlying position of Doukas and Berg is that the family and not the individual patient is the unit of care.[42] They argue that the doctor is responsible for comprehensive family health and that the patient is treated within the family.[43] From the doctors' perspective this leads them to consider the competing interests between family members regarding genetic information. The doctor who practises a family covenant model is not concerned only with the individual patient and his or her personal interests but also with the family members, who want to be part of the medical decision–making process. Also implicit in this model is the impact of the specific characteristics of the familial relationships on the negotiating parties. The personal motives of the family members to reach a common agreement are based on their place in the family and on the nature of the relationship among them. Thus, although the family covenant is based on the individual's choice to enter into a contract, it nevertheless puts the health of the family at the centre, promoting the interests of its members whether they are patients or not.

In developing a model of family covenant Doukas and Berg believe that it should be practised at primary care level. They rely on several assumptions. First, they argue that families receive medical care from a single GP more often than generally realised. They refer to surveys indicating that the majority of families visit the same GP. Second, they argue that GPs are already involved in the provision of genetic services and are likely to become more so as genetic testing becomes more available. They suggest that GPs deal with familial tensions over genetic information. Third, Doukas and Berg appreciate the dominance of the *biopsychosocial* model in family medicine and its contribution to the perception of the doctor–patient relationship.

---

[41] Ibid., at p. 7.
[42] Ibid., at p. 5.
[43] Ibid.

Is a family covenant a practical solution? Theoretically, this model is promising. From an ethical perspective, it addresses the concerns of family members in genetics while not violating the fundamental rights of the individual patient. It gives patients and family members equal discretion to decide how genetic information will be communicated in the family. Relying on the *biopsychosocial* model, it combines both liberal and communitarian conceptions. From a liberal perspective, it relies on the individual's voluntary consent to be part of the covenant. Family members are not forced to join and can withdraw from it whenever they wish. From a communitarian perspective, this model reflects the belief that the interests of individuals in genetic information can be fulfilled by encouraging family members to adhere to collective reflection on this issue of disclosure of genetic information. It is based on empirical data suggesting that approaching genetic testing as a unit can promote familial communication and decrease conflicts.[44] Ultimately, it implies that individuals can fulfil their goals by compromising their wishes for the sake of a collective interest.

Furthermore, this model deals adequately with the complexities involved in genetics mentioned above. It does not express any position with regard to the conflict between the right to know and the right not to know. It leaves it to the parties to the family covenant to determine the circumstances where information will and will not be disclosed. This model is indeed flexible. On the one hand, it is based on the prior consent of patients and family members to disclose information; on the other hand it is sensitive to the interest of patients and family members in sharing information with close intimates.

Undoubtedly, this flexibility derives from the deliberative process this model offers. By highlighting the negotiation process as the most fundamental requirement, the authors appreciate that good communication among the three parties involved is essential if familial tensions over genetic information are to be resolved. Hence, this model is compatible with the conception of familial privacy developed in Chapter 4. It was assumed that family members as a group have a common interest in protecting their familial private sphere from others. When the patient considers whether or not the relatives would like to receive genetic information he or she can rely on his or her familial relationship. Knowing the relatives as no one else does, the patient can arrive at an informed decision based on the mutual communication of thoughts, beliefs, and desires with the relatives. Consequently, a patient who cannot determine in advance what the relatives' interests are with regard to disclosure can find out by approaching the relatives and asking them indirectly for their general views on the subject. This process, described in Chapter 4, wins support in the suggested model of Doukas and Berg. The patient and the family members can gain knowledge about each other's views through a process of communication and deliberation before genetic testing is performed in the private sphere of their family with minimum involvement of

---

[44]   Ibid., at p. 6.

others.

In practice, however, the preliminary assumptions on which Doukas and Berg rely are not entirely accurate.[45] They argue that GPs are *already* involved in the provision of genetic services to their patients. However, recent studies indicate that currently the involvement of GPs is minor.[46] Many GPs do not have the relevant and necessary knowledge to provide comprehensive genetic services, and they often feel they need additional guidance before referring patients to genetic clinics. Yet Doukas and Berg are not entirely mistaken. Policy–makers in the UK are well aware that sooner rather than later family doctors will have to be involved in the provision of genetic services.[47] In any event, GPs are to some extent already involved in the provision of genetic services by referring at–risk patients to genetic clinics and by providing emotional and informational support to patients and their relatives.[48]

The authors' assumption that many families have one family doctor is also inaccurate. Even in the studies they refer to, most respondents' families do not have the same doctor. Moreover, this assumption depends on the definition of the family. Yet, Doukas and Berg fail to provide an explicit and clear definition. The question that arises is who is included in the family. Can first–degree cousins, nieces, and uncles be part to a family covenant? If other family members beyond the nuclear ones are included the assumption that they all visit the same GP will be easily rebutted.

Furthermore, the aim of implementing this model on the primary care level raises the issue of allocation of resources. In the existing health care system it is unlikely that GPs will have the time and resources to engage in formulating a family covenant. In a practice of over 2,000 patients, where doctors spend on average 8.5 minutes with every patient, GPs can hardly have the time to formulate family covenants.[49] Moreover, it is hard to imagine that an extended family will have a comprehensive and detailed discussion about a hypothetical situation that

---

[45] For a broad critique on this model see (2001) 1 (3) *The American Journal of Bioethics* 11–35.

[46] Watson E., et al., "The 'new genetics' and primary care: GPs' views on their role and their educational needs" (1999) 16 (4) *Family Practice* 420; Kinmonth A. et al., "The new genetics: Implications for clinical services in Britain and the United States" (1998) 316 *BMJ* 767; Fry A. et al., "GPs' views on their role in cancer genetics services and current practice" (1999) 16 (5) *Family Practice* 468.

[47] Kumar S., Gantley M., "Tensions between policy makers and general practitioners in implementing new genetics: Grounded theory interview study" (1999) 319 *BMJ* 1410; Lenaghan J., *Brave New NHS?*, London, Institute for Public Policy Research (1998), Ch. 4, pp. 60–77.

[48] Kinmonth et al., supra n. 46, at p. 768.

[49] Hannay D. et al., "Workload of General Practitioners before and after the new contract" (1992) 304 *BMJ* 615; Department of Health, General and personal medical services statistics as at 30 September 2001, www.doh.gov.uk/public/gpcensus2001.htm.

may or may not arise in the future. Convening family members is difficult enough when illness occurs, let alone in times of good health.

Another practical issue that this model raises derives from its preventive nature. This model suggests that family members will discuss their attitudes to a situation they have never encountered and that may or may not occur in the future. It can be argued that even with the help of the doctor they cannot anticipate the various circumstances and complexities that may arise when genetic information becomes available. In addition, they cannot know how they will react to the information. They may change their mind and wish to withdraw from the covenant. Therefore, the question is whether it is effective to discuss issues of disclosure of genetic information in advance when family members have little or no experience of it.

Finally, as Parker and Lucassen point out, family members may share genetic information in destructive ways, for example, during a family dispute.[50] The hypothetical scenario discussed in Chapter 4 of an eight–week pregnant woman who wants to have prenatal testing for Huntington's disease is one example. Doukas and Berg do not seem to provide a mechanism that can deal effectively with such familial tensions. In this respect their perception of the family seems too positive.[51]

Despite these practical difficulties, this model will change the legal attitude to family members in English law. The underlying principle of the family covenant model is that the doctor–patient relationship is not exclusive. Instead, the family and not the individual patient constitutes the unit of medical care. As we have seen, this is not the position of the courts. If this model is adopted a fundamental change in the attitude of the courts to the doctor–patient relationship will necessarily emerge. The courts will have to recognise the family's involvement in the decision regarding communication of genetic information. Put differently, the interests of family members will receive greater legal recognition in this specific area of English medical law.

Furthermore, ethically, the courts will have to change their perception of patient autonomy and confidentiality. They will be obliged to accept that autonomy is a relational concept and that confidentiality can be negotiated in the family. The courts will have to realise that the limitations of patient autonomy exceed the principle of prevention of harm. In the context of genetics this implies that the division of power among the three parties involved will be more balanced. The courts will have to acknowledge that genetic information has various and considerable implications for family members, and that their autonomy should be

---

[50] Parker M., Lucassen A., "Concern for families and individuals in clinical genetics" (2003) 29 *Journal of Medical Ethics* 70, 72; see also: Stock G., "The family covenant: A flawed response to the dilemmas in genetic testing" (2001) 1 (3) *The American Journal of Bioethics* 17.

[51] Parker M., "Confidentiality in genetic testing" (2001) 1 (3) *American Journal of Bioethics* 21, at p. 22 discusses this scenario when criticising the family covenant model.

maintained as well. As for the doctors, the courts will have to recognise the ethical principle of beneficence.

In this book the family covenant model is preferred to all other existing models as it reflects the underlying ethical approach of this study. Yet as we have seen, the implementation of this model may face practical barriers deriving from the structure and limited resources of the health care system in the UK. Therefore, the next step is to develop a model that could surmount these practical barriers. Before such a model is suggested it is necessary to develop the discussion regarding the role of law further, to look at the mechanisms that English law provides when policy and moral issues arise.

6.5 The Role of Law: Sending Indirect Controlling Messages

The mechanism proposed in the remainder of this final chapter relies on a recent perception of law as identified by a few legal commentators. Marc Galanter argues that law is becoming more dominant in Western society.[52] He adds that the law changes as it becomes more influential.[53] The legal discourse increasingly incorporates non–legal arguments and adopts methods of analysis which are not entirely unique to the legal discipline. This process, together with other developments, makes law more complex and creates what Galanter calls islands of temporary certainty in a sea of uncertainty.[54]

Furthermore, Galanter sees the law as an area that like politics provides people the opportunity to have a moral debate. When the law is required to provide answers to moral dilemmas, for example, whether to allow withdrawal of life–supporting treatment, or whether to allow breach of confidentiality, conflicting moral principles such as autonomy, utility, justice, community, and so on are involved. The legal answer, though authoritative in nature, is temporary and changeable.

Finally, according to Galanter the law operates increasingly by 'indirect symbolic controls' through 'radiating messages' rather than by direct 'physical coercion'.[55] Commenting on the state of English family law John Dewar develops this argument further.[56] He argues that family law is developed to influence public attitudes generally and not specifically by setting clear legal rules. One example Dewar discusses is the recent changes in the legislation on divorce. He argues that this legislation is best understood as setting out general guidance on how to divorce

---

[52] See Galanter, supra n. 16.
[53] Ibid., at p. 18.
[54] Ibid., at p. 21.
[55] Ibid., at p. 24.
[56] Dewar J., "The normal chaos of family law" (1998) 61 (4) *Modern Law Review* 467, 470.

well: adults should be reasonable and fully aware of the consequences of their actions for themselves as well as for others.

Galanter's observations apply to English medical law. The legal mechanism often adopted in this area is for Parliament to express its general approach and then to establish an official authority, which is given the discretion to deal with specific cases. One example is the Human Fertilisation and Embryology Authority established under the 1990 Act whose role is to regulate the treatments provided in the area of assisted reproduction.[57] According to section 25 of the 1990 Act, this Authority is required from time to time to publish a code of practice addressing the various aspects of the treatments provided in assisted reproduction.[58] As Mason, McCall–Smith, and Laurie observe, the underlying rationale is to afford the law flexibility when it intervenes in private and familial matters.[59] In Western pluralist society the legislature does not formulate clear rules but only general principles, which will exert influence for change. While in England the legislator sets up governmental authorities, in other countries it establishes ethics committees, which have to follow the general principles and exercise their discretion in particular cases brought before them.[60]

Furthermore, the courts increasingly serve as an arena where a moral debate on medical issues is conducted. Despite the explicit insistence of the courts that society – through the democratic expression of its views in Parliament – will arrive at an accepted moral decision,[61] they are willing to deal with issues that raise significant ethical dilemmas. One example is withdrawal of life–supporting treatment from patients in a persistent vegetative state.[62] In this area the courts

---

[57] The *Human Fertilisation and Embryology Act* 1990, sections 8 & 25.

[58] The Human Fertilisation and Embryology Authority, *Code of Practice*, London, The Human Fertilisation and Embryology Authority, (6th edn., 2003).

[59] Mason J.K., McCall-Smith R.A., Laurie G. T., *Law and Medical Ethics*, London, Butterworths (6th edn., 2002), 24.

[60] Such a mechanism was adopted in Israeli medical law. When there is disagreement between the doctor and the patient about a proposed treatment or disclosure of information to third parties the doctor has to bring the case before an ethics committee, which has the authority to decide and resolve the conflict. This committee comprises a senior lawyer, two consultants, a social worker or a psychologist, and a member of the public. See the Israeli *Patient's Rights Act 1996*, sections 13, 15, 20, 24. However, the view taken in this book is that this mechanism, though it provides flexibility when mediating conflicts about disclosure, is not recommended as it sends a paternalistic message, depriving the parties of the authority to decide in a matter which concerns them personally. The argument put forward in this book is that the decision should be made only by those (patient and family members) who influence it and are affected by it. Ultimately, in this conflict the family's autonomy and privacy should be preserved, and authority should not be given to others however objective they may be.

[61] *Airedale NHS Trust v Bland* [1993] AC 789, 878–879.

[62] *Practice Note (Family Division: Incapacitated Adults: Declaratory Proceedings)* [2002] 1 All ER 794.

discuss various moral principles such as autonomy (of patients), utility (of the futile medical treatment), community (the interests of family members), justice (allocation of resources), and the like. The law becomes what Galanter calls a 'second kind of politics'[63] where the legal claim is used by different groups and organisations as means to participate in the determination of public policy.[64] Moreover, the courts, as this specific area of medical law indicates, reluctantly incorporate non–legal arguments when arriving at a legal decision. Bearing this in mind, the suggested model specified in the next part attempts to reflect this perception of law.

6.6 The Suggested Model: A Process of Communication and Deliberation

As the review in Chapters 3 and 4 reveals, the current legal mechanism for resolving familial conflicts over medical information is based on giving doctors and patients discretion to decide whether or not to disclose information to family members. In exercising their discretion the primary consideration is prevention of physical harm or death to others. When physical harm can be avoided the doctor's decision to breach the patient's right to confidentiality is legally justified. But if the doctor is aware of a serious risk of physical harm to identified relatives the court may hold the doctor liable for the relatives' damages if he or she fails to warn them.

As implied above, the model suggested in this part does not propose to change this legal framework: doctors and patients should have the discretion to decide whether or not to disclose genetic information to family members. The patient's entitlement to make autonomous decisions is appreciated in this book. The new model, however, challenges the existing criteria that guide doctors and patients when considering disclosure. The change is not in the legal framework or method but in the underlying ethical considerations that indirectly influence the legal position.[65] Since medical law is heavily influenced by medical ethics in this area[66] a change in the ethical position will eventually change the law and the symbolic messages it sends to the public.

---

[63] See Galanter, supra, n.16, at p. 23.

[64] Galanter cites Nonet and Selznick, *Law and Society in Transition: Towards Responsive Law*, New York, Harper & Row (1978).

[65] In *W v Egdell* [1989] 1 All ER 1089, the leading authority in this area, the court at first instance began its discussion with the GMC code on confidentiality. The court adopted the mechanism proposed by the GMC, namely that prevention of risk of physical harm to the public justifies disclosure.

[66] Many legal commentators realise that medical law and medical ethics are inseparable when discussing medical issues. See, for example, Mason, McCall-Smith, and Laurie, supra n. 59, at p. 4.

As mentioned earlier, existing professional guidelines currently still rely on a utilitarian mechanism. The Human Genetic Commission recently concluded that disclosure to family members is justified only when the benefit to them outweighs the harm caused to the patient by breach of confidentiality.[67] Furthermore, as we have seen, other proposed mechanisms that take the psychological aspect into account do not reflect comprehensively the ethics of families. Laurie, for example, argues that in the consideration of disclosure the likely emotional reaction of the relative to the news should be taken into account. So when patients consider disclosure to family members their decision is based on *their* prediction of the relatives' reaction. In making this prediction they rely on their *knowledge* of the relatives' inner world. Laurie is correct in considering this criterion, aiming to secure the relative's right not to know. But he ignores the social dimension: usually family members are emotionally attached. Patients do not view the situation from a distance, engaging in an objective assessment of the relatives' likely reaction. Instead, they appreciate that their decisions are made in respect of their relationships with their close family members. This leads them to take into account the effect the decision will have on the familial relationship with them.[68]

The various ethical and professional guidelines in this area advise patients and doctors to take into account the following criteria when familial tensions over access to genetic information arise: (1) the availability of cures or preventive measures; (2) the severity of the disease and likelihood of onset; (3) the nature of the disorder; (4) the availability of genetic testing; (5) the accuracy of testing in assessing the risk; (6) the relatives' likely emotional reaction when given the information. However, an additional criterion, which is omitted from these codes, is: (7) *the effect any decision (to disclose or not to disclose) will have on the familial relationship and on the dynamics of the particular family.*

Adding this social dimension to the existing criteria will accord with the socio–medical literature and with the views of doctors and patients. As discovered in the previous chapter, patients base their decision whether or not to disclose information to family members on the quality and nature of the relationship they have with the relatives, and not so much on the availability of a cure.[69] Doctors too do not emphasise the availability of preventive measures when considering disclosure to family members without consent. In the majority of cases when a disease has no effective cure, and when the likelihood of onset is not certain, this criterion of familial relationship will be dominant.

---

[67]   See The Human Genetic Commission, *Inside Information: Balancing the Interests in the Use of Personal Genetic Data*, London: Department of Health (2002), Ch. 3, para 3.68.

[68]   Reust C., Mattingly S., "Family involvement in medical decision making" (1996) 28 *Family Medicine* 39.

[69]   See, for example: McGivern B. et al., "Family communication about positive BRCA1 and BRCA2 genetic test results" (2004) 6 (6) *Genetics in Medicine* 503; Kenen R. et al., "Healthy women from suspected hereditary breast and ovarian cancer families: the significant others in their lives" (2004) 13 *European Journal of Cancer Care* 169.

This criterion will require doctors and patients to discuss the various aspects of the patient's familial relationship. These may include: the patient's ability to cope with bad news without sharing it with the relatives; the relatives' reaction when they find out that they could have received the information earlier; the relatives' reaction to the possibility that the patient may develop a genetic disease – will they support the patient or will they express resentment and indifference; the patient's reaction to the relatives' decisions, such as undergoing testing, having antenatal testing, terminating a risky pregnancy, and the like; whether the patient's decision derives from his or her relationship with the relatives to whom the information is relevant; whether the nature of the familial relationship suggests that relatives will willingly agree to waive their right not to know, or whether the relationship is based primarily on a strong sense of individual privacy. Considering these aspects will help the patient to decide whether or not to inform family members, and more importantly it will help doctors to solve familial tensions once they arise.

Conducting a serious discussion about these aspects may require that the doctor know well the nature of the patient's familial relationship. In the area of genetics this is satisfied when the patient is referred to a genetics clinic. Genetic clinics have psychologists and counsellors who can discuss thoroughly the various implications genetic information has for the familial relationship as mentioned above.[70] As Angus Clarke, a leading genetic counsellor, recently reported,[71] counsellors and counsellees do discuss these aspects in practice. In addition, at the primary care level GPs are perceived as those who know their patients and their families well. In many cases the nuclear family members has the same GP, who has known them for many years and is trained to mediate familial disagreements and to intervene if necessary.

As with the family covenant model, the implementation of this social criterion requires *a process of communication and deliberation*, which should be conducted both at the doctor's clinic and within the family. As Michael Parker argues, ethical dilemmas in genetics require interpersonal deliberation.[72] It is appreciated that only through discussions and conversations with the doctor will the patient and the relatives be able to gain knowledge about the core values and beliefs of the family and its members regarding confidentiality, privacy, and disclosure of medical information. Communicating with the patient, the doctor will know whether the patient wishes to inform the relatives, whether there are relatives he or she is reluctant to inform and whether he or she knows the relatives' views about disclosure. Communicating with the relatives, the patient will become aware of their opinions on genetic information: whether they wish to receive it or whether

---

[70]   See Harper, supra n. 32, Ch. 1.
[71]   France L., Clarke A., "Professional responses to non–disclosure of genetic information," a paper presented at the *First Interdisciplinary Conference on Communication, Medicine and Ethics*, Health Communication Research Centre, Cardiff University, Cardiff, 26–28 June 2003.
[72]   See Parker, supra n. 51, at p. 22; and also Parker, supra n. 1, at pp. 163–164.

there is information they do not wish to know. When communicating with the patient, the relatives will know whether or not the patient intends to inform them.

6.6.1 The Doctor–Patient Relationship

Focusing on the deliberative process between doctors and patients, the doctor in the vast majority of cases will not have to convince the patient to take a particular decision for gradually the patient will become aware of the implications the information has for the relatives. Clarke reached the same conclusion.[73] He describes four cases where counsellees were initially reluctant to disclose genetic information to family members. Three of them were BRCA carriers while the fourth was the widower of a patient who had died from a rare genetic disorder. Their initial reaction to the bad news was to conceal the information from their adult children because they suspected that they would 'react badly'. However, following a process of deliberation and consultation with the counsellors the counsellees decided to disclose the information, determining the settings of the disclosure. One of them, for example, preferred to wait till she met the relative in person.

Clarke emphasises the benefit of allowing counsellees time to make a decision whether or not to disclose information to their relatives, and argues that if disclosure is forced it might damage the familial relationship. Thus, Clarke promotes a process of deliberation where doctors do not force patients to disclose but discusses with them the dynamics in the family and the likely effect the news will have on the familial relationships. In this process doctors try (but not always succeed)[74] not to lead patients to the decision they prefer. Instead, the doctor or counsellor begins the consultation by asking about the patient's family members and his or her relationship with them, trying to raise the issue of disclosure with the patient as the consultation progresses. In this process the patient not only participates in the decision–making process, he or she also considers the interests of the relatives and his or her responsibility to them. The patient will most probably make the decision that is true to the life–story, background, and core values of his or her family and the doctor will not try to lead him or her to disclose or not to disclose. As Clarke indicates, in some cases the doctor or counsellor does

---

[73] See France and Clarke, supra n. 71; Clarke and his colleagues argue that the doctor's attempt to convince the patient to disclose cannot be perceived as a shared decision–making model because there is no agreement between them about this issue. See Elwyn G., Gray J., Clarke A., "Shared decision making and non–directiveness in genetic counselling" (2000) 37 *Journal of Medical Genetics* 135, 138.

[73] Ibid.

[74] Clarke admits that counsellors 'are sometimes very directive about the benefits of disclosure', although they 'try to work round to this gently...' (Personal communication with Angus Clarke, 14/4/2005).

not even know whether the patient eventually communicated the information to the relatives.

This process leads Clarke to argue that for many patients the choice whether or not to inform family members is not between 'now or never' but between 'now and by the time we next meet.'[75] In addition, as other studies show, it is not a choice between disclosure to all and disclosure to no one, but a decision whether to disclose to one relative or more.[76] Thus, the issue of disclosure which is perceived in law as an absolute question (all or nothing), is in reality more flexible and the decision is made according to the particular circumstances of the case.

Conducting a serious discussion on confidentiality and disclosure the doctor and the patient can agree on the circumstances where genetic information will be disclosed. For example, they can agree that the doctor will disclose the information to one family member, who will pass the information to other relatives. They can also agree that the doctor will notify the relatives' doctor (if they are registered in a different clinic) without disclosing the patient's identity. Or they can agree that the doctor will advise family members to undergo testing, without revealing all the available information. Acquiring an understanding in these circumstances may help doctors and patients to preserve a minimal and essential level of trust, for the deliberation will help patients realise that they have to compromise their interests if they wish to maintain familial relationships.

However, when a serious dispute between doctors and patients emerges, and the doctor decides to disclose genetic information despite the patient's insistence on his or her refusal, a qualified rule of medical confidentiality should be practised based on the justifications presented above. When the patient challenges the doctor's decision to breach his or her right to confidentiality the courts will have to consider not only whether the doctor's decision accords with the utilitarian justification of prevention of physical harm but also whether it accords with the social justifications discussed above, especially when the traditional utilitarian criteria do not provide a conclusive or a satisfactory answer. For example, the doctor's decision to disclose information without consent may be justified if he or she needs the assistance of family members to provide the patient with further treatment, or when he or she has to relieve the relatives' anxiety so that they will be able to give the patient support when receiving the news. However, the doctor will have to consider disclosure without consent cautiously. Having become familiar with the patient's family may assist the doctor in this regard.

The same analysis should apply when family members challenge the patient's or doctor's decision not to disclose. The court will have to examine whether the patient's background and the nature of his or her familial relationship did not

---

[75]   Ibid.
[76]   Green J. et al., "Family Communication and genetic counselling: The case of hereditary breach and ovarian cancer" (1997) 6 (1) *Journal of Genetic Counselling* 45; Forrest K. et al., "To tell or not to tell: Barriers and facilitators in family communication about genetic risk" (2003) 64 *Clinical Genetics* 317.

dictate disclosure even when it could not prevent the onset of the disease. In such cases, when the consideration of prevention of physical harm is not dominant family members will nevertheless be informed and thus their interests will be recognised. This will not be achieved through the formulation of a strict legal rule but indirectly by the inclusion of a social dimension to the criteria that doctors and patients should consider.

In addition, despite the reservations made throughout this book regarding the right not to know, this model is sensitive, to some extent, to the relatives' interest in not receiving genetic information. The doctor and the patient may come to a decision not to disclose, following serious consideration of the moral, psycho-logical and social implications of such a decision. But in the majority of cases patients and relatives will have to realise that this model does not aim to bar a free flow of information in the family. Instead, the underlying philosophy is that familial relationships are based mainly on communication and exchange of thoughts, views and experiences, which leave little room for relatives to fulfil their interest in being left alone and in remaining ignorant. However, this interest will be satisfied when the relatives' views are known or in exceptional cases, for example, when the relative suffers from severe depression. In the end, strengthening a sense of responsibility in the family implies that relatives will have to compromise their personal interest in being in a state of separateness.

Yet, how can a deliberative model deal with a dispute between the doctor and the patient when the doctor believes that the patient's decision adversely affects the interests of the relatives? As explained above the main characteristic of this model is that doctors do not have to convince patients to take the interests of their relatives into account because they usually do. However, in some circumstances, the doctors and the patient may not be able to agree on the circumstances of either disclosure or non–disclosure of genetic information.

In this context we should analyse three examples, two of them already discussed in this book. One is the case of the eight–week pregnant woman who wants to undergo prenatal testing for Huntington's disease, knowing that her husband, from whom she recently parted, refuses to take the test or know the results.[77] The second example is that of the breast cancer patient who was tested to know whether she is a BRCA carrier but resolved not to inform her two daughters if the results were positive.[78] The third example concerns the mother of a four–year–old boy who has Duchenne's muscular dystrophy. Finding out she is a carrier, she refuses to disclose this information to her sister who is ten weeks pregnant and is being treated at the same clinic.[79] In these scenarios, one may wonder how a model based on a process of deliberation can help solve the familial tensions.

[77]   Described in Parker M., Lucassen A., "Concern for families and individuals in clinical genetics" (2003) 29 *Journal of Medical Ethics* 70, box 3.

[78]   Robertson J. et al., "BRCA1 screening in woman with breast cancer: A patient's perspective with commentary" (2001) 11 (2) *Women's Health Issues* 63.

[79]   Parker M., Lucassen A., "Genetic information: A joint account" (2004) 329 *BMJ* 165.

In the first example, where the disease is terminal, learning about the nature of the relationship between the woman and her husband is crucial for understanding the patient's decision to undergo testing. The patient's right to undergo testing should be considered alongside the view that such a decision may destroy the relationship of this family, which is fragile as it is. Indeed, performing the test may put an end to this delicate relationship and may have a serious adverse impact on the lives of the husband and the newborn child. The child may not be able to benefit from living with his or her two biological parents. In addition, it will be very difficult for the mother to conceal the information from her spouse especially if they remain in contact. And when the husband is informed, this may cause him substantial psychological harm.

It must be admitted that such a model does not presume to solve such a serious conflict. However, by embarking on a deliberative process with the doctor, the patient may gradually realise the implications of her willingness to have prenatal testing for her relationships with her husband and unborn baby, even when the patient–husband relationship is dysfunctional. Though the woman will have the final say on this issue, by having a thorough discussion with her doctor she may come to appreciate that to have the test despite her husband's refusal may compromise her other life plans and the relationships that matter to her the most. In the end, the doctor and the patient may come to an agreement where the doctor accepts that the patient took into account the various considerations involved in such a decision.

However, if the doctors refuse to perform the prenatal test they may have to justify the decision in court if challenged by the mother. Undoubtedly, the social criterion suggested above may provide the doctor valid justifications for his or her conduct. Though it may not change the court's decision it will provide more recognition for the relatives' interests.

The second example reflects other difficulties for the doctor and the patient. If the results are positive and the patient insists on her refusal to disclose the information to her two young adult daughters, the availability of some measures to reduce the risk of the daughters' developing inherited breast cancer should be taken into account, together with the nature of the relationship of the particular family. Thus, the mother's instinct to protect her daughters from bad news may be changed through a process of deliberation with her husband and the doctor. Investigating the familial relationship, the common values of the patient's family, and the level of communication among family members, the doctor can indicate to the mother that her initial decision not to disclose may endanger her relationship with her daughters and with her husband, who may favour disclosure. The doctor may also point out to the patient that her responsibility to her daughters may entail disclosure especially when they can take measures to reduce their risk if they test positive. Yet, if the deliberative process does not yield an agreement and the doctor decides to disclose information without consent, the social criterion may add another aspect to the legal discussion even if it does not change the court's decision.

The final example imposes on the doctor a serious conflict between his legal and moral duty of confidentiality to the mother and his legal and moral duty to inform her sister of relevant information to enable her to make an informed reproductive choice. The doctor may ask himself whether one duty should supersede the other. In these circumstances the mother's decision is based on her poor relationship with her sister and on the latter's moral judgement, she having already decided that if the foetus is affected she will terminate the pregnancy. As with the two cases just analysed, the doctor may try to conduct a serious discussion with the mother and ask her whether her decision not to disclose is influenced by her sour relationship with her sister. In the end the mother may come to accept that she should provide her sister with the opportunity to make an informed decision. But if the mother insists on her refusal to disclose the doctor can approach the sister, as she too is his patient, and recommend that she take the test without revealing the source of information. If the pregnant sister enquires, the doctor will have to say that since he is under a conflict of interests he cannot expose the mother's identity. This may spur the sister to contact the mother and uncover her secret, but it would be difficult for either patient to contest the doctor's decision in court, especially as he took into consideration the impact of the familial relationship on his decision to disclose and fulfilled his legal and moral duties.[80]

6.6.2 The Patient–Relatives Relationship

Moving on to the deliberative process within the family, the law can operate indirectly in this realm as well. For example, the law (either through regulations or professional agencies) can direct doctors and other health care professionals to encourage patients to discuss with their families their interests in genetic information. By this process patients and family members will gain knowledge of each other's views on the subject, reaching the conclusion that in the future they may need to compromise their personal interests and respect those of their relatives. Additionally, patients' awareness of the relatives' interests in genetic information can be raised through distribution of leaflets in primary and secondary care clinics or by allocating resources to publish and broadcast advertisements in the media.

Such a policy is adopted in the area of organ donation. The law, through legislation, provides only the general framework, where it requires doctors to consult family members when the view of the dying patient regarding organ

---

[80] Ibid. Parker and Lucassen stand for a family–based approach, seeing genetic information as a joint bank account where the bank manager cannot withhold information from the account holders. They argue that the most convincing ethical principle for disclosure to the relatives is justice.

donation is unknown.[81] The law grants autonomy to patients and family members to decide whether or not to allow donation.[82] However, the law indirectly influences people's decisions by raising their awareness of the substantial gap between the number of patients waiting for a donation and the limited number of organs available, through distribution of leaflets in doctors' surgeries. These leaflets, which are distributed by a governmental authority, urge people to donate and to share their decision with their relatives so that if the occasion arises doctors will know whether organs can be used for transplantation.[83]

The same should apply to genetic information. The law should not determine generally whether or not doctors and patients have to disclose medical genetic information. It should reflect the autonomy of the parties involved to make such a decision. However, the law can indirectly influence people's decisions by presenting the moral, social, psychological, and medical considerations involved in this context and by encouraging people to act responsively for their personal well–being and the well–being of their loved ones.

However, a major difficulty remains when this model requires a deliberative process in the family. It must be admitted that in many families such a process is not possible, either before or after testing. A family whose relationship is dominated by resentment, anger, and frustration will not be willing to conduct a serious discussion about genetic information. This will impose a considerable burden on the doctor, who will have to consider carefully whether the interests of all family members (either the patient or the relatives) are not compromised too much. In that sense the communitarian desire to maintain social relationships in their own right may be outweighed by the particular interests of the individual family member.

A model which may facilitate a comprehensive family discussion about genetic information is suggested by Daly and her colleagues.[84] Although it refers to disclosure of genetic test results, it can be applied even before information becomes available as it aims to deal with the emotional and practical difficulties of the patient vis-à-vis the relatives. In this model the doctor or counsellor guides the patient on how to communicate the information to the relatives step by step. First, he or she learns how to manage the setting in which the information will be disclosed (for example, in person and not by telephone). Second, the patient is advised to probe how much the relatives know about genetic testing generally, about the patient's condition, and about the familial genetic risk. In the third step

---

[81] The *Human Tissue Act* 1961, section 1 (2); The new *Human Tissue Act* 2004 does not change this.
[82] The *Human Tissue Act* 1961, section 1 (1) & (2); and the *Human Tissue Act* 2004, section 3 (6) (c).
[83] United Kingdom Transplant Support Service Authority, Booklet, *Questions and Straight Answers about Transplants* (4th ed., 1998).
[84] Daly M. et al., "Communicating genetic test results to the family: a six–step skills building" (2001) 24 (3) *Family & Community Health* 13.

the patient is shown how to discover whether the relatives would like to receive information (he or she has to wait for a clear–cut invitation to disclose information). At this point, the researchers note, the question is not whether the relatives would like to know, but the level of information they want to know. The patient is taught to ask open–ended questions as these afford the relatives control of the amount of information they want to have. The next step is sharing the information with the family members. In the last two stages the patient learns how to respond to the relatives' feelings and to use written material when answering their questions.

Undoubtedly, this model helps and encourages patients to conduct a family discussion about disclosure of genetic information. It is based on a process of communication and deliberation in the family, whereby the patient gradually learns how to disclose, what to disclose, and to whom to disclose. This six–step model is not limited to a situation where the patient has been already been tested: it can be initiated even before, or before he or she has received the results. However, like other models presented in this chapter, it is based on good familial relationships, especially the patient's willingness to share the information with relatives, something which does not exist in all families.

To sum up, the aim of the deliberative process suggested in this study is not to change the underlying principles of consent and discretion in English medical law but to change the legal position by adopting a relational perception of autonomy. This perception values the right of the individual to make independent decisions but it also appreciates that autonomy can be developed by social relationships and involving others in the decision–making process.[85] Such a perception must lead to relaxation of medical confidentiality and privacy by including a familial social dimension in the utilitarian criteria, which is common in this area of genetics. Consequently, the law will operate indirectly by sending symbolic messages[86] that the interests of family members should be recognised. The law will not set a strict rule of either disclosure or non–disclosure but will rely on ethical criteria that reflect fundamental moral principles accepted by the vast majority of people. This will allow the law to be more flexible. Furthermore, the courts will not need to formulate a new law, something they reluctantly do when there is a legal vacuum, or rely on a single and restrictive rule which forces them occasionally to arrive at unreasonable decisions. Instead they will have the opportunity to conduct an informed legal discussion from a wider perspective, being able to support their decision with a moral judgment and empirical data that reflect the core values of the public. The discussion in the courts will no longer be confined to the question whether the patient poses a serious risk to the public but will encompass other relevant considerations in this context.

---

[85]   See Parker, supra n. 1, at p. 162.
[86]   See Galanter, supra n. 16, at p. 24.

Admittedly, this deliberative process is not free from difficulties. With regard to the doctor–patient relationship, it will require extra resources as the doctor will have to dedicate a substantial amount of time to learn about the patient's familial relationships and to discuss with the patient the decision of whether or not to disclose. In addition, such a process is based on trust and good relations between doctors and patients which may not exist in all cases. Concentrating on the legal aspect, one can argue that adding a social dimension will not provide a clear legal position but will complicate the traditional cost–benefit mechanism especially when physical harm cannot be avoided.

While these are valid arguments, the underlying aim of this approach is to promote the interests of family members. If doctors and patients seriously consider the social implications of genetic information for family members they will reach a sensitive decision which strikes an adequate balance between conflicting familial interests. In addition, engaging in such a process, other interests, beyond the prevention of physical harm, will be legally recognised. Doctors and patients will have to consider disclosure when the relatives consider reproduction or when they consider other major life decisions, such as relocation to another country. If doctors and patients do not disclose information in such circumstances they should be aware that their decision may be challenged in courts.

6.7 Conclusion

Examining the status of family members in English medical law and medical ethics, this book has concentrated on familial tensions over genetic information. Genetic information, perhaps more than any other category of medical information, has considerable impact on people's self–image and identity. It motivates people to exercise their rights to confidentiality and privacy rigorously. They wish to maintain their individuality and control the flow of this sensitive information. Yet genetic information poses a challenge to this individualistic interest for it derives from genetic material people share with their relatives; and it has a considerable effect on blood and non–blood relatives alike. Family members believe that their interests with regard to this information should be legally recognised.

This duality of genetic information symbolises the underlying argument of this book, namely that human identity has two elements: one is a sense of being separate and the other is a sense of belonging.[87] However, this study has discovered that English medical law, and to a considerable extent medical ethics, concentrate on the first element and neglect the second. They highlight an individualistic perception of autonomy while simultaneously overlooking the patient's identity in relationships with others. The view taken in this book is that

---

[87] The Lindemann-Nelsons, supra n. 2, at p. 36 cite Minuchin S., *Families and Family Therapy*, Cambridge, Harvard University Press (1974) 47–48.

this is too narrow an approach to the complexities of human lives generally and with regard to the status of family members in genetics particularly.

Undoubtedly, this one–sided approach has to be balanced; but in light of the duality of human identity and autonomy this study walks a very thin line. On the one hand it admits that patients' rights to self–determination, confidentiality, and privacy have to be respected; but on the other hand it argues that these rights are not absolute and have no meaning outside the community. Therefore, the philosophical approach taken in this book does not challenge the contribution of the liberal tradition; but it emphasises a communitarian perception of the individual and ethics–of–care conceptions that characterise familial relationships. It stresses that the family constitutes part of one's identity and therefore, in the medical context, autonomy should be relational.

The area of genetics raises complex tensions in families. Yet even in this complicated area, and despite the limited capacity of the law to resolve these conflicts, the interests of family members should receive greater legal recognition than they currently enjoy. The complexity of this subject should not lead to a situation where the interests of family members in making decisions are ignored. Both the family covenant model suggested by Doukas and Berg and the deliberative model developed in the last part of this chapter aim to provide a flexible and workable framework where the law supervises adequately the decision–making process in this area and influences doctors and patients to promote the interests of family members. In addition, these models are based on the conclusion reached by this study that people want to decide independently (and alone) whether or not to disclose but in the vast majority of cases they decide to involve the relatives and share the information with them. Reflecting this human tendency these models favour disclosure over non–disclosure.

The deliberative model, which attempts to accord with the current settings of the NHS, suggests that when familial tension over genetic information arises the law should take into account the social dimension of these conflicts. To the traditional utilitarian mechanism of prevention of physical harm, which is common in the legal and bioethical literature, this model adds another fundamental consideration, namely how any decision will affect the familial relationship. Taking into account this criterion this model aims to inspire individuals to maintain their autonomy but at the same time to consider seriously the well–being of their loved ones. Ultimately, when a conflict arises the law can be influential and can promote moral values such as mutual responsibility, accountability, and beneficence.

This book began with the stories of Robert Powell's parents and Dona Safer whose interests were compromised by the doctors. If law and medical ethics change their attitudes to family members according to the suggestions made in this study, the outcome of such cases will be different. In the specific area of genetics, as research develops, the family, rather than the individual, will be seen as the unit of care.

References

Cases

A v Leeds Teaching Hospital NHS Trust [2004] 2 FLR 365, [2004] 3 FCR 324.
AB v Tameside & Glossop HA [1997] 8 Med LR 91.
A–G v Guardian Newspapers (No 2) [1990] 1 AC 109; [1988] 3 WLR 776.
Airedale NHS Trust v Bland [1993] AC 789; [1993] 1 All ER 821.
Alcock v Chief Constable of the South Yorkshire Police [1992] 1 AC 310.
Allin v City & Hackney HA [1996] 7 Med LR 167.
Anderson v Forth Valley HA 1998 SCLR 97.
Anns v Merton LBC [1978] AC 728.
Baker v Kaye (1996) 39 BMLR 12.
Bolam v Friern Barnet Hospital Management [1957] 1 WLR 582.
Bolitho v City and Hackney Health Authority [1998] AC 232; [1997] 4 All ER 771.
C v Dr. AJ Cairns [2003] Lloyd Rep. Med. 90.
Caparo v Dickman [1990] 2 AC 605.
Capital Counties plc v Hampshire CC [1997] QB 1004; [1997] 2 All ER 865.
Carmarthenshire CC v Lewis [1956] AC 549.
Chester v Afshar, (HL), [2004] WL 228913.
Creutzfeldt-Jakob Disease litigation; Group B Plaintiffs v Medical Research Council and another (QB) [2000] Lloyd's Rep Med 161, 41 BMLR 157.
D v East Berkshire Community Health NHS Trust [2004] 2 WLR 58.
Dorset Yacht v Home Office [1970] AC 1004.
Dyson Holdings Ltd v Fox [1975] 3 All ER 1030.
E v United Kingdom [2002] 3 FCR 700.
Emeh v Kensington and Chelsea and Westminster AHA [1985] 1 QB 1012.
Fitzpatrick v. Sterling Housing Association [2001] 1 AC 27; [1999] 4 All ER 705.
Frost v Chief Constable of South Yorkshire Police [1999] 1 AC 455.
Gammans v Ekins [1950] 2 All ER 140.
Ghaidan v Godin–Mendoza [2004] UKHL 30.
Gillick v West Norfolk and Wisbech Area HA [1986] AC 112.
Glass v United Kingdom [2004] 1 FCR 553.
Gold v Haringey Health Authority [1988] QB 481.
Goodwill v BPAS [1996] 1 WLR 1397.
Gorham v BT [2000] 1 WLR 2129.
Grieve v Salford HA [1991] 2 Med LR 295.
Hardman v Amin [2000] Lloyd's Rep Med 498.

Harrogate BC v Simpson (1984) 17 HLR 205.

Hatton v Sutherland, Barber v Somerset CC, Jones v Sandwell MBC, Bishop v Baker [2002] EWCA Civ 76.

Hawes v Evenden [1953] 2 All ER 737.

Hedley Byrne v Heller [1964] AC 465.

Henderson v Merrett [1995] 2 AC 145.

Hill v Chief Constable of West Yorkshire [1989] 1 AC 53.

K v Secretary of State for the Home Office [2001] C.P. Rep. 39.

K v Secretary of State for the Home Department [2002] EWCA Civ 983.

Kapfunde v Abbey National (1998) 45 BMLR 176.

Kent v Griffiths (No. 3) [2001] QB 36.

Marc Rich v Bishop Ltd [1996] 1 AC 211.

McFarlane v Tayside Health Board [2000] 2 AC 59.

McLoughlin v O'Brian [1983] 1 AC 410.

Mendoza v Ghaidan [2003] 1 FLR 468.

MS v Sweden (1997) 45 BMLR 133.

Osman v Ferguson [1993] All ER 344.

Osman v United Kingdom (1998) 5 BHRC 293; [1999] 1 FLR 193.

Palmer v Tees HA [1998] Lloyd's Rep Med 447 (QBD); [1999] Lloyd's Rep Med 351 (CA).

Parkinson v St James & Seacroft University Hospital [2002] QB 266.

Pate v Threlkel (1995) 661 So.2d 278.

Pearce v United Bristol Healthcare NHS Trust (1999) 48 BMLR 118.

Phelps v London Borough of Hillingdon [2001] AC 219; [2000] 4 All ER 504.

Powell v Boldaz [1998] Lloyd's Rep. Med. 116.

Powell v United Kingdom, application no. 45305/99, 4/5/2000.

Pretty v UK [2001] 2 FCR 97, [2002] 2 FLR 45.

R v Chief Constable of the North Wales Police [1999] QB 396.

R v Crozier [1991] Crim·LR 138; (1990) 8 BMLR 128.

R v Department of Health [1999] 4 All ER 185; [2000] 1 All ER 786 (CA).

R (on the application of Burke) v The General Medical Council [2004] EWHC 1879.

R (on the application of S) v Plymouth CC [2002] 1 FLR 1177.

Rand v East Dorset HA [2000] Lloyd's Rep Med 181.

Re A (Children) (Conjoined twins: surgical separation) [2000] 4 All ER 961.

Re B (consent to treatment: capacity) [2002] EWHC 429; [2002] 2 All ER 449.

Re C [1991] 2 FLR 478; [1991] 7 BMLR 138.

Re F (Mental Patient: Sterilization) [1990] 2 AC 1; [1989] 2 All ER 545.

Re R (a child) (adoption: disclosure) [2001] 1 FCR 238.

Re T (adult: refusal of medical treatment) [1992] 4 All ER 649.

Re Wyatt (a child) (Medical treatment: parents' consent) [2004] EWHC 2247.

Rees v Darlington Memorial Hospital NHS Trust [2003] 3 WLR 1091.

Reibl v Hughes (1980) 114 DLR (3d) 1.

Reilly v Merseyside HA [1995] 6 Med LR 246.
Reisner v Regents of the University of California (1995) 37 Cal Rptr 2d 518.
RK and MK v Oldham NHS Trust and Dr B [2003] Lloyd's Rep Med 1.
Rogers v Whitaker [1993] 4 Med LR 79; (1992) 109 ALR 625.
Ross v Caunters [1980] Ch 297.
Safer v Pack (1996) 677 A.2d 1188.
Schloendorff v Society of New York Hospital (1914) 211 NY 125.
Sidaway v Board of Governors of the Bethlem Royal Hospital [1985] AC 871; [1985] 1 All ER 643.
Sion v Hampstead HA [1994] 5 Med LR 170.
Smith v Leurs (1945) 70 CLR 256.
Smith v Littlewoods Organisation Ltd [1987] 1 AC 241.
Spring v Guardian Assurances [1995] 2 AC 296.
Stovin v Wise [1996] AC 923.
Surry CC v M (a minor) [2001] EWCA CIV 691.
Swinney v Chief Constable of Northumbria Police Force (No. 1) [1997] QB 464.
Tan v East London and the City HA [1999] Lloyds' Rep Med 389.
Tarasoff v Regents of the University of California 551 P 2d 334.
Taylor v Somerset HA [1993] 4 Med LR 34.
Thake v Maurice [1986] QB 644.
Topp v London Country Bus Ltd [1993] 1 WLR 976.
TP v UK [2001] 2 FCR 289.
W v Egdell [1990] Ch 359; [1989] 1 All ER 1089 (CH D); [1990] 1 All ER 835 (CA).
W v Essex CC [2001] 2 AC 592; [1998] 3 WLR 534 (CA); [2000] 2 All ER 237 (HL).
White v Jones [1995] 2 AC 207.
Williams v Natural Life Health Food Ltd [1998] 1 WLR 830.
Woolgar v Chief Constable of Sussex Police [1999] 3 All ER 604.
Wyatt v Curtis [2003] EWCA Civ 1779.
X (Minors) v Bedfordshire CC [1995] 2 AC 633.
X v Y [1988] 2 All ER 648.
Yuen Kun Yeu v A–G of Hong Kong [1988] 1 AC 175.
Z v United Kingdom [2001] 2 FCR 246.
Z v Finland (1997) 25 EHRR 371.

Books

Altschuler J., *Working with Chronic Illness: A Family Approach* (London: Macmillan, 1997).
Andrews L., *Future Perfect: Confronting Decisions about Genetics* (New York: Columbia University Press, 2001).

Baider L., Cooper C., Kaplan De-Nour A. (eds.), *Cancer and the Family* (Chichester: Wiley, 2nd edn., 2000).

Bainham A., Sclater S.D., Richards M. (eds.), *What is a Parent? A Socio–Legal Analysis* (Oxford: Hart Publishing, 1999).

Balint M., *The Doctor, His Patient and the Illness* (London: Churchill–Livingstone, 2nd edn., 1964).

Beauchamp T., Childress J., *Principles of Biomedical Ethics* (New York: Oxford University Press, 5th ed., 2001).

Bell D., *Communitarianism and Its Critics* (Oxford: Clarendon Press, 1993)

Bergsma J., Thomasma D., *Autonomy and Clinical Medicine* (Boston: Kluwer Academics, 2000).

Berlin I., *Four Essays on Liberty* (Oxford: Oxford University Press, 1969).

Biegel D., Sales E., Schulz R., *Family Caregiving in Chronic Illness* (Newbury Park, CA: Sage, 1991).

Bloom J., 'The role of family support in cancer control' in Baider L., Cooper C., Kaplan De-Nour A., (eds.), *Cancer and the Family* (Chichester: Wiley, 2nd edn., 2000).

Blustein J., *Care and Commitment: Taking the Personal Point of View* (Oxford: Oxford University Press, 1991).

Brazier M., *Medicine, Patients and the Law* (London: Penguin, 3rd edn., 2003).

Brewin T., *Relating to the Relatives: Breaking Bad News, Communication, and Support* (Oxford: Radcliffe Medical Press, 1996).

British Medical Association, *Human Genetics: Choice and Responsibility* (Oxford: Oxford University Press, 1998).

Buchanan A., Brock D., *Deciding for Others: The Ethics of Surrogate Decision Making* (Cambridge: Cambridge University Press, 1989).

Buckman R., Kason Y., *How to Break Bad News: A Guide for Health–Care Professionals* (London: Papermac, 1992).

Chadwick R., Levitt M., Shickle D., (eds.), *The Right to Know and the Right Not to Know* (Aldershot: Avebury, 1997).

Christie R., Hoffmaster B., *Ethical Issues in Family Medicine* (Oxford: Oxford University Press, 1986).

Clarke A. (ed.), *Genetic Counselling: Practice and Principles* (London: Routledge, 1994).

Cole S., Bird J. (eds.), *The Medical Interview: The Three–Function Approach* (London: Mosby, 2nd edn., 2000).

Cotterrell R., *The Sociology of Law: An Introduction* (London: Butterworths, 2nd edn., 1992).

Cretney S.M., Masson J.M., Bailey–Harris R., *Principles of Family Law* (London: Sweet & Maxwell, 7th edn., 2002).

Deakin S., Johnston A., Markesinis, B., *Tort Law* (Oxford: Oxford University Press, 5th edn., 2003).

Dworkin G., *The Theory and Practice of Autonomy* (Cambridge: Cambridge University Press, 1988).

Dworkin, R., *Taking Rights Seriously* (Cambridge: Harvard University Press, 1977).

Etzioni A., *The Spirit of Community* (London: Fontana Press, 1995).

Faden R., Beauchamp T., *The History and Theory of Informed Consent* (New York: Oxford University Press, 1986).

Fauci A., et al., (eds.), *Harrison's Principles of Internal Medicine* (New York: McGraw–Hill, 14th edn., 1998).

Faulkner A., *When the News is Bad: A Guide for Health Professionals on Breaking Bad News* (Cheltenham: Stanley Thornes Publishers Ltd, 1998).

Feinberg J., *Harm to Others* (Oxford: Oxford University Press, 1984).

Finch J., *Family Obligations and Social Change* (Cambridge: Polity Press, 1989).

Frazer E., Lacey N., *The Politics of Community* (Hemel Hempstead, Harvester, 1993).

Friedman M., *What Are Friends For? Feminist Perspective on Personal Relationships and Moral Theory* (London: Cornell University Press, 1993).

Gibson C., 'Changing family patterns in England and Wales over the last fifty years' in Katz S., Eekelaar J., MacLean M. (eds.), *Cross Currents: Family Law and Policy in the United States and England* (Oxford: Oxford University Press, 2000), pp. 31–55.

Giddens A., *The Transformation of Intimacy* (Cambridge: Polity Press, 1992).

Gilbar O., Ben-Zur H., *Cancer and the Family Caregiver: Distress and Coping* (Springfield, IL: Charles C. Thomas, 2002).

Giliker P., Beckwith S., *Tort* (London: Sweet & Maxwell, 2nd edn., 2004).

Gilligan C., *In a Different Voice* (Cambridge: Harvard University Press, 1982).

———, Ward J., Taylor J. (eds.), *Mapping the Moral Domain* (Cambridge, MA: Harvard University Press, 1988).

Gillon R., *Philosophical Medical Ethics* (Chichester: Wiley, 1986).

Goodin R., Pettit P. (eds.), *A Companion to Contemporary Political Philosophy* (Oxford: Blackwell, 1993).

Gray J., *Liberalism* (Milton Keynes: Open University Press, 1986).

Grubb A. (ed.), *Choices and Decisions in Health Care* (Chichester: Wiley, 1993).

———, *Medical Law* (London: Butterworths, 3rd edn., 2000).

———, (ed.), *Principles of Medical Law* (Oxford: Oxford University Press, 2nd edn., 2004).

Hale B., et al., *The Family, Law and Society: Cases and Materials* (London: Butterworths, 5th edn., 2002).

Harper P., *Practical Genetic Counselling* (Oxford: Butterworth–Heinemann, 5th edn., 1999).

———, Clarke A., (eds.), *Genetics, Society and Clinical Practice* (Oxford: Bios Scientific, 1997).

Hart H.L.A., *Law, Liberty & Morality* (Palo Alto, CA: Stanford University Press, 1963).

Held V., *Feminist Morality* (Chicago: University of Chicago Press, 1993).

Herring J., *Family Law* (Harlow: Longman, 2nd edn., 2004).

Hoffmaster B., 'Morality and the Social Science' in Weisz G., *Social Science Perspectives on Medical Ethics* (Philadelphia, PA: University of Pennsylvania Press, 1991), pp. 241–259

Huygen F.J.A., *Family Medicine: The Family Life History of Families* (London: The Royal College of General Practitioners, 1990).

Jones M., *Medical Negligence* (London: Blackstone Press, 1996).

————, *Textbook on Torts* (London: Blackstone Press, 7th edn, 2000).

Kennedy I., Grubb A., *Principles of Medical Law* (Oxford: Oxford University Press, 1998).

Kubler-Ross E., *On Death and Dying* (New York: Routledge, 1970).

Kymlicka W., *Liberalism, Community and Culture* (Oxford: Clarendon Press, 1989).

————, *Contemporary Political Philosophy: An Introduction* (Oxford: Oxford University Press, 2nd edn., 2002).

Laurie G., *Genetic Privacy: A Challenge to Medico–Legal Norms* (Cambridge: Cambridge University Press, 2002).

Lee S., *Law and Morals* (Oxford: Oxford University Press, 1986).

Lenaghan J., *Brave New NHS?* (London: IPPR, 1998).

Lewis J., *The End of Marriage?* (Cheltenham: Edward Elgar, 2001).

Light E., Niederehe G., Labowitz B. (eds.), *Stress Effects on Family Caregivers of Alzheimer's Patients* (New York: Springer, 1994).

Lindemann-Nelson H., Lindemann-Nelson J., *The Patient in the Family* (New York: Routledge, 1995).

Lunney, M., Oliphant K., *Tort Law: Text and Materials* (Oxford: Oxford University Press, 2nd edn., 2003).

Mackenzie C., Stoljar N. (eds.), *Relational Autonomy: Feminist Perspectives on Autonomy, Agency and the Social Self* (New York: Oxford University Press, 2000).

Macklin R., 'Privacy and control of genetic information' in Annas G., Elias S. (eds.) *Gene Mapping* (New York: Oxford University Press, 1992), p. 157.

Marteau T., Richards M., (eds.), *The Troubled Helix: Social and Psychological Implications of the New Human Genetics* (Cambridge: Cambridge University Press, 1996).

Mason JK., McCall–Smith RA., Laurie GT., *Law and Medical Ethics* (London: Butterworths, 6th edn., 2002).

McLean S., *Old Law, New Medicine: Medical ethics and human rights* (London: Pandora, 1999).

McRae S. (ed.), *Changing Britain: Families and Households in the 1990s* (Oxford: Oxford University Press, 1999).

McWhinney I., *A Textbook of Family Medicine* (New York: Oxford University Press, 2nd edn., 1997).

Mill J.S., *On Liberty and Other Essays* (London, 1859) (Oxford: Oxford University Press, 1991).

Minuchin S., *Families and Family Therapy* (Cambridge: Harvard University Press, 1974).

Montgomery J., *Health Care Law* (Oxford: Oxford University Press, 2nd edn., 2003).

Morgan D., *Issues in Medical Law and Ethics* (London: Cavendish, 2000).

Mulhall S., Swift A., *Liberals and Communitarians* (Oxford: Blackwell, 2nd edn., 1996).

Muncie J., Wetherell M., et al., (eds.), *Understanding the Family* (London: Sage, 2nd edn., 2000).

Murphy J., *Street on Torts* (London: Butterworths, 11th edn., 2003).

O'Donovan K., *Family Law Matters* (London: Pluto Press, 1993).

Okin–Moller S., *Justice, Gender and the Family* (New York: Basic Books, 1989).

O'Neill O., *Autonomy and Trust in Bioethics* (Cambridge: Cambridge University Press, 2002).

Parker M. (ed.), *Ethics and Community in the Health Care Professions* (London: Routledge, 1999).

Parsons T., *The Social System* (Illinois: Free Press, 1951).

Pilnick A., *Genetics and Society: An Introduction* (Buckingham: Open University Press, 2002).

Rawls J., *A Theory of Justice* (Cambridge: Harvard University Press, 1971).

Raz J., *The Morality of Freedom* (Oxford: Clarendon Press, 1986).

Rogers C., *A Way of Being* (Boston, MA: Houghton–Mifflin, 1980).

Sandel M., *Liberalism and the Limits of Justice* (Cambridge: Cambridge University Press, 1982).

Sherwin S. (ed.), *The Politics of Women's Health: Exploring Agency and Autonomy* (Philadelphia, PA: Temple University Press, 1998).

Stoudemire A., (ed.), *Human Behaviour: An Introduction for Medical Students* (New York: Lippincott–Raven, 3rd edn., 1998).

Teff H., *Reasonable Care: Legal Perspectives on the Doctor–Patient Relationship* (Oxford: Clarendon Press, 1994).

Wertz D., Fletcher J., *Ethics and Human Genetics: A Cross–Cultural Perspective* (New York: Springer–Verlag, 1989).

———, *Genetics and Ethics in Global Perspective* (Dordrecht: Kluwer, 2004).

Williams P., *Family Problems* (Oxford: Oxford University Press, 1989).

Wolf S. (ed.), *Feminism and Bioethics: Beyond Reproduction* (New York: Oxford University Press, 1996), pp. 47–66.

240   *The Status of the Family in Law and Bioethics*

Articles

Almqvist el al., 'A worldwide assessment of the frequency of suicide, suicide attempts, or psychiatric hospitalization after predictive testing for Huntington disease', *American Journal of Human Genetics*, 64(1999): 1293.

American Medical Association, Council on Scientific Affairs, 'Physicians and Family Caregivers', *Journal of American Medical Association*, 269(10) (1993): 1282.

American Society of Human Genetics Social Issues, 'Professional disclosure of familial genetic information', *American Journal of Human Genetics*, 62(1998): 474.

Andrews L., 'Torts and the double helix: Malpractice liability for failure to warn of genetic risks', *Houston Law Review*, 29(1) (1992): 149.

Annas et al., 'Drafting the Genetic Privacy Act: Science, policy and practical considerations', *Journal of Law, Medicine and Ethics*, 23(1995): 360 commenting on The *Genetic Privacy Act* 1995, www.bumc.bu.edu/sph.

Ashcroft R., 'The family: Organic and mechanistic solidarity', *The American Journal of Bioethics*, 1(3) (2001): 22.

Baier A., 'Trust and Antitrust', *Ethics*, 96 (1986): 231.

Bailey–Harris R., 'Law and unmarried couple–oppression or liberation?', *Child and Family Law Quarterly*, 8(2) (1996): 137.

Bainham A., 'Homosexuality and the Lords: Shifting definitions of marriage and the family', *Cambridge Law Journal* (2000): 39.

Barker K., 'Unreliable assumptions in the modern law of negligence', *Law Quarterly Review*, 109 (1993): 461.

Baum et al., 'Stress and genetic testing for disease risk', *Health Psychology*, 16 (1997): 8.

Beauchamp T., 'Methods and principles in biomedical ethics', *Journal of Medical Ethics*, 29 (2003): 269.

Beem E.E. et al., 'The immunological and psychological effects of bereavement: Does grief counseling really make a difference? A pilot study', *Psychiatry Research*, 85(1) (1999): 81.

Beeson R., et al., 'Loneliness and depression in caregivers of persons with Alzheimer's disease or related disorders', *Issues in Mental Health Nursing*, 21 (2000): 779.

Bekker H. et al, 'The impact of population based screening for carriers of Cystic Fibrosis', *Journal of Medical Genetics*, 31 (1994): 364

Bell D., Bennett B., 'Genetic secrets and the family', *Medical Law Review*, 9 (2001): 130.

Benatar S., 'Bioethics: Power and injustice: IAB presidential address', *Bioethics*, 17(506) (2003): 17.

———, et al., 'Global health ethics: The rationale for mutual caring', *International Affairs*, 79(1) (2003): 107.

Benson J., Britten N., 'Respecting the autonomy of cancer patients when talking with their families: Qualitative analysis of semi–structured interview with patients', *BMJ*, 313 (1996): 729.

Ben-Zur H. et al., 'Coping with breast cancer: Patient, spouse and dyad models', *Psychosomatic Medicine*, 63(1) (2001): 32.

Berkman L., 'The role of social relations in health promotion', *Psychosomatic Medicine*, 57 (1995): 245.

Berry R., 'The genetic revolution and the physician's duty of confidentiality', *Journal of Legal Medicine*, 18 (1997): 401.

Bloom J. et al., 'Sources of support and the physical and mental well–being of young women with breast cancer', *Social Science & Medicine*, 53 (2001): 1513.

Botelho R., et al., 'Family involvement in routine health care: A survey of patients' behaviours and preferences', *The Journal of Family Practice*, 42(6) (1996): 572.

Bottis M., 'Comment on a view favouring ignorance of genetic information: confidentiality, autonomy, beneficence and the right not to know', *European Journal of Health Law*, 7(2000): 173.

Boyd S.B., 'What is a normal family? C v C (A Minor) (Custody: Appeal)', *Modern Law Review*, 55 (1992): 269

Brownrigg A., 'Mother still knows best: Cancer–related gene mutation, familial privacy and a physician's duty to warn', *Fordham Urban Law Journal*, 26 (1999): 247.

Bundey S., 'Few psychological consequences of presymptomatic testing for Huntington disease', *The Lancet*, 349 (1997): 4.

Burnett J., 'A physician's duty to warn a patient's relatives of a patient's genetically inheritable disease', *Houston Law Review*, 36(1999): 559.

Callahan D., 'Principlism and communitarianism', *Journal of Medical Ethics*, 29 (2003): 287.

Capron A., 'Tort liability in genetic counselling', *Colombia Law Review* 79 (1979): 618.

Chadwick R., Ngwena C., 'The development of a normative standard in counselling for genetic disease: Ethics and Law', *Journal of Social Welfare and Family Law*, 4 (1992): 276.

Chalmers K., et al., 'Reports of information and supports needs of daughters and sisters of women with breast cancer', *European Journal of Cancer*, 12 (2003): 81.

Charles C. et al., 'Decision–making in the physician–patient encounter: What does it mean? (Or it takes at least two to tango)', *Social Science & Medicine*, 44 (1997): 681.

Charles C. et al., 'What do we mean by partnership in making decisions about treatment?', *British Medical Journal*, 319 (1999): 780.

Charles C., et al., 'Decision–making in the physician–patient encounter: Revisiting the shared treatment decision–making model', *Social Science & Medicine*, 49 (1999): 651.

Clarke A., 'Is non–directive genetic counselling possible?' *The Lancet*, 338 (1991): 998.

Clayton E., 'What should the law say about disclosure of genetic information to relatives?' *Journal of Health Care, Law & Policy*, 1 (1998): 373.

Cook D., 'Genetics and the British insurance industry', *Journal of Medical Ethics*, 25 (1999): 157.

Craufurd D., et al., 'Uptake of presymptomatic predictive testing for Huntington's disease', *The Lancet*, (1989): 603.

Cretney S.M., Reynolds F.M.B., 'Limits of the judicial function', *Law Quarterly Review*, 116 (2000): 181.

Croyle R., et al., 'Psychological responses to BRCA1 mutation testing: preliminary findings', *Health Psychology*, 16 (1997): 63.

Curry H., 'The family as our patient', *Journal of Family Practice*, 1 (1974): 70.

Dewar J., 'The normal chaos of family law', *Modern Law Review*, 61(4) (1998): 467.

Doherty W., Baird M., 'Developmental levels in family–centred medical care', *Family Medicine*, 18(3) (1983): 153.

Doukas D., Berg J., 'The family covenant and genetic testing', *The American Journal of Bioethics*, 1(3) (2001): 2.

————, et al., 'How men view genetic testing for prostate cancer risk: Finding from focus group', *Clinical Genetics*, 58(3) (2000): 169.

Duckworth P., 'What is a family? – A personal view', *Family Law*, (2000): 367.

Dudoke De Wit, et al., 'Psychological distress in applications for predictive DNA testing for autosomal dominant, heritable late onset disorders', *American Journal of Medical Genetics*, 34(1997): 382.

Diduck A., 'A family by any other name ... or Starbucks comes to England', *Journal of Law and Society*, 28(2) (2001): 290.

Eisenberg L., 'What makes persons "patients" and patients "well"?', *The American Journal of Medicine*, 69(1980): 277.

Elwyn G., Gray J., Clarke A., 'Shared decision making and non–directiveness in genetic counselling', *Journal of Medical Genetics*, 37(2000): 135.

Engel G., 'The need for a new medical model: A challenge for biomedicine', *Science*, 196(1977): 129.

————, 'The clinical application of the biopsychosocial model', *Journal of Medicine & Philosophy*, 6 (1981): 101.

Fanos J., Johnson J., 'CF carrier status: The importance of not knowing', *American Journal of Human Genetics*, 55(3) (1994): A292

Fanos J., Johnson J., 'Perception of carrier status by Cystic Fibrosis siblings' *American Journal of Human Genetics*, 57 (1995) 431.

Fitzpatrick et al., 'The duty to recontact: Attitudes of genetic service providers', *American Journal of Human Genetics*, 64 (1999): 852.

Forrest K. et al., 'To tell or not to tell: Barriers and facilitators in family communication about genetic risk', *Clinical Genetics*, 64 (2003): 317.

France L., Clarke A., 'Professional responses to non–disclosure of genetic information,' a paper presented at the *First Interdisciplinary Conference on Communication, Medicine and Ethics*, Health Communication Research Centre, Cardiff University, Cardiff, 26–28 June 2003.

Freeman S.J., Ward S., 'Death and bereavement: What counselors should know' *Journal of Mental Health Counseling*, 20 (1998): 216.

Fry A., et al., 'GPs' views on their role in cancer genetics services and current practice', *Family Practice*, 16(5): 468.

Galanter M., 'Law abounding: Legalisation around the North Atlantic', *Modern Law Review*, 55 (1992): 1.

Geller G., et al., 'Physicians' attitudes toward disclosure of genetic information to third parties', *The Journal of Law, Medicine & Ethics*, 21 (1993): 238.

Giliker P., 'Osman and police immunity in the English law of torts', *Legal Studies*, 20 (2000): 372.

Gillon R., 'Defending 'the four principles' approach to biomedical ethics', *Journal of Medical Ethics*, 21 (1995): 323.

————, 'Ethics needs principles – four can encompass the rest – and respect for autonomy should be first among equals', *Journal of Medical Ethics*, (2003): 307.

Glennon L., 'Fitzpatrick v Sterling Housing Association Ltd – An endorsement of the functional family', *International Journal of Law, Policy and the Family*, 14 (2000): 226

Green J. et al., 'Family communication and genetic counseling: The case of hereditary breast and ovarian cancer', *Journal of Genetic Counselling*, 6(1) (1997): 45.

Griffiths J., 'The duty of care in cases of wrongful conception', *Nottingham Law Journal*, (1996): 56.

Grol R. et al., 'Patients' priorities with respect to general practice care: An international comparison', *Family Practice*, 16(1): 4.

Grubb, A., 'HIV transmission: doctor's liability to future partner', *Medical Law Review*, 5 (1997): 250.

————, 'Medical negligence: Duty to third party', *Medical Law Review*, 7 (1999): 331.

Hallowell N., 'Doing the right thing: Genetic risk and responsibility', *Sociology of Health & Illness*, 21(5) (1999): 597.

————, et al., 'Surveillance or surgery? A description of the factors that influence high risk premenopausal women's decisions about prophylactic oophorectomy', *Journal of Medical Genetics*, 38(2001): 683.

————, et al., 'Balancing autonomy and responsibility: The ethics of generating and disclosing genetic information', *Journal of Medical Ethics*, 29 (2003): 74.

Hannay D., et al., 'Workload of General Practitioners before and after the new contract', *BMJ*, 304 (1992): 615

Hans M., et al., 'Huntington's Chorea: Its impact on the spouse', *Journal of Nervous and Mental Disease*, 168(4) (1980): 209.

Hardwig J., 'What about the family', *Hastings Center Report*, March–April, (1990): 5.

Harris J., 'In praise of unprincipled ethics', *Journal of Medical Ethics*, (2003): 303.

Hartmann L., et al., 'Efficacy of bilateral prophylactic mastectomy in women with family history of breast cancer', *The New England Journal of Medicine*, 340(2) (1999): 77.

Hartshorne J., Smith N., Everton R., '*Caparo* under fire: A study into the effects upon the fire service of liability in negligence', *Modern Law Review*, 61 (2001): 502.

Haskey J., 'Demographic aspects of cohabitation in Great Britain', *International Journal of Law, Policy and the Family*, 15 (2001): 51.

Hatcher M., et al., 'The psychosocial impact of bilateral prophylactic mastectomy: Prospective study using questionnaires and semi–structured interviews', *British Medical Journal*, 322 (2001): 76.

Hepple B., 'Negligence: The search for coherence', *Current Legal Problems*, 50 (1997): 69.

Hoffmann, Rt Hon Lord, 'Human rights and the House of Lords', *Modern Law Review*, 62 (1999): 159.

Hoffmaster B., 'The forms and limits of medical ethics', *Social Science & Medicine*, 39 (1994): 1155.

Hollman G. et al., 'Familial hypercholesterolemia and quality of life in family members', *Preventative Medicine*, 36 (2003): 569.

House J.S. et al., 'Social relations and health', *Science*, 241 (1988): 540.

Howarth, D., 'My brother's keeper? Liability for acts of third parties', *Legal Studies*, 14 (1994): 88.

Hoyano L., 'Policing flawed police investigations: unravelling the blanket', *Modern Law Review*, 62 (1999): 912.

Huggins M., et al., 'Predictive testing for Huntington's disease in Canada: Adverse effects and unexpected results in those receiving a decreased risk', *American Journal of Medical Genetics*, 42 (1992): 508.

Hughes J., Louw S., 'Confidentiality and cognitive impairment: Professional and philosophical ethics', *Age and Ageing*, 31 (2002): 147.

Jones M., 'Negligently inflicted psychological harm: Is the word mightier than the deed?' *Professional Negligence*, 13(4) (1997): 111.

————, 'Informed consent and other fairy stories', *Medical Law Review*, 7 (1997): 103.

Julian–Reynier C. et al., 'Cancer Genetic clinics: Why do women who already have cancer attend?' *European Journal of Cancer*, 34 (1998): 1549.

Kennedy I., Negligence: Duty of care; nervous shock; duty of candour', *Medical Law Review*, 6 (1998): 112.

Kent A., 'Consent and confidentiality in genetics: Whose information is it anyway?' *Journal of Medical Ethics*, 29 (2003): 16.

Kessler S., 'Forgotten person in the Huntington's family', *American Journal of Medical Genetics*, 48 (1993): 145.

Kinmonth A. et al, 'The new genetics: Implications for clinical services in Britain and the United States', *British Medical Journal*, 316 (1998): 767.

Kumar S., Gantley M., 'Tensions between policy makers and general practitioners in implementing new genetics: Grounded theory interview study', *British Medical Journal* 319 (1999): 1410.

Kymlicka W., 'Rethinking the family', *Philosophy & Public Affairs*, 20 (1991): 77.

Labrecque M., et al., 'The impact of family presence on the physician–cancer patient interaction', *Social Science & Medicine*, 33 (1991): 1253.

Lako C.J., et al., 'Confidentiality in medical practice', *Journal of Family Practice*, 31(2) (1990): 167.

————, et al., 'Handling of confidentiality in general practice: A survey among general practitioners in the Netherlands', *Family Practice*, 7(1) (1990): 34.

Laurie G., 'The most personal information of all: An appraisal of genetic privacy in the shadow of the human genome project', *International Journal of Law, Policy & the Family*, 10 (1996): 74.

————, 'Obligations arising from genetic information – negligence and the protection of familial interests', *Child and Family Law Quarterly*, 11(2) (1999): 109.

————, 'In defence of ignorance: Genetic information and the right not to know', *European Journal of Health Care Law*, 6 (1999): 119.

————, 'Genetics and patients' rights: where are the limits', *Medical Law International*, 5 (2000): 25.

————, 'Protecting and promoting privacy in an uncertain world: further defences of ignorance and the right not to know', *European Journal of Health Law*, 7 (2000): 185.

————, 'Challenging medical–legal norms: The role of autonomy, confidentiality and privacy in protecting individual and familial group rights in genetic information', *The Journal of Legal Medicine*, 22 (2001): 1.

Lawson et al., 'Adverse psychological events occurring in the first year after predictive testing for Huntington's disease', *Journal of Medical Genetics*, 33 (1996): 856.

Lehmann L. et al., 'Disclosure of familial genetic information: Perceptions of the duty to inform', *American Journal of Medicine*, 109 (2000): 705.

Lerman C., et al., 'Mammography adherence and psychological distress among women at risk for breast cancer', *Journal of the National Cancer Institute*, 85(13) (1993): 1074.

————, et al., 'Attitudes about genetic testing for breast–ovarian cancer susceptibility', *Journal of Clinical Oncology*, 12 (1994): 843.

Lewis J., 'Debates and issues regarding marriage and cohabitation in the British and American Literature', *International Journal of Law, Policy and the Family*, 15 (2001): 159.

Low et al., 'Genetic discrimination in life insurance: Empirical evidence from a cross sectional survey of genetic support groups in the United Kingdom', *British Medical Journal*, 317 (1998): 1632.

Lynch H. T., Watson P., 'Genetic counselling and hereditary breast/ovarian cancer' *The Lancet*, 339 (1992): 1181.

Macklin R., 'Applying the four principles', *Journal of Medical Ethics*, 29 (2003): 275.

Manne S. et al., 'Supportive and negative responses in the partner relationship: The association with psychological adjustment among individuals with cancer', *Journal of Behavioural Medicine*, (1997): 101

————, et al., 'Spousal negative responses to cancer patients: The role of social restriction, spouse mood and relationship satisfaction', *Journal of Consulting and Clinical Psychology*, 67(3) (1999): 352.

Marinker M., 'The family in medicine', *Proceedings of the Royal Society of Medicine*, 69 (1976): 115.

Markesinis B., 'Negligence, nuisance and affirmative duties of action', *Law Quality Review*, 105 (1989): 104 .

————, 'Plaintiff's tort law or defendant's tort law? Is the House of Lords moving towards a synthesis?' *Tort Law Journal*, 9 (2001): 168.

Marteau T., et al., 'Long–term cognitive and emotional impact of genetic testing for carriers of Cystic Fibrosis: The effects of test result and gender', *Health Psychology*, 16(1) (1997): 51.

McBride N., Hughes A., 'Hedley Byrne in the House of Lords: An interpretation', *Legal Studies*, 15 (1995): 376.

McGowan R., 'Beyond the disorder: One parent's reflection on genetic counselling', *Journal of Medical Ethics*, 25 (1999): 195.

McLean S., 'Intervention in the human genome', *The Modern Law Review*, 61 (1998): 681.

Meiser B., et al., 'Psychological impact of genetic testing in women from high–risk breast cancer families', *European Journal of Cancer*, 38 (2002): 2025.

Metcalfe K.A., et al. 'Evaluation of the needs of spouses of female carriers of mutations in BRCA1 and BRCA2', *Clinical Genetics*, 62 (2002): 464.

Michie S., et al., 'Nondirectiveness in genetic counseling: An empirical study', *American Journal of Human Genetics*, 60 (1997): 40.

Minow M., 'Who's the patient?' *Maryland Law Review*, 53 (1994): 1173.

Moller–Okin S., 'Reason and feeling in thinking about justice', *Ethics*, (1989): 229.

Monti G., '*Osman v UK*–transforming English negligence law into French administrative law?' *International & Comparative Law Quarterly*, 48 (1999): 757.

Mullany N., 'Liability for careless communication of traumatic information', *Law Quality Review*, 114 (1998): 380.

Mullis A., 'Wrongful conception unravelled', *Medical Law Review*, 1 (1993): 320.

Murphy J., 'Expectation losses, negligent omissions and the tortious duty of care', *The Cambridge Law Journal*, 55(1) (1996): 43.

Nedelsky J., 'Reconceiving autonomy: Sources, thoughts and possibilities', *Yale Journal of Law & Feminism*, 1 (1989): 7.

Ngwena C., Chadwick R., 'Genetic information and the duty of confidentiality: Ethics and law', *Medical Law International*, 1 (1993): 73.

Northouse L., Swain M., 'Adjustment of patients and husbands to the initial impact of breast cancer', *Nursing Research*, 37 (1987): 221.

———, 'Social support in patients' and husbands' adjustment to breast cancer', *Nursing Research*, 37(2) (1988): 91.

———, et al., 'Couples' patterns of adjustment to colon cancer', *Social Science & Medicine*, 50 (2000): 270.

———, et al., 'Quality of life of women with recurrent breast cancer and their family members', *Journal of Clinical Oncology*, 20(19) (2002): 4050.

Ost D., 'The "right" not to know', *Journal of Medicine and Philosophy*, 9 (1984): 301.

Parker M., 'Public deliberation and private choice in genetics', *Journal of Medical Ethics*, 26(3) (2000): 160.

———, 'Confidentiality in genetic testing', *The American Journal of Bioethics*, 1(3) (2001): 21 .

———, Lucassen A., 'Working towards ethical management of genetic testing', *The Lancet*, 360 (2002): 1685.

———, 'Genetic information: A joint account', *British Medical Journal*, 329 (2004):165.

Philips K. et al., 'Perceptions of Ashkenazi Jewish breast cancer patients on genetic testing for mutations in BRCA1 and BRCA2', *Clinical Genetics*, 57 (2000): 376 .

O'Donovan K., 'Marriage: A sacred or profane love machine?' (1993) 1 (1) *Feminist Legal Studies*, 1(1) (1993): 75.

———, Gilbar R., 'The loved ones: Families, intimates and patient autonomy', *Legal Studies*, 23(2) (2003): 332

O'Sullivan J., 'Liability for fear of the onset of future medical conditions', *Professional Negligence*, 15(2) (1999): 96.

Quaid K., et al., 'Knowledge, attitude, and the decision to be tested for Huntington's Disease', *Clinical Genetics*, 36 (1989): 431.

————, Wesson M.K., 'The effect of predictive testing for Huntington's disease on intimate relationship', *American Journal of Human Genetics*, 55(3) (1994): A294.

Raikka J., 'Freedom and a right (not) to know', *Bioethics*, 12(1) (1998): 49.

Ransom D., Vandervoot H., 'The development of family medicine', *Journal of the American Medical Association*, 225(9) (1973): 1098.

Reust C., Mattingly S., 'Family involvement in medical decision making', *Family Medicine*, 28 (1996): 39

Rhodes R., 'Genetic links, family ties and social bonds: rights and responsibilities in the face of genetic knowledge', *Journal of Medicine & Philosophy*, 23 (1998): 10.

Rhodes R., 'Autonomy, respect, and genetic information policy: A reply to Tuija Takala and Matti Hayry', *Journal of Medicine and Philosophy*, 25(1) (2000): 114.

————, 'Confidentiality, genetic information and the physician–patient relationship', *The American Journal of Bioethics*, 1(3) (2001): 26.

Ritvo P., et al., 'Psychological adjustment to familial genetic risk assessment: Differences in two longitudinal samples', *Patient Education & Counseling*, 40 (2000): 163.

Robertson J., et al., 'BRCA1 screening in women with breast cancer: A patient's perspective with commentary', *Women's Health Issues*, 11(2) (2001): 63.

Rothstein M., Gelb B., Craig S., 'Protecting genetic privacy by permitting employer access only to job–related employee medical information: Analysis of a unique Minnesota Law', *American Journal of Law & Medicine*, 24 (1998): 399.

Ruberman W. et al., 'Psychosocial influences on mortality after myocardial infarction', (1984) 311 *New England Journal of Medicine*, 311 (1984): 325.

Sankar P. et al., 'Patient perspectives on medical confidentiality', *Journal of General Internal Medicine*, 18 (2003): 659.

Schattner A., Tal M., 'Truth telling and patient autonomy: The patient's point of view', *The American Journal of Medicine*, 113(1) (2002): 66.

Shumaker S., Brownell A., 'Toward a theory of social support: Closing conceptual gaps', *Journal of Social Issues*, 40 (1984): 11.

Skene L., 'Patients' rights or family responsibilities?' *Medical Law Review*, 6 (1998): 1.

————, 'Genetic secrets and the family: a response to Bell and Bennett', *Medical Law Review*, 9 (2001): 162.

Smilkstein G., 'The family in family medicine revisited, again', *Journal of Family Medicine*, 39(6) (1994): 527.

Sommerville A., English V., 'Genetic privacy: orthodoxy or oxymoron?' *Journal of Medical Ethics*, 25 (1999): 144.

Spiegel D. et al., 'Effect of psychosocial treatment on survival of patients with metastatic breast cancer', *The Lancet* 2 (1989): 1989.

Spijker A., et al., 'Psychological aspects of genetic counselling: A review of the experience with Huntington's disease', *Patient Education and Counselling*, 32 (1997): 33.

Suter S., 'Whose genes are these anyway?: Familial conflicts over access to genetic information', *Michigan Law Journal*, 31(1993): 1854.

Takala T., 'The right to genetic ignorance confirmed', *Bioethics*, 13 (1999): 288.

———, Hayry M., 'Genetic ignorance, moral obligations and social duties', *Journal of Medicine and Philosophy*, 25 (2000): 107.

Tercyak K., et al., 'Effects of coping style and BRCA1 and BRCA2 test results on anxiety among women participating in genetic counselling and testing for breast and ovarian cancer risk', *Health Psychology*, 20(3) (2001): 217.

———, et al., 'Parental communication of BRAC1/2 genetic test results to children', *Patient Education and Counselling*, 42 (2001): 213.

———, et al., 'Parent–child and their effect on communicating BRCA1/2 test results to children', *Patient Education and Counselling*, 47 (2002): 145.

Tibben A., et al., 'Three–year follow–up after presymptomatic testing for Huntington's disease in tested individuals in partners', *Health Psychology*, 16 (1997): 20.

Toon P.D., Southgate LJ., 'The doctor, the patient and the relative: An exploratory survey of doctor–relatives relationship', *Family Practice*, 4(3): (1987) 207.

Trock B., et al., 'Psychological side effects of breast cancer screening', *Health Psychology*, 10 (1991): 259.

Vernon S. et al., 'Correlates of psychologic distress in colorectal cancer patients undergoing genetic testing for hereditary colon cancer', *Health Psychology*, 16 (1997): 73.

Waaldijk K., 'Taking same–sex partnerships seriously – European experiences as British perspectives', *International Family Law Journal*, (2003): 84.

Watson E., et al., 'Psychological and social consequences of community carrier screening programme for Cystic Fibrosis', *The Lancet*, 340 (1992): 217.

———, et al, 'The 'new genetics' and primary care: GPs' views on their role and their educational needs', *Family Practice*, 16(4): (1999): 420 .

Weir T., 'A Damnosa Hereditas', *Law Quarterly Review*, 111 (1995): 357.

Wertz D., 'No consensus worldwide', *The American Journal of Bioethics*, 1(3) (2001): 14.

———, Fletcher J., 'Privacy and disclosure in medical genetics examined in an ethics of care', *Bioethics*, 5(3) (1991): 212.

Wiggins S., et al., 'The psychological consequences of predictive testing for Huntington's disease', *The New England Journal of Medicine*, 327 (1992): 1401.

Williams K., 'Medical Samaritans: Is there a duty to treat?', *Oxford Journal of Legal Studies*, 21(3) (2001): 393.

————, 'Doctors as good Samaritans: Some empirical evidence concerning emergency medical treatment in Britain', *Journal of Law and Society*, 30(2) (2003): 258.

Witting C., 'Justifying liability to third parties for negligent misstatements', *Oxford Journal of Legal Studies*, 20 (2000): 615.

Woolf, Rt Hon Lord, 'Clinical negligence: What is the solution? How can we provide justice for doctors and patients?' *Medical Law International*, 4 (2000): 133.

————, 'Are the courts excessively deferential to the medical profession?' *Medical Law Review*, 9 (2001): 1.

Official Reports and Guidelines

The Advisory Committee on Genetic Testing, *Report on Genetic Testing for Late Onset Disorders* (London: Health Departments of the United Kingdom, 1998).

The Department of Health, General and Personal Medical Services Statistics: England and Wales, 30/9/2001, www.doh.gov.uk/public/gpcensus2001.htm.

The Department of Health, *Confidentiality: NHS code of practice*, www.doh.gov.uk/ipu/confiden.

The General Medical Council, *Confidentiality: Protecting and Providing Information* (London, General Medical Council, 2000).

The General Medical Council, *Good Medical Practice* (London: General Medical Council, 3rd edn., 2001).

The Genetic Interest Group, *Confidentiality and Medical Genetics* (1998), www.gig.org.uk/policy.

The Human Genetics Commission, *Whose hands on your genes? A discussion document on the storage, protection and the use of personal genetic information* (London: Department of Health, 2000).

The Human Genetics Commission, *Inside Information: Balancing interests in the use of personal genetic data* (London: Department of Health, 2002).

The Law Commission, *Liability for psychiatric Illness: Item 2 of the 6 programme of law reform* (London: Stationary Office, 1998).

The Nuffield Council on Bioethics, *Genetic Screening: Ethical Issues* (1993).

United Kingdom Transplant Support Service Authority, Booklet, *Questions and Straight Answers about Transplants* (4th ed., 1998).

Statutes

The *Human Tissue Act* 1961.
The *Rent Act* 1977.
The *Children Act* 1989.

The *Human Fertilisation and Embryology Act* 1990.
The *Human Rights Act* 1998.
The *Adoption and Children Act* 2002.
The *Civil Partnership Act* 2004.
The *Gender Recognition Act* 2004.
The *Human Tissue Act* 2004.

Foreign Legislation

The *Patient's Rights Act* 1996 (Israel).
The *Genetic Information Act* 2000 (Israel).

Statutory Instruments

The *National Health Service (General Medical Services) Regulations* 1992, SI 1992/635.
The *National Health Service (Choice of Medical Practitioner) Regulations* 1998, SI 1998/668, as amended by SI 1999/3179.
Practice Note (Family Division: Incapacitated Adults: Declaratory Proceedings) [2002] 1 All ER 794.

International Codes and Conventions

Council of Europe, *Convention for the Protection of Human Rights and Dignity of the Human Being with regard to the Application of Biology and Medicine: Convention on Human Rights and Medicine,* 10(2) (1997).
UNESCO, *Universal Declaration on the Human Genome and Human Rights,* 5c (1997).

Index

acts, and tort law 81
Advisory Committee on Genetic
    Testing 49
agency, and autonomy 9
Andorno, R 152, 154
Andrews, Lori 52, 57, 172–3
    and duty to warn 140, 141
Aristotle 36
Ashcroft, Richard 205
assumption of responsibility, and
        doctor's duty of care 84, 101–
        2, 111
autonomy
    and agency 9
    and beneficence 12–13
    and choice 9
    and communication of information
        16–19
    and conceptions of 10
        Beauchamp and Childress 10–12
    and consent 15
    and information 148–9
    and liberalism 6–7, 201
    and medical confidentiality 124
    and medical ethics, liberal
        approach to 9–11
    and refusal of treatment 19–21
    and right not to know 149, 152,
        153–4
    and self-determination 15
    and social context of 25
    and voluntariness 11, 22–3
    see also relational autonomy
awareness, and relatives' claims
    for physical injury 94–6
    for psychological harm 103–5

Baier, Annette 33
Bainham, Andrew 66
Baird, M 159

Balint, Michael 166
Beauchamp, T 88, 149
    and autonomy 9–11
    and right not to know 153
Beckwith, S 117
behavioural sciences, and medicine
        169
Bell, Daniel 8, 28, 29, 30, 205–6
beneficence 12
    and autonomy 12–13
    and Human Rights Act (1998) 96
    and rejection of principle of 203
    and tort law 88
Bennett, B 205–6
Benson, J 192
Bentham, Jeremy 5
Berg, Jessica 38–9, 214, 215, 216,
        217, 218, 232
Berlin, Isaiah 7
    and autonomy 11
Bingham, Lord 127, 128, 130
biomedical model of health care
        164–6
    and disease 164–5
    and doctor-patient relationship 165
    and mind-body dualism 165
    and patients 165–6
    and reductionist approach of 165
biopsychosocial model of health care
        27, 166–70, 203–4
    and characteristics of 170
    and doctor-patient relationship
        168–9
    and family covenant 215, 216
    and family in 166–7, 170
        coping with bad news 173–5
        doctor's obligations to 178–83
        impact of illness on 175–8
        patient decision to seek medical
            advice 172–3

as source of social support 171–2
and illness 167
and influence of behavioural
    sciences 169
and patient autonomy 169
and role of family 168
and systems theory 167–8
see also medical decision-making
    process
Bloom, J 172
Botelho, R 193
Bottis, M 151
Brandon, Lord 81
Bridge, Lord 17, 98
British Medical Association 142
and medical confidentiality 134–5
Britten, N 192
Browne-Wilkinson, Lord 17–18,
    108, 117, 207
Burnett, J 141

Cardozo, J 15
Casadevall, Judge 22
Chadwick, R 25–6, 78–9, 137, 138,
    140–1, 150
Charles, C 184, 185
children, and medical treatment of
    21–2
Childress, J 88, 149
and autonomy 9–11
and right not to know 153
choice
and autonomy 9
and communitarianism 29
and genetic information
    family interest in 137–8
    patient's interest in 69–70
and respect for 202
Christie, R 27, 178–9, 181
Civil Partnership Act (2004) 60
Clarke, Angus 160, 186, 223, 224–5
Clayton, E 83, 143
common good
and communitarianism 29–30, 72
and patient-family conflict 32

communitarianism 28–9
and characteristics of 201
and choice 29
and common good 29–30, 72
and ethics-of-care 33–4
and family-based approach 32, 174
and genetic information
    family access to 36–40
    family covenant 38–9, 215, 216
and identity formation 29
and individuals 29
    oppression of 30
and moral responsibility 29–30
    sharing of genetic information
        70–1
and patient-family conflict 32
and relational autonomy 31–2, 33,
    201
and social relationships 29
and systems theory 168
confidentiality, *see* medical
        confidentiality
conflict
and liberalism 8
and patient-family conflict 32
consent
and autonomy 15
and family members 1–2
and medical law 14–15
    communication of information
        16–19
    legal requirements for 15
    refusal of treatment 19–21
    voluntariness 22–3
consideration, and disclosure of
        genetic information 75–6
Cotterrell, Roger 206, 207

Daly, M 229–30
damages
and economic loss 80
and foreseeability 85
and physical injury 79–80
    doctor not causing damage 91–2
    doctor's liability for patient

conduct 89–91
identification 86–7
liability for failure to act 87–9
policy considerations 113–19
professional awareness 94–6
proximity between doctor and
relatives 85–6, 92–7
and policy considerations 85, 113–
14
changes in attitude 116–18
positive arguments 118–21
traditional considerations 114–16
and proximity 85
relatives' claims for physical
injury 85–6, 92–7
relatives' claims for
psychological harm 98–101,
104–6
and psychological harm 80, 97–8
communication of information
101–4
establishing doctor-relative
proximity 98–101, 104–6
professional awareness 103–5
and relatives' claims for economic
loss 106–8
assumption of responsibility 111
ethical analysis 109–11
Deakin, S 90, 98
decision-making, *see* medical
decision-making process
deliberative model for resolving
familial conflict 221–4, 232
and difficulties with 231
and disclosure of medical
information
doctor-patient relationship 224–8
patient-relatives relationship
228–30
and discretion 221
and familial relationships 222–3
and process of communication and
deliberation 223–4
and relational autonomy 230
and social dimension of 222

Descarte, R 165
Dewar, John 219–20
Diplock, Lord 17
disease
and biomedical model of health
care 164–5
and definition of 164
doctor-patient relationship
and autonomy/beneficence conflict
12–13
and biomedical model of health
care 165
and biopsychosocial model of
health care 168–9
and children, medical treatment of
21–2
and communication of information
16–19
and deliberative model 224–8
and doctor's duty of care 83–5
and exclusivity of 23–4, 203
and family members' interests 1–2,
21
and medical confidentiality 37,
125
and need to abandon perception of
210
and refusal of treatment 19–21
and trust 125, 205
doctor-relative relationship, and
medical confidentiality 123,
135
doctors
and communication of information
16–19
and deliberative model 224–8
and duty of care 83–5
family members 210–11, 213
and duty to warn 139–42, 203
and family covenant 214–15, 217
and professional obligations to
family members 178–83
and relatives' claims for economic
loss 106–8
assumption of responsibility 111

ethical analysis 109–11
and relatives' claims for physical
    injury
    doctor not causing damage 91–2
    doctor's liability for patient
        conduct 89–91
    identification 86–7
    liability for failure to act 87–9
    policy considerations 113–19
    professional awareness 94–6
    proximity between doctor and
        relatives 85–6, 92–7
and relatives' claims for
    psychological harm 97–8
    communication of information
        101–4
    establishing doctor-relative
        proximity 98–101, 104–6
    professional awareness 103–5
see also biomedical model of
    health care; biopsychosocial
    model of health care; doctor-
    patient
    relationship; medical
    confidentiality; medical
    decision-making process
Doherty, W 159
Donchin, A 31
Doukas, David 38–9, 197, 214, 215,
    216, 217, 218, 232
Dugan, B 191–2
duty of care 83–5
    and assumption of responsibility
        84, 101–2, 111
    and family members 210–11, 213
    and policy considerations 113–19
    and relatives' claims for economic
        loss 106–8
    assumption of responsibility 111
    ethical analysis 109–11
    and relatives' claims for physical
        injury
    doctor not causing damage 91–2
    doctor's liability for patient
        conduct 89–91

identification 86–7
liability for failure to act 87–9
policy considerations 113–19
professional awareness 94–6
proximity between doctor and
    relatives 85–6, 92–7
and relatives' claims for
    psychological harm 97–8
communication of information
    101–4
establishing doctor-relative
    proximity 98–101, 104–6
professional awareness 103–5
and third parties 112, 113
and tort law 78
Dworkin, Gerald, and autonomy 10
Dworkin, Ronald, and public interest
    8–9

economic loss 80
and genetic information, family
    interest in 137
and relatives' claims against
    doctors 106–8
assumption of responsibility 111
ethical analysis 109–11
egalitarianism, and liberalism 5
Engel, George
and biomedical model of health
    care 165, 166
and biopsychosocial model of
    health care 168
and systems theory 167
English, Veronica 37, 144
ethics-of-care 33–4
and definition of family 63
and familial relationships 202
Etzioni, A 28–9, 29–30
European Convention on Human
    Rights 93–4, 97, 119
and consent 19–20
and medical confidentiality 129
and privacy 125
European Court of Human Rights
    93–4, 97

and consent 19–20
and medical confidentiality 129–30
and policy considerations 116, 117

Faden, R 10
familial privacy 158, 216
family
  and biopsychosocial model of
      health care 170
    coping with bad news 173–5
    doctor's obligations to 178–83
    impact of illness on 175–8
    patient decision to seek medical
        advice 172–3
    as source of social support 171–2
  and claims against doctors for
      economic loss 106–8
    assumption of responsibility 111
    ethical analysis 109–11
  and claims against doctors for
      physical injury
    doctor not causing damage 91–2
    doctor's liability for patient
        conduct 89–91
    identification 86–7
    liability for failure to act 87–9
    policy considerations 113–19
    professional awareness 94–6
    proximity between doctor and
        relatives 85–6, 92–7
  and claims against doctors for
      psychological harm 97–8
    communication of information
        101–4
    establishing doctor-relative
        proximity 98–101, 104–6
    professional awareness 103–5
  and claims against patients in
      negligence 80–3
  and conflict 32
  and definition of 202–3, 217
    biological 38
    biosocial definition 65–9, 100,
        203

blood ties 51
  in English law 59–65
  legal implications of 51–2, 58–9
  social component of 58, 59, 66–8
and genetic information 3
  access to 25–6
  communitarian models 36–40
  doctor's duty to warn 139–42
  effect on familial relationships
      56–8, 145–6
  impact of 26, 67, 68, 163, 203
  impact on relationships 26
  interest in 51, 65–6, 72–3, 136,
      201
  interest in not knowing 73–6,
      201
  patient's duty to warn 142–4
  patient-spouse relationship 57
  psychosocial implications of 52–
      3, 175–7
  reaction to 55–6
  refusal to share 77
  reluctance to receive 77
  reluctance to share 26–7
  right to know 123, 131–2
  sharing of 70–1
  siblings 56–7
and genetic testing 47
and involvement in patient care 27
and law, changing attitude towards
    207–8
and medical confidentiality,
    qualified principle of 146–7,
    158–9, 188, 211–13, 225
and medical decision-making
    process 36
  disclosure of medical
      information 186–7
  doctors and patient
      confidentiality 187–92, 204
  interests of 210
  partnership model 183–6
  patients' attitudes to disclosure
      192–8, 204
and medical ethics

liberal approach to 12–13
neglect of interests of 1–2, 3
and medical law
  legal change required 208–9
  limited status of 1–2, 3, 21–2,
    204, 208
  promotion of interests of 209–13
  treatment of children 21–2
  undue influence on patient 22–3
and nature of 142, 157–8, 159
and perception of familial
    relationships 34–6
  intimacy 34, 174–5
  justice 35
and relational autonomy 31–2, 33
and right not to know 123, 147–8
  autonomy 149, 152, 153–4
  debate over legal right to 148–52
  deliberative model 226
  familial privacy 158, 216
  as general right 151
  interests of relatives 154–7
  medical confidentiality 152–3
  prevention of harm 150
  privacy 149–50, 154–7
  protection of 152–7
  relational autonomy 159
  as right not to be informed 151
  self-determination 150
and significance of 208
and social aspects of 52
as unit of medical care 113, 174,
    208, 215, 218
see also deliberative model for
    resolving familial conflict
family covenant 38–9, 213–19
feminism
  and communitarianism 28
  and relational autonomy 31, 33,
    201
  and traditional family 61–2
Fletcher, J 151, 153, 190, 191, 192,
    193, 195
Frazer, E 8

Gage, Judge 94
Galanter, Marc 219, 221
Geller, G 189, 190
General Medical Council
  and guidance on good practice 13–
    14
  and medical confidentiality 126,
    129
genetic disorders 44–5
  and polygenic and multifactorial
    disorders 46
  and single gene disorders 45
    autosomal dominant disorders 45
    autosomal recessive disorders
      45–6
    X-linked disorders 46
genetic information
  and communication of 3
  and definition of 50–1
  and dual impact of 231
  and family members 25–6
    biosocial definition 65–9, 100,
      203
    communitarian models 36–40
    coping with bad news 173–5
    definition of 51–2
    doctors and patient
      confidentiality 187–92
    doctor's duty to warn 139–42
    doctor's obligations to 178–83
    family covenant 38–9, 213–19
    family in English law 59–65
    impact on 26, 67, 68, 163, 175–
      8, 203
    interest in 51, 65–6, 72–3, 137–
      8, 201
    interest in not knowing 73–6,
      201
    patients' attitudes to disclosure
      192–8
    patient's duty to warn 142–4
    reaction of 55–6
    reluctance to receive 77
    reluctance to share 26–7
    sharing of 70–1

as source of social support 171–2
and medical confidentiality
  economic loss 137
  family interest in 72–3
  informed choice 137–8
  patient's interest in 72
  patient's motives for insisting on
      144–7
  prevention of harm 131–2, 136–7
  professional guidance 132–5,
      222
  qualified principle of 146–7,
      158–9, 188, 211–13, 225
and patient's interest in 69–71
  confidentiality 70, 201
  economic loss 137
  informed choice 69–70
  not knowing 70, 73–6
  prevention of harm 69, 70
  sharing of 70–1, 201
and patient's refusal to share 77
and privacy 75–6
and psychosocial implications of
      52–3, 73–4
  effect on familial relationships
      56–8, 145–6, 175–7
  effect on patients 53–6
  patient-spouse relationship 57,
      176–7
  siblings 56–7
and right not to know 123, 147–8
  autonomy 149, 152, 153–4
  debate over legal right to 148–52
  deliberative model 226
  familial privacy 158, 216
  as general right 151
  interests of relatives 154–7
  medical confidentiality 152–3
  prevention of harm 150
  privacy 149–50, 154–7
  protection of 152–7
  relational autonomy 159
  as right not to be informed 151
  self-determination 150
and right to know 123, 131–2

breaching medical
    confidentiality 126–31
  medical confidentiality 124–5
Genetic Interest Group
  and medical confidentiality 135
  and right not to know 152–3
genetic testing 47–50
  and advantages of 49
  and adverse consequences of 49–
      50
  and Advisory Committee on
      Genetic Testing 49
  and ambiguity of 50
  and carrier screening 48
  and diagnostic testing 47–8, 49
  and early/late-onset disorders 48–9
  and familial characteristic 47
  and family linkage study 47
  and impact on patients 52–6
  and neonatal screening 48
  and predictive testing 49
  and pre-implantation diagnosis 48
  and prenatal testing 48
  and pre-symptomatic testing 49
  and single gene disorders 47
genetics
  and genes 44
  and mutations 44
  and prevention of harm principle
      131–2
Gibson, Peter 108
Giliker, P 117
Gilligan, Carol 33, 197
Goff, Lord 90, 109, 125
Griffith, Lord 125
Griffiths, Jonathan 108
Grol, R 192
Grubb, A 15–16, 17, 18, 19, 91–2,
      93, 94, 99, 129, 208

Hale, Lady 61, 99, 130
Hallowell, N 194–5, 197
Hardwig, John 31, 32, 35
harm, principle of prevention of 13,
      25–6, 37, 74–5, 119

and breaching medical
    confidentiality 126–9, 221
  family interest in 136–7
  in genetics 131–2
  and patients' interests 69, 70
  and right not to know 150
Harper, Peter 86
health care, and biopsychosocial
    model 27
Hoffmann, Lord 88, 206
Hoffmaster, B 27, 178–9, 181
Hollman, G 175
Hope, Lord 18–19
housing, and definition of family
    62–3
Human Fertilisation and
    Embryology Act (1990) 220
Human Fertilisation and
    Embryology Authority 220
Human Genetics Commission 73
  and medical confidentiality 135,
    222
Human Organ Transplant Act (1989)
    59, 60
Human Rights Act (1998) 63, 117
  and beneficence 96
  and individual rights 97
  and medical confidentiality 129
  and third parties' medical
    negligence claims 93
Human Tissue Act (1961) 59, 60
Human Tissue Act (2004) 59–60
Huntington's disease
  and impact of genetic information
    53–4, 73
  and impact on partners 177
Hutton, Lord 117

identity
  and communitarianism 29
  and dual elements of 231, 232
  and impact of genetic information
    52, 53, 54
  interest in not knowing 75
illness

and biopsychosocial model of
    health care 167
  and definition of 164
individualism, and liberalism 5
individuals
  and communitarianism 29
  oppression of 30
  and justice, Rawls' theory 6–7
  and liberalism
    autonomy 6–7
    pre-social nature of 6
  and public interest 8–9
  and relational autonomy 31–2
information, and communication of
    16–19
  communitarian models 36–40
intimacy, and familial relationships
    34, 174–5
intolerability 21–2

Johnston, A 98
Jones, M 102, 119
justice
  and familial relationships 35
  and liberalism 5
  and Rawls' theory 6–7

Kant, Immanuel 5, 7
  and autonomy 10, 11
Keith, Lord 114
Kennedy, I 15–16, 17, 18, 19

Lacey, N 8
Lako, C J 187, 190
Laurie, Graeme 81, 208, 220
  and duty to warn 143
  and genetic information
    definition of 50
    family access to 39–40
    family interest in 58, 65–6, 69,
      136
    interest in not knowing 75–6
  and genetic testing 50
  and medical confidentiality 126,
    132

and proximity 86
and right not to know 149, 152,
153–4
privacy 154–7
law
and definition of family 59–65,
100
and role in society 52, 61, 64, 206–
8, 209, 219–21
Laws, Lord 112
Lehmann, L 196, 197
liberalism
and autonomy 6–7, 201
and characteristics of 201
and conflict 8
and family covenant 215, 216
and individuals
autonomy 6–7
pre-social nature of 6
and justice, Rawls' theory 6–7
and justifications for 5
and liberty 7
and medical ethics 9–14
autonomy 9–11
beneficence 12–13
family members' interests 12–13
patient-centred 13–14
and medical law 14–25
communication of information
16–19
consent 14–15
refusal of treatment 19–21
voluntariness 22–3
and public interest 8–9
and variations in 5
libertarianism, and liberalism 5
liberty, and Berlin's view of 7
Lindemann-Nelson, H & J 30, 202,
212
and familial relationships 35
and family-based approach 32
and relational autonomy 32
Locke, John 5
Lucassen, A 218
Lunney, M 93

McCall-Smith, R A 81, 220
Mackay, Lord 89–90, 95
McWhinney 181–2
Marinker, M 164, 180–1
Markesinis, Basil 87, 90, 98
Mason, J K 81, 220
Mattingly, S 196
medical confidentiality 203
and duty to warn
doctors 139–42
patients 142–4
and family covenant 214–15
and genetic information
family interest in 72–3
patient's interest in 70, 201
professional guidance 132–5,
222
and justifications for 124–5
and justifications for breaches of
126–31, 204
economic loss 137
genetic information 131–2
informed choice 137–8
prevention of harm 136–7, 221
and medical decision-making
process
disclosure of medical
information 186–7
doctors and patient
confidentiality 187–92, 204
patients' attitudes to disclosure
192–8, 204
and patient's desire for
fear of economic costs 145
fear of impact on familial
relationships 145–6
and qualified principle of 146–7,
158–9, 188, 211–13
deliberative model 225
and right not to know 123, 152–3
and right to know 123
and support for existing position
205–6
medical decision-making process,
and family members 36

and disclosure of medical
    information 186–7
and doctors and medical
    confidentiality 187–92, 204
and family covenant 213–19
and family members' interests 210
and partnership model 183–6
and patient's attitude to disclosure
    192–8, 204
see also deliberative model for
    resolving familial conflict
medical ethics
    and family members 203
        limited recognition of 1–2, 3
    and liberal approach to 9–14
        autonomy 9–11
        beneficence 12–13
        family members' interests 12–13
        patient-centred 13–14
    and patient-relatives relationship 2
medical law
    and doctor-patient relationship 2
        exclusivity of 23–4
    and family members 203
        legal change required 208–9
        limited status of 1–2, 3, 21–2,
            204, 208
        promotion of interests of 209–13
    and liberal approach to 14–25
        communication of information
            16–19
        consent 14–15
        refusal of treatment 19–21
        treatment of children 21–2
        voluntariness 22–3
    and medical practice
        bridging gap between 205–9
        gap between 204
    and patient-centred approach 35–6
    and role in society 206–8, 209,
        219–21
medical models, *see* biomedical
        model of health care;
        biopsychosocial model of
        health care

medicine, and behavioural sciences
    169
Mill, John Stuart 5, 7, 8
    and autonomy 11
mind-body dualism, and biomedical
        model of health care 165
Mullany, N 102
Munby, Judge 20

National Health Service (Choice of
        Medical Practitioner)
        Regulations (1998) 84
National Health Service (General
        Medical Services)
        Regulations (1992) 84
Nedelsky, Jennifer 31
negligence, *see* tort law
Ngwena, C 25–6, 78–9, 137, 138,
    140–1
Nolan, Lord 110
Northouse, L 177
Nozick, Robert 5
Nuffield Council 142
    and medical confidentiality 133

Okin, Susan 35, 61
Oliphant, K 93
omissions
    and failure to warn 142, 203
    and tort law 81, 87–8, 89
O'Neill, Onora 205
    and autonomy 10
organ donation/transplantation 228–
    9
    and definition of family 59–60
Ost, D 152

Parker, M 30, 40–1, 218, 223
patient care, and family involvement
    in 27
patient-relatives relationship 34–6
    and conflict 32
    and deliberative model 228–30
    and family members' interests 2
    and genetic information, effect of

disclosure 56–8, 145–6
and medical confidentiality 123
patients
and biomedical model of health
care 165–6
and biopsychosocial model of
health care 166–7
and claims against in negligence
80–3
and doctor's duty of care 83–5
and duty to warn 142–4
and family definition 58–9
and genetic information
economic interest in withholding
145
fear of disclosing 144–5
impact of 53–6, 73–4
impact on familial relationships
145–6
interest in 69–71, 136
interest in not knowing 73–6,
149
qualified medical confidentiality
146–7, 158–9, 188, 211–13,
225
refusal to share 77
sharing of 70–1, 201
and seeking medical advice, role of
family 172–3
and support from family 171–2,
173–5
see also deliberative model for
resolving familial conflict
patient-spouse relationship, and
impact of genetic information
57, 176–7
policy considerations, and physical
injury claims 85, 113–14
changes in attitude 116–18
positive arguments for duty of care
118–21
traditional considerations 114–16
Powell, Robert 1, 232
privacy 39–40
and genetic information, interest in

not knowing 75–6
and medical confidentiality 124–5
and right not to know 149–50,
154–7
familial privacy 158, 216
proximity
and legal attitude to 112–13
and relatives' claims for physical
injury 85–6, 92–7
and relatives' claims for
psychological harm 98–101,
104–6
and relaxation of requirements
209–10
psychological harm 80
and breaching medical
confidentiality 136–7
and relatives' claims against
doctors 97–8
communication of information
101–4
establishing doctor-relative
proximity 98–101, 104–6
professional awareness 103–5
public bodies, and policy
considerations 114–15, 116–
17
public interest
and breaching medical
confidentiality 126–31
and liberalism 8–9

Raikka, J 150
Rawls, John 5, 215
and justice 6–7
refusal of treatment 19–21, 179–80
relational autonomy 31–2, 33, 201–
2, 232
and British Medical Association
134
and communitarianism 31–2, 33,
201
and deliberative model 230
and ethics-of-care 33–4
and right not to know 159

and sharing of genetic information
70–1
see also autonomy
Rent Act (1977) 62–3
Reust, C 196
Rhodes, Rosamond 36, 51, 138, 148,
149, 151, 205, 206
right not to know 147–8, 203
and autonomy 149, 152
and deliberative model 226
and familial privacy 158, 216
as general right 151
and medical confidentiality 123
and prevention of harm 150
and privacy 149–50
and protection of 152–7
interests of relatives 154–7
medical confidentiality 152–3
privacy 154–7
respect for autonomy 153–4
and relational autonomy, interests
of relatives 159
as right not to be informed 151
and self-determination 150
right to know
and medical confidentiality 123
doctor's duty to warn 139–42
economic loss 137
in genetics 131–2
informed choice 137–8
justifications for 124–5
justifications for breaches of
126–31
prevention of harm 136–7
professional guidance 132–5,
222
qualified principle of 146–7,
158–9, 188, 211–13, 225
and patient's duty to warn 142–4
Rose, Judge 125

Safer, Donna 1, 232
same-sex couples 60, 62, 63
Sandel, M 28, 30
Scarman, Lord 15, 17

Scott, Judge 124, 127
Scott, Rosamund 180
Sedley, Lord 18
self-determination
and autonomy 15
and right not to know 150
sexually transmitted disease (STD),
and failure to disclose 80–1,
82
siblings, and impact of genetic
information 56–7
sickness, and definition of 164
Skene, Loane 37–8, 41, 146
and family definition 51–2
and genetic information
familial nature of 51
family access to 143
Slynn, Lord 63, 116–17
Smith, Adam 5
Smith, Judge 95
social relationships, and reaction to
genetic information 55–8
social support, and family members
171–2, 173–5
social utility, and utilitarianism 8
Sommerville, Anne 37, 144
Southgate, L J 188–9
Steinglass, Peter 171
Steyn, Lord 18
Stuart-Smith, Lord 94, 95, 96, 97,
104, 115, 116
survivor's guilt, and genetic
information 56
Suter, Sonia 137, 142–3
systems theory
and biopsychosocial model of
health care 167–8
and communitarianism 168

Takala, T 150, 152
Tassicker, R 160
Templeman, Lord 17, 114
Tercyak, K 173
Toon, P D 188–9
tort law

and acts 81
and assumption of responsibility
    84, 101–2
and basic principles of negligence
    law 79–80
and beneficence 88
and claims against patients 80–3
and damages
    economic loss 80
    foreseeability 85
    physical injury 79–80
    policy considerations 85
    proximity 85
    psychological harm 80
and doctor's duty of care 83–5
and duty of care 78
and omissions 81, 87–8, 89
and relatives' claims for economic
    loss 106–8
    assumption of responsibility 111
    ethical analysis 109–11
and relatives' claims for physical
    injury
    doctor not causing damage 91–2
    doctor's liability for patient
        conduct 89–91
    identification 86–7
    liability for failure to act 87–9
    policy considerations 113–19
    professional awareness 94–6
    proximity between doctor and
        relatives 85–6, 92–7
and relatives' claims for

    psychological harm 97–8
    communication of information
        101–4
    establishing doctor-relative
        proximity 98–101, 104–6
    professional awareness 103–5
trust, and doctor-patient relationship
    125, 205–6

undue influence, and family
    members 22–3
universalism, and liberalism 5
Unrelated Live Transplant
    Regulatory Authority 59
utilitarianism
    and liberalism 5
    and medical confidentiality 124
        breaches of 129
    and social utility 8

voluntariness
    and autonomy 11
    and consent 22–3

Walker, Lord 18
warn, duty to
    and doctors 139–42, 203
    and patients 142–4
Wertz, D 151, 153, 190, 191, 192,
    195
Williams, P 88, 89
Woolf, Lord 18

Index of Cases Cited

A v Leeds Teaching Hospital NHS
  Trust (2004) 103, 112 n169
AB v Tameside and Glossop HA
  (1997) 101
A-G v Guardian Newspapers (No 2)
  (1988) 125
Airedale NHS Trust v Bland (1993)
  15 n73, 206–7, 220 n61
Alcock v Chief Constable of West
  Yorkshire (1992) 98 n109,
  99, 100–1
Allin v City and Hackney HA (1996)
  101, 103
Anderson v Forth Valley HA (1998)
  137 n69
Anns v Merton LBC (1978) 114
  n172
Application of the President and
  Directors of Georgetown
  College Inc (1964) 179

B v A-G of New Zealand (2003) 24
  n126
Baker v Kaye (1996) 106 n142
Barrett v Enfield LBC 116–17
Beller v Tilbrook (2002) 82 n20
Berner v Caldwell (1989) 81 n13
Blyth v Bloomsbury HA (1993) 17
  n91
Bolam v Friern Barnet Hospital
  Management (1957) 16, 17,
  21
Bolitho v City and Hackney Health
  Authority (1997) 17–18
Brady v Hopper (1984) 139 n82

Caparo v Dickman (1990) 85 n36,
  107
Caparo v Diskman (1990) 114
Capital Counties plc v Hampshire

CC (1997) 23 n123, 84 n30,
  116 n185
Carmarthenshire CC v Lewis (1956)
  90
Chester v Afshar (2004) 18–19
Creutzfeldt-Jakob Disease litigation;
  Group B Plaintiffs v Medical
  Research Council and another
  (2000)
  102, 103, 105 n140

D v East Berkshire Community
  Health NHS Trust (2004) 24
  n126, 117, 119 n199, 120,
  210 n31
DiMarco v Lynch Homes-Chester
  County (1990) 140
Doe v Johnson (1993) 81 n13
Dorset Yacht v Home Office (1970)
  90
Dyson Holdings Ltd v Fox (1975) 62
  n73, 63 n74

E v United Kingdom (2002) 93 n87
Emeh v Kensington and Chelsea and
  Westminster AHA (1985)
  110 n161

Farrell v Avon HA (2001) 102 n131
Fitzpatrick v Sterling House
  Association (1999) 63, 64
  n82, 67 n92
Fosmire v Nicoleau (1990) 180 n85
Frankson and others v Home Office
  (2003) 78 n3
Frost v Chief Constable of South
  Yorkshire Police (1999) 99

Gammans v Ekins (1950) 62 n73
Ghaidan v Godin-Mendoza (2004)

63 n78
Glass v United Kingdom (2004) 19–20, 22
Gold v Haringey Health Authority (1988) 17
Goodwill v BPAS (1996) 86 n44, 91, 107–8, 109–11
Gorham v BT (2000) 107 n149, 109 n156
Grieve v Salford HA (1991) 98 n107

Hardman v Amin (2000) 91 n73, 92 n77, 137 n69
Harrogate BC v Simpson (1984) 63 n75
Hatton v Sutherland, Barber v Somerset CC, Jones v Sandwell MBC, Bishop v Baker (2002) 99 n112
Hawes v Evenden (1953) 62 n73
Hedley Byrne v Heller (1964) 79 n7, 107
Henderson v Merrett (1995) 23 n124, 84 n34, 107 n148, 111
Hill v Chief Constable of West Yorkshire (1989) 86 n40, 114, 115

K v Secretary of State for the Home Department (2002) 95 n97, 112 n168
K v Secretary of State for the Home Office (2001) 95
Kapfunde v Abbey National (1998) 106 n142
Kent v Griffiths (2001) 89 n61, 207 n28

Lee v Taunton and Somerset NHS Trust (2001) 92 n77
Lipari v Sears, Roebuck and Co (1980) 139 n81
Long v Adams (1985) 81 n12

Marc Rich v Bishop Ltd (1996) 85

n37
McFall v Shimp (1978) 12, 82–3
McFarlane v Tayside Health Board (2000) 91 n73, 108 n151, 110
McLoughlin v O'Brian (1983) 98 n105, 99, 100 n117
McPherson v McPherson (1998) 82 n20
Mavroudis v Superior Court of California (1980) 139 n82
Mendoza v Ghaidan (2003) 63 n78
MS v Sweden (1997) 129 n31

Norwood Hospital v Munoz (1991) 179–80

Osman v Ferguson (1993) 95, 114 n176
Osman v UK (1998) 93, 94, 95 n95, 114 n174, 116, 117, 118–19, 207 n29

Page v Smith (1996) 99 n111
Palmer v Tees HA (1999) 79 n8, 85 n38, 86 n40, 94, 96, 97, 115 n181, 117 n190
Parkinson v St James and Seacroft University Hospital (2002) 92 n78, 107 n143, 137 n71
Pate v Threlkel (1995) 131 n39, 140
Pearce v United Bristol Healthcare NHS Trust (1999) 18, 19
Petersen v State (1983) 139 n81
Phelps v London Borough of Hillingdon (2000) 111 n166, 117, 118 n198
Powell v Boldaz (1998) 1, 24, 87 n49, 101, 103–4, 189 n121, 210 n31
Powell v United Kingdom 101 n128
Pretty v UK (2002) 20
Public Health Trust of Dade County v Wons (1989) 180 n85

R (on the application of Burke) v

The General Medical Council
(2004) 20
R (on the application of S) v
Plymouth CC (2002) 130
n35, 145 n121
R v Chief Constable of the North
Wales Police (1999) 125 n12,
128 n27, 130 n35
R v Crozier (1991) 127, 128, 129
R v Department of Health (1999)
125 n8
Rand v East Dorset HA (2000) 91
n73, 92 n77, 137 n69
Re A (Children) (Conjoined twins:
surgical separation) (2000) 22
n118
Re B (Consent to treatment:
capacity) (2002) 19
Re C (1991) 127–8
Re Dubreuil (1993) 180
Re F (Mental Patient: Sterilization)
(1990) 15
Re Farrell (1987) 180 n85
Re J (a minor) (Wardship: medical
treatment) (1991) 21 n116
Re Osborne (1972) 180 n85
Re R (a child) (adoption: disclosure)
(2001) 125 n12
Re T (adult: refusal of medical
treatment) (1992) 22, 23
Re Wyatt (a child) (Medical
treatment: parents' consent)
(2004) 21, 22
Rees v Darlington Memorial
Hospital NHS Trust (2003)
79 n9, 91 n73, 107 n143, 112
n167
Reibl v Hughes (1980) 15 n77
Reilly v Merseyside HA (1995) 98
n108
Reisner v Regents of the University
of California (1995) 82 n21,
140
RK and MK v Oldham NHS Trust
and Dr B (2003) 24 n126, 87

n49, 210 n31
Rogers v Whitaker (1992) 15 n77,
18

S v Gloucester CC (2001) 117 n190
Safer v Pack (1996) 1, 82 n22, 87,
100 n116, 131 n39, 140
Schloendorff v Society of New York
Hospital (1914) 15 n74
Sidaway v Board of Governors of
the Bethlem Royal Hospital
(1985) 15 n79, 17, 18, 23
n122
Sion v Hampstead HA (1994) 100
n118
Smith v Leurs (1945) 89 n62
Smith v Littlewoods Organisation
Ltd (1987) 86 n41, 87 n50,
89–90, 95
Smith v Tunbridge Wells HA (1994)
17 n91
Spring v Guardian Assurances
(1995) 107 n148, 108 n155,
111
Stovin v Wise (1996) 87, 88
Surry CC v M (a minor) (2001) 94
n90
Swinney v Chief Constable of
Northumbria Police Force
(1997) 116 n185

Tan v East London and the City HA
(1999) 100 n118
Tarasoff v Regents of the University
of California (1976) 12, 131
n37, 139, 140, 141
Taylor v Somerset HA (1993) 100
n118
Thake v Maurice (1986) 84 n29, 92
n80, 110 n161
Thompson v County of Alabama
(1980) 139 n82
Topp v London Country Bus Ltd
(1993) 90 n69

W v Egdell (1990) 78 n4, 79 n6,
124, 126 n16, 127, 128, 130,
221 n65
W v Essex CC (2000) 101 n122,
115, 115 n180, 116, 120
White v Jones (1995) 23 n124, 84
n34, 88–9, 107, 108, 109–11
Williams v United States (1978) 139
n81
Woolgar v Chief Constable of
Sussex Police (1999) 125
n12, 128 n27, 130 n35
Wyatt v Curtis (2003) 18

X (Minors) v Bedfordshire CC
(1995) 24 n126, 93, 94 n88,
114–15, 116, 118 n197, 120,
210 n31
X v Y (1988) 124 n2, 125, 128 n28

Yuen Kun Yeu v A-G of Hong Kong
(1988) 114 n172

Z v Finland (1997) 129–30
Z v UK (2001) 93, 115 n178, 116,
117, 210 n31